The Politics of Education and the New Institutionalism: Reinventing the American School

Education Policy Perspectives

General Editor: Professor Ivor Goodson, Faculty of Education, University of Western Ontario, London, Canada N6G 1G7

Education policy analysis has long been a neglected area in the UK and, to an extent, in the USA and Australia. The result has been a profound gap between the study of education and the formulation of education policy. For practitioners, such a lack of analysis of new policy initiatives has worrying implications, particularly at a time of such policy flux and change. Education policy has, in recent years, been a matter for intense political debate – the political and public interest in the working of the system has come at the same time as the breaking of the consensus on education policy by the New Right. As never before, political parties and pressure groups differ in their articulated policies and prescriptions for the education sector. Critical thinking about these developments is clearly imperative.

All those working within the system also need information on policy-making, policy implementation and effective day-to-day operation. Pressure on schools from government, education authorities and parents has generated an enormous need for knowledge among those on the receiving end of educational policies.

This Falmer Press series aims to fill the academic gap, to reflect the politicalization of education, and to provide the practitioners with the analysis for informed implementation of policies that they will need. It offers studies in broad areas of policy studies, with a particular focus on the following areas: school organization and improvement; critical social analysis; policy studies and evaluation; and education training.

The Politics of Education and the New Institutionalism: Reinventing the American School

The 1995 Yearbook of the Politics of Education Association

Edited by

Robert L. Crowson
Vanderbilt University

William Lowe Boyd
The Pennsylvania State University

and

Hanne B. Mawhinney
University of Ottawa

 The Falmer Press

(A member of the Taylor & Francis Group)
Washington, DC • London

UK   Falmer Press, 1 Gunpowder Square, London, EC4A 3DE
USA   Falmer Press, Taylor & Francis Inc., 1990 Frost Road, Suite
             101, Bristol PA 19007

First published 1996

A catalogue record for this book is available from the British Library

Library of Congress Cataloguing-in-Publication Data are available on request

ISBN 0 7507 0532 9 cased
ISBN 0 7507 0533 7 paper

Jacket design by Caroline Archer

Typeset by Keyword Typesetting Services Ltd, Wallington, Surrey

Printed in Great Britain by Henry Ling Limited on paper which has a specified pH value on final paper manufacture of not less than 7.5 and is therefore 'acid free'.

Contents

Politics of Education Association
Yearbook Sponsor

The **Politics of Education Association (PEA)** promotes the development and dissemination of research and debate on educational policy and politics. PEA brings together scholars, practitioners, and policy makers interested in educational governance and politics. It is affiliated as a Special Interest Group with the American Educational Research Association (AERA), and meets each spring in conjunction with AERA's annual meeting. PEA also sponsors its own biennial conferences on current policy issues in education in the fall. The annual membership dues for PEA are $US25.00 (subject to change). Members receive a copy of the annual *Yearbook* and the *Politics of Education Bulletin*, which includes news on member activities and occasional short scholarly pieces. Membership dues should be set to **Louise Adler, PEA Treasurer, EC 552, Educational Administration, California State University, Fullerton; Fullerton, CA 92634–8000, USA**.

A List of Editors and Contributors

William Lowe Boyd is Distinguished Professor in the College of Education at Pennsylvania State University. He is the author or editor of numerous books and articles on educational policies and administration, including several comparative studies and analyses. In 1994, Professor Boyd received one of PEA's first two Stephen K. Bailey awards for his scholarly contributions to the politics of education.

James G. Cibulka is Professor and Chair of the Department of Education Policy, and Administration at the University of Maryland, College Park. His specializations include educatonal politics and policy. He has written widely on urban school policy, private schools, school finance, and education reform. He is currently completing a book on *School Politics: A Crisis of Governance.*

Robert I. Crowson is Professor of Education in the Department of Educational Leadership, Peabody College, Vanderbilt University. His major research interests include large-city school administration, the school principalship, the school district superintendency, and the coordination of children's services. He has authored, co-authored or co-edited volumes on the principalship, organization theory, the politics of administrative reform, and school–community relations.

Mary Erina Driscoll is an Assistant Professor of Educational Administraton in the School of Education at New York University. Her research interests focus on the social organization of schools, with a particular emphasis on school community. She has recently completed a survey of managerial and political issues in collaborative services programs (with colleagues William Boyd and Robert Crowson).

Rick Ginsberg is Director of the School of Education and Professor at Colorado State University. He was co-editor (with David Plank) of the recently released 'Commissions, Reports, Reforms, and Educational Policy' (Praeger 1995). His research interests include organizational and individual change, school reform, and educational policy studies.

Ellen B. Goldring is Professor of Educational Leadership and Associate Dean for Academic Affairs at Peabody College, Vanderbilt University. Her research focuses on the organization and control of schools, and their impact on educational leadership and the principalship. Much of her work examines the changing roles of principals and parents. In an international perspective, she has published in such journals as *Educational Administrative Quarterly, Educational Policy,* and *Urban Education.* She is co-author with Sharon F. Rallis of *Principals of Dynamic Schools: Taking Charge of Change* (Corwin).

Gerald Grant is Hannah Hammond Professor of Education and Sociology at Syracuse University. His last book was *The World We Created at Hamilton High* (Harvard Press, 1988) and he is currently at work with Christine Murray on *Teaching in America: Reinventing a Profession.* Under a grant from the Spencer Foundation, he recently launched a study of the educational life of the Syracuse metropolitan community.

Charles Taylor Kerchner is Professor of Education at the Claremont Graduate School where his work concentrates in the study of educational organizations and   policy. He is currently finishing a book on educational labor relations, co-authored with Julia Koppich and Joseph Weeres. He is also writing and researching the reconvergence of education and city politics.

Ted Kolderie has been in problem-analysis and policy-design all his career; as a newspaper reporter and editorial writer, as executive director of the Citizens League in the Twin Cities area, as a senior fellow at the University of Minnesota's Hubert H. Humphrey Institute of Public Affairs, and as a senior associate since 1989 at the Center for Policy Studies. He has been involved with legislators, governors and others in the policy discussion about new arrangements for K-12 public education; in Minnesota and other states. He is a graduate of Carleton College and has a master's degree from the Woodrow Wilson School of Public and International Affairs at Princeton University.

Hanne B. Mawhinney is the Director of Professional Development Programs in the Faculty of Education, University of Ottawa. She teaches graduate courses in policy and politics of education and leadership. Her current research examines the institutional forces at play in school–community agency linkages.

Douglas E. Mitchell is Professor of Education and Director of the California Educational Research Cooperative at the University of California, Riverside. Educational politics and policy at the local and state levels are the main focus of his research. He has studied issues of social science utilization, state legislative decision-making, local school politics and leadership. He is the author, co-author or editor of six books and more than a hundred journal articles. He was co-editor with Margaret Goertz of the *1989 Politics of Educational Yearbook.* Other major works include: *Culture and Educational Policy in the American States* (with Catherine Marshall and Frederick Wirt, 1989), *The Changing Idea of a Teachers' Union* (with Charles Kerchner, 1988), and *Work Orientation and Job Performance: The Cultural Basis of Rewards and Incentives* (with Flora I. Ortiz and Tedi K. Mitchell, 1987).

Terry M. Moe is Professor of Political Science at Stanford University and Senior Fellow at the Hoover Institution. He has written extensively on American political institutions, organization theory, and rational choice models. His publications include *Politics, Markets, and America's Schools* (Brookings Institution, 1990, with John E. Chubb); 'The new economics of organization', *American Journal of Political Science* (November 1984), 739–777; and 'Political institutions: the neglected side of the story', *Journal of Law, Economics, and Organization* 6 (1990), 213–254.

Kevin J. Moran is currently an Adjunct Assistant Professor and a Post-doctoral Fellow at the School of Education, University of Pittsburgh and the Wilkinsburg School

District. His publications appear in *American Educational Research Journal* and the *World Yearbook of Education*, 1992 and 1995.

Christine E. Murray is Assistant Professor of Education and Human Development at the State University of New York College at Brockport. Her research has focused on the changing roles of teachers, educational policy, and organizational theory. She has published articles in the *Harvard Educational Review* and *Educational Policy* and is currently co-authoring *Teaching in America: Reinventing a Profession* with Gerald Grant.

Mary Anne Raywid is a Professor of Administration and Policy Studies at Hofstra University, where she also directs the Center for the Study of Educational Alternatives. Most of her current work is in the areas of school organization and the politics of education. She has published widely in the broad area of school – society relationships, has been active in a number of educational organizations, and has served on the editorial boards of more than a dozen education journals. For the last two decades she has focused on school reform and restructuring – in the several roles of researcher, developer, consultant, evaluator, and critic.

Jeremy Resnick is a former public school teacher who continues to work with public schools on various change initiatives. He served as coordinator of the Turner School Initiative and is currently the director of the Steel Center AVTS Technical Academy. He has two children who attend public school in Pittsburgh.

Jim Ryan is currently an Associate Professor in the Department of Educational Administration at the Ontario Institute for Studies in Education and a member of the Centre for Leadership Development. His interests include aboriginal education, cultural diversity and postmodernity. Some of his more recent publications can be found in journals such as Language and Education, The International Journal of Educational Reform and the McGill Journal of Education. At the present time he is engaged in a 3-year study of leadership and diversity.

Ken W. Shotts is a doctoral student in Political Economics at Stanford University's Graduate School of Business. His research interests include game theoretic models and computer simulations of American political institutions, as well as empirical tests of these models.

William B. Thomas is Professor of Education at the University of Pittsburgh. He teaches history and sociology of education in the Department of Administrative and Policy Studies. He is co-director of a collaborative between the University of Pittsburgh and the Wilkinsburg School District. His publications appear in *American Educational Research Journal* and the *World Yearbook of Education*, 1992 and 1995.

Joseph G. Weeres is Professor of Education in the Center for Education studies at the Claremont Graduate School. His research and teaching focus on the politics of education, environmental influences on organizations, and education as an institution. He recently spent a year in Asia studying the impact of changing work roles on educational expectations in several developing countries.

Introduction and overview: the new institutionalism and the politics of reinventing the American school

Robert L. Crowson, Vanderbilt University, William Lowe Boyd,
Pennsylvania State University, and Hanne B. Mawhinney,
University of Ottawa

'The more things change, the more they stay the same'. 'There's less real change here than meets the eye'. Comments like these about school reform efforts are common. But, how can this be, considering the bold claims of reformers and the huge array of recent change efforts and reform ideas? This Yearbook addresses this nagging question in light of the mounting efforts to 'reinvent' American education. It suggests that much of the answer about the difficulty of changing schools may be found in insights about the potency of the 'deep structures' embedded in schools as institutions – insights derived from a growing body of social science theory and research called the 'new institutionalism'.

On one hand, the current creativity and variety in reform experimentation seems to demonstrate the nation's firm, continuing belief that 'schools matter', a position thoroughly at odds with the popular conclusions of a few decades ago that in fact they do not. Consider even a short list of current efforts: systemic school reform; standards and high-stakes testing; charter schools, school restructuring; site-based management; home schooling; school choice; privatized schooling; small schools; 'success-for-all' schools; 'accelerated' and 'essential' schools; school-linked, coordinated-services – the list of options for the reform of American education is long and growing longer.

On the other hand, while faith continues in the power of schooling and the search for workable reform is intensifying, our confidence in our ability to produce meaningful school-improvement may be waning. Reports of failed reforms now tend to overpower the literature on school and school district change (Fullan and Miles 1992). Data showing little improvement in student achievement, accompanied by a continuing frustration about 'what works' educationally, may be translating into an emerging trend to *disinvest* in traditionally structured *public* schooling (Boyd 1995). The Goals 2000 effort to approach reform 'systemically', and to solidify school-improvement around national/state goals and standards, appears not to have captured broad support beyond a policy élite. Rather, thinking may be increasingly leaning toward more radical solutions such as privatization or 'breaking up' the system (Boyd, 1995). If indeed the nation continues to believe that schools do matter, that faith may now be receiving expression in a drive toward radical reinvention and renewal in public schooling, impulses far removed from traditional concepts of reform.

If schools matter, it is interesting that the parallel phrase 'institutions matter' has been increasing steadily in scholarly appeal at the same time as the clock seems to be running out on efforts to reform schools in conventional ways. In no small measure,

0268–0939/95 $12 · 00 © 1995 Taylor & Francis Ltd

the rediscovery of the 'institutions' of schooling grows out of the perplexities and frustrations that have been experienced in trying to alter them. The frustration is captured best in just a single, discouraging term from Seymour Sarason (1990), who pointed out the 'intractability' of our schools despite many, often creative efforts to introduce significant change. Similarly, historians David Tyack and William Tobin (1994: 456) have observed that the organizational framework that shapes schooling has remained 'remarkably durable' over time, quite often reflecting a history-laden 'congruence between cultural beliefs and organizational forms' with substantial staying-power. James Cibulka, in this volume, uses the phrase, 'institutional incapacity'.

Thus , inquiry into the 'staying power' of institutions finds common ground, we suggest, with a watershed effort to rethink the reform of public schooling. A rapidly developing literature on the staying power, as well as much of the rest that matters about public-sector organizations, has acquired a common label: 'The New Institutionalism'. The label covers much territory, for the new institutionalism is not yet a very tightly and cleanly defined perspective. Furthermore, the label covers an array of not always compatible conceptual contributions from such differing traditions as political science, economics, history, sociology and organization theory (Zucker 1988, Moe 1990, DiMaggio and Powell 1991).

The central importance of the new institutionalism for educators is that it re-establishes a special interest in the political and social significance of institutions while it simultaneously warns that the reform movement in education must address some 'deep structure' issues in the organization of schooling and in relationships between the schools and the larger society. This Yearbook seeks to provide both an introduction to new institutional theorizing in the study of educational politics and an application of some of this theorizing to the problem of reinventing the American school.

The new institutionalism

In their introductory chapter to *The New Institutionalism in Organizational Analysis*, DiMaggio and Powell (1991) outline some key differences in approach between the old institutionalism and the new. Among the key differences are *first* a focus upon the persistence, 'order', and stability of organizational forces despite pressures for change. *Second*, relatedly, new institutionalism emphasizes 'taken-for-grantedness', 'typifications', and 'common understandings' in organizational life above intentionality and interest-group conflict. *Third*, however, the new institutionalists de-emphasize newcomer socialization processes and the internalization of organizational values/ norms in this taken-for-grantedness in favour of a cognitive-learning interpretation of individual behavior. DiMaggio and Powell (1991: 15) write

> Neoinstitutionalists tend to reject socialization theory, with its affectively 'hot' imagery of identification and internalization. They prefer cooler implicit psychologies: cognitive models in which schemas and scripts lead decision makers to resist new evidence.

Fourth, the new institutionalism recognizes fully that organizations are engaged in a give-and-take with their immediate environments. However, the old environmental emphasis upon negotiation, boundary-spanning, and co-optation gives way under the new to a picture of much deeper, more subtle and all-encompassing environmental relationships. Environments, write DiMaggio and Powell (1991: 13), 'penetrate the organization, creating the lenses through which actors view the world and the very categories of structure, action, and thought'.

Despite these distinctions, theorizing surrounding the new institutionalism is not as clear or as clean as the above comparisons might suggest. To begin with, it is important to note that some confusion remains as to the differences between institutions and organizations. In the main, the new institutionalists do not tend to think in organization-specific terms. Their greater concern, rather, is with categories of organizations (e.g., educational, health-services oriented, or consumer-sales focused). Similarly, their concern is more with environmental fields of forces (impacting upon organizations of common purpose) that with one organization-at-a-time linkages with localities.

Nevertheless, much of the literature does address the value of the new institutionalism in *organizational* analysis, and organization-at-a-time studies have been vital to the development of institutional theory. Two key areas of inquiry have been the deep structures of organizations as reflections of institutionalized elements, and organizations as sources of the institutionalization of new action. Such strange constructs as a 'contagion of legitimacy' and 'infections' (between the elements of organizations) are vital parts of this theorizing (DiMaggio and Powell 1983, Zucker, 1987).

Central to the appeal of the new institutionalism (as well as a source of some confusion) is its multi-disciplinary flavor. Institutional theory is now to be found in the varied forms that grow out of the separate languages of economics, political science, sociology, organizational theory and history. Despite their shared focus upon institutions, the approaches of these disciplines are far from fully compatible.

For example, new institutional economics has attempted to blend the raw rationality and preference-ordering of traditional microeconomics with the constrained-rationality objections of its critics (Moe 1984, DiMaggio and Powell 1991). Similarly, a rational- and/or public-choice movement in political science has focused upon the institutionalized 'rules' and the varying forms of 'order' (e.g., normative, demographic, temporal, etc.) that situationally structure political behavior (March and Olsen 1984; Ostrom 1986). By contrast, much of the theorizing in sociology and organizational analysis has dropped rational-actor assumptions, but has continued a broad focus upon the cultural and historical frameworks that surround individual and group behavior. A key piece of this theorizing has emphasized the 'striking homogeneity of practices and arrangements' across the organizations inhabiting a common institutional environment or field – finding less meaning in the constrained choices of preference-maximizing individuals than in a behavior-driving 'persistence' of practices, processes, and structures 'that are to some extent self-sustaining' (DiMaggio and Powell 1991: 9).

Part I of the Yearbook is devoted to a set of five chapters that examine some reinvention-oriented theorizing for public education, as these theoretical insights relate to the new institutionalism. Given the breadth and complexity of this new field, this edited volume does not attempt to cover the full range of possible new institutional theorizing *vis-à-vis* the politics of education. Nor do the chapters in Part I attempt to provide the thorough coverage of the many disciplinary nuances that would be essential to a deep and full-blown treatment of this field of theory. Rather, the intent in Part I is to provide some illustrative pieces of theoretical framing (from the new institutional literature) around the twin subjects of education politics and reinvented schooling.

Toward this end, in Chapter 1 James Cibulka undertakes a general, introductory look at new institutional theorizing as a source of insights into the incapacities of schools to achieve reform and to satisfy demands for change from their environments.

In Chapter 2, Hanne Mawhinney concentrates with added focus upon the implications of institutional theory *vis-à-vis* the notion of reinvented schooling and the politics of education generally. Next, in Chapter 3, Ellen Goldring reviews the vital topic of environment from the perspective of new institutional theorizing, engaging key questions of the organization-environment relationship in the effort to reinvent schooling. In Chapter 4, Mary Driscoll examines selected themes from the neoinstitutional literature, as this literature relates to differing conceptions of community in education. Finally, in Chapter 5, Terry Moe and Kenneth Shotts use new institutional theory to build a case for radical reinvention of American public schooling and also to critique critics of voucher proposals.

Reinventing the school

What is to be found in new institutional theorizing that can be instructive in the practical task of reinventing schools? Part II provides a set of six chapters that directly address this question. Of course, it is not clear exactly what it means to 'reinvent' anything. The term suggests that much more than 'tinkering' must be involved, that something deep and fundamental is the order of the day. However, the term also suggests a sense of history, or at least some back-to-the-beginnings roots, to *re*-invent that which once was. But, to reinvent (rather than re-create) also suggests a drive toward something innovative or unusual, perhaps a creative and truly 'inventive' solution to an old set of problems.

Each of these notions is well represented in a rapidly developing literature upon which we can draw. In *Reinventing the Factory*, Harmon and Peterson (1990) stress the back-to-the-beginnings importance of *simplification* in manufacturing as a guiding construct, despite the press of our times toward world-class technologies. The elegance of simplicity above the appeal of complex technological wizardry is the 'reinventing it all' message for these authors, a message seemingly quite out-of-step with the trends of the late 1990s. In *Reinventing Government*, on the other hand, Osborne and Gaebler (1992) urge a tinker-no-longer 'revolution' toward entrepreneurial government. Here, the 'reinvent it all' message is very much in step with an anti-bureaucracy mood of the times, a sense that competition, downsizing, and 'customer-driven government' must be among the key ingredients in service renewal. A third example, even closer to education's home, is to be found in let's-get-radical suggestions from Seymour Sarason (1995). The existing governance structure in public education should be abolished, argues Sarason; it has 'proved that it is incapable of initiating and sustaining other than cosmetic changes' (p. 163). It is time now to initiate a new political principle in education, a principle that reinvents institutionally through a newly accorded respect for individual rights and interests.

The six chapters in Part II cover just a sample of the reinventing-the-schools topics that could be addressed and could be instructively analyzed from the new institutionalism perspective. Taken together, these chapters provide a rich introduction into the potentialities of the new institutionalism and the applicability of this theorizing to changing-the-schools issues. Chapter 5, by Gerald Grant and Christine Murray, provides an important historical backdrop to the reinvention idea. In Chapter 6, Mary Anne Raywid applies new institutional thinking to an analysis of a school-within-a-school innovation in one case-study setting. Chapter 7, by William Thomas, Kevin Moran and Jeremy Resnick, presents a case study of the institutional politics surrounding efforts to initiate the contracted-out-management of a single, troubled school in Wilkinsburg, Pennsylvania. In Chapter 8, Ted Kolderie argues that reinvented schooling must 'get radical', with a break-up of big-city districts. Relatedly, Charles Kerchner and Joseph Weeres, in Chapter 9, examine the need for new thinking about the relationships between city schools and their urban environments, as these can be derived from new institutional analyses. Part II closes with a chapter by Rick Ginsberg on the necessary reconceptualization of schools as organizations, amidst the promise of a technology-unleashed twenty-first century.

The new institutionalism under critique

While new institutional theorizing is suddenly a hot topic (Scott, 1995), it is still unclear how much utility it offers in the strategic task of improving public education. If institutions matter, what is yet to be learned in depth about their politics, social structures and performances before we can begin to employ these insights effectively in school improvement? What are the key connections between the broader institutional and the narrower organizational processes of school renewal that are central to our managerial understanding? What are the pitfalls, the dangers, the down side of new institutional theorizing that should be of special concern to the school-improvement community?

Part III includes a set of chapters that offer a critique and analytical appraisal of new institutional thinking *vis-à-vis* the politics of education and school renewal. In Chapter 11, Douglas Mitchell offers a thorough critique of institutional theorizing in organizational analysis, and points in some new directions in understanding the social structure of education. James Ryan, in Chapter 12, brings a postmodern perspective to the appraisal of new institutional theorizing. Finally, in the closing chapter, Robert Crowson and William Boyd try to pull together the strands of new institutional theorizing and insights about school reform for a clearer picture of our contemporary understanding of the politics and potential for reinventing schools.

References

BOYD, W. L. (1995) 'Productive schools from a policy perspective: desiderata, designs, and dilemmas.' Keynote address presented at the annual conference of the International Congress for School Effectiveness and Improvement, Leeuwarden, The Netherlands, January 3–6.

DIMAGGIO, P. J. and POWELL, W. W. (1983) 'The iron cage revisited: institutional isomorphism and collective rationality in organizational fields', *American Sociological Review*, 48, 147–160.

DIMAGGIO, P. and POWELL, W. W. (1991) 'Introduction,' in W. W. Powell and P. J. DiMaggio (eds), *The New Institutionalism in Organizational Analysis* (Chicago: University of Chicago Press), pp. 1–38.

FULLAN, M. G. and MILES, M. B. (1992) 'Getting reform right: what works and what doesn't', *Phi Delta Kappan*, June, 745–52.

HARMON, R. L. and PETERSON, L. D. (1990) *Reinventing the Factory: Productivity Breakthroughs in Manufacturing Today* (New York: Free Press).

MARCH, J. G. and OLSEN, J. P. (1984) 'The new institutionalism: organizational factors in political life' *American Political Science Review*, 78(3), 734–49.

MOE, T. M. (1984) 'The new economics of organization', *American Journal of Political Science*, 28(4), 739–777.

MOE, T. M. (1990) 'Political institutions: the neglected side of the story' *Journal of Law, Economics, and Organization*, 6, 213–53.

OSBORNE, D. and GAEBLER, T. (1992) *Reinventing Government: How the Entrepreneurial Spirit is Transforming the Public Sector.* (Reading, MA: Addison-Wesley).

OSTROM, E. (1986) 'An agenda for the study of institutions' *Public Choice*, 48, 3–25.

SARASON, S. B. (1990) *The Predictable Failure of Educational Reform* (San Francisco: Jossey-Bass).

SARASON, S. B. (1995) *Parental Involvement and the Political Principle* (San Francisco: Jossey-Bass).

SCOTT, W. R. (1995) *Institutions and Organizations: Theory and Research* (Thousand Oaks, CA: Sage).

TYACK, D. and TOBIN, W. (1994) The 'grammar' of schooling: why has it been so hard to change? *American Educational Research Journal*, 31 (3), 453–79.

ZUCKER, L. G. (1987) Institutional theories of organization, *American Review of Sociology*, **13**, 443–464.

ZUCKER, L. G. (1988) (ed.) *Institutional Patterns and Organizations: Culture and Environment* (Cambridge, MA: Ballinger).

Part 1

1. The reform and survival of American public schools: an institutional perspective

James G. Cibulka

Introduction

In the early years of the education reform movement, no one contemplated the demise of the nation's public schools. While the rhetoric was flamboyant ('a nation at risk') and the diagnosis of critics was severe indeed (William Bennett declared Chicago's schools in 'educational meltdown'), no one prognosticized a doomsday scenario for public education. Yet it is just that prospect which has become commonplace in the mid-1990s. Warnings that the future of public education is in jeopardy are heard almost daily, particularly from public school defenders.

There is a very significant problem embedded here. How is it that in the space of roughly a decade, since the publication of *A Nation at Risk*, there has been such a steady escalation of these predictions of imminent decline? Is there something in the reaction of the educational establishment which, by virtue of equivocation or error of judgment, has worsened its political condition? This problem of institutional responsiveness, or *un*responsiveness, will be my focus. As one might expect in a volume devoted to the new institutionalism, I shall argue that this line of analysis is a helpful way to understand public school responses to the reform demands thrust upon them.

First, however, I review two conventional explanations for why school reform has proceeded at such a slow pace.

Utility maximization: individual self-interest

One of the most popular theoretical frameworks for analyzing organizational behavior is public choice theory, which is a specific variant of rational choice theory. Of course, public choice theorists did not invent the idea that actors in politics and organizations operate from self-interest. Pluralist bargaining theory (Dahl 1960, Truman 1951) and pluralist models of organizational behavior (Pfeffer 1991) also begin from the same premise. Variants are applied to organizational analysis by Allison (1971) and Peterson (1976). Choice theorists, however, represent an important departure in the attempt to model utilitarian behavior in organizational and political contexts. First, such models are unitary. They seek to characterize political or organizational behavior not as a collectivity of competing interests but as a single preference schedule. The unit of analysis is the individual bureaucrat. Woking from this approach, a bureaucrat seeks to optimize benefits through the budget (Niskanen 1971).

Second, in the public choice approach self-interest is defined as the pursuit of *selfish* ends: personal gain in the form of higher salaries and benefits, as well as per-

0268–0939/95 $12 · 00 © 1995 Taylor & Francis Ltd

quisites which benefit the individual. Organizational economists emphasize that this is a form of goal displacement; the owners of the firm (in the case of public agencies, the voting-qualified public) have their rights displaced by the managers (Barney and Ouchi 1986).

Depending on which public choice theory one confronts, its core assumptions may be embellished. According to Chubb and Moe (1990), for instance, public education has become so politicized that schools are ridden with rules, principals spend most of their time handling external problems not germane to tasks of teaching and learning, and they are preoccupied with career advancement. Michaelsen (1981) argues that boards of education are unable to check administrative self-aggrandizement because they lack information and are unable to determine public preferences, particularly in socially heterogeneous communities which present schools with conflicting demands and expectations, leaving policy setting prey to control by administrators with self-serving goals. Both of these versions of public choice theory, however, work from the same core assumption upon which the entire public choice perspective is built – that school officials are self-interested and act in pursuit of those selfish ends, resulting in reduced goal effectiveness.

There is a serious problem with this core premise, however, and it affects explanations for why school officials resist school reform. Rational theorists working in the public choice tradition assume that the ends are given and rational behavior is the *strategic* pursuit of those ends. Surely this is a serious distortion. Actors' commitments to institutions are *goal oriented*, not merely strategic. Institutions embody legitimizing values or ends of political action, such as equality or liberty. Accordingly, insofar as actors strive to influence events or control others, their actions often are instrumental to the maintenance of cherished goals and values. Indeed, strategies and goals become hopelessly mixed. For example, school officials often are concerned with preserving their autonomy, whether it is structural independence from city government or reluctance to work collaboratively with other service providers and parents. Such actions are simultaneously strategic and goal oriented. Utility maximization is not pursuit of self-interest alone, but both strategic and goal/value-oriented activity.

It follows that utility-maximization, or preference setting, is influenced by institutional context. Structures and norms frame the way officials (and the public) act, the way they perceive problems and envision solutions. The system of collective bargaining, for instance, institutionalizes labor-management disputes but also imposes sharp constraints on opportunities for innovation, merely because of the procedural requirements it imposes. Norms of standardization, often defended as equitable treatment for children, limit experimentation. The looseness of decision making in educational bureaucracies also provides opportunities for enterprising principals who know how to get what they want for their school from the system, although role socialization to avoid conflict or controversy creates counter-incentives for compliant behavior.

Actors' preferences also reflect a political context. Who lines up for and against policies is critical to how they are perceived. The alliances and coalitions may be shifting or stable, but they do influence the decision whether to favor or oppose a policy, or even whether a situation is defined as a problem requiring a solution. For example, the positions toward reform taken by particular groups may change over time because the group's allies change. The strength of opposing groups may require a change in calculus. In the early 1980s the Wisconsin Association of School Boards (WASB) opposed much legislation increasing state standards for public schools. By the late 1980s, under new leadership and a changing political context, the organization began to alter its posture so that it could not be labeled as reactionary and opposed to all reforms. By becoming an ally of Governor Tommy Thompson on some education reform issues, WASB has been able to increase its influence. Another example: In 1993 the Wisconsin Education Association Council (WEAC) abruptly changed course and decided to stop stonewalling education reform proposals. It saw an opportunity to reach a modus operandi with Thompson on his proposed changes in the collective bargaining law. In exchange for the Governor's promise to pull back on such proposals (as it turned out, only for a year), WEAC agreed to support some of the Governor's proposals the group heretofore had resisted. This 'change of heart' was in fact self-interested, but understandable only within a broader political context. Public choice models, at least as developed thus far, do not take us very far in explaining how and why these changes occur over time. If preferences are determined in a social context, utility-maximization must be portrayed as a dynamic and fluid process of agenda-setting, mobilization of support, and brokering of interests. Preference formation is filtered through a complex institutional system which rational choice theorists ignore, to their peril.

To recap the analysis so far, public choice theory, while clearly focusing our attention on individual self-interest as a key feature of the behavior of school officials, does so at the price of introducing serious distortions. In particular, by offering a model of utility-maximization stripped of value-oriented behavior and of organizational and political context, this theory cannot explain how school officials actually form preferences and why they act as they do.

Organizational dysfunction theory

Another theoretical perspective, which I shall label *organizational dysfunction theory*, is an important corrective to the atomistic assumptions of public choice theory. However, to preview my argument, the theory, too, has its problems, evetually leading us to examine institutional theory.

I admit at the start to taking some liberty in pulling together and treating under the label organizational dysfunction theory (hereafter simply dysfunction theory) what are in reality a number of different theories of bureaucratic behavior. I am not the first to have done it, however. Allison (1971) and Peterson (1976) found much use for this perspective. Organizations fail because of problems of coordination and control. These problems, in turn, are a consequence of organizational complexity, such as specialization of function, subsystem loyalties, and organizational routines (standard operating procedures), all of which prevent bureaucrats from clearly framing organizational problems which might enable them to adopt appropriate policies, or implement them effectively.

March and Olsen's (1986) 'garbage can' theory and Lindblom's (1959) theory of disjointed incrementalism also fit well within this dysfunction model. Owing to the disorderly way in which organizational problems present themselves, and the limited capacity of actors to act within the most rigorous assumptions of a rational decision model, much organizational behavior can be described by non-decisions and problems chasing solutions. Adherence to past policies and tradition outweighs problem-finding and solution-oriented behavior. Only by the farthest stretch of the imagination can adherence to routines, inaction, and so on, be made compatible with the view of organizational actors as utility-maximizing. On the contrary, amidst these normative, structural, and cognitive constraints, they can hardly be expected to optimize anything.

This is such a pervasive view of why organizations fail that it has fueled radical restructuring of private-sector market firms, so that they might become simpler and leaner in management structure, more focused on productivity, and more oriented toward customer satisfaction. Efforts to 'reinvent government' (Osborne and Gaebler 1992) strike the same themes.

There is an important limitation of the dysfunction thesis, however. Problems of organizational responsiveness are seen as emanating from inside the organization. External problems confronting the organization are treated as givens. Why problems appear as they do, prompted by what constellation of external forces, is of relatively little concern to dysfunction theorists. This fact suggests that it is the relationship of the organization to its environment, not principally the internal dynamics of organizational behavior, which must be understood more clearly to solve this puzzle. To be sure, dysfunction theory does not ignore the interface of the organization with its larger environment entirely. Instead, the focus is on the inability of organization actors to perceive problems clearly, respond to them strategically, or process policies in a manner likely to lead to goal achievement.

To understand fully the response of school officials to reform proposals, we must have another theory which captures more directly how problems in the environment affect organizational structures and processes, how actors respond to their environment, and the structures of power relations embedded in both the organization and its environment. This angle of vision provides a broad corrective to the view that implementation breakdowns are principally endogenous (internally driven). A strength of institutional theory is that it can focus on the interpenetration of organizations and their environments, and how strategies for controlling those environments must shift to accommodate the environmental changes. As will be seen, it is this problem which is, in my view, at the heart of the current crisis of legitimacy for public schools.

An institutional model: a brief synopsis

As institutions schools are embedded in a societal environment and a specific institutional environment.[1] The societal environment's key components are the international context within which the society and nation-state operate, the demography of the society, its economic wealth, the structure of social organization, organization of social space, and societal values. In short, this societal environment provides the overall context for institutional actors. Frequently there is little or nothing they can do to alter these societal forces. At best they can hope to anticipate and perceive how changes in this societal environment will impact on the institution, and act accordingly. Some examples of exogenous societal changes which have profoundly reshaped America's public schools are the Cold War, the globalization of the economy, decline of traditional family structures, diversification of the population, suburbanization, and increasing individualism.

By contrast, the more proximate institutional environment, while permeable with the larger societal environment, consists of authoritative and exchange relationships which enable school officials to carry out their mission, however defined. Institutional environments consists of stakeholders who lay legitimate claim to that outcome – producers, consumers, students, taxpayers, interested citizens, as well as social, economic, and political elites. Other institutions such as the media also are important elements within this institutional environment. Perhaps the most important are governmental institutions (which we shall use synonymously with 'the state'), such as bureaucratic regulators, the courts, governmental funding sources, and so on.

The organization's structures can be seen as part of this institutional environment, although in fact the structures typically have evolved in response to pressures from *both* the broader societal environment and the immediate institutional environment. Thus, urban and suburban schools have evolved quite different organizational structures to deliver public education because demographic and class differences between cities and suburbs, rooted in the societal environment, helped shape the organizational structures. At the same time, both urban and suburban schools responded to pressure from teachers' unions in the 1960s by acceding to a system of collective bargaining, which in turn profoundly influenced the bureaucratization of schooling in both contexts.

Institutionalization is the process by which the adaptation of environment occurs and shapes organizational structure. Institutionalization, however, is not only reactive. It can be a highly proactive attempt to shape the environment to serve the institution. Actors, furthermore, can act in pursuit of goal achievement, survival, or legitimacy. Distinguishing among these three forms of *raison d'être* can be difficult (just like distinguishing between goal-oriented and strategically oriented activity), even for those directly engaged in the pursuit of these ends. Suffice it to say here that organizational actors engage in utility-maximization at various times to advance one or another end, quite apart from their own calculus of personal self-interest (the public-choice theorist's premise). Whether institutionalization in fact helps to assure legitimacy and survival, independent of goal achievement, is an empirical question, although most theorists would say the driving force behind institutionalization is precisely that dynamic. To complicate matters further, there is evidence that some institutionalization processes are accidental, and this lack of intentionality complicates change processes (March and Olsen 1989).

The problem of change for public schools: an institutional interpretation

A central feature of institutionalized organizations such as the public schooling enterprise is that the boundaries between organization and its environment are blurred. Theorists may disagree as to whether the institution is its environment or the internal structures and processes of organizations.[2] The dichotomy is a false one, for organizations strive to shape their environments and in turn adapt to them, seeking to imbue themselves with the legitimacy which societal and institutional environments require yet also shaping the (institutional) environment in a way helpful to their ends (goal achievement, legitimacy, or survival). Thus, it has become increasingly difficult to identify the web of interrelationships tying organizational actors to their environments.

This blurring has power implications, of course. The politics of institutionalization is in many respects the aggregation of interests in the service of legitimacy and survival. In the case of schools these interests have been many. In the early years of Progressive reform, business was a dominant influence, although the coalitions of power varied from city to city and over time, sometimes including organized labor, political parties, and reformers of one kind or another. Two significant interests which have expanded their influence in the post-Second World War period are teachers and racial minorities. Teachers won bargaining rights in many regions of the country in the 1960s and 1970s. Civil rights reformers demanded an end to racial segregation in schooling from the 1950s onward, but particularly in the 1960s.

The changes wrought for public schools cannot be underestimated. Gradually there occurred a shift from a political order built on integration to one built on aggregation. Here I borrow terminology from March and Olsen (1989: 117–119), although the concepts are mirrored in political theory, in sociology, organizational theory, and elsewhere. A political system built on integration emphasizes rational deliberation by citizens and elites who pursue the general welfare working from a common set of values (Mashaw 1985, quoted in March and Olsen 1989: 118). History and group obligation assume paramount importance. An alternative approach to popular sovereignty is to construct institutions by electoral processes and bargaining among groups and individuals pursuing self-interest through voluntary exchange, working within established norms and rules such as majority will, individual rights, and so on. We will recognize this legitimizing order as interest-group liberalism or pluralist politics. March and Olsen further argue that leadership is very different in these two governing orders. Integration requires leaders capable of acting as trustees who educate the citizenry and who focus on the common public interest and on tradition. Leaders working within a political system leaning toward aggregative processes must be responsive to emergent sentiments and skillfully build coalitions from these diverse interests, through bargaining, brokering, and compromise.

The Progressive reform ideology, which laid the foundations for the public school institution as we know it today, epitomized an integrative approach to governance. It was an ideology of rational deliberation, application of technical information, and consensus building. School boards and school administration were to be cleansed of partisan self-interest in pursuit of the common public interest. Recruitment of businessmen to serve on school boards (who were presumed to be neither provincial nor self-serving citizens), and depoliticization of school policy setting by creation of politically and fiscally independent school districts were devices to restore a tradition of small-town civility to school politics which many Progressives nostalgically sought to recreate in reaction to the urbanization and industrialization of America.

In practice, the American public system was never fully transformed in the Progressive image. Schools could not avoid social conflict altogether, even behind the mantle of professionalism. The 1930s, for example, proved an early challenge to the Progressive ideology, as the labor movement became increasingly radical and sought a stronger voice on school boards, particularly in cities, while at the same time businesses sought to use the ideology of efficiency to economize, with the Great Depression as a backdrop.[3] These partisan political struggles thus invaded the Progressive ideal of school policy making as the pursuit of a unitary public interest. In these respects, the governance of public schooling was always a mix of integration and aggregation. Nonetheless, at the level of governing structures the reform of American public schools was remarkably complete. Most school systems became politically independent, if not fiscally independent, of municipal governments, and operated largely outside the elctoral processes employed elsewhere in our political system.

It was not until the post-Second World War period that this legitimizing order built on political integration began to unravel and incorporate to an increasing degree the elements of aggregative politics. Perhaps the two major forces responsible for this shift were the racial crisis which began in the 1950s and the organization of teachers into unions in the 1960s. Both served to undercut the legitimacy of professional management of our schools built on technical competence and disinterested expertise. School boards became battlegrounds for civil rights struggles and the organizing efforts of teachers. School superintendents, while attempting to stay above the fray, were unable to avoid conflict. At the time their frequently inept management of these complex problems was blamed on their rural backgrounds. In retrospect, however, it can be seen that the institution of public schooling, created from this ideology of governance, was an important independent contributor to the problems school officials had in managing conflict.

The transformation which schools have been experiencing toward a new system of governance has roughly paralleled the changes in the American political system in recent decades. However, the nation's public schools were not merely examples of this transformation, but were in fact a key institution driving the transformation in the larger social order. Once teacher won the right to bargain collectively, many other public employee and service provider groups (social workers, hospital employees, etc.) followed suit. Once schools became a battleground for civil rights, there was no stopping the expansion of civil rights demands to other institutions such as housing and the labor market.

It is worth reviewing some of the important elements of this shift toward interest aggregation as a mode of governance.

School boards

First, school boards now increasingly look like collections of special interests rather than maintaining the image of public trustees sharing a unitary vision of the public interest. In the 1970s and 1980s pressures occurred from minority communities to reduce the number of at-large seats on school boards in order to increase the chance that minority candidates could be elected (Danzberger *et al.* 1992). At the same time that district and ward representation helped make school boards more diverse, it made them more responsive to geographically specific constituencies. Indeed, these structural changes made it easier for 'one-issue' candidates with narrow agendas to win election, although the proliferation of special-interest candidacies has occurred even without such formal changes in school board election laws. Some of the groups who have demanded and won representation include parents of special education students, parents of the gifted, citizens favoring or opposing particular curricular approaches such as basal readers, teaching of evolution, school prayer, outcome-based education, and so on.

This is a very different picture of school boards from the one painted in the early 1970s by Zeigler *et al.* (1974), who described school board elections as commonly uncontested and issueless. This description may still hold in some suburbs and small towns, although probably far less so even there, and certainly this quiescence does not characterize urban school districts at all.

As school boards have become battlegrounds for many special interests, it is less credible for them to argue that they speak for the community as a whole. Instead, policies increasingly represent bargained compromises among teachers' unions, administrators, other employee groups, and contending external constituencies such as business, African-Americans, Mexican-Americans, and many others.

Regulatory federalism: external dependence and fragmented bureaucratization

The governance system of public schooling also has been evolving away from an integrative model because of two closely related developments. On the one side, governmental regulation of public schools increased rapidly in the 1960s and 1970s and even in the 1980s. Despite considerable rhetoric about 'deregulating' state and federal education policy, only modest steps in this direction have been taken by federal officials, and only a handful of states have begun repeal or even scaling back on their voluminous state education codes. Concerns about accountability, which appeared in the Sputnik debates of the late 1950s, fueled a good deal of the legislation. Battles over racial segregation led to extensive involvement of the federal courts, as well as numerous federal and state laws regulating various aspects of race in the teaching, administration, and governance of the public schools. Such developments prompted Arthur Wise (1979) to lament that these attempts at external regulation of schools were having a negative effect on them and leading to a condition of 'hyperrationalization.'[4] Throughout the 1980s the local share of school funding continued to decline, in the nation as a whole, and by the late 1980s state support exceeded local support, often in response to legislative and court actions intended to improve the equity of funding. Consequently, by the 1980s, amidst state education reform activism, it had become common to point out that local control of public schools, long a cherished value in America, was little more than popular mythology. Public schools may be local institutions in a technical sense, but 'regulatory federalism' made them creatures of state and federal governments. By regulatory federalism in this context I mean simply the use of state and federal power to influence and control local school districts. This regulation touched virtually every aspect of schooling, from the technical core of teaching and learning, to personnel, buildings and grounds, food operations, transportation, health and safety, and so on.

The second development which proceeded hand in glove with this regulatory growth and resulting dependence on external actors was the further bureaucratization of public schools, but along fragmented lines. Bureaucratization, of course, preceded the growth of state and federal regulation. Indeed, it was part of the unitary model of governance favored by Progressives and endorsed by the fledgling discipline of educational administration. Long before external demands mounted for further regulation of schools beginning in the late 1950s, school administrators were committed to the perfection of the bureaucratic apparatus. In Milwaukee, for example, the 1950s witnessed the expansion and addition of numerous new bureaus and departments with the mission of improving curriculum, staff development, testing, and so on (Cibulka and Olson 1993). Indeed, the professionalization of education, grounded in claims of technical expertise and backed by experts in schools of education and regional accrediting associations, provided the legitimacy for this bureaucratization. During this period, the claim was made that education policy should be informed by these experts rather than subject to 'political' influences by politicians and community activists, who presumably represented narrow, special interests rather than the broad public interest.

Regulatory federalism and federal and state grants-in-aid did not so much challenge this bureaucratization as give it new life, at least for a time. Expanded intergovernmental aid and regulation of schools by state and federal governments led educational bureaucracies, never especially strong and always fragmented in their authority, to become Byzantine in form. Federal court orders for desegregation in some school systems such as that in Boston created a separate and duplicative administrative machinery, often outside the direct control of the school board and superintendent and reportable to the federal judge or court-appointed monitoring panel. After the Elementary and Secondary Education Act (ESEA) was passed, a separate bureau or department had to be created in most school systems to administer the law. In a matter of years these offices acquired enormous power, partly because of the supplementary resources they controlled, providing access to jobs, perquisites, and badly needed educational supplies and equipment, but also because the ESEA office was supported by parents and community activists determined to protect their benefits. Reflecting elements of the War on Poverty philosophy of the Kennedy–Johnson administrations, federal law even required that such groups he consulted and sign off on grant applications. ESEA was the largest of these federal programs, but scores of other federal and state policies followed, each of which required some management. Federal policy encouraged a fragmented approach to the management of such programs, because of their categorical nature, and auditing requirements that the funds supplement local (and state) dollars rather than supplant them, among other things. Not until the 1980s did this piecemeal approach to federal policy come in for substantial criticism, because of the tendency it created to overidentify students as possessing special needs, as well as the many coordination problems it created at the local school level. Yet by this time, the particular bureaucratic dysfunctions created by this intergovernmental aid and regulation were firmly in place. Whatever problems the centralized bureaucratic model of governance possessed, well in place by the 1950s, to these were added fragmentation and significant dependence on external constituencies who sought control over these bureaucratic appendages.

To recap, I have argued that the institutionalization of public schooling in the USA has led to a model of governance which, while still officially an integrative model, is in fact aggregative. The ineffectiveness of school boards, the advent of regulatory federalism, evidenced by external dependence and fragmented bureaucratization, are all examples of this trend toward an aggregative order. The fact that this aggregative model has been 'tacked on' to an earlier integrative model of governance contributes to the incoherence of the present institutional system. It has led to an *institutional incapacity* to act decisively with a set of reforms which might satisfy the demands for change coming from the environment.

Milwaukee: an example of institutional incapacity

Two brief case scenarios drawn from the Milwaukee Public Schools (MPS) illustrate this institutional incapacity. The first deals with the school system's attempt to decentralize its operations and the second with its resistance to efforts to provide greater school choice. Both of these examples show how the school system displays residues of the earlier integrative system, which was able to set policy autonomously, but now operates *de facto* as an aggregative unit, where policies are bargained over incrementally and lack any overall coherence.

Context

In June 1995 Howard Fuller resigned as Superintendent of Schools, even though he had been offered a renewal of his contract by the Board of School Directors. Fuller cited

irreconcilable differences with the board over his goals to restructure the school district. Four years earlier in 1991 Fuller had been recruited by Milwaukee business leaders
and supported by the State Superintendent Herbert Grover and Governor Tommy
Thompson. An African-American who was a one-time community activist, Fuller
had assumed leadership roles as a state cabinet officer and vocational college administrator. He had received his doctorate in education from Marquette University but
lacked the normal qualifications for licensure as a superintendent. At the urging of
the State Superintendent, a special law was passed to grant him this license in order
that he might qualify for the Milwaukee school post.

Fuller had not been recruited by the board of education. Indeed, the board
expressed some reluctance to alter its superintendent search procedures to accommodate Fuller's application. However, the board was experiencing difficulty recruiting
other candidates (a number of prominent ones had withdrawn). Further, there was
considerable pressure brought to bear from the business community, metropolitan
newspapers, and most of the African-American leadership in the city. So Fuller eventually was selected. It is fair to say, however, that from the start Fuller was the business
community's candidate.

Despite his reform credentials and his recruitment from outside the public school
establishment, Fuller was no more successful than his predecessors in reforming MPS.
Reform is a prevalent theme in MPS, and scarcely a year goes by without some new
ambitious reform being announced, quietly displacing the discussion of earlier reform
agendas. Meanwhile, very little reform actually reaches the implementation stage or,
having done so, receives enough long-term support to enjoy any likelihood of success.

Issue No. 1: decentralization

Discussons over decentralization of MPS provide a good illustration of institutional
incapacity. As early as 1967 the Academy for Educational Development conducted a
study for the school system recommending decentralization as a means of addressing
the district's ineffective inner-city schools. Despite an effective schools experiment
'Project Rise' begun in 1979 in 18 schools, the school system remained highly centralized. Later in 1985 then Superintendent Lee McMurrin sought to inaugurate an
effective schools model system wide, known as Project Care, but significantly there
was no attempt to decentralize decision making or authority to the school level. In
1988 another Superintendent, Robert Peterkin, divided the school system into six
service delivery areas (SDAS).[5] This regional decentralization plan bore little relationship
to the prevous effective schools efforts or to another policy established by the school
board in the previous uear (1987) to create school-based management (SBM).

The school board adopted guidelines for a voluntary pilot SBM program.[6] From
the beginning the policy was crippled by opposition from the teachers' union the
Milwaukee Teachers Education Association (MTEA) and from reluctant principals who
had a voice through the Administrators and Supervisors Council (ASC). After several
years of debate, the school board mandated in June 1990 that some form of shared decision making should be in place in every school by 1994–95. Giving schools four years
to come up with a plan may seem like a long time, but it took until 1993 to develop a
clarifying memorandum of understanding with the teachers' union, which worried
that SBM would require teachers to assume management responsibilities, and argued
that this model should not be forced on school faculties. These fears existed despite

provisions of the SBM experiment which restricted the powers of SBM Councils; the councils had to comply with all collective bargaining agreements and had decision-making authority over only a small portion of the budget and a few limited areas of the curriculum, such as homework policies, report card format, field trips, recess schedules, and so on. In addition there were some provisions for waiving 47 district requirements.[7]

Indeed, the contractural provisions for SBM which had been adopted, and which guaranteed such things as a minimum of 51% teachers on the SBM councils and pay for staff who participated in SBM, were allowed to 'sunset' in 1992, thereby terminating the SBM arrangements at 70 schools. In the 1993 memorandum reinstateing Part XIII of the Teacher Contract relative to SBM, a compromise was struck in which it was stated that 'all schools shall have a system of local school governance.'[8] This policy for the first time imposed a   system-wide mandate for SBM but was deliberately so broad that schools wanting to implement 'shared decision making' instead of SBM had wide latitude to do almost   anything they wanted. While the school administration and some members of the school board, as well as the Greater Milwaukee Committee (representing the city's business leadership), had been pushing for some system-wide initiative, they had to settle for something which was more symbolic than substantive.

In many cases school principals have been as reluctant as teachers to move forward with SBM. For example, in 1992–93 Superintendent Fuller attempted to equalize budget allocations and to give school principals more budget authority. However, individual principals and the ASC consistently expressed reluctance to accept more budget authority, fearing the work involved and not wishing to be accountable for budget development and management. When Fuller left the school system in 1995, budgeting still had not been decentralized, despite years of study and discusson.

The school system could point to the fact that it had a policy in place for SBM and shared decision making at every school. However, the policy was so lacking in substance and therefore credibility that the school system no longer referred to SBM as a central feature of its reform initiative in its planning and public relations documents. SBM had been neutralized by a reluctant union and bureaucracy and had become by 1994–95 (the original target date for full implementation of the reform set by the school board) a non-issue and non-event.

This case scenario exemplifies a school system which is committed to maintaining its autonomy, which operationally is taken to mean *free from accountability to others for one's actions.* Even moderate reforms such as the SDAs and SBM ran into opposition from teachers and administrators. The school board, influenced by these negative voices, was often divided and indecisive, epitomizing the highly incremental politics of pluralist bargaining, and also at times was ambivalent about relinquishing authority to regions or individual schools. The fragmented bureaucratic structure, reflecting regulatory requirements generated both inside the school system's bureaucracy and from myriad external agencies, also contributed to inaction. Central office officials, and even the school board itself, resisted attempts by SDAs and SBM schools to be treated differentially, citing traditional standardized operating procedures, collective bargaining requirements, and allegiance to external mandates.

Issue No. 2: school choice

A synopsis of the school system's actions regarding school choice suggests that the central issue has been the school system's desire to maintain its autonomy. Because school choice would involve *loss of autonomy (control) to parents by school authorities,* and increased accountability, it has been resisted in several contexts. For example, the school board established a system of specialty and magnet schools in 1976 to respond to a federal court order to desegregate its schools, creating 52 speciality elementary schools (59 remained attendance area schools).[9] Many of these speciality schools were persistently oversubscribed, but school authorities made few efforts to open additional 'high-demand' speciality schools, despite the fact that most speciality schools cost no more to operate than a traditional attendance-area school. Instead, parents were forced to send their children to schools which were their second and third choices. In other words, the system of speciality schools was not intended to carry choice so far that student assignments would be based primarily on parental choice. Put differently, school officials did not approach the task of student assignment from a market or consumer perspective. In 1993 a school board member attempted to win support for this policy shift, but lacked sufficient votes.

MPS was also reluctant to contract with community agencies lest this lead to significant autonomy for parents and their children. In 1980 the Wisconsin state legislature, responding to pressure from a coalition of community-based organizations in the Milwaukee area, had funded an experimental program allowing MPS to contract with these agencies to educate children 'at risk'. Because the school board and administration were very reluctant to enter into any contractual arrangements with these organizations, the latter lobbied the state legislature to create a new state law. MPS was specifically empowered to contract with community organizations to serve up to 30% of its at-risk population. Superintendent Lee McMurrin and the school board did not welcome this opportunity, and entered into contracts to serve fewer than 1000 youth, less than one-fourth the number of youth eligible. The MTEA also was a staunch opponent, even after winning a concession requiring one certified MPS teacher at each site. Opponents on the school board also alleged poor quality in some of the programs, after commissioning a study from a known community critic of the program (Biaz 1992).

Howard Fuller encountered this same internal resistance when he proposed that MPS be allowed to create charter schools and that such schools be open to private contractors. After several years of opposition from the board, Fuller eventually won board endorsement of a weaker proposal for charter schools, subsequently enacted by the Wisconsin legislature in 1994. MTEA and its state affiliate the Wisconsin Education Association Council (WEAC) managed to cripple the law with a requirement that the school board must be the employer. Fuller and the school board had a falling out in 1995 over Fuller's desire to further strengthen the charter law, an effort labeled simplistically by his opponents as 'privatization.' The state legislature did strengthen the law in 1995, but did not go as far as Fuller wanted. In the meantime, Fuller decided to resign, when several school board members were elected on anti-privatization planks. Fuller's opponents were convinced that his policies, if adopted, would destroy public schooling as a guarantor of equal opportunity, thereby linking claims of autonomy to larger societal ends.

In sum, MPS has resisted any efforts or opportunities to extend greater choices to parents and students.[10] While the administrative decentralization of the school system was interpreted as a challenge to the tradition of autonomy enjoyed by all actors – principals, teachers, central bureaucrats, and even the board – as each of these parties related to one another, school choice represents to many school officials not only a loss of autonomy to the environment but a threat to public education itself.

Both the SBM and choice issues, while hardly exhaustive of all the reform issues facing MPS, portray a school system both reluctant to change and, it would seem, incapable of reforming itself. The behavior of the school system indicates a lack of accountability both internal to the school system and to external publics, particularly to parents (a majority of whom are dissatisfied). School officials fight to stave off further influence by parents, or even further authority and accountability for themselves. Ironically, despite evidence that schools have become captive of the special interests of teachers' unions and administrators, their commitment to autonomy persists and is at the root of much institutional incapacity.

The reform of school systems in the early 20th century dominated by professional voices was a successful strategy for consolidating environmental support. Today, however, school officials remain committed to a legacy of structural and normative autonomy which cripples efforts to reform the system. A strategy of institutionalization appropriate to an earlier era is debilitating now and threatens the institution's survival. Yet in the case of MPS, despite warnings by the Governor and members of the state legislature that MPS may be dismantled, the school board and most of the central administration proceed as though environmental support is guaranteed. Further, the system has evidenced a capacity to resist regime changes. Since 1976 Milwaukee has had no fewer than four superintendents who were mandated to achieve major reforms (not counting interim superintendents). Even when the business community successfully installed its own reform superintendent, Howard Fuller, he was unable to prevail.

An institutional model helps capture the problem at hand in a more accurate way than either a public choice, utility-maximization model or a dysfunction model. In their opposition to fundamental reforms of the school system, MPS officials exhibit undoubted self-interest. But that self-interest is modulated by a powerful institutional context, rooted in structural and normative autonomy, which blinds them to alternative policies. Their commitment to the idea that the school system requires autonomous control to operate effectively is a powerful impediment to fundamental reform.

By the 1960s MPS had evolved in point of fact so that it could no longer operate so autonomously and many relationshps with the environment portrayed attributes of an aggregative political order. Officially, however, the system continues to be structured and its normative culture stresses the assumptions of the earlier integrative approach to politics. Thus, there is a significant lag between the institutional environment as it has been transformed and the institutional structures and norms continuing to govern the school system.

Conclusion

Institutional theorists have turned their attention to how institutions change. Perhaps the most popular theory is Krasner's (1984) model of 'punctuated equilibrium,' which posits that institutions change abruptly, due largely to external environmental influences, followed by long periods of quiescence. Moreover, such fundamental change is likely to occur when a number of other institutions within which the institution is embedded also provide opportunities for change, rather than act as an impediment to such fundamental reform.[11]

Have we reached this historical moment with respect to the institution of American public education? Certainly the external environmental forces which public school officials once were able to contain, and the conflict the institution was once able to channel or suppress now appear to be overwhelming it. There is little evidence to suggest that public school officials understand that a fundamental transformation is at hand and that it requires an entirely new approach to organizing and delivering educational services. If that continues to be the case, the fate of the institution of public schooling will be determined largely by forces in the societal and institutional environment, such as the performance of economic institutions in our society, the mobilization of bias for and against the welfare state, and the evolving status of families. Here institutional theory points us in the right direction, by emphasizing the interpretation and interdependence of public schools with other key institutions in our society.

What the theory has not yet resolved, and may never be able to, is how to predict outcomes of attempts to reform institutions, precisely because such outcomes depend not only on complex often unpredictable events but also on agency – the way actors perceive their preferences and options. This analysis has emphasized how institutionalization of schools has proven to be a destabilizing force at the present moment of environmental turbulence, robbing school officials of the capacity to *perceive* their options clearly. It is still within the grasp of public school officials to influence the public school institution's outcome rather than be passive actors in their own possible demise. Whether the institution can summon the capacity for self-insight and self-correction is a chapter of institutional theory – and institutional history – which is still unwritten.

Notes

1. The following section is a synopsis of a lengthier discussion in Cibulka (1995).
2. Meyer and Rowan (1977) and Powell and DiMaggio (1991) frame their analyses to explain how organizations such as schools seek to respond to an institutionalized environment external to the schools. Working within this tradition, Scott and Meyer (1994: 115) argue that institutional theorists call attention to the way cultural rules, i.e. cognitive and normative frameworks, spur the growth of formal organizations. By contrast, Zucker (1987:446–447) argues that institutional elements often have their origins in processes internal to the organization.
3. For these developments in Chicago, see Katznelson and Weir (1987). Mirel (1984) captures the same developments in Detroit. Cibulka and Olson (1993) analyze Milwaukee.
4. In a related vein, in the 1960s and 1970s, there was much talk among experts of so-called growing 'nationalizing influences' on public education, which included not simply laws but extra-governmental influences such as the growth of a national testing industry and national textbook markets, as well as accreditation agencies.
5. Shortly after Peterkin's premature departure several years later, Howard Fuller decided to eliminate the SDAs because of principals' complaints of duplication and confusion.
6. 'Guidelines on School Based Management,' Milwaukee Public Schools, adopted 24 June, 1987.
7. This policy was established in December, 1989, 'Implementation of the Forty-Seven Waivers for SBM Schools.' The central administration assigned schools to one of five levels of autonomy, depending on the school's previous experience with SBM. However, some SBM schools did not participate in the experiment because they believed they had more autonomy outside the experiment. Quoted in Mitchell (1994: 43).
8. 'Memorandum of Understanding Between the MBSD (Milwaukee Board of School Directors) and the MTEA (Milwaukee Teachers Education Association),' adopted 23 September, 1993.
9. Each middle school and high school also has a specialty focus.
10. In the meantime, there was considerable evidence that MPS parents wanted exactly that. A poll conducted by the Wisconsin Policy Research Institute (1994) indicated that 65% of Milwaukee residents supported vouchers, and support was even higher among African-Americans. Residents of the city of Milwaukee are especially likely to prefer parochial schools (33%) or private schools (31%) over public schools (31%). (Others had no

preference.) A private poll conducted for MPS in 1992 indicated that 89% of respondents rated MPS unfavorably, and a majority favored either a complete overhaul (29%) or major change (43%). (Quoted in Mitchell 1994: 47). At the level of overt evidence of parental displeasure with what MPS offers, in 1993 voters rejected a $474 million facilities plan by a three-to-one margin. Also, one can cite a private scholarship program known as Partners Advancing Values in Education (PAVE) funding low-income parents to attend private sectarian schools, which has consistently been oversubscribed. It is important to note that Milwaukee's best-known choice program, which permits a limited number of low-income children to attend qualified, non-sectarian private schools, also was thrust upon MPS by the Wisconsin state legislative, over MPS' opposition. In 1995 when the state expanded its choice law to include parochial schools, the school system was inundated with parent applications, before the Wisconsin Supreme Court put a stay on the implementation of the law, pending a challenge to its constitutionality by the ACLU and other groups. MPS's school board president Mary Bills was publicly sympathetic to the challenge.

11. Not everyone is convinced of the accuracy of this model. For a critique, see Thelen and Steinmo (1992: 15).

References

ALLISON, G. (1971) *Essence of Decision* (Boston: Little, Brown).

BARNEY, J. B. and OUCHI, W. G. (1986) *Organizational Economics* (San Francisco: Jossey-Bass).

BIAZ, T. (1992) *MPS Partnership Schools Qualitative Evaluation: Findings and Recommendations* (Milwaukee: Center for Economic Development, University of Wisconsin-Milwaukee).

CHUBB, J. E. and MOE, T. M. (1990) *Politics, Markets, and America's Schools* (Washington: Brookings Institute).

CIBULKA, J. B. (1995) The institutionalization of public schools: the decline of legitimating myths and the politics of organizational instability, in R. T. Ogawa (ed), *Advances in Research and Theories of School Management and Educational Policy* (Greenwich: JAI Press), pp. 123–158.

CIBULKA, J. G. and OLSON, F. I. (1993) The organization and politics of the Milwaukee public school system, 1920–1980, in J. L. Rury and F. A. Cassell (eds), *Seeds of Crisis: Public Schooling in Milwaukee since 1920* (Madison: University of Wisconsin Press), 73–109.

DAHL, R. (1960) *Who Governs?* (New Haven: Yale University Press).

DANZBERGER, J., KIRST, M. and USDAN, M. (1992) *Governing Public Schools: New Times, New Requirements* (Washington: Institute for Educational Improvement).

KATZNELSON, I. and WEIR, M. (1987) *Schooling for All* (New York: Basic).

KRASNER, S. D. (1984) Approaches to the state: alternative conceptions and historical dynamics. *Comparative Politics*, 16(2), 223–246.

LINBLOM, C. (1959) The 'science' of muddling through, *Public Administration Review*, 19 (Spring), 79–88.

MARCH, J. G. and OLSEN, J. P. (1986) Garbage can models of decision making in organizations, in J. G. March and R. Weissenger-Baylon (eds), *Ambiguity and Command: Organizational Perspectives on Military Decision Making* (Cambridge, MA: Ballinger).

MARCH, J. G. and OLSEN, J. P. (1989) *Rediscovering Institutions* (New York: Free Press).

MASHAW, J. L. (1985) Prodelegation: why administrators should make political decisions. *Journal of Law, Economics and Organization*, 1, 81–100.

MEYER, J. W. and ROWAN, B. (1977) Institutionalized organizations: formal structure as myth and ceremony. *American Journal of Sociology*, 83, 340–363.

MICHAELSEN, J. B. (1981) A theory of decision making in the public schools: a public choice approach, in S. B. Bacharach (ed.), *Organizational Behavior and Representative Government* (New York: Praeger).

MIREL, J. (1984) The politics of educational retrenchment in Detroit, 1929–1935. *History of Education Quarterly*, 24(3), 323–358.

MITCHELL, S. B. (1994) *Why MPS Doesn't Work: Barriers to Reform in the Milwaukee Public Schools*, Vol. 7, No. 1 (Milwaukee: Wisconsin Policy Research Institute).

NISKANEN, W. A. (1971) *Bureaucracy and Representative Government* (Chicago: Aldine-Atherton).

OSBORNE, D. and GAEBLER, T. (1992) *Reinventing Government: How the Entrepreneurial Spirit is Transforming the Public Sector* (New York: Addison-Wesley).

PETERSON, P. E. (1976) *School Politics: Chicago Style* (Chicago: University of Chicago Press).

PFEFFER, J. (1981) *Power in Organizations* (Marshfield: Pitman).

POWELL, W. W. and DiMAGGIO P. J. (1991) *The New Institutionalism in Organizational Analysis* (Chicago: University of Chicago Press).

SCOTT, W. R. and MEYER, J. W. (1994) *Institutional Environments and Organizations: Structural Complexity and Individualism* (Thousand Oaks: Sage).

THELEN, K. and STEINMO, S. (1992) Historical institutionalism in comparative politics, in S. Steinmo, K. Helen and F. Longstreth (eds), *Structuring Politics: Historical Institutionalism in Comparative Analysis* (Cambridge, UK: Cambridge University Press), 1–32.

TRUMAN, D. (1951) *The Group Process: Political Interests and Public Opinion* (New York: Alfred A. Knopf).

WISCONSIN POLICY RESEARCH INSTITUTE (1994) *The Wisconsin Citizen Survey: August 1994*, Vol. 7, No. 6 (Milwaukee: Author).

WISE, A. (1979) *Legislated Learning* (Berkeley: University of California Press).

ZEIGLER, L. H., JENNINGS, M. K. and PEAK, G. W. (1974) *Governing American Schools: Political Interaction in Local School Districts* (North Scituate: Duxbury).

ZUCKER, I. G. (1987) Where do institutional patterns come from?: organizations as actors in social systems, in L. G. Zucker (ed.), *Institutional Patterns and Organizations: Culture and Environment* (Cambridge: Ballinger)

2.   The new focus on institutions and the reinvention of schooling

Hanne B. Mawhinney

The politics of reinventing schooling in America

As North Americans approach a new millennium, the concern with reinventing public schooling that has swept into discourse on educational policy change shows few signs of losing its imaginative appeal to reformers and researchers (Ball 1994, Borman and Greenman 1994, Moorman and Egermeier 1992, Murphy 1991, Osborne and Gaebler 1992, Ravitch and Vinovskis 1995, Tyack 1995). In the United States, for example, a 'growing perception that fundamental educational change is not only desirable but necessary to the economic, social, and political well being of the nation' led to the passage of the Goals 2000: Educate America Act, in 1994 (O'Day 1995: 99). This legislation seemed to signal a new era of federal involvement in setting a national agenda for reform. It was to represent a new effort to incorporate the learning of two decades of educational policy analysis into a framework for systemic reform which aligned incentives for change at each level of government: federal, state, and local (Riley 1995).

Just prior to the recent Republic Party sweep of the United States Congress, Robert Riley, the United States Secretary of Education, described the enactment of the Clinton administration's legislation, Goals 2000: Educate America Act as 'nothing less than landmark legislation' (1995:23). It was, he stated, 'the first time in the nation's history [that] a statutory framework defining an appropriate role for the federal government in education has been enacted' (p. 4). Goals 2000 was called notable for not only setting out a systemic policy framework linking schools with state and federal educational bodies, but also for the unprecedented bipartisan support it generated for a new approach to reform 'built around high standards and community participation' (Riley 1995: 23).

O'Day (1995: 100) described the potential for Goals 2000 to reinvent schooling through a systemic reform strategy, focused on 'improved student learning through clear, common standards and coherent policy support for school-based change'. It is, according to O'Day, a strategy which combines 'the vitality and creativity of bottom-up change efforts with an enabling and supportive structure at more centralized levels of the system' (p. 100). In less than a year, the belief that Goals 2000 signaled the start of a new era of educational improvement in the USA expressed by Riley, and O'Day, and other supporters, has proven more than overly optimistic. The legislation appeared to have all the elements to successfully address the constraints imposed on federal policy making by what Skowronek (1982), in his historical study of the expansion of national administrative capacities, determined was an enduring bias toward localism in American political ideology. Despite this design, conservatives in Washington are

0268–0939/95 $12 · 00 © 1995 Taylor & Francis Ltd

now calling for its abolition. Secretary of Education Riley expressed his dismay at recent charges that the legislation could 'result in an unprecedented federal intrusion' in state responsibility for schooling by noting 'All we [federal government] do is say, you – the states and local schools – have to develop your own reform plan to try to reach broad national goals. I don't think people quarrel with the goals. They're very broad practical goals' (Feldman 1995: 1). Despite Riley's efforts, Goals 2000 has become a 'lightening rod' for discontent with federal involvement in education. The discontent even threatens the Department of Education, which is under scrutiny by the Republican-controlled Congress.

An institutional focus for politics of education inquiry

The politics surrounding Goals 2000 in the USA, and those engendered in the many other western countries currently in the throes of reinventing schools, pose challenges for students of the politics of education seeking to examine the institutional forces at play in systemic and national educational reform. A new focus on institutions is among the array of approaches to analyze various dimensions of proposed reforms that students of the politics of education are offered in the social science disciplines. New institutionalism represents a revision of the behavioralist paradigm which in previous decades directed researchers in the social sciences to examine the observable beliefs and behaviors of groups and individuals, diminishing 'the attention once given to institutional context and actual outcomes' (Shepsle 1986: 52). Although the social science disciplines share the assumption that institutions 'matter' in ways not captured by behavioralism, important differences are evident among institutionalists in the disciplines of political science (Hall 1992, March and Olsen 1989, Skocpol 1985, Steinmo *et al.* 1992), economics (Moe 1990, Williamson 1995), anthropology (Berger and Luckmann 1967) and sociology (Powell and DiMaggio 1991, Scott and Meyer 1994, Scott 1995).

Students of the politics of education have begun to incorporate these diverse conceptual perspectives into their analyses of different dimensions of reform with the same eclectic pragmatism that has characterized their field of study during the past quarter century. In the process they have, however, not been overly concerned with examining the contradicting assumptions evident in various disciplines regarding the institutional forces at work in educational reforms. Any new insights forthcoming from the institutional analyses of educational reforms may be undermined by the failure to grapple with these contradictions. New institutional theories may contribute less to our conceptual understanding of the politics of education than they do to the further diffusion of an already disparate field of inquiry. Indeed they may exacerbate an effect observed by Scribner and Layton (1995), who reflect that during the course of its 25-year history, the politics of education has become 'a rich and maturing field of research and study, albeit disparate, fragmented, and perhaps at times even schizophrenic' (p. 1).

My argument in this chapter is that given this fragmented conceptual foundation, those who wish to enlighten our understanding of the politics of education must maintain the critical stance which has also characterized much work in the field (see Peterson 1995), in exploring the conceptual opportunities offered by the divergent thrusts of institutional theorizing. The trends of institutional thinking that I explore here are intended to identify some challenges for institutional research on reinventing schooling that builds on the tradition of critical conservatism in politics of education scholarship.

The changing study of politics of education

In recent years those who have analyzed the politics of educational reform have examined the claims of reformers offering solutions to the apparent stagnation in educational change. They have explored proposals for vouchers to enhance parental choice (Boyd and Walberg 1990), decentralizing control of education, equalizing expenditures, chartering schools, contracting schools to private providers, detracking classrooms, credentialing teachers (Popkewitz and Brennan 1994), and professionalizing teaching. According to Peterson (1995) these analyses, exemplified in successive yearbooks of the Politics of Education Association, share a 'skeptical conservatism' rooted in the traditions of political theory. Peterson observes that the 'discipline of the politics of education' that has emerged is

> . . . both critical and conservative . . . it is skeptical of the institutions it studies, but it is cautious about proposing changes. If its treatment of those in authority is often sardonic, it is not less dubious of proposed remedies and reforms. (p. xiii)

The critical stance of politics of education scholarship extends to its links with the parent discipline of political science. While students of the politics of education have tracked the theoretical developments in that discipline, they have done so selectively and critically (Wong 1995). They have largely avoided the limitations of focusing essentially on 'what is' imposed by the conceptual orientation to behavioralism which dominated political science. Instead they have consistently acknowledged the importance of history or 'what has been,' and the importance of normative discourse on 'what ought to be' (Wong 1995: 22).

Reassessments of the state of study of politics of education by contributors to the *Politics of Education Association 25th Anniversary Yearbook* place the field at a point of departure into new realms of theoretical analysis of the rapidly changing domain of education. The essays in the yearbook reach into disciplines of anthropology, sociology, economics and organizational theory for theoretical guidance in analyzing the social processes evoked in the current era of educational reform. At the same time some contributors ask us to keep sight of the longstanding concerns of political science-based inquiry in examining the new terrain of educational change (Stout *et al.* 1995).

Both directions have been taken by educational analysts during the past decade. We have a growing body of research and writing on: changing American education (Borman and Greenman 1994), the changing contexts of teaching (Lieberman 1992), the problems and prospects of restructuring schools (Lane and Epps 1992), the changing patterns of power evident in teacher education reform (Popkewitz 1993), the more generic change forces at play in reform (Fullan 1993), new images of schools (Bacharach and Mundell 1995), and on the potential of learning from past reform efforts (Ravitch and Vinovskis 1995). Although these, and other studies, share a preoccupation wth the dynamics of changing the institutional structures and processes of education, their link with the new institutional theorizing in the social science disciplines is not always explicit. Educational analysis of reform has not fully benefited from the new directions in institutional theorizing.

The failure to incorporate conceptual directions from new institutional theories into current analyses is significant because the research to date suggests that the process of institutional revision is more fundamental than past attempts at educational reform (Murphy 1991). Basic elements of public schooling as we have come to know it are under revision. Reformers call for efforts to decentralize the organization, management, and governance of schooling; empower those closest to students in the classroom (i.e. teachers, parents, and principals); create new roles and responsibilities for all the players in the system; and transform the learning–teaching process that unfolds in the classroom.

These changes challenge our understanding of the relation of schools to their environments, of the nature of change and conflict in public organizations, of organizational behavior and its relation to individual action, and of the deep institutional forces at play and their relation to changing ideologies defining public schooling. During the past decade similar challenges have been the focus of inquiry for new institutional theorists of various persuasions who have explored different social processes and structures in a number of contexts. That their efforts are only now being examined by educational researchers seeking new approaches to analyzing these phenomena in school reform is partly because of the very diversity of theorizing that is currently underway in the name of new institutionalism.

Conceptual dimensions of institutional theorizing

Educational researchers can hardly be faulted for puzzling over the differences among the strands of institutional theory that even proponents such as DiMaggio and Powell (1991) describe as ambiguous and paradoxical. Like other institutional theorists, DiMaggio and Powell acknowledge the differences among orientations in the meaning attributed to the concept of 'institutions,' the emphasis placed on micro and macro features, the different weighting accorded cognitive and normative aspects of institutions, and the importance attributed to 'interests and relational networks in the creation and diffusion of institutions' (p. 1). Students of the politics of education may find the conceptual pluralism of new institutionalism in keeping with the traditions of their field of study. Different conceptions of institutions and institutional processes offer opportunities to analyze the processes of revision of core elements of schooling from various perspectives. However, the difficulty in gaining understanding of the differences among new institutional perpectives is that until recently there have been few attempts to examine these differences systematically. This condition presents a challenge to researchers concerned with contributing to a more focused dialogue on emerging issues in the study of politics of education.

Although there is no definitive analysis of new institutional perspectives, students of the politics of education may now examine different accounts of their differences by organizational sociologists Powell and DiMaggio (1991), Scott, Meyer and their associates (1994) and Scott (1995); and by political scientists March and Olsen (1989), Thelen and Steinmo (1992), Krasner (1984) and Robertson (1993). DiMaggio and Powell (1991) express a view that most analysts of new institutionalism share:

> There are, in fact, many new institutionalisms – in economics, organization theory, political science and public choice, history, and sociology – united by little but a common skepticism toward atomistic accounts of social processes and a common conviction that institutional arrangements and social processes matter. (p. 3).

Conceptions of exactly how institutions 'matter' vary among different perspectives, according to those who have examined new institutional theories. Analysts identify several strands of institutional theorizing, some within the same discipline. For example, Scott (1995), who has developed perhaps the most formalized typology of institutional theories, identifies three contrasting models of institutions based on different assumptions regarding the nature of reality and how to account for behavior. Perspectives vary in the assumptions they make about the nature of reality and in their assumptions about whether there is a reality external to the individual or whether actors and actions are social constructed. Scott also distinguishes among assumptions regarding how actors make choices and the type of logic used to determine social action. These assumptions are evident in different views of the basis of compliance, the mechanisms for diffusion of social processes, the logic of action adopted, the cluster of indicators of institutionalization, and the foundation for legitimacy claims. Scott argues that differences among these dimensions account for what he calls regulative, normative and cognitive models of institutions. Regulative models depict institutions as legally sanctioned rules, laws and sanctions that operate through coercive action to achieve desired ends. According to Scott, theorists focusing on regulative elements are more likely to adopt a social realist ontology and to emphasize a rational choice model of action. He classifies the new historical institutionalism found in the work of political scientists such as Thelen and Steinmo (1992) and the neo-institutional approaches to economics taken by Moe (1990), North (1990), and Williamson (1985) as illustrative of regulative institutionalism. In contrast, normative models, adopted by traditional institutional sociology, describe institutions as systems tied together by social obligation and rules of appropriateness. The new institutionalism in the work of sociologists such as DiMaggio and Powell (1991) and Scott and Meyer (1994) takes a cognitive turn, emphasizing a social constructionist set of assumptions, and embracing a theory of practical action in which 'taken for grantedness' forms the basis for compliance.

These general dimensions outline the framework of Scott's (1995) approach to identifying the basis of some of the confusion and controversies among new institutional perspectives over questions such as: are the "pillars" of institutions bundles of sanctions, collections of norms, or clusters of cognitions? Do institutions vary in their reliance on one or another of these pillars? Do different institutional forms have different effects on the constituent units? How do institutions arise and persist? decline and collapse? Scott's analysis is not definitive; however, it does suggest that the scope of institutional theorizing underway captures the range of concerns of researchers studying the politics of reinventing schools. The typology hints at the conceptual issues of change, power and efficiency with which new institutional theorists of all persuasions are currently grappling (DiMaggio and Powell 1991).

These are exactly the issues confronting students of the current politics of educational reform in examining the problems and prospects for the reinvention of schooling. As educational analysts Moorman and Egermeier (1992) suggest, the agenda for reinvention focuses attention on the new dynamics of institutional performance and change. These dynamics pose conceptual challenges for educational analysts that can be informed by different strands of institutional theory. In the following sections of the chapter I set out directions for institutional research on some of these dimensions of reinvention. I illustrate ways in which strands of institutional theory focus our attention on different sets of assumptions about reinventing schools, define different questions as salient, focus on different levels of aggregation, and raise different challenges to established orientations to the study of the politics of education. My intention in pointing to the institutional forces at play is to set out some of the challenges on the frontiers of institutional theorizing that have the potential to contribute to a new generation of politics of education scholarship.

The institutional dynamics of reinventing education

New institutionalists in both sociology and political science agree that the pervasive tendency in both fields to emphasize institutional constraints has produced better explanations of what change efforts are not possible than what might promote change. Beyond this common focus on constraints there are substantial differences in new institutional approaches to the problems of change implied by current reform initiatives. The notion of 'reinvention' conveys a sense of the dynamics of institutional and organizational change. It suggests change of a scope to challenge the basic assumptions underlying conceptions of schooling:

> . . . the values and beliefs that dictate the establishment of a certain kind of order, control, accountability, legitimacy, and pattern of relationships. (Moorman and Egermeier 1992: 47).

New institutionalist analyses in organizational sociology and in alternative approaches in political science focus on various of these dimensions in their conceptualizations of the problems of change. In the following sections of this chapter, four orientations to change, each grounded in a unique interpretation of why institutions matter, are discussed. First, Jepperson and Meyer's (1991) conception of the nature of knowledge systems giving impetus to change provides a rationale for subsequently examining organizational sociology and public choice theorizing, two orientations to institutional theorizing which have each been incorporated by educational analysts constructing the knowledge system for reinventing schools. Finally discussed is a fourth orientation by the school of political science known as historical institutionalism. It refocuses our attention on the traditional concerns of politics of education inquiry by offering a conception of the interaction of institutions, ideas and interests that gives impetus to the dynamism implied by the reinvention agenda.

Reinvention as constructed by agents of change

Although sociologists such as Jepperson and Meyer (1991) acknowledge that some forces of change may be seen as exogenous to institutions, they focus specifically on institutional sources of change in formal organizing, because they believe that 'non institutional accounts greatly exaggerate its less-institutional features' (p. 225). They distinguish between institutional sources of change that are internal to a given polity from those which are external. They describe institutional changes, such as those in the reinvention of school agenda, which call for a new focus on accountability through setting national educational goals and assessing outcomes of those goals, as given impetus by conditions external to a given polity. Their approach to institutional analysis suggest directions that could be taken in examining how the concept of educational accountability through standards and outcomes has become widely diffused among western nations. Jepperson and Meyer direct researchers to look for evidence of cultural isomorphism which facilitates local change through competition and diffusion. Such analysis would examine the forces giving impetus to the diffusion of outcomes-based assessment processes across states and provinces, and among western nations.

The analysis would necessarily look at the role of educational policy researchers and domains of inquiry such as the politics of education in defining accountability as a problem of change. Jepperson and Meyer (1991) describe both researchers and the associations where their conceptions are legitimized as 'agents of institutional change' by virtue of their playing 'empowered roles, particularly in importing changes from the external system and interpreting them as producing public goods for the local collective' (p. 226). These sociologists note, as an example, the diffision of doctrines of new forms of equality and versions of economic thinking among social scientists throughout the world. In western political systems where 'justifications rest so heavily on doctrines of effectiveness and justice in an evolving real world, the carriers of knowledge have high standing as agents of collective interest . . . [and] their justifications are crucial to most institutional changes' (p. 226).

These arguments set an agenda for new institutional inquiry into the politics of constructing the problem–solution mix that has become defined as reinventing schools. Although long-time scholar of the politics of education Paul Peterson (1995) describes the domain as characterized by a critical conservatism, the 'sardonic' stance to which he refers has most often been directed toward politicians and policy makers. Researchers in the field have not generally turned their analytic gaze toward the involvement of their colleagues in defining educational problems and the changes required for their solution. Jepperson and Meyer's (1991) research suggests that inquiry into the empowered roles accorded educational analysts would examine the impact of the turn to the study of policy that overtook politics of education inquiry during the past two decades. Contributors to the recent *Politics of Education Yearbook* who examined this turn are equivocal in their assessment of its impact on politics of education inquiry, some faulting the failure to focus on traditional political issues in policy analysis (Sroufe 1995, Stout *et al.* 1995), others describing a lack of strong theoretical basis for analysis (Cibulka 1995).

The new institutional theorizing exemplified in the propositions of sociologists such as Jepperson and Meyer (1991) suggests a different line of inquiry into the transformation of the domain of politics of education into the study and, increasingly, the practice of policy analysis and policy making. They describe the special 'licensing' of social scientists, and of their associations, to define problems and justifications for particular solutions. Their concern is with the influence of different polity forms in creating such licensed social actors. They argue that national polities differ in their social organization, and in the dominant sources of institutional change in formal organizing. Liberal systems such as the USA and Canada, 'lacking a specified definition of social interests and functions, elaborate knowledge systems that support and stabilize interests' (p. 227). As new issues arise these systems organize them in characteristic ways. For example, Jepperson and Meyer argue that in the USA, with its licensed actors and interests, 'change is pursued by individuals who speak as interested citizens with a bit of technical expertise, rather than as direct embodiments of central authority' (p. 227). These propositions assume that there is some underlying definition of the common good; however, Jepperson and Meyer acknowledge that their theorizing does not specify how such definitions are produced. They do recognize that conceptions of the common good are contested and propose that political change, and subsequent organizational change, is generated by a basic contradiction in the 'empowerment of both collectives and individual persons as rational moral projects' in modern polities (p.229).

A critical analysis informed by the new institutionalism conceived by Jepperson and Meyer would examine the creation of knowledge systems by educational policy analysts. Following their propositions suggests that politics of education researchers engaged in policy analysis, and in some cases policy advocacy, on the requirements for reinventing schools not only participate in creating knowledge systems for the common good, but also act as licensed agents of change for the polity. An institutional analysis would look for the ways in which educational researchers have informed the current proposals for reinventing schools. In the USA this research would examine the construction of the concept of 'systemic change' in educational research communities, and its transformation by politicians and policy makers into an agenda for reinventing schools. This analysis would examine the links between educational research, policy analysis, and policy advocacy, and proposed systemic changes encompassing what O'Day (1995) describes as

> . . . a unifying vision and goals, including ambitious learning outcomes for all students; coherent instructional policies aligned in support of achieving that vision; and a restructured system of governance and resource allocation that places greatest authority and discretion for instructional decisions on those closest to the students – that is teachers and others at the school site. (p. 100)

An institutional analysis would find that these elements of systemic reform have been informed not only by new research findings on the nature of the teaching–learning process, but also by the understanding of the symbolic and structural characteristics of schools gained through a generation of educational research on the constraints to planned educational change that has itself been informed by institutional theorizing.

One of the potential contributions of new institutional thinking is its capacity to focus our analytic gaze on the ways in which all kinds of theorizing, even the new institutional sort, has been used to guide the construction of educational policy solutions. Two orientations to new institutional theorizing have found particular favor among students of the politics of education, one drawn from the sociology of organization, and the other from the public choice school of political science. As the following discussions suggest, both have informed the knowledge system seen as a legitimate basis for guidance by educational policy makers, analysts and researchers.

Conceptions of constraints to reinvention from organizational sociology

Educational policy analysts have found the focus on organizational constraints by new institutional sociology to be congruent with their conceptions of the problems of changing schools. Their work has been influenced by the work of American organizational sociologists such as Meyer and Rowan (1977), Meyer *et al.* (1983), and Weick (1979). These theorists forged new directions in institutional theorizing on the structural characteristics of schools, and their relations to education systems, that influence their capacity to change. They highlighted the organizational characteristics of loose coupling and tight integration as influencing the capacity of schools to change. Their research, and more recent studies, provide an institutional analysis of the common observation that although schools are relatively autonomous from the larger educational system and from environmental forces, the system as a whole is remarkably uniform. Being loose coupled preserves a degree of flexibility and variety in schools, both valuable tendencies if the purpose of the change effort is to ensure pluralism of outcomes, or if there is a need to promote local responsiveness to new circumstances, or to ensure a degree of stability and predictability in the entire system (Moorman and Egermeier 1992).

Institutional sociologists studying schools have contributed a new understanding of institutional forces giving impetus to systemic integration. They have theorized that institutions like schools gain legitimacy and societal support by incorporating the rational myths of the society. The myths of 'real school' are incorporated as taken-for-granted roles and rules concerning classroom structure, accreditation, grade structure and grading, established texts, testing and accountability functions (Meyer *et al.* 1983). Analysts of educational change have examined the implications of these structural characteristics for the policy approaches required to reinvent schools. Moorman and Egermeier (1992) speculate, for example, that loose coupling and tight integration are conditions that reflect 'opposing cultural orientations embedded within a common cultural field' (p. 50). They see loose coupling as an organizational expression of American values of 'opposition to centralized authority, individuality and autonomy, diversity, and local innovation . . . [and] tight integration is the expression of cultural myths concerning technical rationality and control, the "melting pot" that creates one out of many, and the power of institutions to subdue and engineer a desired future' (p. 50).

Loose coupling and tight integration reflect the oppositional drives and constraints embedded in common cultural assumptions about schools. Policy change efforts focused only on responding to the imperative for tight integration will result in 'hyperrationalization,' or increasing efforts to control and mandate change by policy makers. This, they argue, will ultimately produce increasing loose coupling by those targeted for control. Moorman and Egermeier conclude that these tendencies suggest that successful educational reform requires the creation of an integrative myth that 'emphasizes coordination and enablement and that stimulates behavior more in line with the loosely coupled nature of the education system' (p. 52).

The institutional arguments laid out by Moorman and Egermeier have been used by educational analysts who take a professional orientation to reinventing schools. They argue that changing teachers' working conditions, including introducing greater control by members of the profession over teaching quality and competence and enhancing norms of collegiality, will improve schooling (Wise 1990). The strategy for change that follows from the professional imperative in current reform initiatives directs policy makers to adopt bottom–up strategies that focus on classroom and school-level changes that enhance the professionalization of teaching. A new institutionalism of politics of education inquiry would examine the interaction of these, and other forces, giving impetus to the construction of the problem of reinventing schools as one of enhancing teacher professionalism. It would also look at the basis upon which enhanced teacher professionalism is contested by alternative constructions of the problem of reinventing schooling.

Reinventing schools through public choice

One of those alternative constructions is based on the application of a market approach to changing schooling incorporating the new institutionalism in political science known as rational choice theory. This approach has been the focus of much of the institutional analysis by scholars of the politics of education (see Boyd *et al.* 1995). However, unlike the widely diffused and accepted knowledge system of the institutional constraints inherent in the structure of schools and schooling generated by the new institutional sociology, rational choice theorizing remains a contested and poorly understood approach. Educational analysts have been quick to seize upon school choice through vouchers, one of the policy strategies that the approach has generated, but less direct in examining the institutional rationale that public choice is based upon. In recent years, for example, educational analysts and policy makers have been drawn to the argument that schools would improve if the match between consumer preferences and educational programs were determined through market forces of supply and demand. They argue that educational choice ensures the most efficient service and the most accountable operation. Choice made possible by participation entitlements, or vouchers, would allow attendance at different schools on the basis of the preferences of consumers. The assumption is that schools will be motivated to reinvent themselves in the image desired by consumers, by the need to survive in a competitive market.

Although vouchers and public choice strategies have been incorporated into the knowledge system for reinventing schools, just how these strategies for changing schools reflect a new institutionalism in political inquiry is less well articulated. Politics of education inquiry has largely ignored the attention this theory pays to the institutional framework within which citizens, politicians and bureaucrats determine the allocation of resources. It has not explored the assumption that each of these groups of actors will manipulate elements of the institutional framework to their advantage. Some of these ideas are well known in traditional politics of education inquiry, but little effort has been made to explore the arguments of rational choice theorists such as the proposition that politicians will favor the use of hidden taxes, will enact unpopular policies early in their mandate, and will provide selective benefits to specific groups that ensure their re-election.

Nor have students of the politics of education incorporated into their analyses the rational choice analysis of bureaucratic decision making and the problem of state autonomy. Rational choice theory depicts bureaucrats as displaying a pattern of behavior unrelated to the preferences of citizens. An influential early rational choice analysis suggested that independent of serving the public interest, bureaucrats sought to maximize their 'utilities' (e.g. salary, public reputation, power patronage, output of the bureau, ease of making changes and managing the bureau) by increasing the budget allocated to their bureau by the governmental sponsors (Niskanen 1971).

These, and more recent public choice conceptualizations, have the potential to set new directons for politics of education inquiry into the impact of state autonomy on efforts to reinvent scools. In the USA such an inquiry could, for example, examine the role of federal legislators and state governors in supporting and contesting Goals 2000 and other federal efforts to reinvent schools. The analysis would be guided by the depictions by public choice theories of the policy process as relatively insulated from public preferences and demands by a number of systemic elements including: the decision rule structure of a society (simple majority, plurality), the length of time between elections, and the range of potential policy interventions that a citizen chooses by voting for a representative or for a political party. The analysis would consider the proposition that governments are insulated from citizen demands, and are thus, made more autonomous by periodic elections and bureaucratic autonomy, and by the resources at their disposal to manipulate the political environments. These institutional features of state interventions are important in rational choice theory because they impose constraints on self-interested behavior.

Politics of education inquiry into reinvention of schools using these, and other propositions of rational choice theory, would construct a more robust knowledge base for assessing a market approach to reinvention. This inquiry would examine the basis upon which the theory contrasts the institutional constraints operating within the public sector with idealized conceptions of the market. To date, much of the use of rational choice theory in education has argued for the use of mechanisms such as vouchers to stimulate the development of pseudo-market conditions in the public sector of education (Chubb and Moe 1990). The basic argument is that state actions are less efficient than market operations. However, closer examination of the rationale undergirding this argument would lead educational analysts to consider the arguments by critics who suggest that it may neglect the institutional structure of markets, and that the resulting organizational frameworks may vary among different market operations substantially. Hall (1986), for example, concludes that 'many public choice theorists may be guilty of juxtaposing an idealized conception of market operation to more institutionally nuanced views of government behavior' (p. 12). Analyses such as suggested here may find that although the ambitious theoretical propositions set out by public choice theorists have received considerable attention by politics of education researchers, the rational political behavior predicted by the theory is not always evident in their findings. Empirical studies in other domains have found that the 'ruthless elegance of these models often seems to founder on the complexities of political motivation and economic behavior' (Hall 1986: 10). Even political scientists such as Moe (1990), who see in this economic orientation to new institutionalism the promise for a general rational choice theory of social institutions, recognize the limitations of an approach that does not account well for the informal, indirect, unintentional and systemic control aspects of political behavior.

Students of the politics of education acknowledge that these are important aspects of the kind of educational policy changes that are proposed to reinvent schools. Nor does rational choice theory provide an adequate framework for analysis of the contested conceptions of the common good that create the institutional dynamism evoked by the interaction of institutions and political processes across time. These phenomena are more directly the focus of inquiry by the historical institutionalism that has developed in political science. The final section of this chapter turns to consider historical institutionalism as an approach which extends the traditional concerns of politics of education inquiry into a new conceptual terrain.

Conceptual issues in analyzing institutional dynamism

Historical institutionalism shares with rational choice theory the assumption that institutions provide the context in which political actors define their strategies and pursue their interests (Hall 1986). It differs from rational choice institutionalism in its orientation to the problem of the 'state,' which in contemporary political theory concerns the bases of state autonomy and its relations to configurations of power in civil society (Pal 1993: 34). Neo-institutional theories adopting a historical perspective do not assume an essential relation between the state and civil society. It follows that the state has the capacity to act independently, although the degree and strength of autonomy and capacity to act are constrained by historical context and current forces. Thus 'individual state officials operate within structures and circumstances that are to some extent given' (Pal 1993: 35). In neo-institutional theories these structures and circumstances include 'a host of factors from organizational context to availability of ideas for policy responses' (p. 35).

The state in this sense is conceived narrowly as state officials with their own preferences and capacities to effect public policy. Or, it may also be seen from a macro-perspective as encompassing the organizational configuration of state officials. Skocpol (1985) argues that this approach is important, not just because of the implications of the choice of governing instruments by state officials, but also because:

> . . . their organizational configurations, along with their overall patterns of activity, affect political culture, encourage some knds of group formation and collective political actions (but not others), and make possible the raising of certain political issues (but not others). (p. 21)

Thus, the design of political institutions is as important to political democracy as are economic and social conditions. Institutions such as legislatures and courts are not only arenas for power struggles between proponents of different models of schooling, but they also embody 'collections of standard operating procedures and structures that define and defend interests' that characterize particular types of state/society relations and engender particular dynamics (March and Olsen 1984: 738).

Although these and other conceptions found in historical institutionalism have been less directly incorporated into the knowledge system constructed by educational analysts to define the problem of reinvention, they offer insights into the interaction of the institutions, ideas, and interests involved. These interactions refocus politics of education inquiry on aspects of the reinvention agenda which have traditionally informed studies of political and policy change. Particularly important for inquiry into the politics of reinvention is the capacity of historical institutionalism to frame our analytic gaze on sources of institutional dynamism. This turn to analysis of processes of change is new to institutional analysis, which has tended to produce mechanical, static accounts. Recent developments in historical institutionalism move beyond comparative statics to explore the political conditions under which particular institutions have specific consequences, and to consider how institutions are formed and change (Thelen and Steinmo 1992). This final section of the chapter describes some of the new directions for inquiry into the politics of reinventing schools suggested by research focused on these dimensions of dynamism.

One of the contributions of the historical approach to institutional analysis is the emphasis it places on changes over time and its consequent refinement of our understanding of those institutional forces which generate path-dependent development, and the conditions of crisis that give impetus to rapid and sometimes substantial change. Thelen and Steinmo (1992) use an historical frame for analysis to describe a number of conditions of dynamism encompassing both path-dependency and crisis-punctuated change which can inform new institutional analyses of the politics of educational change.

These political scientists describe the condition where the same institutions produce different outcomes over time as occurring when changes in socioeconomic or political contexts result in previously latent institutions suddenly becoming salient. They cite the example of the transformation of the European Court of Justice from a minor actor in European politics into a locus for conflict and cooperation, by recent cross-nation legislation. Similar phenomena may be evident in an analysis of the new role for American courts generated by Goals 2000. Heise (1995) anticipates the kind of analysis that will be required of scholars of politics of education exploring this new role when he suggests that 'it is clear that standards, a cornerstone of Goals 2000, will serve as a catalyst for the next generation of educational legislation' (p. 55). Heise argues that 'by converging with emerging legal doctrines forged by school-finance litigants at the state level, educational standards even voluntary ones, will attract litigation designed to turn standards into legal entitlements' (p. 55). His argument is hypothetical; however, it does underline the potential for institutions such as the courts to become active interveners in a process of educational change. Politics of education inquiry into policy change could consider what social and political realignments underlying the reinvention proposals lead to the salience of the courts as an arena for the conflicts that Heise predicts.

Another condition giving impetus to institutional dynamism occurs when changes in the socioeconomic context or in the political balance of power result in elements of existing institutions being made to serve new ends. Political scientists who have examined this source of dynamism describe the condition where new actors emerge who pursue their goals through existing institutions. Dunlavy's (1992) comparative analysis of public infrastructure development in 19th-century Prussia and America illustrates how the relative degree of federal and state-level intervention changed as the scale of the task of providing infrastructures, such as railroads, grew. Her analysis suggests that as the problem of railroad regulation across state governments grew more complex and more salient to the economic growth of the country, it was transformed into a national issue requiring federal involvement. Dunlavy's institutional analysis suggests that the shift of conflict to the federal level opened new veto points in courts and in the federal legislative structure for various interests to   challenge and change the emerging regulatory framework.

Similarly Immergut's (1992) analysis of health care policy illustrates how a nation's electoral rules and constitution provide the institutional rules of the game in which political battles are fought. She shows how, by making some courses of action more difficult and facilitating others, the institutions she studied redefined the political alternatives and changed the array of relevant actors. Actors are, however, not depicted as without agency in historical institutional thinking. Immergut, for example, distinguishes between political actors and their strategies, and the institutional framework in which they act. Contradictions and uncertainties arise in policy change because the institutional frameworks in which the changes must occur have typically been created in previous political struggles by long-gone actors. While conflict over policy outcomes may follow from such institutional effects, the line of analysis laid out by both Dunlavy (1992) and Immergut (1992) also suggests that broad policy paths are created by institutional choices. At the same time it is clear that those engaged in political battles over institutional changes cannot be certain that their intentions will have effect in subsequent political changes. March and Olsen (1989) argue that:

> Understanding the transformation of political institutions requires recognizing that there are frequently multiple, not necessarily consistent, intentions, that intentions are often ambiguous, that intentions are part of a system of values, goals, and attitudes that embeds intention in a structure of other beliefs and aspirations.

March and Olsen focus our attention on perhaps the most critical element of innovation, the relationship between new policy ideas, such as those calling for quality education for all students in the reinvention agenda, and the institutional configurations which influence their potential impact on policy outcomes. Thelen and Steinmo (1992) describe this orientation as emphasizing 'ideational innovation under institutional constraints' (p. 22). It is the orientation Hall (1992) takes in tracing the interaction of institutions, ideas and interests in the development of monetarist policies in the UK in the 1970s. Hall illustrates that the institutional characteristics of the British parliamentary system, which give significant power and autonomy to ruling governments, allowed the prime minister to make policy changes that would have been more difficult in the American federal institutional structures. Contrary to the common emphasis on the constraints on innovation imposed by institutions, Hall's research suggests that some institutional configurations may actually enhance system change. Thelen and Steinmo (1992) observe that 'we tend to think of institutions as bureaucracies that are conservative and biased toward continuity . . . [but] some institutional structures may establish a dynamic tension that inspires creativity and encourages innovation' (p. 24).

At the same time, there is substantial evidence of the constraining nature of institutions in the research of political scientists such as Weir (1992) who examines how, during the evolution of employment policy from the 1920s to the 1980s, the structure of the American state narrowed the possibilities of policy innovation. Weir argues that the fragmentation of the American political institutions made the government relatively open to a wide range of innovations, often those which first developed outside the mainstream of the politics of the day. She describes American policy change as 'bounded innovation' because the institutional features of the political system 'created opportunities for some kinds of innovation [but also] set boundaries on the types of innovations possible' (p. 192). For politics of education scholars interested in uncovering how particular systems of knowledge about problems with schooling emerged to guide current policy making aimed at reinventing schools, Weir offers an historical approach which looks for connections among policies over time, and which assumes that 'individual innovations are part of a "policy sequence" in which institutional development renders some interpretations of problems more persuasive and makes some prospective policies more politically viable than others' (p. 192). Innovation appears path dependent, where decisions at one point in time set 'policy off onto particular tracks, along which ideas and interests develop and institutions and strategies adapt' (p. 192).

Capturing these trends requires that researchers look for broader patterns of politics across different domains where policies may shape thinking about the problem under consideration or create politics which collide to produce unanticipated effects. Weir cautions that such collisions may create turning points in a policy sequence by 'creating opportunities for political actors seeking to promote new ideas and different visions of politics' (p. 192). In order to capture these interactions, institutional analysts conceptualize policy as part of a larger 'package' which relates particular changes to past policies and other issues on the current political agenda. Analysts focus on the relational patterns of policy emerging from opposing and supporting forces in the political environment.

Along with these analytic conceptions Weir's analysis of the institutional features of American politics offers guidance for students of the politics of federal government involvement in reinventing schools. She argues that the American practice of recruiting into the federal policy-making bureaucracy individuals whose primary identification and prospects lie in their professional expertise, 'provides a hospitable setting for introducing new ways of looking at a problem' (p. 193). These features mean that a wide range of ideas have the potential to influence federal policy making in the USA. At the same time Weir recognizes that actual choices of ideas by politicians are influenced by the fragmented nature of national political institutions, which creates many opportunities for mobilizing opposition. This condition encourages policy makers to adopt short time lines ignoring the longer term impacts of policy choices. Related to these constraints is the structure of the American federal system which creates formidable procedural barriers to policy ideas requiring negotiation through its multiple levels. Weir concludes that in the USA:

> . . . policies that depend on reforming existing institutions or building new institutional capacity are less attractive than those that funnel distributive benefits through existing institutions, those that bypass existing institutions altogether, or those that rely on private activity, since they may be more easily launched. (p. 193)

This approach to institutional analysis addresses the traditional concern of politics of education inquiry for the forces at play in defining the policy interests. Institutional features of the American political institutions mean that policy ideas vulnerable to political attacks will not reach the national agenda unless supportive alliances for them are built. Weir's analysis differs from traditional pluralist models of interest articulation in seeing the construction of alliances to be the product of political processes, not the pre-existing preferences of interests. Groups do not always know what their interests are in particular policy areas, and 'the process by which a group forms around support for a specific set of policy preferences cannot be taken for granted; instead questions must be asked about why one policy is favored over another' (p. 194). The organization of political institutions such as parties, legislative and legal processes are instrumental in determining how groups define their policy interests. These institutions channel the interactions of different groups and affect the possibilities that they will have some common interest.

The approaches suggested by Weir, Hall, Dunlavy and Immergut offer insights into the dynamics of reinventing schools for those who wish to contribute to a new institutionalism in politics of education inquiry. Such inquiry could, for example, examine the interaction of institutions, ideas and interests that led to the passage of Goals 2000 in the USA. The analysis would look at the ways in which the institutional features of American politics influenced the construction of ideas linking national progress to educational attainment. This link was clearly articulated by the Clinton administration as the rationale for its Goals 2000: Educate America Act in an argument linking the 'relative decline in the economic power of the United States [with] a similar decline in American academic achievement' (Graham 1995: 5). An institutional analysis would look for the policy sequence which made this particular interpretation of the problem of schooling more persuasive than others.

It would find that Clinton's declaration was not new in American educational politics, rather it extended arguments expressed in previous decades in a number of national reports on the state of education in the USA. The 1983 report *A Nation At Risk* argued, for example, that: 'the educational foundations of [American] society are presently being eroded by a rising tide of mediocrity that threatens its very future as a Nation and a people' (cited in Martin 1994: 138).The same rationale was articulated at the 1989 'Education Summit' by George Bush, and the attending governors (including then governor Bill Clinton), who based their proposals for reforms on the argument that 'the caliber of the educational system and the nation's economy are inextricably intertwined' (cited in Martin 1994: 142). An institutional analysis would view these preferences for linking educational reform to economic progress as setting the path taken in current reforms.

An institutional analysis of efforts to reinvent schools would look at the impact of the American federal system on the evolution of the policies calling for a new national role in setting standards and supporting local innovation. It would look at the way in which new ideas of how to overcome the mischiefs of the American federal system were brought into the stream of possible policy options. The analysis would consider, for example, how the concept of systemic reform was carried into the American federal policy-making system by educational analysts such as O'Day and Smith (1993) recruited by Secretary of Education Riley (1995) who was, himself, influenced by the institutional tradition of incorporating a wide range of professional expertise into the policy-making stream. The analysis would also consider the influence of the fragmented structure of national political institutions in the USA which create substantial opportunity for mobilizing opposition. It would consider the effect of the Republican electoral success in transforming federal policy making in education, and the collision of the ideas expressed in that party's 'Contract with America' platform with the path to reinventing schools set out in Goals 2000.

These, and other directions for analyses suggested by the new historical institutionalism in political science focus politics of education scholarship on questions of how institutional forces shape people's ideas, attitudes, and even their preferences, about how to reinvent schools. The approach suggests that the professional, market, and political impetuses to reinvention identified by Moorman and Egermeier (1992) have been structured by institutional arrangements. The new historical institutionalism recognizes that the contested nature of such ideas fuels the dynamism of reinvention.

New institutional inquiry in politics of education

In this chapter I have examined only a few of the directions for productive inquiry into the politics of reinventing schools being forged by new institutional approaches in sociology, political science and economics. I have suggested a number of ways in which the conceptual problems posed by key elements of the reinvention agenda can be informed by new institutional theorizing and research. Educational analysts have already begun to incorporate some of the directions suggested by institutional theories into their analyses. Many of these analyses focus on the institutional constraints to changing schools suggested by the work of organizational sociologists (see Ogawa 1993). Others have examined the potential of public choice theory to inform their analyses of the potential of vouchers to transform schooling (see Boyd *et al*. 1995). Some sociologists of education have undertaken the kind of broad institutional analysis suggested by Meyer (1994) in examining the emergence of the idea of credentialing teachers as a means of reforming schools (Popkewitz and Brennan 1994). A few scholars of the politics of education have undertaken the kind of analyses of political institutions suggested by political scientists who take a historical approach to institutional analysis (Wong 1989).

The evidence for the emergence of a new institutionalism in politics of education inquiry is, however, spotty. Much of the institutional inquiry undertaken by educational analysts focuses on the patterns of institutional constraints identified by organizational sociologists such as Scott and Meyer (1994). There is a troubling tendency to incorporate the most general conclusions from new institutional sociology into analyses of the deep structural dimensions of schooling which constrain their capacity to change. Similarly, as this chapter has suggested, the general rationale for market mechanisms such as vouchers taken from public choice theory has been incorporated into research on changing schools.

Surprising little politics of education research has taken direction from the other institutional orientation to political science that emerged in the 1970s through the research of graduate students and faculty at Harvard and the University of Chicago who were examining the role of the American state in the development of social and economic policy. Theda Skocpol (1985) and her associates from these schools have been instrumental in calling for state-centered approaches to public policy inquiry and analysis which examine the influence of past decisions on the institutional constraints and opportunities of later periods of policy making. Robertson (1993), in reviewing the return to history and new institutionalism in political science, observes that the impact of Skocpol's work is substantial; since 1975 she has been cited more frequently in political science journals than any other individual. The interest in historical institutionalism in political science is hardly evident in politics of education research.

One of the reasons for the lack of strong affiliation of politics of education scholarship with political science theorizing is that those who have contributed to this new field have been trained in educational administration rather than political science (Cibulka 1995). Reflecting the multidisciplinary bias of their schooling in educational administration, they have sought theoretical guidance in diverse disciplines, and in recent years multidisciplinary inquiry has become the norm in studies of educational politics. Politics of education researchers have adopted institutional perspectives from the disciplines of sociology, anthropology, public administration, economics, and organizational theory (Wong 1995). This eclectic borrowing of institutional theorizing suits the pragmatic bent that has in recent years directed politics of education scholarship to focus on the study of policy (Cibulka 1995).

If there is any commonality among the multidisciplinary studies undertaken under the rubric of politics of education it is the focus on policy inquiry and analysis that many researchers adopt more or less explicitly (Cibulka 1995). The shift from political to policy inquiry in politics of education research is consistent with the pragmatic orientation that has defined the field from its inception. Politics of education scholars have often been active participants in educational policy communities engaged in problem solving on important policy issues such as service integration, accountability systems, race and gender equity issues, and school finance (Wong 1995). Critics argue that the policy focus that has pervaded politics of education scholarship has, however, added little to the cumulative knowledge base about politics. Cibulka (1995) blames this limitation on the reliance on descriptive case study methodologies, the largely atheoretical but multidisciplinary approaches taken, and the 'provincial' or non-comparative character of much of the work on educational policy.

Sroufe (1995) is similarly critical of the tenuous link between policy analysis and political analysis. He describes the failure to take into account the political concerns of federal politicians relating to a policy analysis which proposed a revision of the American legislation (Chapter 1 of the Elementary and Secondary Education Act) which would have redistributed funding for poor children from their districts to districts which had the highest concentrations of child poverty. The political fact that such redistribution would have reduced funding for the districts represented by key members of the House of Representatives ensured that the policy change was not supported. Sroufe concludes that policy analysis is different from political analysis, and warns that the latter is prone to focus on 'static snapshots of phenomena that are more accurately represented as being in motion' (p. 79). He suggests that students of the politics of education have not adequately focused on political structures and processes and have undertaken comparative studies in analyzing educational reform. Stout and his colleagues (1995) agree, arguing that the policy analysis that has been undertaken has often been framed too narrowly to take into account the interaction of political ideas and institutional elements of schooling.

A similar argument is made by Cibulka (1995), who cites Wirt's observations on this problem:

> [politics of education] studies are too much focused on the administration and evaluation of school policies. Leadership studies continue to be framed narrowly, political socialization is ignored, intergovernmental politics are underplayed, the role of the media is unexamined, the study of electoral politics has fallen dormant, there is little scholarly analysis of the courts, cross-national comparisons remain rare, and so on. (Wirt cited in Cibulka 1995: 121)

The studies that have been undertaken do adopt an eclectic and pragmatic approach which some of the recent contributors to the *Politics of Education Yearbook* have found troubling (Stout *et al.* 1995). The research explicitly incorporating institutional thinking from different disciplines largely ignores their substantial differences in fundamental assumptions about the nature of institutions. Indeed it appears that the range of directions for analysis offered by institutional theorizing poses a threat to the development of the field of study in the politics of education which some describe as increasingly fragmented. There is a real danger that the new institutionalisms being incorporated into politics of education inquiry will enhance this trend.

At the same time, the students of the politics of education do have a tradition of critical inquiry which can be applied to the problem of determining the relevance of new institutional theorizing for their concerns (Peterson 1995). Stout (1995) and his colleagues ask us to recall that 'politics of education ultimately involves distributive questions in a material sense, as well as in terms of the citizenry's competing values, attitudes, and ideologies' (p. 16). These traditional concerns suggest that proposals for reinventing schools will raise the fundamental questions concerning the ideological basis of institutional change in schooling outlined by Stout and his colleagues (1995):

- Who should go to school?
- What should be the purpose of schooling?
- What should children be taught?
- Who should decide issues of school direction and policy?
- Who should pay for schools? (p. 16)

The analysis undertaken in this chapter suggests some potential directions that a new institutionalism in the politics of education could take in making sense of the ideological dilemmas that are evoked by these questions, and in examining the dynamics at play in current efforts at reinventing schooling.

References

BACHARACH, S. B. and MUNDELL, B. (1995) *Images of Schools* (Thousand Oaks: Sage).

BALL, S. (1994) *Education Reform* (Buckingham: Open University).

BERGER, P. L. and LUCKMAN, T. (1967) *The Social Construction of Reality* (New York: Doubleday).

BORMAN, K. M. and GREENMAN, N. P. (1994) *Changing American Education: Recapturing the Past or Inventing the Future?* (Albany: SUNY).

BOYD, W. L., CROWSON, R. L. and VAN GEEL, T. (1995) Rational choice and the politics of education: promise and limitations, in J. D. Scribner and D. H. Layton (eds), *The Study of Educational Politics* (Washington: Falmer), 127–145.

BOYD, W. L. and WALBERG, H. (1990) *Choice in Education: Potential and Problems* (Berkeley: McCutchan).

CHUBB, J. E. and MOE, T. M. (1990) *Politics, Markets and American Schools* (Washington: Brookings Institution).

CIBULKA, J. G. (1995) Policy analysis and the study of politics of education, in J. D. Scribner and D. H. Layton (eds), *The Study of Educational Politics* (Washington: Falmer).

DIMAGGIO, P. J. and POWELL, W. W. (1991) Introduction, in W. W. Powell and P. J. Dimaggio (eds), *The New Institutionalism in Organizational Analysis* (Chicago: University of Chicago Press), 1–38.

DUNLAVY, C. A. (1992) Political structure, state policy, and industrial change, in S. Steinmo, K. Thelen and F. Longstreth (eds), *Structuring Politics: Historical Institutionalism in Comparative Analysis* (Cambridge: Cambridge University Press), 114–154.

FELDMAN, L. (1995) Conservative questions 'true goal of Goals 2000 education guidelines. *Christian Science Monitor*, 8 June, 1.

FULLAN, M. (1993) *Change Forces* (New York: Falmer).

GRAHAM, P. A. (1995) Assimilation, adjustment, and access: an antiquarian view of American education, in D. Ravitch and M. A. Vinovskis (eds), *Learning From the Past* (Baltimore: Johns Hopkins University Press), 3–24.

HALL, P. (1986) *Governing the Economy* (New York: Oxford University Press).

HALL, P. (1992) The movement from Keynesianism to monetarism, in S. Steinmo, K. Thelen and F. Longstreth (eds), *Structuring Politics: Historical Institutionalism in Comparative Analysis* (Cambridge: Cambridge University Press), 90–113.

HEISE, M. (1995) The courts vs. educational standards. *The Public Interest*, 120, 55–63.

IMMERGUT, E. M. (1992) The rules of the game, in S. Steinmo, K. Thelan and F. Longstreth (eds), *Structuring Politics: Historical Institutionalism in Comparative Analysis* (Cambridge: Cambridge University Press), 55–89.

JEPPERSON, R. L. and MEYER, J. W. (1991) The public order and the construction of formal organizations, in W. W. Powell and P. J. DiMaggio (eds), *The New Institutionalism in Organizational Analysis* (Chicago: University of Chicago Press), 204–231.

KRASNER, S. D. (1984) Approaches to the state: alternative conceptions and historical dynamics, *Comparative Politics*, 16(2), 223–246.

LANE, J. J. and EPPS, E. G. (1992) *Restructuring the Schools: Problems and Prospects* (Berkeley: McCutchan).

LIEBERMAN, A. (1992) *The Changing Contexts of Teaching* (Chicago: University of Chicago).

MARCH, J. G. and OLSEN, J. P. (1984) The new institutionalism: organizational factors in political life. *American Political Science Review*, 78, 734–749.

MARCH, J. G. and OLSEN, J. P. (1989) *Rediscovering Institutions: The Organizational Basis of Politics* (New York: Free Press).

MARTIN, S. R. (1994) The 1989 education summit as a defining moment in the politics of education, in K. M. Borman and N. P. Greenman (eds), *Changing American Education: Recapturing the Past or Reinventing the Future?* (Albany: SUNY), 133–159.

MEYER, J. W. (1994) Rationalized environments, in R. W. Scott and J. W. Meyer (eds), *Institutional Environments and Individualism* (Thousand Oaks: Sage), 28–54.

MEYER, J. W., BOLI, J. and THOMAS, G. M. (1994) Ontology and rationalization in the western cultural account, in R. W. Scott and J. W. Meyer (eds), *Institutional Environments and Organizations: Structural Complexity and Individualism* (Thousand Oaks: Sage), 9–27.

MEYER, J. W. and ROWAN, B. (1977) Institutionalized organizations: formal structure as myth and ceremony. *American Journal of Sociology*, 83, 340–363.

MEYER, J. W., SCOTT, W. R. and DEAL, T. E. (1983) Institutional and technical sources of organizational structure, in J. W. Meyer and W. R. Scott (eds), *Organizational Environments: Ritual and Rationality* (Beverley Hills: Sage), 45–67.

MOE, T. (1990) Political institutions: the neglected side of the story. *Journal of Law, Economics and Organizations*, 6, 213–253.

MOORMAN, H. and EGERMEIER, J. (1992) Educational restructuring: generative metaphor and new vision, in J. J. Lane and E. G. Epps (eds), *Restructuring the Schools: Problems and Prospects* (Berkeley: McCutchan), 15–59.

MURPHY, J. (1991) *Restructuring Schools: Capturing and Assessing the Phenomena* (New York: Basic Books).

NISKANEN, W. A. (1971) *Bureaucracy and Representative Government* (Chicago: Aldine Aterton).

NORTH, D. (1990) *Institutions, Institutional Change, and Economic Performance* (Cambridge: Cambridge University Press).

O'DAY, J. (1995) Systemic reform and goals 2000, in J. F. Jennings (ed.), *National Issues in Education: Goals 2000 and School-to-Work* (Washington: Phi Delta Kappa), 99–115.

O'DAY, J. A. and SMITH, M. S. (1993) Systemic school reform and educational opportunity, in S. H. Fuhrman (ed.), *Designing Coherent Education Policy: Improving the System* (San Francisco: Jossey-Bass), 250–312

OGAWA, R. T. (1993) *The Institutional Sources of Educational Reform: The Case of School-Based Management*. Paper presented to the annual meeting of the American Educational Research Association (Atlanta, April).

OSBORNE, D. and GAEBLER, T. (1992) *Reinventing Government: How the Entrepreneurial Spirit is Transforming the Public Sector* (Reading: Addison-Wesley).

PAL, L. A. (1993) *Interests of State: The Politics of Language, Multiculturalism and Feminism in Canada* (Montreal: McGill-Queen's University Press).

PETERSON, P. E. (1995) Forward to the study of educational politics, in J. D. Scribner and D. H. Layton (eds), *The Study of Educational Politics* (Washington: Falmer), xiii–xiv.

POPKEWITZ, T. S. (1993) *Changing Patterns of Power* (Albany: SUNY Press).

POPKEWITZ, T. S. and BRENNAN, M. (1994) Certification to credentialing: reconstituting control mechanisms in teacher education, in K. M. Borman and N. P. Greenman (eds), *Changing American Education: Recapturing the Past or Inventing the Future?* (Albany: SUNY Pres), 33–70.

POWELL, W. W., and DiMAGGIO, P. J. (1991) *The New Institutionalism in Organizational Analysis* (Chicago, University of Chicago Press).

RAVITCH, D. and VINOVSKIS, M. A. (1995) *Learning From the Past* (Baltimore: Johns Hopkins University Press).

RILEY, R. W. (1995) The Goals 2000: Educate America Act. Providing a world-class education for every child, in J. F. Jennings (ed.), *National Issues in Education* (Bloomington: Phi Delta Kappa International), 3–25.

ROBERTSON, D. B. (1993) The return to history and the new institutionalism in American political science. *Social Science History*, 17(1), 1–36.

SCOTT, R. W. (1994) Institutions and organizations: towards a theoretical synthesis, in R. W. Scott and J. W. Meyer (eds), *Institutional Environments and Organizations: Structural Complexity and Individualism* (Thousand Oaks: Sage), 55–80.

SCOTT, W. R. (1995) *Institutions and Organizations* (Thousand Oaks: Sage).

SCOTT, W. and MEYER, J. W. (1994) *Institutional Environments and Organizations: Structural Complexity and Individualism* (Thousand Oaks: Sage).

SCRIBNER, J. D. and LAYTON, D. H. (1995) Introduction and overview, in J. D. Scribner & D. H. Layton (eds), *The Study of Educational Politics* (Washington: Falmer), 1–2.

SHEPSLE, K. (1986) Institutional equilibrium and equilibrium institutions, in H. Weisburg (ed.), *Political Science: The Science of Politics* (New York: Agathon), 51–82.

SKOCPOL, T. (1985) Bringing the state back: strategies and analysis in current research, in P. B. Evans, D. Rueschmeyer and T. Skocpol (eds), *Bringing the State Back* (Cambridge: Cambridge University Press), 3–37.

SKOWRONEK, S. (1982) *Building a New American State: The Expansion of National Administrative Capacities* (Cambridge: Cambridge University Press).

SMITH, M. S. and O'DAY, J. A. (1990) Systemic school reform, in S. H. Fuhrman and B. Malen (eds), *The Politics of Curriculum and Testing* (Philadelphia: Falmer), 233–267.

SROUFE, G. E. (1995) Politics of education at the federal level, in J. D. Scribner and D. H. Layton (eds) *The Study of Educational Politics* (Washington: Falmer), 75–88.

STEINMO, S. K., THELEN, K. and LONGSTRETH, F. (1992) *Structuring Politics: Historical Institutionalim in Comparative Analysis* (Cambridge: Cambridge University Press).

STOUT, R. T., TALLERICO, M. and SCRIBNER, K. P. (1995) Values: the 'what?' of the politics of education, in J. D. Scribner and D. H. Layton (eds), *The Study of Educational Politics* (Washington: Falmer), 5–20.

THELEN, K. and STEINMO, S. (1992) Historical institutionalism in comparative politics, in S. Steinmo, K. Thelen and F. Longstreth (eds) *Structuring Politics: Historical Institutionalism in Comparative Analysis* (Cambridge: Cambridge University Press), 1–32.

TYACK, D. (1995) Reinventing schooling, in D. Ravitch and M. A. Vinovskis (eds) *Learning From the Past* (Baltimore: Johns Hopkins University Press) 191–216.

WEICK, K. E. (1979) *The Social Psychology of Organizing*, 2nd edn (Reading: Addison-Wesley).

WEIR, M. (1992) Ideas and the politics of bounded innovation, in S. Steinmo, K. Thelen and F. Longstreth (eds), *Structuring Politics: Historical Institutionalism in Comparative Analysis* (Cambridge: Cambridge University Press), 188–216.

WILLIAMSON, O. E. (1985) *The Economic Institutions of Capitalism* (New York: Free Press).

WISE, A. E. (1990) Six steps to teacher professionalism, *Educational Leadership*, 47, 57–60.

WONG, K. K. (1989) Policy-making in the American states: typology, processes, and institutions, *Policy Studies Review*, 8(3): 527–548.

WONG, K. K. (1995) From political science to multi-disciplinary inquiry, in J. D. Scribner and D. H. Layton (eds), *The Study of Educational Politics* (Washington: Falmer), 21–35.

3.   *Environmental adaptation and selection:*
where are the parents and the public?

Ellen B. Goldring

Despite a public and professional claim that America's schools are not changing at a rapid enough pace, a rather significant list of reform efforts can be mentioned: school-based management, integrated social-service delivery, and revised standards (e.g. National Council Teachers of Mathematics) to name just a few. The extent to which these reforms have actually improved education is not clear; but they have created an outcry from many parents and the public-at-large. It is by no means apparent that the public understands and supports the drive toward systemic reform and coherent educational policy that is behind Goals 2000. For some parents, such recent reform efforts have brought into question, once again, public confidence in education.

Indeed, there is a growing trend which suggests that large numbers of parents do not support these reform efforts. 'Education-reform ideas favored by government and business leaders are badly out of sync with the general public's top concerns' (Walsh 1994:6). Parents do not support such initiatives as portfolio assessments and cooperative learning, suggesting an 'enormous disconnect between the leadership and the public' (Walsh 1994:6). The public is concerned with safe and orderly schools and a return to basics according to one study. In Kentucky, for example, citizens are urging the legislature to overturn parts of the school-reform law. 'Ivory-tower education theorists...began mandating ideas that many parents and teachers don't support' (Harp 1994:15). These trends seem to suggest that reform initiatives are not taking the direction that parents and the public prefer.

This lack of support from the public can be explained in terms of beliefs about what constitutes a 'real school', a school that matches the prevailing cultural beliefs of what schools should be (Metz 1990). Reforms that go against the public's notions of 'real schools' are hard to sustain. It seems that without a concerted effort to enlist the support of the public so that they understand and embrace the reforms, public support for educational change will not be forthcoming (Tyack and Tobin 1994).

For reforms to succeed, support and actual pressure for educational change must come from parents. Parents and the public-at-large must be informed citizens – to request, and in fact, demand, higher expectations for public schools, expectations that will lead to more implementation of reform efforts to improve our nation's schools. Thus, for example, Don Davies (1994: 44) recently stated, 'Significant changes at the school level are most likely to happen when there is consumer demand for change and when the reform effort includes families and communities in partnership with educators'. He claims local schools will not act on new initiatives, such as Goals 2000, unless there is 'greatly increased consumer demand for local action', and there will not be local action unless schools include parents and communities in the reform process. Demand refers to 'advocacy for changed policies and practices, a willingness to become aware of existing

0268–0939/95 $12 · 00 © 1995 Taylor & Francis Ltd

conditions in the educational system – results, needs, problems, limitations, assets, resources'. Similarly, Jim Guthrie, Director of the Education Policy Center at Vanderbilt University recently stated that educational reform will most likely not succeed unless the expectations of the public are heightened. He contrasted the lack of public awareness of educational issues to the heightened public understanding in areas of public health, such as the national stop-smoking campaign promoted by the Surgeon General (Guthrie 1994).

Thus, on the one hand, much of the public and many parents do not 'like' the educational reforms they see, and therefore feel that the schools are not meeting their needs. Perhaps the schools need to *adapt* more effectively to parents' expectations. On the other hand, reforms are not succeeding because parents are not bringing enough pressure to bear on the system, and do not have clear enough understandings about the reforms. The paradox is that reformers and the public do not see eye-to-eye on the nature of educational changes, so how can we say that we should enlist the public to 'require' these changes?

One way of interpreting and understanding these intricate, complex relationships between the public and school reform is to study the interrelationships between schools and their environments: parents and the public-at-large are key actors in the environments of schools. Theoretical lenses can inform the study of the relationships between parents and the public and schools. This chapter will present a brief theoretical overview of two particular perspectives of organization-environment relationships: institutional theory and population ecology. These theories are representative of two classes of theory: adaptation and selection (Hannan and Freeman 1989). Adaptation theories, such as institutional theory, suggest that individual organizations adapt in response to environmental norms, opportunities and threats. Selection theories, such as population ecology, are concerned with populations of organizations, rather than individual organizations, and concentrate on the impact of environments in terms of founding, merging and disbanding organizations. These theories suggest that environments 'select' specific organizational forms for continued survival.

Any volume on institutional theory would be incomplete without attention to 'environment as institution'. However, closely interrelated with institutional theorists' interests in environments is ecological theorizing, hence these two lines of thought must be addressed together. This chapter focuses on these two theories and then suggests that for parents and the publics' voices to be heard in education, there must be links to existing institutions and interest groups.

Institutional theory: adapting to environments

What are the institutional environments of organizations? This section briefly reviews the 'environment as institution' perspective on institutional theory. Institutional theory has many strands and facets. One particular aspect, the focus of this chapter, is *environment as institution*, which is quite different from the analysis of organizations as institutions (Zucker 1987). 'Perhaps the single most important contribution of institutional theorists to the study of organizations is their reconceptualization of the environments of organizations' (Scott 1991: 165). Institutional perspectives on environments go beyond the narrow notion of environment as source of resources and information, as suggested in a resource-dependency approach (Pfeffer and Salancik 1978).

Previous conceptions of environments focused on a rational-technical exchange between organizations and environments. The attributes of an environment that impact organizational structure, from an institutional perspective, differ from those referred to as the technical environment in the resource dependency perspective.[1] While the rational, resource-dependency theorists focused on the environment in terms of complexity, stability, homogeneity, and resource availability, the institutional theorists focus on the 'powerful institutional rules' held by public opinion, important constituents, and the laws themselves (Meyer and Rowan 1977). For instance, from a resource-dependency perspective, schools apply for a grant for a special project from a local business to procure much needed resources. From an institutional perspective, however, the relationship with the business providing the grant may have a more far reaching impact on the school beyond the monetary. The school may begin to respond to some of the cultural norms of the operating procedures of the business as well. Similarly, the school may be adapting to new institutional rules which suggest that *all* schools should engage in partnerships with businesses, even though these partnerships may not always be favourable for the school (Goldring and Sullivan 1995).

An institutional view of environments embraces both 'the rules and belief systems as well as the relational networks that arise in the broader societal context of organizations' (Scott 1983: 14). A focus on institutional environments highlights institutional elements that come from outside the organization and asks how these elements change and impact organizations. Institutional theory is an adaptive perspective of organizations; organizations change themselves to be congruent with their environments.

Recently, Scott (1995) has suggested that institutional environments can be analyzed in terms of three pillars: regulatory, cognitive and normative. The regulatory pillar, highly connected to the role of the state, emphasizes the 'rule-setting, monitoring and sanctioning activities of institutions' (p. 35). According to this view, organizations adapt to their environments to comply with the prevailing regulations in a rather rational, cost-benefit type of decision frame. Institutional environments are portrayed as 'the elaboration of rules and requirements to which individual organizations must conform if they are to receive support and legitimacy' (Scott and Meyer 1983: 149). Institutional theory suggests that organizational structure evolves in order to conform to and reflect institutionalized rules and codes. 'Their survival is not based on effectiveness and efficiency of market transactions but rather on conformity with eternally defined rules' (Scott 1983: 125). Consequently, structural conformity is more important than what actually takes place inside the organization. For instance, schools may be following the site-based management bandwagon in order to conform to wide-spread guidelines and popular beliefs about restructuring (often mandated by the state) even though evidence about its relationship to student learning is limited.

The cognitive pillar refers to an 'internal representation' of the symbols and meanings of the environment and the activities associated with these activities (D'Andrade 1984: 88). Thus, organizations adapt to socially constructed, common understandings of their environments. Institutional environments include 'socially defined categories' (Meyer *et al.* 1981). Consequently, institutional theorists recognize that there is not just one institutional environment, but multiple institutional environments (Scott 1987), depending on the perceptions and construction of social reality of participants both inside and outside the organization. The actual rules and regulations governing organizations are as crucial as the interpretations and constructions of meanings surrounding these rules and regulations. 'Institutionalization is the process by which a given set of units and a pattern of activities come to be normatively and cognitively held in place, and practically taken for granted as lawful (whether as a matter of formal law, custom, or knowledge.)' (Meyer *et al.* 1987: 13). The movement towards devaluation of power from central office to individual school sites in big urban school districts, what Kerchner and Caufman (1995) have termed 'regime overthrow', has rapidly been adopted across the country following Chicago school reform efforts. These ideas fit the normative and cognitive perceptions of many groups in other cities, including politicians, community groups and parents.

Since the rules, regulations and procedures are not objectively tested, collective socially constructed realities are central. It is not the objective existence of rules, norms and regulations that impact organizations, but a common definition of social reality agreed upon by individuals (Scott 1992: 31). From an institutional perspective, then, organization structure mirrors or adheres to externally legitimated formal structures. 'By designing a formal structure that adheres to the prescriptions of myths in the institutional environment, an organization demonstrates that it is acting on collectively values purposes in a proper and adequate manner.'

The normative pillar of institutional environments specifies shared values and norms that guide organizational actors' adaptations. Organizations conform to external norms and the collective normative order, thus strengthening 'long-run survival prospects' (Meyer and Rowan 1977: 252, Zucker 1987). These external norms are referred to as myths because they are widely held beliefs. They are believed to be true by a majority of individuals even though they are not objectively tested (Scott 1992). From an institutional perspective, the structure of schools under recent reform and restructuring movements is in response to institutional processes rather than in response to technical needs for efficiency. Thus, schools are restructuring in response to 'ritually defined meanings and categories supplied by the environment but do not attempt seriously to implement them at the operational level' (Scott 1992: 279). These ritually defined meanings and categories include the rhetoric and legislation surrounding such ideas as teacher empowerment and school site management. As M. Meyer (1979) points out, these changes in structure are highly visible but are much less costly than actually trying to change behaviour. Therefore, it is less costly to restructure governance systems that include teachers than it is to have teachers implement, for example, empowerment in the classroom through such ideas as constructivism.

The general view is that institutional environments are dominated by three groups, or institutional agents (Scott 1995): self-interested regulators (Niskanen 1971), professionals (Scott 1983) and other organizations (Peltzman 1976). Self-interested regulators of schools include state bureaucracies and their affiliates, such as accrediting bodies. These agencies provide the institutional rules, policies and regulations that govern organizations.

Professional groups give legitimacy to the actions, beliefs and norms of organizational members. 'In a resource-dependence or social exchange approach to organizations, legitimacy is sometimes related as simply a different kind of resource. However, from an institutional perspective, legitimacy is not a commodity to be possessed or exchanged but a condition reflecting cultural alignment, normative support, or consonance with relevant rules or laws' (Scott 1995: 45). Hasenfeld (1992) suggests that professionals in human service organizations select 'service technologies' according to what is legitimate in the view of their professional colleagues. Treatments that are consistent with the dominant values and norms of professional groups are largely adapted as what is 'good' for the client. Similarly, teachers can more easily oppose reform efforts, such as privatization, when they are supported by their professional groups (e.g. teachers' unions), without entering into a complete analysis about the effectiveness of these reforms.

Newly organized groups, part of the institutional environments of schools, have been entering the educational arena, for example the conservative right and its affiliated associations. These groups are promoting a number of curricular and policy concerns, particularly those which would lead to changing the relationships between church and state. Thus, questions regarding prayer in school have been on the agenda in many communities because of pressure from these groups.

In the next section, another theoretical lens, organizational ecology, is presented. It emphasizes the selection of organizations by environments, rather than adaptation.

Selection theory: organizational ecology

Organizational ecology is a theoretical view of organizations that suggests 'most organizational change occurring in any historical period is the result of a process of organizational selection and replacement rather internal transformation and adaptation' (Carroll 1988: 2). Organizational ecologists study organizations at various levels; most are interested in population ecology, the best developed of the organizational ecology theories (Hannon and Freeman 1989). As the name of the theory suggests, population ecologists are concerned with *populations of organizations* as the unit of analysis, rather than individual organizations. Individual organizations are referred to as member organizations of a certain population. Those studying organizations from an ecological perspective are primarily interested in changes in populations of organizations that occur through organizational creation and mortality, rather than change at the individual level. Population ecologists claim that individual organizational change does not contribute much to population change (Hannan and Freeman 1977, 1984, Singh and Lumsden 1990). Hence, population ecologists study schools as a population of organizations, not schools as individual sites.

The definition of a population is often complex and open to interpretation. The term population often 'refers to an aggregate of organizations that are homogeneous on some relevant dimension' (Pennings 1980: 138). However, this delineation is not always clear. For example, 'Did the implementation of Montessori's ideas result in a new population of nursery schools or did it merely result in an educational innovation that augmented the diversity of nursery schools?' (Pennings 1980: 142).

Populations of organizations are also defined in terms of a unitary character (Hannan and Freeman 1988). Unitary character refers to 'a common dependence on the material and social environment. A population of organizations has a unitary character in this sense if its members are affected similarly by changes in the environments (including other populations)' (p. 9). This definition suggests that environmental changes impact populations of organizations more rapidly and more forcefully than they do individual organizations. This perspective is useful in charting the connections between the changing demographics of a nation's children and certain trends in public schools over long periods of time, such as the expansion of social service programmes in schools.

Other definitions of populations of organizations include, three important components: the similarity of members, the sharing of materials and competence within populations of organizations, and the absence of sharing among populations of organizations (McKelvey and Aldrich 1983). In other words, organizations are part of populations when members have similar training, credentials and job descriptions. The unique socialization experiences of teachers sets public schools apart from other educating institutions, such as universities. In addition, organizational members have a common core 'technology' that is shared and known within the population but is not shared with populations in other organizations. One would expect to find more variability between organizational populations than between organizational members within populations. For example, one of the difficulties in meshing schools with other social service organizations is that this type of partnership requires merging two separate organizational populations, populations whose members have unique socialization experiences, and different mechanisms for work.

The focus from the population ecology perspective on environmental selection is related to issues of change. Selection occurs as organizations compete for various pools of resources. It is assumed that organizations do not change because of high levels of structural inertia due to the selection process (Hannan and Freeman 1984). Structures that are reproducible and relatively stable over time, are favoured by a selection process (Singh et al. 1986), 'Selection-based approaches treat organizations and their attributes as relatively fixed and hold that through selective elimination those organizations prevail which are congruent with their environment' (Pennings 1980: 135). Thus, in contrast to an adaptive stance, the 'selection models emphasize organizational inertia and a passive, compliant and submissive organizational orientation to the environment' (p. 144). This perspective typically gives a long historical explanation of environmental patterns to account for the founding or disbanding of organizations. Following this perspective, Meyer et al. (1988) examined changes in elementary and secondary schools in the USA from 1940 to 1980. They found that schools and schools districts became more and more similar over time in terms of the structure and internal staffing patterns. This finding can be used to support an ecological selection model.

What are the factors that seem to decide an organization's selectability by the environment? One selection factor is organizational age. This perspective, termed the liability of newness perspective, suggests that 'organizational forms that have high levels of reliability and accountability are favoured by selection processes' (Singh and Lumsden 1990: 168). That is, older organizations with their established patterns, procedures, and reproducibility are less likely to die and hence face the liability of newness. Schools that have long established histories within a given community are often supported, while newer, innovative programmes brought to new schools are often pushed out by the community (see Raywid, this volume).

Others have referred to the relationship between selection and age as the liability of aging hypothesis (Aldrich and Auster 1986). This hypothesis suggests that older organizations are less likely to change due to internal processes, such as vested interests, power distributions and homogeneity of 'thinking'. Externally, older organizations are less likely to change because of established exchange relationships and dependencies which limit autonomy and selection processes that do not 'select' change.

Another factor related to environmental selection is structural inertia. 'Greater reproducibility of structure also leads to greater inertia, however, organizations become increasingly inert with age' (p. 168). Environments select organizations that resemble other organizations in the same population. Schools that are similar to other schools will be selected for survival (see Raywid, this volume).

Another important selection factor includes size: larger organizations have lower mortality rates than smaller organizations. This is referred to as the liability of smallness (Freeman et al. 1983). The explanation for this is related to inertia and age. Organizational inertia, age and size are highly interrelated and all point to environmental selection. For instance, the liability of smallness is usually related to the liability of newness, since new organizations are usually small. The nature of the selection process is such that organizations with inert features are more likely to survive, and older organizations have more inert features (Hannan and Freeman 1984). This perspective helps explain why small change may not lead to substantial educational reform, to the spread of innovation that reform proponents increasingly refer to as 'going to scale'. Population ecologists may suggest that small changes are not selected by environments because they are not noticed by the environment.

Taken together, these perspectives suggest why schools as a population are rather impermeable to innovation. The population ecologists submit that the environment does not select schools that are small, new or different from those of the past. In contrast, the environment would select schools that continue to resemble 'real schools' of the past.

Criticism of the population ecology perspective revolves around the view that this theory is highly deterministic: there is not much free will, adaptation, or change because organizations wait around for the inevitability of environmental conditions that will select them out (Astley and Van de Ven 1983, Singh and Lumsden 1990). Population ecologists respond to this criticism by stating that the main issue is one of the unit of analysis: a selectionist approach emphasizes the population level of analysis instead of the adaption of a single organization (Singh and Lumsden, 1990). Therefore, if one is interested in the rate of change of a single organization, an adaptation perspective may be useful, while if one is interested in the population level, selection perspectives are important. In the next section, the interrelations between the adaptation and selection theories are presented.

Interaction of institutional and ecological dynamics

The relationships between organizational adaptation and selection are closely linked, connecting institutional and ecological theories (Tucker *et al.* 1988). The main question examined in relating institutional theory and ecological perspectives is: How do institutional forces shape the ecology of organizations (Barnett and Carroll 1993)? This line of questioning is a relatively new development in organizational theory (Scott 1995).

Population ecologists have begun to consider institutional processes in two ways. One perspective relies on the informal norms of institutions, while the other approach focuses on the formal rules and regulations to explain organizational selection processes (Barnett and Carroll 1993).

Informally constructed norms of institutions are used by population ecologists to explain the density of organizations in populations (Hannan and Freeman 1989). This is known as the density dependence model, a model explaining the evolution of the number of organizations in a population.

> According to this theory, an organizational form is legitimated or institutionalized to the extent that it is 'taken for granted' by relevant actors and publics. By this view, legitimation involves the emergence and acceptance of norms about the organizational form and the activities it encompasses. That is, norms develop informally about the proper ways to organize for particular activities and the institutional environment sanctions organizations on the basis of these norms. (Barnett and Carroll 1993: 173)

Thus, the density model claims that the early evolution or founding of specific organizational forms is based upon legitimation norms within a given population. These norms explain the evolution of organizational forms when there is little competition. From the population ecology perspective,

> norms about the organizational form are not imposed from the outside by actors or agencies but are instead constructed informally as a result of the growth and diffusion of the population. As the population initially expands in numbers, its organizational form gets defined, codified and promulgated. After a certain density is reached, norms have developed about the organizational form. This means that the form is taken for granted, and further increases in the population have no additional effects of this kind. (Barnett and Carroll 1993: 174)

In sum, density legitimizes organizational forms themselves, and takes into account both the cognitive and normative pillars of the institutional environment (Scott 1995). This suggests that perhaps the notion of 'scaling up' from single school demonstration sites to wider implementation may not be effective. Perhaps widespread implementation must initially be promoted in ways that allow new norms to reach a level of density that will impact the population.

This view puts legitimacy at the core of population ecology perspectives, as it helps explain how selection pressures impact organizations. And, as noted earlier, it is just this matter of public legitimacy that may be the most problematic about a large part of the school reform movement. Specifically, organizations with institutional support from the environment have access to more resources and in turn can 'live longer'. For instance, 'in organizational ecology one of the important reasons young organizations have a liability of newness is that they lack external legitimacy and institutional support' (Singh and Lumsden 1990: 184). It should be noted that convincing empirical tests about the relationships between legitimacy to density are not widespread (Zucker 1989).

Population ecologists also relate to institutional theory by exploring the impact of formally constructed rules and regulations (the regulatory pillar of institutional environments) on the evolution of organizational populations rather than informal norms (Barnett and Carroll 1993). Thus, researchers have explored institutional constraints, such as new laws on organizational founding, mortality and competition. This approach views institutional changes in terms of laws and formal rules as exogenous to the organizational population (Barnett and Carroll 1993). Specific areas of research centre around the structure of formal regulatory institutions, as well the content of new regulations. Research questions include such matters as the extent to which the authorities behind the laws and institutional constraints are centralized, fragmented and coordinated (Meyer *et al.* 1987), and the extent to which new regulations are particularistic or universalistic with respect to a given population of organizations (Barnett and Carroll 1993).

Adaptation and selection: where are the parents and the public?

The beginning of this chapter claimed that there is misalignment between educational reformers and the parents and the public. What can institutional theory and population ecology suggest about this dilemma? It seems that parents and the public are not considered a fundamental part of the regulatory, normative, or cognitive pillars of the institutional environments of schools, for if they were, schools would be attending to their voices and adapting to their needs. It also seems that parents and the public are not impacting the environmental selection criteria of the population of schools, or even individual schools within that population.

It is important to note that some school reform ideas, such as school choice, charter schools and home schooling, are developing support among some parent groups. These reforms rely heavily on 'market' ideas, an individualist perspective, rather than institutional or population dynamics. These efforts are based on individual options to enter and exit the schooling arena, and individual 'voicing' of dissatisfaction, in a consumer type relationship (Hirschman 1970). These reforms provide parents with individual freedoms, but do not promote an 'institutionalized force' for change.

What have we learned? It seems that in order for parents and the public to have a place in school reform, they must become an institutional force in the environments of schools. Since most accounts suggest that parents have been unsuccessful in doing this on a school by school basis, it may be time for parents and the public to join other organizational bodies that are already part of the institutional environments of schools. I suggest that through affiliation and strong partnerships with existing organizations and groups, parents will be heard.

Elsewhere I have written (Goldring 1991) that in Israel, for example, parents have little influence at the local school site level, but have considerable influence through affiliation with national organizations. Parents in Israel have gained a voice in education by forming action committees or coalitions with key organizations that schools do adapt to. These committees are initiated by small groups of parents who mobilize a wider group of interested people from the public-at-large and other parents. This group in turn is joined in its struggle by a stable, 'institutionalized' organization, political party, or interest group. Thus the parents and members of the public are bonded together as a nucleus, with the support of the institutionalized organizations, to press for change. For example, parents who felt that girls were not being given educational opportunities similar to boys mobilized alongside national women's organizations. Peterson (1976) has referred to such partnerships as ideological bargaining units. These units are comprised of parents and others who, as individuals, share a common ideological outlook. Because the parents and other members are linked to groups that are already part of the institutional environments of schools, they become part of the adaptive framework for change.

Similarly, I believe that for parents to be heard in the USA they must become interwoven into the fabric of the institutional environments of schools. This can be accomplished by linking with existing institutions. There is evidence of this as schools respond to back-to-basics movements and other causes that have been picked up by certain affiliated groups. Could parents have influenced the changes in many schools regarding outcome-based education without the involvement of existing, well-organized groups? For parents to successfully influence educational decision-making, a large proportion of them would have to seek out organizations and groups that fit their views on particular issues, such as teachers' unions, political parties or religious organizations. A possible by-product of parents and the public putting educational issues on the agenda of existing organizations is that the overall importance and visibility of education could be raised. As parents and the public redefine the agendas of regulatory organizations, normative groups and interest groups, the populations of schools may also change if we heed the new developments in organizational theory that have begun to link ecological selection with adaptation.

Note

1. Although beyond the scope of this chapter, it is important to note that organizations *do* operate in both technical and institutional environments; these two environments are interrelated (Scott 1993).

References

ALDRICH, H. E. and AUSTER, R. E. (1986) Even dwarfs started small: liabilities of age and size and their strategic implications, in B. M. Staw and L. L. Cummings (eds), *Research in Organizational Behavior*, vol. 8, (Greenwich: JAI), 165–98.
ASTLEY, W. G. and VAN DE VEN, A. H. (1983) Central perspectives and debates in organization theory. *Administrative Science Quarterly*, 30 (2), 245–73.

BARNETT, W. and CARROLL, G. R. (1993) Organizational ecology: approaches to institutions, in S. Lindenberg and H. Schreuder (eds.), *Interdisciplinary Perspectives on Organization Studies* (Oxford: Pergamon), 171–81.

CARROLL, G. R. (1988) Organizational ecology in theoretical perspective, in G. R. Carroll (ed.), *Ecological Models of Organizations* (Cambridge, MA: Ballinger), 1–6.

D'ANDRADE, R. G. (1984) Cultural meaning systems, in R. A. Shweder and R. A. LeVine (eds), *Culture Theory: Essays on Mind, Self, and Emotion* (Cambridge: Cambridge University Press), 88–119.

DAVIES, D. (1994) Partnerships for reform. *Education Week*, 12 October, p. 44.

FREEMAN, J., CARROLL, G. R. and HANNAN, M. T. (1983) The liability of newness: age dependence in organizational death rates. *American Sociological Review*, 48, 692–710.

GOLDRING, E. B. (1991) Parents: participants in an organizational framework. *International Journal of Educational Research*, 15 (2), 215–28.

GOLDRING, E. B. and SULLIVAN, A. S. (1995) Privatization: integrating private services in public schools, in P. Cooksone and B. Schneider (eds), *Transforming Schools* (New York: Garland), 533–556.

GUTHRIE, J. (1994, October) Education reform: Does it work? *Education Policy Series*. Vanderbilt University (unpublished).

HANNAN, M. T. and FREEMAN, J. (1977) The population ecology of organizations. *American Journal of Sociology*, 82, 929–64.

HANNAN, M. T. and FREEMAN, J. (1984) Structural inertia and organizational change. *American Sociological Review*, 49, 149–64.

HANNAN, M. T. and FREEMAN, J. (1988) Density dependence in the growth of organizational populations, in G. R. Carroll (ed.), *Ecological Models of Organizations* (Cambridge, MA: Ballinger).

HANNAN, M. T. and FREEMAN, J. (1989) *Organizational Ecology* (Cambridge, MA: Harvard University Press).

HARP, L. (1994) KERA foes push to overturn Kentucky school outcomes. *Education Week*, 12 October, 15.

HASENFELD, Y. (1992) The nature of human service organizations, in Y. Hasenfeld (ed.), *Human Services as Complex Organizations* (Newbury Park: Sage), 3–23.

HIRSCHMAN, A. O. (1970) *Exit, Voice and Loyalty* (New York: Viking).

KERCHNER, C. T. and CAUFMAN, K. D. (1995) Schools as decision-making arenas, in S. Bacharach and B. Mundell (eds), *Images of Schools* (Thousand Oaks: Corwin), 43–70.

MCKELVEY, B. and ALDRICH, B. (1983) Populations, natural selection and applied organizational science. *Administrative Science Quarterly*, 28, 101–28.

METZ, M. (1990) Real school: a universal drama amid disparate experience, in D. E. Mitchell and M. E. Goetrz (eds), *Education Politics for the New Century* (New York: Falmer), 75–91.

MEYER, M. (1979) Organizational structure as signaling. *Pacific Sociological Review*, 22, 481–500.

MEYER, J. W. and ROWAN, B. (1977) Institutionalized organizations: formal structure as myth and ceremony. *American Journal of Sociology*, 83, 340–63.

MEYER, J. W., BOLI, J. and THOMAS, J. M. (1987) Ontology and rationalization in the western cultural account, in G. M. Thomas, J. W. Meyer, F. O. Ramirez and J. Boli (eds), *Institutional Structure, Constituting State, Society and the Individual* (Newbury Park: Sage), 43–63.

MEYER, J. W., SCOTT, W. R. and DEAL, T. E. (1981) Institutional and technical sources of organizational structure, in Herman D. Stein, *Organizations and human services: Cross disciplines reflections* (Philadelphia: Temple University Press), 66–82.

MEYER, J. W., SCOTT, W. R. and STRANG, D. (1987) Centralization, fragmentation and school district complexity. *Administrative Science Quarterly*, 32, 186–201.

MEYER, R. W., SCOTT, W. R., STRANG, D. and CREIGHTON, A. L. (1988) Bureaucratization without centralization: changes in the organizational system of US public education, 1940–1980, in L. G. Zucker (ed.), *Institutional Patterns and Organizations: Culture and Environment* (Cambridge, MA: Ballinger), 139–68.

NISKANEM, W. A. (1971) *Bureaucracy and Representative Government* (Chicago: Aldine-Atherton).

PELTZMAN, S. (1976) Toward a more general theory of regulation. *Journal of Law and Economics*, 19, 211–40.

PENNINGS, J. M. (1980) Environmental influences on the creation of processes, in J. R. Kimberly and R. H. Miles (eds), *The Organizational Life Cycle* (San Francisco: Jossey Bass), 135–60.

PETERSON, P. E. (1976) *School Politics Chicago Style* (Chicago: University of Chicago Press).

PFEFFER, J. and SALANCIK, G. (1978) *The external control of organizations* (New York: Harper & Row).

SCOTT, W. R. (1983) Health care organizations in the 1980s: the convergence of public and professional control systems, in J. W. Meyer and W. R. School (eds), *Organizational Environments* (Beverly Hills: Sage), 157–72.

SCOTT, W. R. (1987) The adolescence of institutional theory. *Administrative Science Quarterly*, 32, 493–511.

SCOTT, W. R. (1991) Institutional arguments, in P. DiMaggio and W. W. Powell (eds), *The New Institutionalism in Organizational Analysis* (Chicago: University of Chicago Press), 164–82.

SCOTT, W. R. (1992) Organizations: Rational, Natural and Open Systems (Englewood Cliffs: Prentice-Hall).

SCOTT, W. R. (1995) *Institutions and Organizations: Theory and Research* (Newbury Park: Sage).

SCOTT, W. R. and MEYER, J. W. (1983) The organization of societal sectors, in J. W. Meyer and W. R. Scott (eds), *Organizational Environments: Ritual and Rationality* (Beverly Hills: Sage), 129–53.

SINGH, J. V. and LUMSDEN, C. (1990) Theory and research in organizational ecology. *Annual Review of Sociology*, 16, 161–195.

SINGH, J. V., TUCKER, D. J. and HOUSE, R. J. (1986) Organizational legitimacy and the liability of newness, *Administrative Science Quarterly*, 31, 171–93.

TUCKER, D. J., SINGH, J. V., MEIHARD, A. G. and HOUSE, R. J. (1988) Ecological and institutional sources of change in organizational populations, in Glenn, R. Carrol (ed.), *Ecological models of organizations* (Cambridge, MA: Ballinger), 127–152.

TYACK, S. and TOBIN, W. (1994) The 'grammar' of schooling: why has it been so hard to change? *American Educational Research Journal*, 31 (3), 453–80.

WALSH, M. (1994) School experts found out of sync with public. *Education Week*, 12 October, 6.

WEST, P. (1994) Report links increased enrollments in math, science to reforms of 80's. *Education Week*, 12 October, 11.

ZUCKER, L. G. (1987) Institutional theories of organization. *American Review of Sociology*, 13, 443–64.

ZUCKER, L. G. (1989) Combining institutional theory and population ecology: no legitimacy, no history. *American Sociological Review*, 54, 542–45.

4.   'We have the right to be different': educational community through a neoinstitutional lens

Mary Erina Driscoll

During a recent trip to Montreal, Québec, I spent a fair amount of time on the Metro, the city's underground public transportation system. My visit occurred a few months before a referendum in which voters would be asked about the sovereignty of the province, a step that would make Québec quasi-independent from the rest of Canada. Frequently, I encountered advertisements that attempted to explain the notion of sovereignty to the voters and to persuade them that it was an idea of some merit. In particular, this highly partisan campaign was designed to allay voters' fears about impending changes in the newly independent Québec. Each of these explanatory posters concluded with a phrase that I, equipped with at best rudimentary French, translated as 'We have the right to be different'.

This slogan, I realized upon reflection, aptly invoked a multitude of images. The polemics I encountered were intended to explain the ways in which institutions and norms for organizational behaviour might be altered under the new framework of a sovereign Québec, mini-rhetorics of a sort that focused on the fate of well known conventions and institutions. For example, the advertisements discussed the potential fate of existing currencies and financial instruments, the consequences for the pensions earned by retired government workers, and even the likelihood of further changes in the national constitution. Their concise but powerful arguments were designed to assure voters that the formal, state-supported institutions on which they had come to rely would remain strong and that their connection to these institutions would not change to their disadvantage. Indeed, their persuasive techniques relied on the readers' understanding of democracy and voters' rights under such a system, sovereign or not.

Yet at the same time, the advertisements implicitly called upon the readers' patriotism and commitment to the quasi-national community of the province. The case was made in French, not only the official language of the province but one so widely shared among the desired targets that no benefit of translation was provided for the linguistically uninitiated. The advertisements appealed directly to the voters' deeply seated sense of identity as members of the Québecois community, and the differences implied between the voting reader and the rest of the country were asserted to be both meaningful and sources of some pride.

This juxtaposition of the languages of communitarianism and institutionalism, if you will, remains on my mind while framing this chapter on the 'new' institutionalism and the 'new' communitarianism. My task is to consider, albeit briefly, how these literatures 'fit' with one another, and in particular, to ascertain if our emergent understanding of neoinstitutionalism can inform our understanding of community, especially as the latter has been construed in educational settings.

0268–0939/95 $12 · 00 © 1995 Taylor & Francis Ltd

The juncture is at best complicated, made doubly so because both terms are defined in many ways and are thus freighted with various (and at times conflicting) meanings. In this chapter, I will eschew any serious attempt to demonstrate the variety of ways in which institutionalism has been constructed, leaving that to the able hands of others (Powell and DiMaggio 1991, Scott 1995). For my purposes, however, I would like to make reference to some themes from this literature for our consideration. After contrasting these in a global fashion with some of the themes that emerge in community, I would like to explore some connections between these two concepts using three distinct views of community that are very different from one another. In each of these cases, I will conclude with some of the questions that this exercise suggests, offering not a set of answers but rather some emerging directions for further thought and inquiry.

I shall simplify this task further by focussing the discussion of community on the literature that has envisioned community in educational organizations. Thus our discussion of communitarianism will reflect work that has been related to schooling and to the institutional arrangements that support public and private education.

Themes of neoinstitutionalism: a selective view

Paul DiMaggio and Walter Powell's (1991) overview of the field termed 'new' or neo-institutionalism provides a compehensive discussion of the ways in which institutions have been conceptualized, including traditional scholarship, from the first part of this century to more recent work across disciplines that includes economics, political science, international relations, sociology and organizational analysis. Drawing on their work as well as that of John Meyer and Brian Rowan (1977), I would like to delineate three themes, found largely in the sociological domain of this literature, that will be helpful in our subsequent discussion of community.

As DiMaggio and Powell note, there is a robust tradition in sociology that has focused on institutions. One of the features that distinguishes the 'new' institutionalism from the old, they suggest, is the former's debt to the 'cognitive revolution' in psychology (DiMaggio and Powell 1991: 22). Earlier traditions of institutional theory emphasized the intentional aspects of institutions and the importance of values, norms and modes of behaviour that were created and learned by individuals coalesced in a group. They suggest that the 'new' institutionalism takes a less intentional view of such constraints on behaviour and thought. These new rubrics assert that institutions so shape our cognitive structures and options that the rule-like behaviour and modes of thought in which individual actors engage is ingrained to the degree that actors cannot conceive of other ways of knowing or being. Institutions play a major part in providing the cognitive realities that shape the way we come to know and experience our world. The 'taken-for-granted' rules that govern behaviour in them are not known or experienced as such by the participants. As DiMaggio and Powell write, 'Institutions do not just constrain options; they establish the very criteria by which people discover their preferences'. (DiMaggio and Powell 1991: 11).

A second theme germane to our discussion is derived from the work of Meyer and Rowan (1977). In their seminal piece, 'Institutionalized organizations: formal structure as myth and ceremony' they note institutionalized organizations decouple the work of the organizations from the kind of ceremonial action that sustains the societal myths from which the organization derives legitimacy.

> By designing a formal structure that adheres to the prescription of myths in the institutional environment, and organization demonstrates that it is acting on collectively valued purposes in a proper and adequate manner (Dowling and Pfeffer, 1975; Meyer and Rowan, 1978). . . . The organization becomes, in a word, legitimate, and it uses its legitimacy to strengthen its support and secure its survival. (50)

Thus, although much of the technical work of the organization may take place out of sight and with relatively little fanfare, the ceremonial aspect of the organization is usually quite prominent. It is evident not only in formalized events such as organization charts but especially in the kinds of symbolic activities that build confidence in the organization and promote commitment to it. Such ceremonial activities are not intended to accomplish the actual 'work' of the organization and would meet few criteria for efficiency. Rather, this ritualistic aspect of organizations helps to 'celebrate institutionalized myths' (Meyer and Rowan 1977/1991: 55).

Third, DiMaggio and Powell suggest (1991) that the new literature on institutions construes the environments of organizations in ways that are very different from earlier work. Moreover, they argue that this literature tends to view institutions themselves at a more global level, and the new theorists see institutions embedded in the macro-structures of society:

> Authors of older works (Selznick, 1949; Gouldner 1954; Dalton 1959; Clark 1960a) describe organizations that are embedded in local communities, to which they are tied by the multiple loyalties of personnel and by interorganizational treaties (''co-optation'') hammered out in face-to-face interaction. The new institutionalism focuses instead on nonlocal environments, either organizational sectors or fields roughly coterminous with the boundaries of industries, professions or national societies (Scott and Meyer, 1991). Environments, in this view, are more subtle in their influence; rather than being co-opted by organizations, they penetrate the organization, creating the lenses through which actors view the world and the very categories of structure, action and thought . . . . (13)

We will return to each of these themes – the cognitive constraints institutions create, the importance of ceremony in institutionalized organizations, and the ways in which organizations and environments are conceptualized – in a new context below, exploring their relevance as we discuss three well articulated visions of community. We turn now to a brief overview of some of the recent literature on community and a preliminary juxtaposition of these institutional themes with those found in the literature on educational community.

A diffuse literature on community

Much as is the case with the study of institutions, the study of communities has a long tradition. Many current conceptions of community build on the classic distinction between *Gemeinschaft* and *Gesellschaft* developed by the nineteenth-century German sociologist Ferdinand Tonnies (first published in the USA in 1957). Tonnies, and Weber (1947) after him, categorized the associative relationships in organizations formed from the common bond of shared technical tasks as *Gesellschaft* (of society). These associative relationships are based on rational assessments of common interests and purposes. In contrast, communal relationships (termed *Gemeinschaft*, or of the community), are based on subjective feelings, sentiments or traditions that bind people together in community.

In the past decade scholars in education and in other disciplines have invoked the image of community with increasing frequency in their calls for the revitalization of American education (for example, Bellah *et al.* 1985, Raywid 1988, Wehlage *et al.* 1989, Cuban 1992). Multiple theoretical perspectives have resulted in an array of conceptualizations of community. While they have produced some confusion about what is meant by the term and about the manner and extent to which this concept is useful in education, it is possible to identify common themes across much of the literature.

Even a brief review of the literature related to community published during the past decades reveals both the richness and the diversity in this body of work. For example, the philosopher Alasdair Macintyre's powerful idea of the living traditions embodied by communities calls attention to the role of narrative in community (Macintyre 1981). In Macintyre's view, the individual is shaped by a community of memory even as he or she participates in creating the stories and practices that help to perpetuate it. Macintyre's ideas have greatly influenced Robert Bellah and his colleagues (Bellah *et al.* 1985, 1991), who argue for a public language that recognizes the importance of these communal ties and for the creation of a common discourse that develops the institutions and practices necessary to a 'good society'.

In contrast, a tradition of inquiry in sociology has focused on how schools as institutions shape the society and, in turn, on how social mores are reflected in these complex organizations. Etzione (1993), a staunch proponent of the 'new communitarian-ism', proposes a vision of community that is girded as much by responsibilities as by rights, in which the interests of the individual are carefully weighted against the prerogatives of the communal society. In this scheme, schools become essential organs of democracy, shaping the social and moral values that are necessary for a society to survive.

Other work in the sociology of education has investigated the ways in which the relationship between schools and their communities affects children's learning. Coleman and Hoffer (1987) postulate that students accrue a kind of communal social capital in the 'functional communities' created by extra-school ties such as membership in a parish. This social capital, they argue, greatly enriches the educational resources available to children.

The topic of community is of long-standing interest to the field of education. Nearly one hundred years ago, Dewey (1897) sketched a vision of a school as a small society that nurtured and shaped democratic ideas. The theme of community in schools is one to which he returned often (Dewey 1956, 1916), and his seminal work is still of enormous value as we grapple with these visions of education and community.

In the 'school effects' literature of the past twenty years, several researchers note they have also found evidence of a positive ethos (Rutter *et al.* 1979) or a 'sense of community' (Goodlad 1984, Lightfoot 1983) in schools where effective teaching and learning appear to be occurring. Evidence of 'communal school organization' has likewise been linked to a beneficial set of outcomes for students and teachers, including greater engagement by teachers and students, fewer incidences of negative behaviours, increased teacher satisfaction, and even improved student achievement (Bryk and Driscoll 1988, Driscoll 1989, Bryk *et al.* 1993).

Other recent work germane to the topic includes Noddings' studies of the ethic of caring (Noddings 1988), which have focused attention on the ways in which schools can become caring communities. In this vision, schools are places that bring students and teachers together in interactions about more than just the technical aspects of teaching and learning. Similarly, scholars studying teachers' professional lives have developed a robust concept of professional community in schools, focusing on the structures of collegiality that shape teachers' work (Johnson 1990, Louis 1990, Little 1992, Lieberman 1992, McLaughlin *et al.* 1990).

It is not surprising, then, that among the clarion calls for reform in the 1980s, several discussed the importance of creating communities of learners and teachers (Holmes Group 1986). Nor is it startling that this tradition has been popularized to the extent that some recent work (Sergiovanni 1993) translates the concepts of *Gemeinschaft* and *Gesellschaft*

(Tonnies 1957) into a primer for 'building community' in schools.

The idea of community in school is not without troubling issues as well. One set of questions pertains to the elements that most of these visions of community shared and the so-called 'dark side of community' (Noddings 1994) thus created. The concept of membership inherent in most visions of community, for example, leads us towards unanswered questions about criteria for membership and raises issues of diversity and exclusion that must be reconciled with a public education system that has prided itself on moving towards greater inclusion. In most cases, however, community has been presented as an unmitigated good, and the attributes shared by these visions are presented as worthy goals for all schools.

Perhaps the most common theme in the educational literature on community, then, has been the value of this image as an alternative organizational metaphor to guide schools that have become bureaucratic, hierarchical places. But other themes resonate. Most of this literature emphasizes the importance of caring, the primacy of diffuse relationships among individuals, and the development of a clear and widely shared set of purposes and values for schools.

When comparing these themes with those identified from the neoinstitutional literature, there are clearly some notes in common. The role of community in shaping one's understanding of oneself and the world through the creation of one's personal narrative (Macintyre 1981) has much in common with a view of institutions as the entities that provide the cognitive context for behaviour and understanding. While some theorists may argue that community emphasizes an intentionality and commitment that is not central to institutional views, there is general agreement that community members do not engage in all aspects of communal life with forethought. Indeed, the very pervasiveness of meaningful activities and the preponderance of daily, nearly unnoticed routines embodying common values are seen to invest community with its power in shaping human lives (Bellah *et al.* 1985).

Moreover, the ceremonial action that Meyer and Rowan ascribe as a hallmark of institutionalized organizations plays an important role in most delineations of community. Students of community suggest that one cannot over-emphasize the role of symbols, myths and communal activities in forming a sustaining community. It is through these emblems of shared meaning and through participation in these common activities that commitment to the community is built and through which all members, new and old, are socialized (Bryk and Driscoll 1988, Driscoll 1995). Meyer and Rowan (1977) themselves note that while ceremonies and symbols may be decoupled from the technical work of an organization, the commitment they create may be real.

But there is dissonance among these themes as well, especially with respect to the third theme identified in the neoinstitutional literature – the ways in which institutional environments are construed and the levels at which institutions are defined. In order to better explore the questions raised by these connections, it will be helpful to turn to more explicit formulations of community, notably the 'communitarian agenda' of Amitai Etzioni (1993); the concept of functional community as explicated by James S. Coleman and Thomas Hoffer (1987); and, finally, the concept of teachers' professional community, building on a diverse literature with particular attention to recent work by Karen S. Louis and others (1995).

Etzione and the communitarian agenda

In his book, *The Spirit of Community: Rights, Responsibilities and the Communitarian Agenda*, the sociologist Amitai Etzioni (1993) presents a manifesto for a communitarian agenda, what he defines as an 'environmental movement dedicated to the betterment of our moral social and political environment'. A central tenet of this movement is that rights must be linked with responsibilities. For too long, he argues, democratic societies have protected the rights of individuals without stressing at the same time that individuals bear obligations and responsibilities to the society in which those rights are earned. The balance between the two, he suggests, has been sadly lacking in modern society. Yet his manifesto does not concentrate solely on the diagnosis of the disease, and much of his work has been focused on the prescriptions for change that must be undertaken in order to realize fully his communitarian vision of a democratic society. Educational organizations have a vital role to play in building this society, and achieving the social goals of this movement is in a large part dependent on the communitarian school.

Etzione suggests that an understanding of the communitarian school must begin with agreement on the qualities that must be developed in all citizens.

> Although there are long lists of what our youngsters require, we Communitarians argue that two requirements loom over all others, indeed are the foundation of most other needs: to develop the basic personality traits that characterize effective individuals and to acquire core values. In the sizeable educational literature on the subject, both are sometimes referred to as "developing character". We mean by character the psychological muscles that allow a person to control impulses and defer gratification, which is essential for achievement, performance, and moral conduct. The core values, which need to be transmitted from generation to generation, contain moral substances that those with proper basic personality can learn to appreciate, adapt, and integrate into their lives: hard work pays, even in an unfair world; treat others with the same basic dignity with which you wish to be treated (or face the consequences); you feel better when you do what is right than when you evade your moral precepts. (90–91)

Since schools have such a central role in developing the values essential to a communitarian democracy, Etzioni asserts that it is the society, and not the family, that bears the final responsibility to ensure that students are properly educated. He writes,

> Schools are left with the task of making up for undereducation in the family and laying the psychic foundation for character and moral conduct. This is where the various commissions that have studied educational deficits missed a major point. By and large they argued for loading students with more hours of science, foreign language, maths and other skills and bodies of knowledge. *But you cannot fill a vessel that has yet to be cast.* (92)

Etzioni's vision of a communitarian school encompasses far more than merely classrooms. Thus 'the first step toward enhancing the moral educational role of schools is to increase the awareness of the school as a set of experiences. Schools should be seen not as a collection of teachers, pupils, classrooms, and curricula'. (103). When we think of the school community, he argues, we must recognize the importance of the extracurriculum, the overall atmosphere of the schools, the physical condition and surroundings of the school, and the structural arrangements that allow for bonding between teachers and students. He also suggests a mandatory year of national service after high school in order to develop a sense of responsibility for the larger social community.

In many ways, Etzioni's vision of a communitarian school is consonant with a traditional view of institutional theory. The organizations that shape behaviour must be created through human intention to conform to the principles of the democratic society. Etzioni's view of 'communitarianism' envisions a distinct and crucial role for the institution that we know as public education. In fact, the public school is the linchpin in this effort to reinvigorate and rebuild our notions of a democratic society, since it is in this organization where the values that characterize this larger national community are imbued in, and enacted by, young citizens. Moreover, education and its institutional structures not only shape values, but continue to provide an arena in which those values are discussed and debated. In this sense, Etzioni has much to share with Henig (1994), who has also identified schools as an essential agents of a democratic government. As Henig asserts,

> For all its exasperatingly slow pace, democratic government plays an absolutely critical role in airing alternative visions, encouraging compromise, and enticing disparate groups to redefine their interests and find common ground . . . .Because education is a process through which individuals come to richer and broader understandings of their interests and how they relate to those of others, and because public schools are the vehicle for educators most feasibly and appropriately subject to democratic control, government policy toward public schools is the major opportunity that democratic societies have for upgrading the quality of insight and sensitivity on which future majority decisions will rely. (10)

Viewed through a traditional institutional lens, then, Etzioni's vision of community in schools leads us towards questions of how best to reinvent and reinvigorate the institutional character of public education. Since the institutional framework necessary to support this vision of community is already in place, it requires only re-imagining.

But it is critical to note that there is steel in this vision of community as well. Because the school is so central in developing a core set of democratic, communitarian values, this view of school community requires a level of moral standardization among schools that may be difficult to achieve, especially if Etzioni's assessment of the present sad state of citizens' understanding of community and democracy is accurate. Etzioni's view of schooling, I would suggest, clearly id *not* compatible with a view that would allow every school to develop a unique core of values shared and expressed by each member of the community. Schools *must* teach those values he deems necessary for the sustenance of the larger national community. No mandate here for a thousand flowers to bloom: this is a relatively orderly garden that he envisions, with each school undertaking essentially the same mission.

Neoinstitutional theory as delineated by DiMaggio and Powell (1983/1991) may be helpful in identifying one of the key issues that must be faced if the manifesto is to become reality. In an early paper on institutions, they consider the mechanisms through which institutional sectors achieve remarkably high levels of homogeneity among organizations, and focus on why organizations look so similar to one another. In exploring this 'institutional isomorphism', or homogeneity of organizations within an organizational field, they postulate three processes through which standardization occurs. One process is 'coercive' isomorphism, in which organizations standardize in response to political influence and the need to maintain legitimacy. Alternative mechanisms are mimetic processes, in which competition spurs imitation, and professionalization (DiMaggio and Powell (1983/1991: 68–69).

After completing an extensive study of American schools, Goodlad (1984) noted this isomorphism when he observed that one of the most striking features of schools was their similarity to one another. One could argue that it is the coercive processes of standardization at the state and federal levels that have contributed to this isomorphism far more than the professionalism of schools' staff or the competitive nature of school organizations. This standardization has occurred despite the fact that the hallmark of American education is its decentralization. Recreating a new communitarian school on a nation-wide basis would require similar coercive mechanisms to produce the kind of widepsread dissemination of this ideal institution that Etzioni suggests. But many calls for reform are moving in exactly the opposite direction, either by exhorting the value of school choice in the public and private sector by all families (Chubb and Moe 1990) or by suggesting that only through radical decentralization can troubled schools survive and succeed (Hess 1991).

I do not wish to overstate this point. Etzioni would hardly endorse a centrally-controlled Ministry of Democratic Values that inspects and sanctions schools, and it is unlikely that any mechanisms devised to standardize the core values of schools would be truly coercive. But it is important to note that the task of revitalizing institutions along democratic lines, if indeed they fall so far below the mark now, is an enormous one, and there are tensions among the current designs for reform, our notions of what constitutes democratic education, and the kinds of processes that DiMaggio and Powell (1983/1991) suggest may be at operative in any movement to change schools.

Coleman and Hoffer's functional community

Another view of 'communitarianism' in education is found in the conceptual framework developed by James Coleman and Thomas Hoffer (1987) in their comparative study of public and private high schools. Their discussion of this theory begins with a reference to the 'functional communities' observed in classic studies of small-town youth and the connections early sociologists made between those communities and what they observed in schools (Lynd and Lynd 1929, Hollingshead 1949). Coleman and Hoffer write

> Parents knew who their children's friends were and knew their parents. The norms that pervaded the school were in part those dictated by the needs of the youth themselves (attractiveness to the opposite sex, for example) but in part those established by the adult community and enforced by the intergenerational contact that this closure brought about. This structural consistency between functional community, a community in which social norms and sanctions, including those that cross generations, arise out of the social structure itself, and both reinforce and perpetuate that structure. (7)

While acknowledging that this closeness can be limiting, 'partly through inheritance of the parents' reputation by the child', they argue there is a positive effect on the

> opportunity of children from different social backgrounds.... A functional community augments the resources available to parents in their interactions with school, in their supervision of their children's behavior, and in their supervision of children's associations, both with others their own age and with adults. The feedback that a parent receives from friends and associates, either unsolicited or in response to questions, provides extensive additional resources that aid the parent in monitoring the school and the child, and the norms that parents, as part of their everyday activity, are able to establish act as important aids in socializing children. (7)

Coleman and Hoffer believed that the differences that they saw between Catholic and public high schools were attributable to the fact that Catholic schools were located in 'functional communities', centred on Catholic parishes. Unlike the small-town schools observed at the beginning of the century, however, modern public schools were far less likely to be embedded in communities where multiple generations shared ties of work, family and friendship. But in the functional communities that supported Catholic schools, the parents of students and students themselves had oportunities to interact around many different non-educational activities, and shared a similar value system. Such interactions resulted in multiple connective relationships among the school families, often reaching across generations, as well as a deeply embedded common core of beliefs.

Functional community, they argued, is different from community created by a group of people who coalesce merely around educational choices and share little else in common (resulting in an educational version of what Bellah *et al.* (1985) term a 'lifestyle enclave').

> A functional community is neither a necessary nor a sufficient condition for value consistency, though the two have some affinity.... At the same time, there are collections of people who exhibit value consistency, but who constitute no functional community at all.... We will use the term 'value community' to describe a collection of people who share similar values about education and childrearing but who are not a functional community. As the preceding examples indicate, some public schools of choice and some private schools in the independent sector have

students whose parents are members of a value community, but not a functional community. (Coleman and Hoffer 1987: 10).

Coleman and Hoffer assert that schools that have a true *functional* community (in which parents and students are linked outside of as well as through the school) have the richest array of resources available to children and increase their opportunities the greatest amount.

It is not incidental that the Coleman and Hoffer theory animates a study that explored the workings of religious versus non-religious high schools, in particular, focusing on the Catholic sector. As noted above, they postulate that such schools are located in a strong institutional matrix in which the school is a natural, organic extension of the larger institution of the Church. Such close connection between school and this larger context provides a dense network of social ties around a variety of issues germane to the institution, resulting in a 'social capital' for the child that is available as an educational resource.

Once again, we see that the Coleman and Hoffer formulation of community has deep roots in traditional theories of institutions. They posit that it is precisely the strength of the extra-school institutional ties that results in social capital for the child. An interesting question arises, however, when we try to imagine an institutional context supporting functional community that wields the power of a traditional religious organization, given that over ninety percent of the schoolchildren in the United States attend schools that are publicly funded and operated. In some ways, we are begging the question that Durkheim grappled with in late nineteenth century French society: absent the Church, what institutions can provide the context for behaviour and understanding that Coleman and Hoffer term social capital?

It is difficult to identify, in the environment of the modern high school, a traditional institution that approximates the coherence and density of the ties produced by either a religious organization or a closely knit small town. Yet here neoinstitutionalist theory may be helpful in encouraging us to think about institutions in a somewhat more amorphous fashion and to envision the environmental influences in more creative ways.

Recall that one of the themes identified at the outset of this discussion was that environments have subtle influences on organizations, 'creating the lenses through which actors view the world and the very categories of structure, action and thought...' (DiMaggio and Powell 1991: 13). Recent work by Heath and McLaughlin (1994) suggests that schools have been extraordinarily myopic in their attempts to identify the institutional forces in adolecent lives that may be turned to advantage in educational enterprise. They argue that community-based organizations which operate outside the purview of bureaucratic schools provide experiences in which urban youths develop their creativity and engage in productive activity in ways that prepare them well for their future. These 'non-standard', highly diverse organizations are located throughout urban communities but often have few if any connections with schools, even though, as Heath and McLaughlin argue, they are able to succeed in capturing the attention, talents and skills of children that conventional institutions have deemed 'at risk'. Heath and McLaughlin's work suggest that if schools are to build on the functional urban communities in which their students live, they must move beyond standard educational outreach strategies and begin to appreciate and learn from the powerful institutional forces that shape their students' lives, attending to the many positive benefits that such nontraditional organizations may have for student learning.

The contexts of teachers' work and the creation of professional community

Finally, we turn to a third conception of community that is emerging from theory and inquiry that focuses on the context of teachers work. The study of the profession of teaching is hardly new; over sixty years ago, for example, Willard Waller's seminal work on the sociology of the teaching profession initiated a kind of formal scrutiny of teachers' work that attended carefully to the nature of that work as it was framed by the contexts of both the school and the community (Waller 1932). But the conceptions of the task of teaching which animated continuing study in the decades that followed varied greatly. Within recent memory, for example, dominant modes of research such as explorations of 'effective schools' and school climate have often reduced the task of teaching to a set of variables in a regression equation predicting student achievement (Bossert 1988). Clearly, exceptions to these reductionist conceptions exist, such as Lortie's sociological portrait of the profession (1975) or Jackson's ethnography of life in classrooms (1968). But as McLaughlin and Talbert (1990) indicate, a complex and reflective vision of teaching has at times been overshadowed by what they term 'relatively mechanistic' ideas of the tasks of teaching that 'spawned an industry of teacher-proof curricula' (McLaughlin and Talbert 1990: 2).

In the past decade, the vision of teaching as a complex enterprise has been framed in significant ways by the context in which teachers' work has become more widespread. McLaughlin and Talbert note an increasing 'recognition of teaching as a *professional enterprise* [emphasis mine] requiring individual judgement' which, in turn, has led to an increased understanding that

> Effective teaching depends on more than just teachers' subject-matter knowledge and general pedagogical skills or even pedagogical content knowledge. Effective teaching depends significantly on the contexts within which teachers work – department and school organization and culture, professional association and networks, community educational values and norms, secondary and higher educational policies. (2)

Discussions of the demands of teachers' work and, concomitantly, their status as professionals, have gained momentum in the past decade. Although teachers' professionalism has been championed by professional and collective bargaining associations such as the National Educational Association and the American Federation of Teachers throughout most of the twentieth century, one of the most powerful arguments for recognizing teaching as a profession is found in the 1986 report by the Carnegie Foundation for the Advancement of Teaching, *A Nation Prepared*. Through the establishment of a National Board of Professional Teaching Standards, two-thirds of which is comprised of classroom teachers, the Carnegie Corporation sought to replicate its earlier success with the 1911 Flexner Report, which spurred the development and codification of the medical profession.

The extent to which teaching fits a classical sociological definition of a profession has provoked a good deal of debate. Louis, Kruse and Bryk (1995) suggest that the sociological literature distinguishes 'true' professions from other highly educated occupations on the basis of whether or not they have a technical knowledge base, whether or not the profession itself has control over entry to the profession and conditions of work, and whether or not the profession has a strong client orientation. Teachers rarely have sole control over entry into their profession or the conditions under which they work. Thus the calls to 'increase professionalism' in education have usually been accompanied by demands for increased teacher control over their work (Louis *et al.* 1995: 12).

An interesting development in the literature on teacher professionalism is a recent attempt by Karen Seashore Louis and her colleagues to bring this work together with that on community in schools. As they note, these traditions have been blended infrequently.

> The sociological writings on professionalism and community remain distinct and offer different premises about the attainment of social goals. The classical literature on professionalism emphasizes that such work is selective, requires high levels of training, and addresses a task of recognized value to society. Virtually any definition of a profession emphasizes the nonroutine character of the work that must be done, namely, that it requires considerable individual judgment in how to apply the expertise of the profession to a given problem. Because of the emphasis on judgment, professions often emphasize a form of social control that requires members of the profession to regulate the conduct of their peers.
>
> The community literature, on the other hand, focuses on the primacy of sustained face-to-face relationships and the activities that support such relationships. In the community literature, social control is established through the norms and values espoused by the community. Social integration within and across subgroups is achieved by aligning important norms and values while simultaneously creating a supportive environment for individual development. (11)

Louis and her colleagues argue that the emphasis on community as well as professionalism is necessary for school improvement because merely 'empowering' teachers will not result in the kind of commitment to teaching and to educational reform that is necessary to change urban schools:

> The available data suggest that school-based decision making and teacher empowerment is an important but insufficient stimulus for developing teachers' performance as professionals . . . . We contend that for empowerment to work to the advantage of students and teachers, a shared commitment to a fundamental change of teaching practice must emerge. For this to happen, we argue, requires the addition of a focus on community. (13–14)

Louis, Kruse and Bryk draw on a range of work in developing their conception of professional community. Earlier studies of schools as communities (Bryl and Driscoll 1988, Bryk *et al.* 1993) suggest that the three 'key features' of community in schools are a core of shared values, a common set of activities that structure interactions and provide shared experiences, and the specific organizational structures that will promote such activities, including expectations for collegial exchanges (cited in Louis *et al.* 1995: 16).

Terming their concept of professional community an 'emerging framework', the authors suggest that professional communities 'share five core characteristics: shared values, reflective dialogue, deprivatization of practice, focus on student learning, and collaboration' (Kruse *et al.* Bryk 1995: 34). Professional community is supported by structural conditions such as time for teachers to meet and talk, physical proximity to one another in shared work spaces, interdependent teaching roles, communication structures and professional networks, teacher empowerment, and school autonomy. Professional community is also supported by social and human resources such as openness to improvement, a sense of trust and respect, access to professional expertise, supportive leadership, and socialization processes that induct new members and maintain community. The benefits of school-based community, they argue, include an increased collective responsibility for student learning. (For a fuller explication of each of these elements, see Kruse *et al.* 1995.)

A connection can easily be made between the effort to develop teaching as a profession and the traditional institutional literature, much of which includes studies of professions. But it may be that this early sociological framework on the professions is less productive than is the case with newer formulations. The cognitive emphasis of neoinstitutionalism may be far more compatible with the most recent work that has explored teachers' worlds. As Susan Moore Johnson writes in her study of the physical, structural, sociological, economic, political, cultural and psychological features of teacher workplaces, 'Workplaces are not inert boxes that house practice. Rather, they are

complex sets of features that interact with practice. They convey information about what
is expected. They influence what is possible. They determine what is likely'. (9).

Similarly, what DiMaggio and Powell (1991) call the 'cognitive sunk costs' of
institutions resonantes with McLaughlin and Talbert's (1990) work that investigates the
'multiple embedded contexts' of teaching:

> In our view, a social constructionist perspective on teachers' work and workplace is critical if we are to understand
> how context shapes teaching and to craft productive organizations and policy environments in education. What
> we call here the "bottom-up" perspectives on the teaching workplace asks *what* and *how* particular context
> conditions are significant to teachers' perceptions and experiences of their work environment and their conceptions
> of teaching goals and tasks. (McLaughlin and Talbert 1990: 3)

At the very least, we could learn much from institutional case studies focusing on this
recent development of the teaching profession, similar to those done by neoinstitutional-
ists such as Galaskiewicz (1991) on corporate philanthropy, Brint and Karabel (1991) on
community colleges, and DiMaggio (1991) on art museums (cited in Powell and
DiMaggio 1991).

In part because recent work on professional community is indeed 'emergent', it is a
complicated task to determine how the neoinstitutional literature can be of assistance. As
observed earlier, the insights provided by Meyer and Rowan (1997) on the critical role of
ceremonial actions in organizations fit well with the kinds of common activities that are
presumed to shape professional community. This work suggests that even as we pay
attention to the place where teachers' technical work is accomplished, the classroom, we
cannot neglect the activities that legitimate the status of the professional community and
project the logic of confidence necessary for its survival.

Our grasp of the many forces that shape professional community at the school site
may be helped by emerging frameworks in neoinstitutionalism that broaden our
understanding of institutions beyond traditional conventions to include a multiplicity of
powerful societal forces. Ann Lieberman (1992) summarizes much of this new perspective
on the context of teaching as she widens the lens through which these contexts should be
observed. She notes, echoing Louis and Johnson, that

> teaching is affected by not only what the teacher does, but by the context within which teaching takes place: the
> kinds of students, the content of the curriculum, and *political and social forces within as well as surrounding the school*
> [italics mine] . . . . Teachers are powerfully affected by changes in context, both in their ability to be successful
> with students and their own feelings of adequacy.

Additionally, the features noted by Kruse, Louis and Bryk (1995) that support community
imply an understanding of, as well as an ability to influence, the complicated political and
social contexts that currently govern American public education. A neoinstitutional
perspective would suggest that a commitment to developing professional community
demands that a substantial amount of attention must be given to these macro-structures
that shape education at the site level.

Some final thoughts

In this chapter, I have tried to bring together selected themes from the neoinstitutional
literature with three different conceptions of community in education. Although many
areas of compatibility between the two literatures have been noted, this juxtaposition has
also introduced a number of areas for further thought. The insights provided are thus both
intriguing and inchoate. In brief, this exercise suggests that a sophisticated rendering of
the institutional environments of school communities must be developed if we are to

comprehend fully their consequences or explore their potential. At a minimum, such an effort requires an understanding of the embedded contexts of urban schools which attends to the diverse realities of student and teacher lives. Similarly, it implies that the political and social institutions that provide the context for school must be considered as critical factors in any attempt to 'build community' in schools.

References

BELLAH, R., TIPTON, S., SWIDLER, A., and SULLIVAN, W. (1985) *Habits of the Heart* (New York: Basic).

BELLAH, R. *et al.* (1991) *The Good Society* (New York: Knopf).

BOSSERT, S. (1988) School effects, in N. Boyan (eds.), *Handbook of research on educational administration* (New York: Longman), 341–354.

BRINT, S. and KARABEL, J. Institutional origins and transformations: the case of American community colleges, in W. Powell and P. DiMaggio (eds), *The New Institutionalism in Organizational Analysis* (Chicago: University of Chicago Press), 337–360.

BRYK, A.S. and DRISCOLL, M.E. (1988) *The High School as Community: Contextual Influences and Consequences for Students and Teachers*, National Center for Effective Secondary Schools at the University of Wisconsin.

BRYK, A.S., LEE, V. and HOLLAND, P. (1993) *Catholic Schools and the Common Good* (Cambridge, MA: Harvard University Press).

CARNEGIE FORUM ON EDUCATION AND THE ECONOMY (1986) *A Nation Prepared: Teachers for the 21st Century*, Report of the Task Force on Teaching as a Profession (New York: Carnegie Foundation).

CHUBB, J. and MOE, T. (1990) *Politics, Markets and America's Schools* (Washington: Brookings Institute).

CLARKE, B.R. The 'cooling-out function' in higher education, *American Journal of Sociology*, 65, 569–76.

COLEMAN, J. and HOFFER, T. (1987) *Public and Private Schools: The Impact of Communities* (New York: Basic).

CUBAN, L. (1992) Managing professional dilemmas while building professional communities, *Educational Researcher*, 21, 4–11.

DALTON, M. (1959) *Men Who Manage* (New York: Wiley).

DEWEY, J. (1897) My pedagogic creed, *School Journal*, 54, 77–80.

DEWEY, J. (1916/1966) *Democracy and Education* (New York: Free).

DEWEY, J. (1956) *The School and Society* (Chicago: University of Chicago Press).

DIMAGGIO, P. Constructing an organizational field as a professional project: U.S. art museums, 1920–1940, in W. Powell and P. DiMaggio (eds), *The New Institutionalism in Organizational Analysis* (Chicago: University of Chicago Press), 267–292.

DIMAGGIO, P. and POWELL, W. (1983) The iron cage revisited: institutional isomorphism and collective rationality in organization fields, *American Sociological Review*, 48: 147–60. Reprinted in W. Powell and P. DiMaggio (eds). *The New Institutionalism in Organizational Analysis* (Chicago: University of Chicago Press), 63–82.

DIMAGGIO, P. and POWELL, W. (1991) Introduction, in W. Powell and P. DiMaggio (eds), *The New Institutionalism in Organizational Analysis* (Chicago: University of Chicago Press), 1–40.

DRISCOLL, M.E. (1995) Thinking like a fish: the implications of community for parents and schools, in B. Schneider and P. Cookson, (eds), *Transforming schools* (Greenwood).

ETZIONI, A. (1993) *The Spirit of Community: Rights, Responsibilities and the Communitarian Agenda* (New York: Crown).

GALASKIEWICZ, J. (1991) Making corporate actors accountable: institution-building in Minneapolis-St. Paul, in W. Powell and P. DiMaggio (eds), *The New Institutional in Organizational Analysis* (Chicago: University of Chicago Press), 292–310.

GOODLAD, J. (1984) *A Place Called School: Prospects for the Future* (New York: McGraw Hill).

GOULDNER, A.W. (1954) *Patterns of Industrial Bureaucracy* (Glencoe: Free).

HEATH, S.B. and MCLAUGHLIN, M.W. (1994) The best of both worlds: connecting schools and community youth organizations for all-day, all-year learning, *Educational Administration Quarterly*, 30 (3), 278–300.

HENIG, J.R. (1994) *Rethinking School Choice: Limits of the Market Metaphor* (Princeton: Princeton University Press).

HESS, G.A. (1991) *School Restructuring, Chicago Style* (Newbury Park CA: Corwin).

HOLLINGSHEAD, A. B. (1949) *Elmtown's Youth* (New York: Wiley).

HOLMES GROUP (1986) *Tomorrow's Teachers* (East Lansing: Holmes).

JACKSON, P. (1968) *Life in Classrooms* (New York: Teachers College Press).

JOHNSON, S. M. (1990) *Teachers at Work: Achieving Success in our Schools* (New York: Basic).

KRUSE, S. D., LOUIS, K. S. and BRYK, A. S. An emerging framework for analyzing school-based professional community, in K. S. Louis and S. Kruse (eds) *Professionalism and Community: Perspectives on Reforming Urban Schools* (Thousand Oaks: Corwin), 23–44.

LIEBERMAN, A. (1992) Introduction: the changing context of education, in A. Lieberman (ed.), *The Changing Contexts of Teaching* (Chicago: University of Chicago Press), 1–10.

LIGHTFOOT, S. L. (1983) *The Good High School* (New York: Basic).

LITTLE, J. (1992) Opening the black box of professional community, in A. Lieberman (ed.), *The Changing Contexts of Teaching* (Chicago: University of Chicago Press), 157–170.

LORTIE, D. C. (1975) *Schoolteacher* (Chicago: University of Chicago Press).

LOUIS, K. S. (1990) Social and community values and the quality of teachers' work life, in M. McLaughlin, J. Talbert and N. Bascia (eds), *The Contexts of Teaching in Secondary School* (New York: Teachers College Press), 17–39.

LOUIS, K. S., KRUSE, S. *et al.* (1995) *Professionalism and Community: Perspectives on Reforming Urban Schools* (Thousand Oaks: Corwin).

LOUIS, K. S., KRUSE, S. and BRYK, A. (1995) Professionalism and community: what is it and why is it so important in urban schools? in K. S. Louis and S. Kruse (eds), *Professionalism and Community: Perspectives on Reforming Urban Schools* (Thousand Oaks: Corwin), 3–22.

LYND, R. and LYND, H. (1929) *Middletown* (New York: Harcourt).

MACINTYRE, A. (1981) *After Virtue* (South Bend: University of Notre Dame Press).

McLAUGHLIN, M. and TALBERT, J. (1990) The contexts in question: the secondary school workplace, in M. McLaughlin, J. Talbert and N. Bascia (eds), *The Contexts of Teaching in Secondary Schools* (New York: Teachers College Press).

McLAUGHLIN, M., TALBERT, J. and BASCIA, N. (eds). (1990) *The Contexts of Teaching in Secondary Schools: Teacher Realities* (New York: Teachers College Press).

MEYER, J. and ROWAN, B. (1977) Institutionalized organizations: formal structure as myth and ceremony, *American Journal of Sociology*, 83 (2): 340–363. Reprinted in W. Powell and P. DiMaggio (eds), *The New Institutionalism in Organizational Analysis* (Chicago: University of Chicago Press), 41–62.

NODDINGS, N. (1988) An ethic of caring and its implications for instructional arrangements, *American Journal of Education*, 96, 215–230.

NODDINGS, N. (1994) The dark side of community. Invited address, Annual Meeting of the University Council for Educational Administration, Philadelphia, October.

POWELL, W. W. and DiMAGGIO, P. (eds) (1991) *The New Institutionalism in Organizational Analysis* (Chicago: University of Chicago Press).

RAYWID, M. A. (1988) Community and schools: a prolegomenon, *Teachers College Record*, 90, 198–210.

RUTTER, M., MAUGHAN, B., MORTIMORE, P., OUSTON, J. and SMITH, A. (1979) *Fifteen Thousand Hours: Secondary Schools and Their Effects on Children* (Cambridge, MA: Harvard University Press).

SCOTT, W. R. (1995) *Institutions and Organizations: theory and research* (Thousand Oaks: Sage).

SCOTT, W. R. and MEYER, J. (1991) The organization of societal sectors: propositions and early evidence, in W. Powell and P. DiMaggio (eds), *The New Institutionalism in Organizational Analysis* (Chicago: University of Chicago Press), 108–142.

SELZNICK, P. (1949) *TVA and the Grass Roots* (Berkeley: University of California Press).

SERGIOVANNI, T. (1993) *Building Community in Schools* (San Francisco: Jossey Bass).

TONNIES, F. (1957) *Community and Society* (East Lansing: Michigan State University Press).

WALLER, W. (1932) *The Sociology of Teaching* (New York: Wiley).

WEBER, M. (1947) *Theory of Social and Economic Organization* (New York: Macmillan).

WEHLAGE, G., RUTTER, R. A., SMITH, G. A., LESKO, N. and FERNANDEZ, R. R. (1989) *Reducing the Risk: Schools as Communities of Support* (Philadelphia: Falmer).

5.   Computer models of educational institutions: the case of vouchers and social equity

Terry M. Moe and Kenneth W. Shotts

The new institutionalism has transformed social-science theory over the past decade or two, and, as it finds its way into the education field, there is every reason for optimism about the prospects for a theory of educational institutions. Progress will not be easy or straightforward, however, for the new institutionalism is not a single theory that can simply be applied to education. It is a diverse intellectual movement whose schools of thought range from rational choice to garbage can theory, from Marxism to institutional sociology. The challenge for education scholars is to make productive use of this eclectic body of work, selecting its most promising theoretical tools and adapting them to the substance and concerns of their own field.

We will not be arguing here that one path to theory is clearly better than the others. Instead, we want to highlight a methodology that, even within the new institutionalism, has attracted less attention than it deserves, and we want to suggest how it might be instrumental in moving toward a theory of educational institutions.

The methodology is computer modelling. Its great advantage is that it allows for the development of formal, clearly specified theories whose implications can be logically derived and tested, even when applied to complex situations that standard modelling approaches cannot handle (because, without radical simplification, they often cannot generate mathematical solutions). While there are certain drawbacks associated with computer models as well—their parameters must take on actual numerical values, for instance, which limits their generality and makes their validity more difficult to assess—the trade-off is well worth it. Institutions are complex, and computer modelling offers a powerful, enormously flexible analytic means of managing this complexity, promoting theory, and exploring key issues that most formal models would be forced to ignore or trivialize (e.g., Cyert and March 1963, Cohen *et al.* 1972, Bendor and Moe 1985).

A foundation for this line of theory-building already exists within the education field. In a recent article, Charles Manski (1992) developed a computer simulation of a voucher system, with special attention to its effects on equal opportunity for the poor. Manski construes his analysis narrowly, as a simple contribution to the ongoing debate over vouchers—and the fact is, for reasons we will soon discuss, we disagree with much of what he says and does here. But we also think his work should be appreciated as a pioneering effort to develop computer models of alternative institutional systems—namely, the existing education system and a voucher system—and to compare the outcomes they generate for students, schools, and society. This is precisely the sort of exercise that progress toward a theory of educational institutions requires. The focus on vouchers, moreover, is a perfect vehicle for theory-building: for the voucher debate is really a debate about the merits of alternative institutional systems, and the only way to address the major points at issue is to model these systems and compare them.

Our purpose here is to solidify and build upon this early foundation, in the hope that it might serve as a springboard for a new research programme on educational institutions. There are perhaps many ways to do this. The one we have chosen involves four basic elements, all built around Manski's pioneering application of computer models to the voucher issue.

(1) We will clarify, in step-by-step fashion, how Manski goes about building his analysis, so that readers unfamiliar with his article, and especially those unfamiliar with computer modelling as a methodology, can gain perspective on what this kind of analysis involves (and perhaps begin to think about doing it themselves someday).

(2) We will push for theoretical progress by challenging—in what we think is a constructive, forward-looking way—key aspects of Manski's analysis: the way he characterizes the (institutional) theory of vouchers, the assumptions on which he bases his models, the interpretations he attaches to the simulation results, and the policy recommendations he ultimately embraces. The point is not simply to criticize, but to move toward a more balanced, defensible, and productive foundation for theory.

(3) We will present a new analysis, derived (by us) from Manski's own computer program, that takes the theoretical argument a step further—and points to conclusions about the relative performance of institutions (the existing system versus vouchers) that are quite at variance with the Manski's.

(4) Finally, we will look beyond the specific framework adopted by Manski to suggest other approaches—based on different assumptions about who the relevant actors are, how they are motivated, what they know, how the institutional context is structured, and so on—that might offer more plausible or fruitful paths for pursuing a broader theory of educational institutions.

At this point, it is too early to know which analytic approach is best. This is the beginning of what stands to be an innovative process of theory-building in which, with any luck, many researchers will begin to generate new models and debate their relative merits. The potential payoffs are substantial: not just a better understanding of vouchers, but genuine progress toward coherent theories of education systems as a whole—how they operate under specified conditions, what their broader consequences are, and how better outcomes might be engineered through wise policy choices. In an education field that has produced few powerful theories, this is an exciting prospect indeed.

Theory and vouchers

Manski prefaces his computer model with a lengthy introduction in which he assesses the literature on vouchers and argues the need for theory. What he has to say here is worth highlighting, both because it seriously mischaracterizes the theory of vouchers and because it reveals an unwarranted perspective on what counts as theory in the first place.

Manski centers most of his discussion on various arguments that have been made on behalf of vouchers, and his assessment is overwhelmingly negative. It is not just that, in his view, these arguments are unpersuasive or empirically unsupported. It is that they are theoretically unfounded—which, of course, is the key point: this is a paper about the need for theory. The only theoretical basis for vouchers, he argues, is a 'straightforward application of elementary principles of classical economics (p.354). This was so when Milton Friedman (1955) first proposed vouchers in the 1950s, and it remains so today.

Beyond classical economics, as Manski sees it, the argument for vouchers is more a reflection of conservative ideology than theory. Voucher proponents, including academics who claim to be doing serious research, are often just engaging in 'rhetoric' and 'advocacy' to promote the cause; their arguments do not really deserve to be taken seriously. Among the offenders are John Chubb and Terry Moe, whose *Politics, Markets, and America's Schools* (1990) is passed off (without discussion) as symptomatic of the 'present rhetoric of choice' (p.355). Manski sums it up this way:

> During the past 30 years, the basic intellectual argument for systemic choice has not notably advanced beyond the classical economic ideas sketched by Friedman. If anything, recent writing advocating choice views the matter more simplistically than did Friedman. It seems enough today to declare that choice promotes consumer sovereignty and competition. (p.355)

Having isolated classical economics as the target theory, Manski then devotes himself to attacking its validity. His argument is familiar: that its idealized assumptions do not hold in the real world, where information costs, monitoring costs, externalities and the like produce problems that undermine the theory. This, he believes, destroys the only theoretical basis that choice proponents have for forwarding their claims. Once beyond these idealized notions 'we are in the messy real world of trade-offs' (p.357) in which government provision and control may be preferable.

He goes on to argue, via an interesting shift in terminology, that progress requires getting away from the 'qualitative' analysis of voucher advocates by pursuing a 'quantitative' analysis instead. This would enable theorists to 'pin down magnitudes' (p.357) — e.g., regarding how much information parents actually possess or how difficult public monitoring actually is. To Manski, the absence of such work is but another indication of how frivolous the arguments for choice have been.

> It is disappointing and frustrating that serious attention has not been given to these questions of magnitudes during the 30 years in which choice has been actively debated . . . In the absence of quantitative analysis, rhetoric reigns. (p.357)

Manski has every right to criticize vouchers on scientific grounds. Indeed, such criticism is usually helpful, because it promotes the kind of debate that theoretical progress depends upon. But much of what he has to say about the theory of vouchers is misleading and at times even offensive to the professional integrity of its proponents.

For starters, Manski's disappointment and frustration with the state of voucher theory seem more than a little out of place. The fact is, theory of any kind has so far made little headway within the field of education, which has long been woefully underdeveloped in this regard. Education is an intensely practical field, driven by practitioner-oriented concerns. Anything resembling coherent theory is often disparaged, even by many education researchers. This is particularly true when it comes to issues of an institutional or systemic nature.

The voucher debate is unusual precisely because there *is* a clear theoretical perspective at work, one that speaks not simply to vouchers *per se*, but also to broader issues of politics, markets, and the structure and operation of educational institutions. This perspective, moreover, is potentially very powerful, rooted as it is in microeconomics, which has been productively applied to a whole range of social behaviours and which, by almost any account, represents the most successful and well-developed theory in all the social sciences. Given the weakness of theory in the education field, Manski ought to be applauding voucher proponents for having a coherent theory at all, particularly one with such analytic power and potential. And whether he agrees with the theory or not, he should see it as a tremendous opportunity for moving toward a genuinely theoretical understanding of the educational system and its institutions.

A second problem with Manski's critique is that he mischaracterizes the theoretical argument for vouchers. There are really two lines of theory at work here, one a theory of markets and the other a theory of politics, both of them arising from rational choice foundations. The theory of markets, which is the only part that Manski recognizes, is not based solely on classical economics, as he claims. Economics has come a long way since the rarified models of classicism reigned supreme. Today, the sorts of issues Manski raises as somehow contradicting the economic argument for vouchers—imperfect information, monitoring and control, public goods—are in fact well integrated into modern economic theory, and whole subfields are devoted to them.

These days it is the rare economist or voucher proponent who argues that free, entirely unregulated markets will automatically lead to the promised land. Rather, information costs, monitoring costs, externalities, and other concerns are an integral part of their theoretical thinking. Precisely because they are so equipped, they know that free markets can indeed produce undesirable problems, they know why problems tend to arise, and they know what sorts of conditions they need to create—often via institutional design—to promote better outcomes. As a result, voucher proponents are best thought of not as free-marketeers, as Manski portrays them, but as institutional designers whose designs arise in part from theoretical arguments about why free markets do *not* work optimally if left totally unregulated.

The other line of theory, which Manski overlooks entirely, is the theory of political institutions. This is essential to any debate over vouchers, because the claims to be made or criticized are always comparative in nature. The question is not whether vouchers are good in some absolute sense, but whether a voucher system is better than the system of political institutions by which the schools are currently governed. An answer, whether positive or negative, cannot emerge out of a theory of markets alone, even with its modern extensions. It requires a companion theory of education's political institutions.

This is where Chubb and Moe's *Politics, Markets, and America's Schools* comes in. Beginning from first principles, they go to some lengths to develop a clear, coherent theory of the political control and governance of American schools—showing, among other things, that debilitating bureaucracy and ineffective organization are unavoidable products of the system. As is true of the economic theory of vouchers, this political theory grows logically out of broader rational-choice literature of demonstrated power and promise. In their case, the broader literature is the positive theory of political institutions (e.g., Shepsle 1986, Moe 1990a, 1990b, Horn 1995), which is itself deeply anchored in the 'new institutional economics' (Williamson 1985), or what political scientists often call the 'new economics of organization' (Moe 1984).

Manski may not like what Chubb and Moe have to say about government. But he does the field (and the authors) a disservice by dismissing their arguments as sheer advocacy and rhetoric. The fact is, Chubb and Moe have a theory of government rooted in a powerful theoretical tradition, and their conclusions about educational institutions flow logically from those foundations. This, again, is unusual for the field and ought to be regarded as an opportunity for theoretical debate and progress. A serious assessment of vouchers would see their theory for what it is and address what ought to be the real issue: its validity. If Manski doubts what Chubb and Moe say about government, his task is to show exactly why they are wrong and, just as importantly, to point the way toward a coherent, alternative theory of government that does a better job.

There is, finally, one other aspect of Manski's prefatory treatment of the voucher literature that deserves mention here before we move on to discuss his model. This is his view of 'qualitative' and 'quantitative' analysis and how they fit into the theoretical enterprise. As Manski tells his story, 'qualitative' is a perjorative term. When he says that voucher arguments are qualitative, he means that they are not theoretical, that they are imprecise and unscientific, and that anything goes. What Manski brings to the table, on the other hand, is true science: quantitative analysis, in the form of a computer model. This is sophisticated, rigorous, objective and quite necessary if the voucher debate is to move beyond the value-driven claims of choice advocates. 'In the absence of quantitative analysis, rhetoric reigns' (p.357).

We agree that quantitative analysis is generally a good thing, and that education and the other social sciences need more of it. Yet Manski goes off the deep end here, and what he says is both misleading and, purely from the standpoint of scientific methodology, unwarranted. In the first place, qualitative analysis is entirely compatible with proper science and contributes enormously to scientific progress. Qualitative arguments can provide clear, coherent, logically rigorous expressions of theory. Indeed, throughout social science this is the most common vehicle by which theory is developed and debated.

Second, there is nothing magical about quantitative analysis. While it is presumably rigorous, it needn't—and often doesn't—express anything interesting or important in terms of theory, and it is just as vulnerable to the underlying values of the theorist as qualitative argument is. Indeed, a technically sophisticated modeller with an ideological agenda is probably more dangerous to science than her qualitative counterpart, because formal models have the appearance of objectivity and dispassionate theory, and are more difficult for the larger audience to evaluate.

Without belabouring the point, our bottom line is that Manski gives a very distorted introduction to the theory of vouchers. He mischaracterizes the literature, trivializes serious efforts at theory construction and weaves a methodological argument that confuses science with quantification. Not a propitious beginning for an analysis that really does have something to contribute and could, with better packaging, have prepared readers to appreciate what it is.

Manski's computer model

Manski is on firmer ground when he builds his computer model. As in any modelling effort, his challenge is to make assumptions that reduce complexity, capture essential features of the system, and generate interesting implications on important issues. This is not an easy thing to do. Educational institutions are extraordinarily complicated, and it is not at all clear from the outset what modelling strategies are likely to prove most productive. Countless analytic choices have to be made, yet there are few guidelines to go by.

Manski handles this challenge well. His assumptions are plausible in most respects, especially as a first stab at the problem, and they allow him to fashion a coherent model from which a range of implications can be derived. We would have done it differently, but this is to be expected at such an early stage. The important thing is that Manski succeeds in crafting a useful starting point for future analysis.

In this section, we briefly describe the basic structure of the model, and then suggest how Manski puts it to use in generating conclusions about vouchers.

Overview

Manski's model world has three types of actors: a public sector, a private sector and students (or families). The public and private sectors each behave as single actors who make decisions about the provision of educational services to students. (Individual schools are not modelled.) Students, in turn, choose whether to attend school in one sector or the other.

The basic question is: how are the decisions of students and sectors affected by the introduction of vouchers, and what are the consequences, especially as they bear on low-income families?

The public sector

Now for a little more detail. The public sector is modelled as a single, unitary actor that provides an identical education to all of its students and receives a fixed, exogenously determined amount of funding, V_o, for every student it enrolls. Some part of this, E_o, will actually be spent on things students value. The rest, V_o-E_o, either goes to bureaucratic waste or to promote social goals that students don't care about. The public sector's choice problem is to pick its optimal value for E_o, thereby deciding how much of its per-pupil budget will go toward students and how much will go toward other things.

How the public sector chooses its optimal E_o depends on what kind of decision-maker the public sector is assumed to be. Manski explores two possibilities:

1   It might be competitive, trying to attract as many students as possible by 'efficiently' (in this sense) spending all its funding on things students value. It would thus set $E_o = V_o$.
2   It might be wasteful, maximizing the difference between its budget and the amount it spends on students. It would thus maximize the total surplus, $n(V_o - E_o)$, where n is the total number of students it enrols.

Manski does not embrace either of these behavioural models. He sees them as anchoring opposite ends of a motivational continuum and simulates the effects of vouchers under each scenario separately.

The private sector

Manski's private sector is also a unitary decision-maker that offers a homogeneous set of educational services to all families. Its services are not free, as the public sector's are, but are offered at a single price (tuition) which is uniform throughout the sector.

Manski assumes the private sector always behaves competitively, due to the effects of market forces. It will thus be driven to spend all of its revenues on things valued by students. It will also be driven to set its tuition at a level that maximizes the number of students enrolled in the sector.

To put this in mathetmatical terms, the private sector's per student revenues consist of tuition, T_1, plus whatever voucher funds, V_1, may be provided by the government. Its first decision rule, as a competitive actor, is thus to set $E_1 = T_1 + V_1$, where E_1 is spending on things valued by students. Since V_1 is set exogenously by the government, however, the optimal value of E_1 will be strictly determined once the optimal value of T_1 is known. Its key strategic problem, then, is to identify its optimal T_1, which it does by figuring out which level of tuition maximizes student enrollment.

Students

Students choose between the public and private sectors based on a comparison of the utilities they associate with each. How they carry out this evaluation turns on the nature of their utility functions, of course, and Manski assumes that these vary across students as a reflection of three underlying characteristics, all of them exogenously determined:

1 Family income. Students with higher incomes place less value on the marginal dollar. This means that upper-income students will find private schooling less costly and more attractive than lower-income students. It also means, however, that lower-income students will place higher value on vouchers than upper-income students, because the value of money is greater to them.
2 Motivation level. Some students are more highly motivated to get a good education than other students, and they accordingly place greater weight on school quality in making their comparisons of schools across sectors. Manski treats this as a binary variable, with half the students randomly labeled high motivation and the other half low motivation.
3 Private school preference. This one doesn't make any sense to us, but for now we will simply present it without comment. Manski assumes that each student has a built-in preference for one sector or the other, quite aside from considerations of cost or quality. He also assumes that the distribution of these sectoral preferences is biased: the average student is assumed to be averse to private education, and thus to prefer public education.[1]

These are general background factors that lend shape to student utility functions. In order for students to evaluate the two sectors, however, they also need to take account of specific features of schooling in each, features that bear on educational cost and quality. Manski focuses on three: private school tuition, the amount of money each sector spends on students (a measure of school quality), and the positive 'student interaction effect' arising from the fraction of students in each sector who are highly motivated (another measure of school quality). While tuition is an obvious cost consideration, the way he goes about measuring school quality is debatable; but again, we will not take up these issues just yet.

The assumptions, together with his guesses as to what the numerical values of parameters ought to be, allow Manski to arrive at a mathematical expression for student utility functions. These are the functions that guide student choices within the model. (See Appendix A.)

Communities

How vouchers work out in practice will presumably depend on the community context, including, among other things, the characteristics of its students and the level of
funding it provides for its public schools. To get at these contextual differences,
Manski applies his model separately to three simple types of communities: poor,
average, and wealthy.

1   The poor community has an income distribution weighted toward the low
    end of the scale and spends $4000 per student on its public schools (that is,
    V_0 = $4000).
2   The average community has a balanced income distribution and spends $6000
    per student.
3   The wealthy community has an income distribution skewed toward the high
    end and spends $10,000 per student.

A summary of Manski's results

Manski's analysis is based on 18 separate simulations. Each describes how a particular
type of community (poor, average, or wealthy) would be affected by a particular
type of voucher policy (no voucher, a $2000 voucher, or a $4000 voucher) under a particular assumption about public-school behaviour (competitive or wasteful). Together
they cover every possible permutation.

This is potentially very complicated. There are lots of variables here: many determinants that might be looked at, many effects that might be explored, and many relationships that change with their surrounding context. It would be easy to write a
whole book outlining all the implications. Much of this, however, would clearly be
overkill. For while some of these things are worth pursuing, the fundamental point
of all this is to understand the effects of vouchers on students, especially those from
low income families. There is one overarching question, then, that stands to simplify
and lend orientation to the entire enterprise: does the introduction of vouchers leave
low-income students better or worse off than they were before? This is the crux of
the matter.

Surprisingly enough, Manski never really addresses the issue. He never asks
whether vouchers make students better or worse off. Instead, his focus is on a variety
of sociological variables and school characteristics that presumably tell us something
about the bigger picture of how vouchers affect the two sectors and their mixes of
students. His analysis is devoted, as a result, to exploring how vouchers influence the
percentages of kids choosing public or private schools, the amount of funding each
sector devotes to students, the level of private school tuition, the fraction of high
motivation kids in each sector, segregation of students by income, and the like.

These issues are interesting in their own right. They bear on matters that have
been debated in the literature on choice, and they are certainly part of a larger perspective on the effects of vouchers. But what do they say about whether students have
been made better or worse off? They do not speak to this issue directly. Rather, they
speak to it indirectly – which, in the 'qualitative' literature (as Manski puts it) is the
way they often figure into the choice debate: they are commonly used as proxies for
student well-being. Critics often claim, for instance, that vouchers allow high-

motivation students to escape from public to private schools and that this is bad. The suspicion is that many of the remaining public students, especially those with low incomes, will be worse off as a result. Similarly, critics claim that vouchers lead to greater income segregation of students, and that this is bad too. The suspicion, again, is that income segregation leaves low-income students worse off.

However important issues like income segregation and the motivational mix of students might be on other grounds, their use as proxies for student well-being is questionable and in this case entirely unnecessary. Manski doesn't need proxies. The fact is, he has direct measures of student utility within his model. He just doesn't use them to answer the question at hand.

What he does do is to explore virtually everything else of possible relevance. He juggles a variety of variables, relationships, and contextual settings, and in the process arrives at findings about the effects of vouchers that, not surprisingly, are complicated and contingent. Based on all this, he then ends his article with a set of 'policy lessons' built around two general conclusions about vouchers: their effects on low-income kids 'appear to be neither uniformly positive nor negative', and vouchers 'would not come close to equalizing educational opportunity across income groups' (p.368). His bottom line is that vouchers cannot be counted upon to help poor kids, that they are bad policy, and that 'our nation should not rush to implement voucher programs' (p.368).

Let's take the second of these general findings first, because it is so easily dealt with. It is quite true, as Manski claims, that vouchers do not equalize educational opportunity across income groups in his model. But who ever claimed that they would? Voucher proponents argue that vouchers will promote *greater* opportunity across income groups, that they will make low-income kids *better off*, not that they will achieve some kind of impossible dream of total equality. The only relevant yard-stick is whether vouchers represent an improvement over the *status quo*. Clearly, this is the yardstick used by proponents of compensatory education, special education, and other programmes for the disadvantaged which promote equity, but do not even come close to equalizing opportunities across income groups. Should these policies be opposed because they do not achieve the ideal? We doubt that Manski, or any other reasonable person, would say so. Why should vouchers be held to a different standard?

Manski's other summary finding is that the effects of vouchers are sometimes positive, sometimes negative. In the abstract, this is pretty much what ought to be expected for any policy: effects will vary with conditions and some effects under some conditions could well be negative. The practical issue is what weight ought to be attached to the various analytic possibilities. Manski chooses to highlight the nega-tive and to see his analysis as damning evidence against vouchers. But we think this is unwarranted, even within the context of his own model. This is clearly true when it comes to the actual well-being of poor kids, which he ignores (and we'll discuss below). But it is also true for the sociological and school issues that he explicitly investigates.

Although he doesn't present it this way, Manski's analysis shows that vouchers have their most positive effects when the communities are poor and the public schools are wasteful. This is just what voucher proponents would expect. When vouchers are introduced, Manski's public schools do indeed become more responsive to students, wasting less and spending more on things students value. There is a clear and beneficial competitive effect. Income segregation of poor kids in the public sector goes down as more are empowered to seek out preferable schools in the private sector. As they do so, the fraction of high-motivation kids in the public sector declines—but the kids who are left find that their schools, now disciplined by competition, are more responsive to their needs.

This suggests that vouchers might work quite well indeed to expand opportunities for low-income kids. But for Manski, things are more complicated. In particular, he emphasizes that the effects of vouchers are less positive (and sometimes negative) in wealthier communities, where the public schools are already competitive—so that, taken as a whole, the end results are rather mixed. Given his concern for low-income kids, these sorts of complications are more distracting than helpful.

Consider the finding that, when the public schools are already perfectly competitive, vouchers do not work as well to improve educational opportunity. From an analytical standpoint, this is obvious: if the public schools are maximally solicitous of student needs, providing maximum quality for each dollar spent, then there is far less room for vouchers to improve things. Students and schools are already doing great. So what exactly is the relevance of this 'finding' when it comes to drawing substantively meaningful inferences about vouchers? The driving force behind the education reform movement during the last ten years is precisely that the public schools are doing a mediocre job of educating students, and that they are heavily bureaucratic and unresponsive—especially in urban areas, where low-income children are trapped in our nation's worst schools. The whole point of reform, including vouchers, is to do something about this: to engineer better schools, and better opportunities for kids, within a system that desperately needs improvement.

Under the circumstances, it is more than a little odd to argue against vouchers because they don't always have positive effects when the schools are perfectly competitive. Who cares? The real question is: how well can vouchers (and other reforms) do when there is a serious need for improvement? This is all the more central given Manski's overarching concern for low-income students. Empirically, these kids are segregated in schools that surely come closer to the model's wasteful ideal than any other group of schools in America (e.g., Peterson 1990). For them, it is of no real relevance that vouchers don't work well when the public schools are perfectly competitive. It is of major relevance, on the other hand, that vouchers stand to be highly beneficial when the public schools are wasteful and in great need of improvement. To say, as Manski does, that the effects of vouchers are 'mixed' simply misses the point.

Much the same applies to his analysis of the mixed effects of vouchers across communities. Manski notes, for instance, that the introduction of vouchers causes spending on low-income kids to increase within all communities where the public schools are wasteful. (There is no effect when the latter are competitive.) But he complains that the amount spent on these kids varies less with the size of the voucher than with community type, for there are big differences as one moves from poor to average to wealthy communities. This he portrays as a negative reflection on vouchers—they don't correct for cross-community inequities.

Whoever thought they would? As he sets it up, wealthy communities spend $10,000 per pupil on their schools, while poor communities spend only $4000. Even if we assume schools are equally wasteful in these communities, wealthy communities are going to spend much more money on things students value than poor communities, with or without vouchers. Vouchers cannot—and cannot be expected to—eliminate the class structure of American society, nor the political advantages (e.g., the more favourable tax bases) that flow from it. No feasible reform is going to turn poor kids into Rockefellers. What we really want to know is whether vouchers help to improve opportunities for these kids, particularly those in poor communities, who are sequestered in schools that are lower in quality and meagerly funded by comparison to those in other communities.

For these and other reasons, we think Manski's analysis often does more to confuse the central issues than to clarify them. When all the permutations he introduces are put in perspective, and when weight is properly attached to those most relevant to the conditions actually faced by poor children, his model sheds much more favorable light on vouchers than comes through in his account.

We should note, finally, one aspect of Manski's analysis that ought to raise legitimate concerns among voucher advocates. This is his conclusion that vouchers have negative 'student-interaction effects' on low-income kids who remain in public schools. The logic is that, when vouchers are introduced, high-motivation students are the ones most likely to use them to go private; this lowers the fraction of high-motivation kids in the public sector, which in turn (by assumption) lowers the quality of education for those remaining.

This argument gets at a creaming phenomenon that is potentially very real (Moe 1995). Clearly, high-motivation kids do put more value on education, and, all else equal, they are more willing to take advantage of the new options that vouchers offer. Under some conditions, then, vouchers may drain off the most motivated kids from the public sector, leaving it with the kids who care the least, are the most difficult to educate, are discipline problems, and so on – which could then reduce the quality of education for all remaining students, even those who are highly motivated and well behaved.

There is nothing mysterious here. This is a definite possibility, and voucher advocates ignore it at their own peril. Their reforms need to be designed with these creaming problems, and solutions to them, in mind. Having said as much, though, we should add that Manski's line of reasoning cannot simply be accepted at its face value. Empirically, high-motivation kids are not randomly distributed within the existing (pre-voucher) system. They tend to be from high-motivation families, who see that they are placed within the best schools the *status quo* has to offer. Often, they will actually have the *least* to gain from vouchers, and will have little incentive to move, even though they value education a lot. The converse holds for low-motivation kids. They will tend to be in the very worse schools under the *status quo*, have the most to gain from change, and have the greatest incentive to leave, even if they value education less. Manski's model does not capture this.[2]

Second, Manski has no empirical justification, and gives none, for moving 'student interaction effects' to centre stage as one of only two determinants of educational quality. Three decades on research of student achievement and effective schools have shown that many factors shape the quality of education a child receives in school, notable among them the child's socioeconomc background and varous organizational aspects of the school. While student body composition and peer effects are often relevant, the evidence of their impact and relative importance is mixed and offers little basis for the kind of exalted causal status that Manski confers on them (e.g., Bryk *et al.* 1990, Bliss *et al.* 1991).

Third, even if a negative 'student-interaction effect' emerges, it may be more than compensated for, indeed swamped, by the effects of other changes that are brought about by vouchers, e.g., that schools are prompted to spend more of their money on things students value. This is especially likely if, empirically, the role of peer groups is less formidable than Manski assumes here.

And fourth, the only way to tell is to look at the bottom line: given all the changes that vouchers set in motion, are low-income kids better or worse off? Maybe there is some creaming, and maybe this does, all else equal, have negative consequences for school quality. But what we want to know is whether, when everything is taken into account, kids are better off than before. This is the question Manski never answers and to which we now turn.

The utility of vouchers

We obtained a copy of Manski's computer program, kept all its original features and assumptions (whether we liked them or not), and simply put it to use in exploring whether vouchers leave low-income kids (defined as kids whose families are in the lowest income quintile) better or worse off in this particular model world.[3]

To simplify matters, and to target what is truly important, we focus here on poor and average communities and ignore the wealthy communities. By Manski's definitions, there are very few low-income kids in wealthy communities anyway, and those lucky enough to live there already benefit from the spending of $10,000 per child. They get a high quality education with or without vouchers. It is the low-income kids in the other communities, especially the poor communities, that merit our attention.

Our simulation results are summarized in Table 1. In a gross sense, they confirm Manski's claim that the effect of vouchers on low-income kids is 'neither uniformly positive nor negative'. If the public sector is competitive, most low-income students lose utility in both the poor and average communities. If the public sector is wasteful, on the other hand, all students gain utility. Yet to suggest that these results are 'mixed', and to leave it at that, obscures what is really going on here.

As we pointed out earlier, there is no reason to expect vouchers to have much impact when the public schools are competitive, and that is precisely what we find when we look at student utilities. Introducing vouchers into an ideal world of terrific public schools does not increase utility for most low-income students, and indeed, usually makes them worse off, but the negative shift in utility is close to zero.

In the average community, for example, regardless of the voucher level, all low-income students lose utility. But they lose at most 0.04 utiles, which translates into a monetary amount of $32 for a family earning $20,000 per year. This is a trivial sum. The only nontrivial losses for poor students occur when a $4000 voucher is implemented in the poor community. Here, students who stay in the public sector lose either 0.1 or 0.2 utiles, which correspond to monetary losses of $80 and $160 for a family earning $20,000 per year. These losses aren't quite trivial, but they are clearly rather small, and this is the worst case scenario. In general, therefore, when the schools attended by low-income children are already terrific—which, of course, is painfully far from reality—vouchers have very little effect.

When the public schools are wasteful, on the other hand, vouchers have room to bring about improvement. And they do. In both poor and average communities, regardless of the voucher amount, huge gains in utility are registered by every student. This is true not just of students who transfer to the private sector. It is also true of

Table 1. Simulated effects of vouchers on low income students.

	$2000 Voucher		$4000 Voucher	
	Public Schools Competitive	Public Schools Wasteful	Public Schools Competitive	Public Schools Wasteful
POOR COMMUNITY				
% of low income students who gain utility	0	100	9	100
% of low income students who lose utility	0	0	91	0
Average utility change for low income students	0	+1.11	−0.073	+3.13
Range of utility changes for low income students	0 to 0	+0.68 to +3.35	−0.20 to +2.00	+1.59 to +6.00
Significant concentrations of utility changes for low income students	No low income student's utility changes	48% gain 0.68 utiles 40% gain 1.36 utiles	50% lose 0.10 utiles 41% lose 0.20 utiles	22% gain 1.59 utiles 11% gain 3.18 utiles
AVERAGE COMMUNITY				
% of low income students who gain utility	0	100	0	100
% of low income students who lose utility	100	0	100	0
Average utility change for low income students	−0.03	+1.11	−0.03	+1.99
Range of utility changes for low income students	−0.04 to −0.02	+0.74 to +2.05	−0.04 to −0.02	+1.28 to +4.65
Significant concentrations of utility changes for low income students	50% lose 0.02 utiles 50% lose 0.04 utiles	50% gain 0.74 utiles 49% gain 1.48 utiles	50% lose 0.02 utiles 50% lose 0.04 utiles	50% gain 1.28 utiles 49% gain 2.55 utiles

students who remain in the public sector, despite Manski's concerns about 'student–interaction effects'.

These utility gains are particularly dramatic when compared with the tiny losses associated with the competitive situation. In the average community, for instance, the introduction of a $4000 voucher leads to utility gains of at least 1.28 utiles for every low-income student and to an average gain of 1.99 utiles. This average gain is 50 times greater than the largest losses associated with the competitive situation. Even greater gains are realized by low-income kids in poor communities. There, when the voucher amount is $4000, every student's utility increases by at least 1.59 utiles, and the average utility gain is 3.13 utiles, equivalent to a $2400 increase in income for a family earning $20,000 per year. By any standard, this is an enormously positive impact.

The most reasonable way to assess these results is to treat the competitive and wasteful ideals as opposite poles of a continuum, with real systems falling somewhere in between. When vouchers are introduced into competitive systems, the impact on the well-being of low-income students is essentially nil: this is the worst-case scenario. When vouchers are introduced into wasteful systems, the impact is extremely beneficial: this is the best-case scenario. For virtually *all* systems falling somewhere between the competitive and wasteful poles—and thus for virtually all real-world systems—we should therefore expect the impact of vouchers on low-income students to be positive, and to be especially large in magnitude for systems closer to the wasteful end of the continuum, as many poor inner-city communities almost surely are.

The key issue is whether vouchers leave low-income kids better off. But a related issue is also important, especially to Manski and other critics, whose focus often seems to be less on the kids and more on society. The issue is one of relative opportunities: how do vouchers affect the gap between rich and poor? Even if low-income kids are better off under a voucher system, is it possible that upper-income kids do even better still, so that the gap between the two social groups actually increases and society becomes, by this measure, less equitable?

We put Manski's model to use in exploring this issue as well, again maintaining its original structure. In most discussions of relative opportunities, the focus is not on utility *per se*, but specifically on the quality of the school available to kids in different income groups and how this might change with vouchers. That is our concern here.

Following Manski, we assume that educational quality is a function of two factors: the amount a school sector spends on things students value and the fraction of high-motivation kids in the sector, both of which vary with the introduction of vouchers. We then measure how much students benefit from varying levels of school quality by referring to the utility function Manski posits for them, which, when shorn of their concerns for income, tuition, and 'private school preference', gives us a student utility index for school quality alone. The question is how this quality index differs across poor and rich students and whether the initial gap between them is widened or narrowed by the introduction of vouchers.

When the public schools are already competitive, and thus spending all their resources on things students (including low-income students) value, there is not much of a gap between the poorest and richest kids to begin with, and vouchers don't have a large impact one way or the other. As Figure 1 indicates, vouchers succeed in reducing the quality gap somewhat in poor communities, whereas in average communities they increase it a little. As was true in other aspects of Manski's analysis (and our own), the results are mixed when the public schools start out uniformly high in quality. This is to be expected.

It is a different matter, however, when the public schools are wasteful – which, again, is surely the reality for most low-income kids. Here, as Figure 1 shows, the *status quo* produces a sizeable quality-gap between the schools attended by rich and poor kids, and vouchers actually have some room to bring about change. The result is a significant reduction in the quality gap across income groups. In the average community, a large initial quality gap is cut in half by a $4000 voucher, with low-income kids realizing much greater gains than their wealthy counterparts. And in the poor community, the results are even more dramatic: a similarly large initial gap between income groups is completely eliminated by a $4000 voucher, equalizing school quality across groups.

Overall, then, Manski's own model suggests that vouchers can play very positive roles indeed in the promotion of educational equity. Assuming again that real-world schools are distributed between the competitive and wasteful poles of the continuum, the most reasonable inference is that vouchers are likely to leave low-income kids better off than they were under the *status quo*, and to reduce the quality gap between rich and poor, perhaps quite significantly. The magnitude of these effects is especially

Poor Community

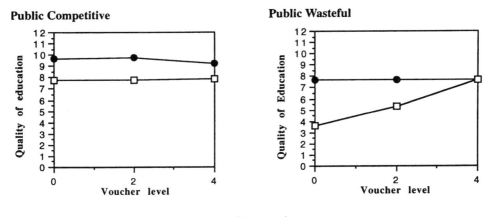

Average Community

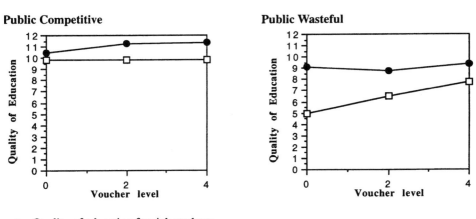

—●— Quality of education for rich students.
—□— Quality of education for poor students.

Figure 1.   Equality of educational opportunity. The upper line in each graph represents average educational opportunities for students from families in the highest income quartile. The lower line represents educational opportunities for students from families in the lowest income quartile. The quality of education is measured by an index derived from Manski's student utility function.

strong in low-income communities, where schools are the worst and the need for reform the greatest.

Suggestions for the future

None of this proves anything, of course, about how vouchers actually work in the real world. We believe, given the broader background of economic and political theory, that vouchers would indeed tend to promote social equity (if the institutions were properly designed). And we are not surprised that Manski's model points in the same direction. But any model's conclusions, as well as the kinds of explanations it provides, are only as valid as the model itself. And while Manski's model is a reasonable first step toward a new computer methodology for theory-building, its original structure

leaves a lot to be desired as a tool for understanding how a voucher system would operate. Whatever it has to say about vouchers, negative or positive, should be entertained
only tentatively and with healthy skepticism.

There is no magic formula for creating a better model. If there is any magic at
all, it is to be found in the collective enterprise of social science. As new researchers
enter the field, try out a variety of assumptions and analytic frameworks, and assess
their merits, we are likely to learn a great deal and arrive at superior theories along
the way. Where this will lead, however, is anyone's guess.

What we can say, at this point, is that a number of theoretical issues are unavoid-
ably central to this process. They need to be addressed, and how they are addressed—
and whether they can be dealt with in a simple, formal way—will determine the
kinds of models that are developed and pursued. In this section, we want to discuss
some of these issues and outline some of our views on them.

The actors

Manski simplifies matters by treating the public and private sectors as unitary actors
that offer uniform services to all kids in their domains. We think too much is lost by
this assumption. This is especially true for the private sector, whose great dynamism
and diversity are rooted in flexible, decentralized decision-making—in the autonomy
of individual schools (and potential entrants) and their incentives to seek out
specialized niches in the marketplace. These supply-side dynamics are fundamental
to the way a voucher system works, and to ignore them, particularly by treating the
private sector as a centralized monolith, virtually guarantees that vouchers will be
poorly understood. The key decision-makers are the individual schools, and a good
model should recognize this.

The public sector, on the other hand, can more reasonably be treated as a centralized structure, since district and state governments make most of the important
decisions for the local schools. One strategy is to model the sector as a unitary decision-maker, much as Manski does. Another is to model it as a simple, two-level hierarchy, with schools making decisions subject to constraint by their political superiors.

Motivation

Manski does not make much effort to justify his motivational assumptions, nor to be
clear about what they really mean. It is plausible enough, for instance, to assume that
the private sector behaves 'competitively', but he proceeds as if this has an obvious
meaning: that it acts to maximize enrollment. In fact, private schools can behave competitively on the basis of all sorts of very different utility functions. One does not dic-
tate the other. Moreover, most real-world private schools surely do *not* maximize
enrollment; their small size and sense of community are central to their educational
success (Bryk *et al.* 1993). It would be more plausible to assume that they try to maximize school quality, subject to attracting enough students to cover costs. Quality
may mean somewhat different (and not necessarily academic) things to schools of different types. There are other possibilities as well.

With regard to the public sector, Manski's reliance on the 'competitive' and
'wasteful' assumptions serves as a substitute for serious discussion of what actually

motivates public decision-making. There is little basis, theoretical or empirical, for the 'competitive' model (Lieberman 1993). The 'wasteful' model is far closer to reality, but even here Manski lays only a meagre foundation for understanding why officials would behave in this way (and get away with it). Any reasonable model of public-sector motivation must begin at the beginning: by recognizing that the public schools are part of government and thus inherently shaped by the politics of democratic control. Whatever simplified motivational model we might adopt for explaining school behaviour must, in the end, be compatible with the driving forces of politics and bureaucracy (Chubb and Moe 1990).

Students (and families) can be modelled in a variety of ways. Manski assumes they care about school quality and income (and thus tuition), which is simple and reasonable. It is important to recognize, however, that the definition attached to school 'quality' thereby has profound consequences for everything that happens within the model; and Manski's definition, in terms of money and student-interaction effects, is debatable. He makes no reference here to the huge literature on 'effective schools' that provides empirical evidence on school quality, nor does he justify the factors he chooses as rightly taking priority over all others. It would be preferable to define school quality with closer attention to this research literature, which would probably not lead to the two factors he embraces. Another approach would be to get away from quality *per se*, and to emphasize instead different things about schools—such as size, types of programs, reputation, religious affiliation, proximity—that students value (and that different students may value differently).

There is one assumption Manski makes about student motivation that we have to reject outright. In addition to quality and income, he assumes their utility is shaped by a 'private school preference' which biases them toward one sector over the other. Operationally, he assumes most students have a bias for the public sector and that, for reasons having nothing to do with school quality or income, their utility would decline if they chose a private school. Manski apparently introduced this mysterious factor in order to make his initial distributions of kids across the two sectors come out right. On technical grounds, this is understandable. But it is far preferable, obviously, to specify explicitly what it is that students value about the two sectors and their schools, and to explain their behaviour on that basis. As Manski sets it up, many kids will not use a voucher because they are biased against the private sector (receive negative utility from it) for no apparent reason. This is simply unnecessary; it gets in the way of explanation, and it threatens to promote misleading conclusions.

Information and beliefs

Interestingly enough, given his attack on neoclassical economics, Manski takes the neoclassical path of assuming all players are perfectly informed. Presumably, this is to simplify his model. Empirically, however, it is obvious that issues of bounded rationality are absolutely central to the voucher debate.

A standard claim is that students (and families) are likely to be poorly informed about the schools available to them, the quality of school programmes, and so on, and that information on these scores varies inequitably across social groups, with upper-SES students far better informed than lower-SES students. On the other hand, any economist would be quick to point out that people will gain information over time, often through direct experience with schools and the choice process, and that, partly as a result, schools will develop reputations that convey useful information to everyone, even those without any direct experience.

All of this can be modelled rather easily, especially with the benefit of computer technology (e.g. Cyert and March 1963, Bendor and Moe 1985). Doing so would help us understand how the accuracy, social distribution, and learning of relevant information affect the operation of a voucher system. It would also suggest what kinds of auxilliary institutions, such as parent information centers, might make vouchers work better and more equitably.

Choice

Manski's model is too complex to allow for analytic solution by standard neoclassical methods, which is presumably why he resorts to computer modelling. Within his computer model, however, he retains a number of common neoclassical components. Perhaps the most basic of these is that all actors are optimizers, making choices so as to maximize their utility (although he does not always call it that or clearly specify what it is). Combined with the perfect information assumption, the result is a model that is quite traditional indeed. Like neoclassical models, moreover, it does not really have a time component or pay attention to dynamics. It is essentially an exercise in comparative statics.

While optimization is often a powerful analytic tool, it is not the only way to go. A more realistic, and perhaps more predictive, approach is to recognize, as Herbert Simon (1947) did long ago, that cognitive limitations make it impossible for people to engage in sophisticated optimization, and that instead they engage in more simple-minded processes of adaptation and adjustment over time, making incremental changes in their behaviour (doing more of what works, less of what doesn't work) in response to environmental feedback on their choices and the choices of others. This approach to choice obviously fits much more comfortably into a model of bounded rationality, in which people may be very poorly informed about their choices and about their decision context.

An adaptive model of this sort also doesn't assume, as comparative statics models often do, that the system automatically moves to a globally optimal equilibrium. Instead, it focuses attention on the dynamics of adaptive adjustment, generating a time path of behaviour that can be substantively important in its own right and that may or may not lead to a global optimum. Indeed, it may show how, given certain conditions and the 'path-dependent' nature of collective choice, society can get stuck with educational arrangements that are highly stable and yet wholly unsatisfactory (David 1988). This sort of thing clearly happens a good deal in the real world, and computer models of adaptive adjustment are good ways to explore them.

Social context

No model can capture the richness of American society, nor should it try. But certain features are central to an understanding of vouchers and need to be considered. American society, for instance, is highly segregated by race and class, and so is the exist-ing school system. Even within communities, poor and minority kids tend to be sequestered in the worst schools, and, when fortunate enough not to be, often find themselves segregated anyway by virtue of the tracking system, where they receive a qualitatively different education from kids who are college-bound. As a result, they have much more to gain from reform than more affluent kids, and our models need to reflect this.

Another major feature of American society is that people with money already have a great deal of choice under the current system. This is not just because they can send their kids to private schools. It is because they have residential mobility: they can move to areas with good public schools, while people without money remain stuck in the bad public schools. Residential mobility is one of the most fundamental forces driving the inequities of the existing American educational system. For all intents and purposes, moreover, it cannot readily be stopped. It will always be a fact of life, and we need to incorporate it into our models.

Still another basic property of American society is its heterogeneity. People are different. Significant variations in income, education, occupation, geography, ethnicity, ideology, language, culture and a host of other factors have produced a population that is enormously diverse, and diverse in its notions of what makes for a good school. On a whole range of issues—curriculum, teaching methods, school size, moral values, religion, sex education, bilingual education—different Americans clearly value schools of different types. One of the most fundamental questions that can be asked about an educational system is whether it provides Americans with the kinds of schools they value. A standard criticism of the existing public school system is that it fails to do that very well, that it is too uniform and unresponsive. A standard argument for vouchers, on the other hand, is that parental choice and private-sector supply are especially valuable in heterogeneous settings, promoting a far richer variety of schools to match the diverse values of the American population. Whether either is true is a subject for theory. But our models cannot explore these issues unless the heterogeneity of our society is explicitly taken into account.

Manski's social context is too homogeneous. He does capture important features of the American class structure by distinguishing among his three community types, which differ by income and school spending. This is useful, but it leaves out too much. Whether vouchers improve things depends in great measure on the social conditions to which they are applied. The kinds of social conditions Manski simplifies away are precisely the conditions under which we would expect vouchers to work especially well.

Institutional design

Manski proceeds as though there is one standard design for a voucher system: all kids get vouchers of equal value, which they can apply toward private school tuition. This is a free-market version favored by Milton Friedman and other libertarians. While this design has clear relevance to the real world—a number of voucher reform efforts, including California's Proposition 174, have essentially been of this simple type— there are in fact many other ways to design a voucher system. In particular, it is possible to design a voucher system for the specific purpose of promoting equity.

For instance, vouchers might be given only to low-income and special-needs kids, or the size of the voucher might vary inversely with income, so that poor kids get bigger vouchers than more affluent kids. Parents might not be allowed to add on to the voucher; and, if schools want to participate, they might be required to accept the voucher as payment in full. States might be required to provide transportation for low-income kids, and to set up local 'parent information centers'. Private schools might be required to set aside a certain percentage of their slots for poor kids, or to admit a number of children by random draw.

These sorts of ideas, along with many others foreign to the free-market model, are an integral part of modern thinking about the design of voucher systems. They have been seriously proposed in scholarly writings (Chubb and Moe 1990, Coons and Sugarman 1992); they are the foundation of the nation's only operating voucher system (in Milwaukee); and they are at the forefront of ongoing efforts to bring about choice-based reform.

Researchers need to recognize this. It is meaningless to talk, as Manski does, about the generic effects of a voucher system. And it is misleading to suggest that, when vouchers seem to have undesirable consequences, these are somehow inherent in vouchers *per se*. The term 'voucher system' properly refers to a large family of possible institutional designs, and different designs can be expected to have very different effects. Whatever the effects of a free-market design may be, a system purposely constructed to promote equity would almost surely generate very different outcomes. Researchers need to explore this. The task is not to vilify a particular version of vouchers. It is to see the voucher issue from the standpoint of institutional design and to build theories capable of connecting alternative designs with their corresponding effects.

One final point. In this section, we have questioned some of Manski's central assumptions and suggested why alternative approaches would seem more productive. We are not arguing, however, for greater complexity or 'realism' in the modelling enterprise. The power and success of modelling depend on drastic simplifications of reality, and the task for researchers is always to strip away as much complexity as possible by making the *right kinds* of simplifications. The suggestions we have offered here are intended to raise important issues and point the way toward productive modelling strategies. But to the extent they introduce new complexities (and they do), they will ultimately have to be dealt with in highly simplified form. As in all modelling, the challenge for the future is not just to recognize what is relevant, but to find some simple way of capturing its essence and putting it to use.

Conclusion

Computer modelling is a technology whose time has come. The challenge for education researchers is to take advantage of it in moving toward new, more powerful theories of the structure and performance of educational institutions – theories that stand to tell us not only how these institutions operate and what can be expected of them, but also how they can be reformed (by means of new designs) to bring about better schools and more equal opportunities for our nation's children.

Charles Manski has been instrumental in pointing researchers down this important new path. Indeed, it is precisely because his work signals a productive new research tradition that we focused on it here. While we have been critical, our overriding purpose has been to clarify what Manski has done, in the hope that this will provide a stronger, more productive foundation for future progress. Without this kind of clarifying assessment, we think his contribution is likely to be misunderstood, especially by readers unfamiliar with his formal technology, leaving misguided notions about vouchers and theory-building in its wake.

Above all else, it is essential to distinguish between Manski's methodology and the analysis that accompanies it. There is nothing in the methodology that leads inexorably to the strongly negative perspective on vouchers that pervades Manski's analysis. In fact, much of what he actually has to say about vouchers is misleading or incorrect.

This is a problem from the outset, when he prefaces his own efforts at theory-building by mischaracterizing the theory of vouchers. Among other things, he stereotypes its economic arguments as simplistic mixtures of classical economic theory and conservative ideology. He ignores the political theory of government that animates its expectations about the existing education system. He dismisses clear, coherent theoretical arguments as mere advocacy and rhetoric. And he argues that qualitative arguments about vouchers are inherently inferior to his own quantitative approach and have little scientific merit. All of this is unwarranted and leaves readers with scant basis for appreciating the key issues of theory and methodology that ought to lie at the heart of this new and exciting enterprise.

In developing his formal analysis, Manski does a rigorous job of identifying assumptions, setting up the model, carrying out the simulations, and exploring the impact of vouchers on various social indicators of equity under a variety of conditions. The result is a complex analysis that shows, not surprisingly, that vouchers have mixed effects. From this he draws the policy lesson that they cannot be counted upon to enhance the educational opportunities of poor kids and should be avoided by wise policymakers.

Even if Manski's model is taken at face value, the thrust of his analysis here is misleading. In the first place, he tends to treat all the various conditions as equally relevant to the lives of poor kids, when in fact they are not. If we turn our attention to the conditions that matter most—poor communities, wasteful schools—vouchers have very positive consequences. This gets entirely lost, when it should be front and center. In the second place, Manski focuses on numerous social indicators of the well-being of low-income kids and fails to ask what ought to be the key question of his entire analysis: are poor kids better or worse off as a result of vouchers? When we put his own model to use in generating an answer, vouchers have an impact on these kids that ranges from virtually zero at one extreme (when the public schools are terrific) to enormously beneficial on the other (when they are in need of improvement). This suggests, again, that Manski's own conclusions and policy lessons are unwarranted.

Throughout, Manski offers his readers little perspective on the modelling exercise itself, proceeding as though the particular assumptions he makes and the particular conclusions he arrives at are pretty much what 'quantitative theory' has to say about vouchers. In fact, of course, countless analytic choices have been made along the way in designing the model—choices about who the relevant actors are, what motivates them, what they know, how they make rational choices, and what their social and institutional contexts are, among other things—and there is nothing sacrosanct about the way Manski deals with these issues. Indeed, as we discussed above, there are good reasons for adopting very different assumptions on these scores and for remaining skeptical of a model based on the kinds of assumptions Manski relies upon.

In the grander scheme of things, what is important about Manski's model is not what it specifically assumes or implies, nor even that the analysis surrounding it is unduly negative. The important thing is that it offers a promising methodology for future work and serves as a stimulus for other researchers to grapple with these issues.

When this begins to happen, computer models of voucher systems—and all sorts of other institutional arrangements, for that matter—will probably develop along many different paths, depending on how theorists choose to address the issues that face them. Even apparently simple issues, like who the relevant actors are and what motivates them, are not really simple at all and do not have obvious solutions. Plausible arguments can be made for dealing with each of them in a host of different ways, and it is not possible to identify a best approach that clearly dominates. As alternative assumptions are pieced together into alternative models, the number of permutations is potentially enormous, and virtually all of them might initially seem quite reasonable.

This sort of uncertainty is inevitable at the beginning of any new scientific enterprise. But it is also exciting, and sets the stage for a burst of new research activity that stands to be tremendously beneficial over the long haul: generating new ideas, developing and testing out a variety of assumptions, debating the merits of alternative models, and amassing a storehouse of new information about which approaches seem to work best. These are the basic elements of theoretical progress, and there is every reason to think that computer modelling will soon bring them to the study of educational institutions.

Notes

1. Manski introduces this term in order to ensure that, in a model world without vouchers, initial student choices lead to a distribution of students across sectors that roughly correspond to their distribution in the real world.
2. Among other things, Manski does not allow public schools to vary in quality within communities, which means that high and low motivation kids attend the same public schools; no account is taken of tracking, which, empirically, gives high motivation kids a different experience in public schools than their low motivation peers receive; lower, middle and upper income communities are all assumed to have the same mix of low and high motivation kids; and high motivation kids are not allowed to escape inadequate public schools in one community for better public schools in another, which, empirically, is clearly a major force in American education— promoting 'white flight', the concentration of high motivation kids in suburban schools, the further decline in urban schools, and so on.
3. To facilitate analysis, however, we did make one technical adjustment worth noting. In his original model, Manski sought to simplify matters by assuming the public and private sectors make their monetary decisions in increments of $1000. A sector currently spending $3000 on things students value, for instance, could only increase its spending by moving all the way up to $4000—no smaller increments were allowed. We simply give the schools more flexibility, allowing them to set monetary values in $200 increments. This in no way alters the basic logic of Manski's model, but rather permits it to operate more smoothly and with greater precision. We assume the only reason Manski did not allow for a finer grid of adjustments himself is that it takes a tremendous amount of computer time to include them in the simulation.

References

BENDOR, J. and MOE, T. M. (1985) An adaptive model of bureaucratic politics. *American Political Science Review,* 79, 755–74.

BLISS, J. R., FIRESTONE, W. A. and RICHARDS, C. E. (1991) *Rethinking Effective Schools: Research and Practice* (Englewood Cliffs: Prentice-Hall).

BRYK, A. S., LEE, V. E. and SMITH, J. L. (1990) High School organization and its effects on teachers and students, in W. H. Clune and J. F. Witte (eds), *Choice and Control in American Education,* vol. 1 (Philadelphia: Falmer), 135–226.

BRYK, A. S., LEE, V. E. and HOLLAND, P. B. (1993) *Catholic Schools and the Common Good* (Cambridge: Harvard University Press).

CHUBB, J. E. and MOE, T. M. (1990) *Politics, Markets, and America's Schools* (Washington: Brookings Institution).

COHEN, M. D., MARCH, J. G. and OLSEN, J. P. (1972) A garbage can model of organizational choice. *Administrative Science Quarterly,* 17, 1–25.

COONS, J. E. and SUGARMAN, S. D. (1992) *Scholarships for Children* (Berkeley: Institute for Governmental Studies).

Cyert, R. M. and March, J. G. (1963) *A Behavioral Theory of the Firm* (Englewood Cliffs: Prentice-Hall).

David, P. (1988) The future of path-dependent equilibrium economics. CEPR Discussion Paper Series, Stanford University.

Friedman, M. (1955) The role of government in education, in R. Solow (ed.), *Economics and the Public Interest* (New Brunswick: Rutgers University Press), 123–144.

Horn, M. J. (1995) *The Political Economy of Public Administration* (Cambridge: Cambridge University Press).

Manski, C. F. (1992) Educational choice (vouchers) and social mobility. *Economics of Education Review*, 11, 351–69.

Moe, T. M. (1984) The new economics of organization. *American Journal of Political Science*, 28, 739–77.

Moe, T. M. (1990a) The politics of structural choice: toward a theory of public bureaucracy, in O. E. Williamson (ed.), *Organization Theory: From Chester Barnard to the Present and Beyond.* (New York: Oxford University Press), 116–153.

Moe, T. M. (1990b) Political institutions: the neglected side of the story. *Journal of Law, Economics, and Organization*, 6, 213–54.

Moe, T. M. (1995) School choice and the creaming problem, in T. A. Downes and W. A. Testa (eds), *Midwest Approaches to School Reform.* (Chicago: Federal Reserve Board).

Peterson, P. E. (1990) Monopoly and competition in American education, in W. H. Clune and J. F. Witte (eds), *Choice and Control in American Education* (Philadelphia: Falmer), 47–48.

Shepsle, K. A. (1986) Institutional equilibrium and equilibrium institutions, in H. F. Weisberg (ed.) *Political Science: The Science of Politics.* (New York: Agathon), 51–81.

Simon, H. (1947) *Administrative Behavior* (New York: Macmillan).

Appendix A: Manski's Utility Functions.

For a low motivation student who chooses public sector schooling:
$$U_{n0} = 2.5 \log (E_0) + H_0 + 25 \log (Y_n)$$

For a low motivation student who chooses private sector schooling:
$$U_{n1} = 2.5 \log (E_0) + H_0 + 25 \log (Y_n - T_1) + p_n$$

For a high motivation student who chooses public sector schooling:
$$U_{n0} = 5 \log (E_0) + 2H_0 + 25 \log (Y_n)$$

For a high motivation student who chooses private sector schooling:
$$U_{n1} = 5 \log (E_0) + 2H_0 + 25 \log (Y_n - T_1) + p_n$$

The variables used in these equations are defined as follows:
E_0: the amount of money per pupil that the public sector spends on things valued by students.
E_1: the amount of money per pupil that the private sector spends on things valued by students.
H_0: the fraction of high motivation students in the public sector.
H_1: the fraction of high motivation students in the private sector.
T_1: the level of tuition charged by the private sector.
Y_n: the student's family income.
p_n: the student's private school preference. It is a normal random variable with mean -0.5 and variance 1.

Part 2

6. *The second academic revolution*

Gerald Grant and Christine Murray

If the first academic revolution was the revolt of the professoriate against the entrenched power of a largely clerical nineteenth century college presidency (Jencks and Riesman 1968), the second is a less clear-cut struggle to overturn a system of elementary and secondary education that has its roots in the same era.

That system, aptly named the One Best System by David Tyack, has proved to be both remarkably stable and highly resilient (Tyack 1974). The age-graded, centrally controlled and highly bureaucratized system of public schools has survived largely in the form in which it was invented in the late nineteenth century. Virtually all of the successful changes in the system could be classified as those that helped the system to expand, to extend its services or to become more efficient. It gradually expanded to provide universal schooling through 13 levels; it extended services to the disabled, to the disenfranchised and to those of all ability levels. It elaborated the curriculum to serve children who would work in farms, factories, shops and hospitals. It added a wide array of other courses of instruction to serve every interest group and a wide range of utilitarian and recreational aims. The reforms that succeeded were often those like the Carnegie Unit that helped to improve the functioning or efficiency of the system and to provide a universal medium of exchange for its services. Even the teacher and union militancy of the 1960s and 1970s did not fundamentally alter the system so much as expand the rights of one set of participants.

Contemporary reformers and educational change agents tend to underestimate the reasons for this stability and resilience. They often fail to appreciate how extraordinarily well the system has functioned to accomplish what its designers wanted it to achieve. And they are likely to forget the religious and revolutionary zeal of its founders who wanted to create a system that would serve all children of a country that was seen as the world's greatest democratic experiment. It was a system that was founded on the core values of a highly individualistic, democratic nation. It resolved the tension between liberty and equality on the side of freedom, or opportunity for all to achieve, rather than an emphasis on more equal outcomes. It married that to a system of individual achievement and effort that allowed for wide expression of individual belief, although the schools were deeply Protestant in their origins. Finally with the aid of mass systems of psychological and cognitive testing refined in the early twentieth century, the system gained legitimacy as the central sorting and selection agency of the society.

The reformers tend to be grudging about the success of the system. But in fact the system served as the foundation of the long-term success of both the economic and democratic development of the country, while also preserving and enhancing the religious freedom that its founders had cherished. Defenders of the system are not dissuaded by data of poor average outcomes when compared, for example, with math and science achievement in other modern nations, because they believe the system has served to provide opportunity and has allowed a sufficient number to achieve the highest academic

0268–0939/95 $12 · 00 © 1995 Taylor & Francis Ltd

levels. They are likely to point to the undisputed world-wide preeminence of the American college and university system as evidence of this. The K–12 system, they would argue, was never intended or expected to provide equal group outcomes or even necessarily high average outcomes. It was to provide the opportunity and the incentive for those who wished to reach the highest levels of academic achievement, but it was not to command it.

It is the complex struggle to change the sentiments of the American people about these very basic values that is at the heart of any understanding of the issues of educational change.

Think of the enormous change in beliefs that is required to move to the new set of principles that underlies most contemporary educational reform efforts. It involves nothing less than a shift from the system of sorting and selecting and tracking to one of inclusion that aims to raise the average achievement of all children and to assure that none fall below an acceptable minimum. This does not require the invention of new values but an important shift in the relative weights of individualism and cooperation on the one hand and liberty and equality on the other. These have always existed in uneasy tension in American society, though until recent decades the greater emphasis in the schools has been placed upon individualistic achievement and the opportunity to be unequal rather than on cooperative endeavours to create more equal outcomes for all.

Our talk about change is often confused and our efforts are often piecemeal. Sometimes we are trying to change the children, more often the teachers. At other times, change is focused on the social structure or the conditions of work. But in the end significant change in schools involves changing the ethos or basic values and norms in the sense just elaborated. And that means that the beliefs of the individuals responsible for the operation of those schools must change in these ways. To say the least, we are often naïve about what is required or involved.

Consider, for example, three organizations which have had great success in changing the beliefs of individuals towards more cooperative behaviours. The Jesuits are a radical example of the kind of conversion that is brought about in many religious orders. A novice begins what is usually a 15-year course of training with a thirty-day retreat in which silence is imposed and contact with the outside world is forbidden. There is a daily examination of conscience and conferencing with one's spiritual guide about one's progress in incorporating new values. One's faults and shortcomings are examined and acknowledged in public before one's peers. One is examined in all respects for one's sincerity, devotion and adherence to central beliefs and norms.

Young Marine recruits who land on Parris Island may not be allowed to sleep for the first thirty-six hours, during which time they are stripped, their heads are shaved and they are subjected to a series of humiliations. In three months the fat ones may lose thirty or forty pounds and the thin ones gain as much. Their bodies, voices, and posture will change radically. They will be pushed to the limits of their physical endurance and then beyond. They will be forced to fail at tasks they will soon succeed at. They will gain in confidence and competence. They will eat, sleep, shower, run in groups and literally carry each other across many physical obstacles, recognizing that to do less might someday cost them their lives. They will be relentlessly observed and relentlessly criticized for failure to conform to group norms.

Those who enter the offices of psychotherapists do not seem to cross such daunting thresholds. Yet most psychotherapists operate at least under the aura of the medical establishment and it special authority. The essential condition for continuing therapy is that one open one's deepest thoughts and secret feelings to inspection by others. One is guided into a new way of seeing and of constructing and valuing or reframing one's own behaviour. Drugs and other medicines may be used to aid treatment. Modern therapy often takes place in small groups in which strong bonds are formed that facilitate the process of behavioural change.

One need not belabour the comparisons with most efforts at educational reform. But seldom do they incorporate many of the factors that are common to these three examples. In each case the effort is voluntary. There is a giving over of the self to a new authority that will help one achieve a desired status. There is a belief in great rewards to be had by undergoing the rigours of a conversion process – to save one's soul, or one's country, or one's sanity. A significant period of time is devoted to the change effort. Support structures and intricate reinforcing mechanisms and practices are common to all three.

There are scores of studies that have produced a litany of reasons why change has so often been frustrated in schools: desire or motivation is lacking; there's no investigation of the need for change or a diagnosis of what may be wrong; teachers are not involved or consulted; no consensus exists about the path the change should take; even when there's a clear need and a good plan has been developed, there's no surplus capital to invest in the change or time for adequate training to carry it out; change efforts are plagued by staff turnover and burnout; the cost/benefit ratios are skewed and the rewards for the effort required are inadequate; necessary changes in social structure are not made (Fullan 1991).

Most of the radical change that has occurred in schools has occurred on the periphery of the system, in isolated hot spots, or what earlier writers of a leftist persuasion such as Herbert Marcuse might have called repressive tolerance. It has usually occurred when there was some combination of charismatic principal leadership with conditions conducive for a fresh start. The latter would include magnet schools, or schools that were failing so badly that radical action was required, or some surplus capital that was insufficient for system change but adequate to make a major difference in a few schools. Kim Marshall (1993) provides a persuasive account of such change in an elementary public school in Boston. Marshall describes a six-year effort of seventy-eight hour work weeks that have been required to achieve a genuine consensus about the kind of value change towards greater cooperation and towards the belief that all children can learn to read and write at high skill levels. He describes the relentless work that is involved to communicate to all members of the school community that teaching and learning come first, and to provide the kind of transformative experiences and training for teachers that enables them to move away from a sorting-and-selecting system to one that truly embraces a higher level of competence for all. Marshall explains how these changes are linked with changes in assessment and even more importantly changes in the beliefs of pupils as well as teachers so that they come to believe that effort not innate ability is what counts. And his account makes clear that this change often proceeded in the face of, rather than with the cooperation of, the central system.

We have numerous accounts of such heroic efforts. But unfortunately they are scattered and isolated and, as mentioned a moment ago, tolerated rather than adopted by the larger system. Although their value is great in extending our vision of what is possible, we do not think that large-scale change will be achieved in this way. We believe that more widespread institutional change is likely to come about as a result of some combination of these three factors: technological transformation, the rise of competing systems, and a reformation if not a revolution of the teaching profession. We shall deal briefly with the first two and develop the third more fully, drawing on recent research.

Technological transformation. Though creative software applications are still in their infancy, even skeptics like Larry Cuban who have chronicled the boom and bust cycle of previous technological innovations (Cuban 1986), believe that the personal computer revolution may be different both in its quality and impact (Cuban 1993). It can offer all students access to a wider range of print and video sources. It enables mastery learning by establishing feedback loops to help reteach material that testing identifies students have not learned. It multiplies the opportunities for peer tutoring and wider collaboration among pupils over electronic networks.

Computers had spread to 98 per cent of American schools by 1991; in one decade the ratio of computers changed from 125 students per computer to 18 students for each computer. While there were imaginative uses of computers in some classrooms, particularly in assisting blind, deaf and multiple disabled students, most pupils used them to learn *about* computers rather than to learn to think and inquire *with* them.

Unlike previous technological innovations, however, which were usually marginal to major educational reform movements, computers have become deeply associated with the reform movements of the 1980s and 1990s. Yet adoption of computers for instruction has been slow and the presumed benefits as much a matter of rhetoric as of research, though there are some stunning examples of what Seymour Papert calls 'oases of learning' (Papert 1993: 3). Cuban argues that in the last decade when the computer met the traditional classroom, the classroom won. Where the computer advanced it was more likely to be used to enhance what traditional teachers in the age-graded system have always done. In other words, like the overhead projector, it was adapted to what teachers were already doing rather than becoming a means to new forms of learning. Deeply ingrained beliefs about the nature of teaching and learning (that knowledge is received rather than constructed, for example), are slow to bend. Cuban remains highly skeptical of a rapid incorporation of new instructional technology, especially at the secondary level where commitment to the sorting and selection function of the system is strongest. We agree with him that change will come first in a hybrid mix of new and old technology in elementary and middle schools, but even there, cautiously and slowly, in the absence of some major change in the political and social environment that would provide a shock to the system. But, in decades if not years, the schools will be forced to adapt to the nature of work in an increasingly technological society.

The rise of competing systems. In the last decade several nationally prominent educators have established new networks of schools engaged in radical reform. Among these are James Comer at Yale, Henry Levin at Stanford and John Goodlad at the University of Washington. The Coalition of Essential Schools, founded by Theodore Sizer with headquarters at Brown University, may be the most promising of these efforts. The Coalition has attempted to integrate structural, pedagogical, and value change through a set of nine overarching principles.

The genius of Sizer's Coalition lies in the creation of a teacher-to-teacher reform network, in which teachers act as peer coaches in developing, sharing, testing and teaching each other what it means to articulate these nine principles in restructured schools. It wouldn't work at all, however, without the opportunity for teachers to test their beliefs. The principles define a more participatory and interdisciplinary form of education, summed up as 'student as worker, teacher as coach', as well as new forms of demonstrating what one has learned, or 'graduation by exhibition' in the Coalition rubrics. The belief that all children can learn to use their minds well by deeper engagement in a more sinewy, less broad curriculum, is at the heart of the Coalition's work. Although the Coalition cannot provide teachers with the powerful forms of resocialization developed by the Marines or the Jesuits, it does ask schools attracted to the Coalition to take at least a year to test their commitment to the Coalition vision. At the end of this year of exploration, three-fourths of the teachers must agree they want to join in order to become a member school.

Though each of these new systematizers has established a separate organization with independent funding from foundations and other sources, they are all essentially outside-in efforts. That is, they had small amounts of incentive money and expertise to offer existing schools. They have rarely been able to initiate even one new school. They are dependent upon cooperation, collaboration and seduction of existing schools and school systems.

The impact and possibilities of change through such means could be revolutionized given major sources of new funding through voucher plans or broad adoption of charter school reforms or other robust forms of public schools of choice in a significant number of states. The excitement generated by the Annenberg Foundation gift of $500 million for basic school reform is suggestive of the energies that might be unleashed. However, it remains a suggestion, for five hundred million dollars would not fund even one urban school system for one year.

The revolt of the teachers. Our own work during the past five years of careful observation of teachers in nine schools in four school districts has convinced us that a slow revolution is under way. This second academic revolution is proceeding in fits and starts and with frequent slippage, but it is a genuine revolution that probably cannot be stopped. Our work was conceptualized as a study of teachers in new roles. These four districts were selected because teachers there had taken on new roles as mentors, school site managers, and policy makers of various kinds. We have come to see the central metaphor of this study as the teachers' struggle to take charge of their practice.

It is not too far-fetched to conceive of the construction of the modern public school system as an aggregation of one-room school houses into a newly centralized system of education in which a mostly male administrative class established top down direction of teachers. Teachers themselves had almost no say in the shaping of the system. Their classrooms were brought together in an egg crate fashion side-by-side down long school halls, but no genuine communication among the teachers themselves was established about the nature of their own practice. That conversation has begun, and has been expanding and raising the consciousness of teachers about their roles over the past decade. It will continue. It has been infused by feminism. Teachers are no longer willing to let a patriarchy write the rules and control the cheque-book. It is partly a result of higher levels of education and training: most teachers in the USA now have a master's degree whereas before the Second World War most did not have even a bachelor's. But at heart a new concept of the teaching profession is emerging. The conviction is growing among teachers that the kinds of reforms that are being demanded for children – namely that all of them become competent problem solvers and critical thinkers – cannot be fulfilled if the teachers themselves are not similarly empowered with respect to inquiring into the nature of their own practice.

Comparisons with the first academic revolution – that of the academic professoriate – are instructive. For most of the nineteenth century, college professors operated under the thumb of often autocratic presidents. In the twentieth century they overthrew that administrative authority and established the rights of academic freedom and control of the tenure process. Although formal authority continued to rest with presidents and boards of trustees, the recommendations of faculty committees were rarely overturned, and top management in universities saw themselves primarily as representatives of the faculty. Essentially the professors asserted that only our peers are fit to judge who is qualified to be a physicist or a philosopher, and to decide what physics and philosophy are. Only we have the knowledge to decide what the curriculum should be and how to teach it and how to prepare future philosophers and physicists. Moreover the progress and prosperity of the society depends upon our developing new knowledge. We have the exclusive right to carry out research and conduct inquiries into the nature of that knowledge. The professoriate took charge of the curriculum and of the recruitment, training, induction and assessment of new members of their profession. They assumed the exclusive right to define the objects of their research and the nature of their practice.

At the same time as the professoriate was redefining the academic profession in this way, school administrators established themselves as the certified experts of the educational system under the guise of scientific management. And as progressive school administrators with newly earned doctorates carried out massive school surveys early in the twentieth century, they also succeeded in establishing themselves in the public eye as the experts. They developed elaborate curriculum guides and wrote the rules and regulations that govern modern school bureaucracies.

In the last decade, elementary and secondary school teachers have moved beyond traditional union demands for improving the conditions of work to assert analogous claims. They cannot convincingly claim to be the discoverers of basic knowledge in a way that is true of university professors. But in ways that are analogous to the vast majority of college teachers, many of them can assert that they have genuine expertise in their subject matter and that there is a body of pedagogical content knowledge that is specific to their work. Most importantly, they are no longer willing to let the administrative class define themselves as the exclusive experts in the content of the curriculum and as the sole decision-makers about who is fit to teach it.

The outcomes of this slow revolution of the schoolteachers are far from clear. While analogous to the revolt of the professoriate, the schoolteachers' revolution differs in important respects and renders prediction more hazardous.

Critical to the success of the first academic revolution was the ability of the professoriate to deliver on its promises. A higher education system that in the nineteenth century was not sharply distinguished from good secondary schools (or academies as they were then more commonly known) moved to world-wide pre-eminence by the middle of the twentieth century. The fruits of academic freedom combined with an emphasis on the discovery of new knowledge produced a higher level of expertise that was there for all to see, whether measured in Nobel prizes or advances against disease or great feats of engineering. Not only the Manhattan Project, but many other breakthroughs achieved by American scientists in the Second World War, raised the status of American universities in the public eye. Federal funding for university research soared, first in the physical sciences and then in the biological sciences. By the 1960s, major funding flowed to the social sciences, then enlisted in President Johnson's War on Poverty. The professorial élite commanded high salaries and presidents courted them to prevent them leaving for competing institutions offering better conditions for their work. While schoolteachers are better trained now and can justifiably point to an expanded knowledge base underlying their practice, teaching is still perceived as a low-tech field with a relatively modest base of expertise as compared with the high status professions. Teacher demands for continued salary growth are meeting more skepticism, if not anger, from a public that feels teachers who have won higher salaries in the last decade have not delivered the goods. In Rochester, New York, where a new contract offering 40% raises and more decision-making power for teachers won front page attention in the *New York Times* in 1987, the new mood is reflected by a 1995 citizens' task force report entitled 'No More Excuses'. Moreover, even within the teaching profession, there is an insistent minority that warns against the over-professionalization of the field and the negative effects of asserting the privileges of expertise.

A second, perhaps more critical, difference is that the first academic revolution produced a new tracking system in higher education. It established more rigorous qualifications and meritocratic grounds for appointment of faculty to leading institutions. As Jencks and Riesman (1968) pointed out, one of the first things these faculty did in leading colleges and universities was to eliminate both unscholarly students and unscholarly faculty. The formula for success was to hire the most distinguished PhD scholars who would be the basis for attracting the best students. Lesser institutions tried to emulate them. Thus, the most ambitious systems of public higher education imitated the California master plan that assigned students to one of three levels of the state university and college system on the basis of their school grades and scores on standardized tests. The push behind the second academic revolution is to do just the opposite: to untrack the schools and to educate all students to higher levels in more inclusive settings.

The third salient difference between the first and second academic revolutions is that the first was accompanied by the professoriate's demand that they have more time for research and the responsibilities of running the university. Not only were teaching loads dramatically reduced in research-oriented institutions, but all college faculty largely shed the custodial and *in locus parentis* functions characteristic of the earlier era. They had time both to pursue their own scholarly agendas and to take on the work of evaluating their colleagues and deciding their fates in promotion and tenure committees. The schoolteachers, even those who have most eagerly embraced new policymaking and mentoring responsibilities, seldom have been granted any major relief in either teaching or custodial responsibilities. After a year or two on school site-based committees they are more than ready to relinquish such 'privileges'. It is analogous to asking General Motors workers to invent the Saturn plant while they are still working a 40-hour week producing Pontiacs.

It should be no surprise that the public remains skeptical about the ability of teachers to assume responsibility for evaluating the competence of their colleagues. To deny tenure and stay malpractice requires long hours of observing and evaluating the work of one's colleagues, to say nothing of the time required to change practice and bring new knowledge to bear on the quality of teaching.

In summary, we have tried to sketch the course of a second academic revolution. We began by pointing out the tendency of most educational reformers to underestimate the staying power of the 'one best system' as well as the enormous effort required to bring about major changes in belief systems. Neither similar incentives nor similar levels of effort are commonly found in recent reforms aimed at transforming the ethos of schools. Major system and school change is likely to be fostered by some combination of new technology, the rise of competing models of education, and a reformation if not a revolution of the teaching profession.

This second revolution of the schoolteachers is in some ways similar to the academic revolution effected by the professoriate early in this century. But there are stark differences, namely in the ability of teachers to achieve major gains in educational outcomes while operating within the structure of the 'one best system'. Moreover, the aims of the second revolution embody values about which there is yet no firm consensus among either the public at large or the teachers themselves. Even our colleagues who write most passionately about the need to untrack the elementary and secondary schools convey to their own children at the dinner table that they should be aiming for entrance to Harvard or Berkeley, and anything less is really second best. There is a struggle for the soul of the teaching profession that mirrors in large measure the tensions in the broader society about how to strike the right balance between the values of individualism and cooperation, on the one hand, and liberty and equality on the other.

Acknowledgement

We are grateful to the Spencer Foundation for their support for the work leading to this essay.

References

CUBAN, L. (1986) *Teachers and Machines: The Classroom Use of Technology Since 1920* (New York: Teachers College Press).

CUBAN, L. (1993) Computers meet classroom: classroom wins, *Teachers College Record*, 95 (2), 185–210.

FULLAN, M. G. with SUZANNE STIEGELBAUER (1991) *The New Meaning of Educational Change* (New York: Teachers College Press).

JENCKS, C. and RIESMAN, D. (1968) *The Academic Revolution* (New York: Doubleday).

MARSHALL, K. (1993) Teachers and schools: what makes a difference: a principal's perspective, *Daedalus*, 22 (1), 209–242.

PAPERT, S. (1993) *The Children's Machine: Rethinking School in the Age of the Computer* (New York: Basic).

TYACK, D. B. (1974) *The One Best System: A History of American Urban Education* (Cambridge, MA: Harvard University Press).

7.   *The Wadleigh Complex: a dream that soured*

Mary Anne Raywid

The Wadleigh Complex in Harlem – the nation's most famous African-American community opened in the Fall of 1993 with high expectations: a set of three middle schools and one incipient high school, all housed in a single building. The grand day had been several years in the making, and in excess of $38 million had been invested in renovating the building and the school's programme and organization. The effort had involved considerable external support – including that of then-Governor Cuomo and Congressman Rangel – as well as political help from within New York City. Large numbers of people had worked on the 'New Wadleigh' – a school district-community task force and three teams of teachers, each with its own separate, hardworking advisory committee.

Three separate and distinctive instructional programs had been fashioned, one emphasizing the visual and performing arts, another writing and publishing, and a third, science and technology. All three had been launched and 'incubated' elsewhere before the 'new' Wadleigh building opened, and two of the three were highly imaginative and already successful before moving into their new quarters.

In the fall of 1993, the immaculate, refurbished-to-order building opened with high hopes on the part of its teachers, the community, the local school district, and city officials. Today, not two years later, the staffs of at least two of the three programmes are extensively demoralized, the creator-directors of the two innovative ones are preparing to leave, along with their core staff, and the shiny new building is beginning to show signs of wear and tear.

It is possible to point to some explanations, although one could wish that by and large they offered more by way of clear advice as to what should have been done differently. As the school's story will show, its auspices were unusual, locating it structurally within two different authorities: one of New York's 32 community school districts, and at the same time within the city's centralized High School Division. (Since its decentralization in 1969, New York's community school districts are responsible for K–8, sometimes K–9 schools, the High School Division is responsible for grade 9–12 and 10–12 secondary schools.)

Method and framework

The data and perceptions yielding this case history were accumulated in the course of several separate inquiries. Over a three-year period, I conducted research in one of Wadleigh's three schools-within-a-school, the Alternative Arts Middle School, looking primarily at the professional lives of teachers there. The study, which entailed two weeks of observation within the school each year, was conducted under the auspices of the

0268–0939/95 $12 · 00 © 1995 Taylor & Francis Ltd

National Center on the Organization and Restructuring of Schools. Additionally, this case history of Wadleigh is illuminated by research conducted several years ago in New York's District 4, under a Secretary's Discretionary Grant from the US Department of Education, and also by a study of New York City school governance in 1991 sponsored by the Manhattan Institute for Policy Research. Perceptions and conclusions are based largely on observations, conversations, and interviews in Wadleigh and in the District 3 office. To date, there have also been several analytic accounts of the planning process for the Wadleigh complex (Sostre 1991, Elwell 1993); a detailed examination of the early history of one of the three schools-within-a-school, the Science and Technology Middle School (Sostre 1992), and an interpretive article describing the developments that are the major focus here (Elwell 1994). These several studies have informed this inquiry.

The Wadleigh story is a controversial and a sensitive one, and those involved do not agree on the facts, let alone on a single interpretation of its evolution. Two kinds of efforts have been made to accommodate to these circumstances in this study. One is an unusually extensive although not entirely successful attempt to verify factual reports across the several groups involved. And the second is an explicit effort to characterize the evolution described from the several quite different perspectives of major adult participants: staff within the schools-within-a-school, parent leaders, principal, and district superintendent. The story is told largely from the vantage point of the teachers and directors in the two innovative programmes. But a shift to the perspective of others is introduced and made explicit at several points in the narrative.

The story told in succeeding pages – moving from high hopes and promising prospects to a dream soured, in less than two years' time – is illuminated by institutional theory. This body of literature underscores the power of pressure to conform exerted on organizations in institutionalized fields such as education. It describes forces that compel even would-be innovative organizations to assume the features of uniformity marking the conventional, despite their contexts and despite their goals (Zucker 1987). Such pressures can take the form of laws and regulations; of influences toward regularity and homogenization brought to bear by professional associations; of what have become accepted, 'standard' solutions to situations of ambiguity and unclear goals; and of normative values that have become attached to practices and arrangements, quite irrespective of their effectiveness (DiMaggio and Powell 1983). It is not only the laws and bureaucratic regulations, and the professional associations which operate to bar innovation, but also the 'social fact' type status which the alleged preferability of many organizational arrangements have come to enjoy – imbuing them with a value that their contributions to effectiveness could never warrant (Zucker 1987).

In the case of Wadleigh, it has been the voices of vocal parents, as well as of professionals, that have championed the values of conventional organizational arrangements. They have demanded conformance to the organizational format of 'real school' (Metz 1989), wherein a principal governs a formal hierarchy and faculty and staff are subordinate and appropriately deferent to him. And as will be seen, vocal parents have rejected the idea of three extensively independent schools within a single building, reasserting instead the merits and tradition of the old Wadleigh which was unitary in structure.

The beginnings

The story of the new Wadleigh began in 1987 when the Acting Chancellor of New York

City schools decided to simply close the school. This sometimes happens to New York schools when they get bad enough, and things had reached that point at Wadleigh. The student population had dwindled to 450 – in a facility built for 1500–2000 – and only a portion of the 450 attended on any given day. The building appeared almost beyond repair, with whole unused areas sealed off and one entire wing closed after students set fire to two classrooms. In other sections of the building, plaster flaking from leaks vied with graffiti to cover the walls. And the condition of the instructional programme was an apt complement to that of the physical plant. Students roamed the halls, hat-and-coat-clad all day. Teachers struck misbehaving youngsters – with baseball bats, according to some (Elwell 1993: 333). One veteran inner-city school administrator who visited declared it the worst school he had ever seen. State Governor Cuomo called it 'an insult to children'.

But Wadleigh, which had first opened in 1901, had some loyal alumni who joined with neighbourhood people, community groups, and some Wadleigh teachers in wanting to see the school remain open. These several groups formed a 'Task Force' to keep it alive, and the group managed to get the attention of political figures, moved in part by fears that in addition to a school, the survival of a neighbourhood was at stake. An unusual collaboration between New York Community School District 3, and the City's centralized High School Division, managed to keep Wadleigh alive, closing it instead in 1989 for redesign. The 'redesign' anticipated was to include both physical plant and programme.

But it would be a mistake to conclude that the interested parties were agreed as to what was in order. Despite the erosion in the educational programme, as well as in the condition of the building, there were people who felt that all that was necessary was a fresh start, perhaps with some curricular assistance and some key teacher replacements. Some of the Wadleigh staff were of this persuasion and were evidently surprised to learn that the project director had been charged with programme as well as plant redesign. Some tried to promote an arrangement that would have kept the old staff intact while temporarily located elsewhere as the building was being renovated. But school officials were agreed that more was necessary, and when the old Wadleigh was closed for redesign, most of its staff were reassigned.

The circumstances recommended an atypical planning process. The redesign of failing New York City high schools is standardly tackled by a single individual assigned the role of 'project director', who sometimes seeks help from a local university. But to convert Wadleigh (then functioning as a middle school of grades 7–9) into a combined middle and high school, called for a different strategy. To arrive at a programme with enhanced promise for an extraordinarily challenging student population also called for a different strategy. A project director was hired to plan the new Wadleigh, who took very seriously the design *process* itself. His charge was redesign of the school plant and programme. His office was in District 3 (actually in the Wadleigh building), but half his salary was to come from the High School Division.

The project director selected was an individual who had been part of the pioneering efforts of District 4 in creating its famed 'alternative concept' schools – small, autonomous, themed programmes multiply-housed in single buildings that contain as many as five such programmes. He had been an alternative school director in District 4 and also, later, a part of the central office staff. He shared the District 4 idea that good schools must be small, independent, and designed by those who will operate them – and who have chosen to do so. But the project director was a man in a hurry, under pressure to complete the planning in short order. So he could not wait, as District 4 had done, for volunteers. Moreover, he felt that he might be able to improve on the District 4 process in several ways: by offering sufficiently extensive support to make extraordinary leadership unnecessary (Sostre 1991), and by simultaneously providing each new school with political support and needed help (both expertise and resources) from the start. He felt this could emerge by assembling carefully chosen groups to participate in the design process.

These convictions became the starting point for the design. Not all of them were foreign to District 3, which already had several alternative schools firmly ensconced as separate, autonomous programmes housed in other schools. But the previously existing alternatives were elsewhere in the District and had attracted relatively few Harlem students. Thus the alternative school concept remained largely unfamiliar to people in the Wadleigh area.

The project director decided to divide the new Wadleigh into four units: three themed, alternative middle schools, and a small high school. He then assembled an advisory group to participate in designing each of the themed programmes. As members, he invited teachers he thought able, and potentially perhaps willing, to assume leadership of each, plus individuals who could provide some theme-related or organizational expertise, and some carefully chosen civic organization and corporate representatives. One advisory group, for instance, for the Alternative Arts Middle School, included the executive director of the Lincoln Center Institute (of the well-known Center for the Performing Arts), an official of a respected advocacy group, the Public Education Association, and the personal representative of the president of the Colgate-Palmolive Corporation. The hope was for these groups not only to aid in the planning but to remain intact as Advisory Boards to the new schools-within-a-school – and as crucial political allies in protecting them from external threats emanating primarily from elsewhere in the system (Elwell 1994).

Thus the planning was broad-based, it involved at least the prospective teacher-directors of two of the three programmes, and it involved strong expertise, prospective resources and support for them. What it did not involve, however, was representatives of the 'Task Force', which had had its own ideas about programme for an improved Wadleigh. Although some of their ideas were reflected in the three themed programs that emerged from the design, not all of the Task Force's curricular recommendations had been incorporated. The attempt to do so might well have proved problematic since, as the group's proposal acknowledged, '[t]here is no mistaking the fact that this proposal is a compromise' (Wadleigh... in the Year 2000: A Community and School Respond, n.d.: 2).

But perhaps more fundamentally, a different model of school planning had been adopted than that which the Task Force exemplified: a teachers plus experts model, rather than a multiple stakeholder model. Thus, despite the fact that school officials and at least some key members of the three planning groups met with the Task Force repeatedly, and innundated it with information, the community group was not a real part of the planning.

The design scheme succeeded in the cases of two of the three projected programmes, in that in both the Arts, and the Writing and Publishing groups, teacher leadership emerged in the course of the design process and began to direct the theme's elaboration. However, for the third programme, the Science and Technology Middle School, leadership was, from the start, a greater challenge. No director emerged from within the planning group, defeating the hope for staff ownership in the plans that is central to the strategy. Leadership has continued to be a challenge and the programme has so far had four teacher-directors. Reportedly, no theme has ever been elaborated with sufficient clarity or comprehensiveness to guide the program, and of the three Wadleigh schools this one is generally perceived weakest and least successful. (Both the other two, for instance, have more applicants than they can accommodate. In comparison, this one has very few.)

The other two programmes, however, have achieved considerable success with respect to eliciting student attendance, response and engagement. Test scores do not indicate the gains that might be hoped. But that students attend regularly, do not drop out, and in many cases are enthusiastic about school are in themselves positive and significant accomplishments.

The Wadleigh Complex – refurbished to meet the specifications of the three programs – was to re-open in 1992. Actually it was 1993 before the renovation was completed. Meanwhile, however, the three programmes were launched in 1990 and began operating in rooms made available to them in three separate elementary schools in the area. There were inconveniences and annoyances in the temporary arrangements, although they compared well with the accommodations of the District's other alternative schools. But space was sometimes a problem, as was adapting to a host's schedule and regulations. On the other hand, this enforced physical distance from each other proved an advantage. By the time they moved into their permanent quarters, each of the new programmes was three years old. Although only two of the three had managed to take full advantage of it, each had been given opportunity to test and elaborate its theme, and establish its own culture and procedures – in short to become a school.

The new Wadleigh

Once in the new building, however, it did not take long for stresses and strains to emerge. Coordination and control versus autonomy proved the major tension, but there were others. As earlier suggested, the Wadleigh Complex was made part of two jurisdictions, District 3 and the City's High School Division, with the District responsible for the middle schools and the Division responsible for the high school grades. The building administrator was to be selected by representatives from both levels and to be responsible to both the District 3 and the Manhattan High School offices.

The original design for the new Wadleigh had called for a 'campus director' in lieu of a principal – to permit and to underscore the programmatic independence of the three schools-within-a-school, each of which was to control its own instructional programme (Concept Paper 1989). The high school was to have a single theme, 'The High School of Communications Media and Technology', which seemed broad enough to accommodate the interests of the youngsters choosing any of the three middle schools – the group that was expected to constitute the bulk of the high school's student population. (Plans for the high school have since changed, with the notion of a single high school having been replaced with the idea of extending the three middle schools as three separate grade 6–12 programmes. Subsequently the design has reverted to a single high school, but one with three strands, intended to represent the themes of the three middle schools.)

Between the design's emergence and adoption, there were changes in the governance plan. Perhaps the most significant was the shift from 'campus director' to 'principal'. The Council of Supervisors and Administrators – the collective bargaining agent for city school administrators – had insisted on that. But so had the United Federation of Teachers, the teachers' bargaining agent, as well as the High School Division. Some community members, too, also found it important. In Wadleigh circles the story is still told of the local school board member who, before the principalship appointment was made, publicly bewailed the delay and the resulting predicament of 'those poor children [Wadleigh's] who don't even have a principal'.

The appointment process for the principal (as well as for other staff) was to reflect a modification of standard procedure. Both the District Superintendent and the Superintendent of Manhattan High Schools were to participate in the selection. Subsequently, the evaluating officer for the principal was to be 'the Manhattan High School Superintendent in consultation with the District 3 Superintendent'. (Memorandum of Understanding, 4.) The official Memorandum of Understanding made clear that the principal would 'head Wadleigh Secondary School and supervise high school instruction'. But it less explicitly added that this official would also 'handle building concerns, personnel, and . . . be held responsible and accountable for these and any other programs, policies, and activities expected of a building principal'.

Unfortunately, neither the project designer nor any of the three directors was involved in the interviewing and selection process, so there was no opportunity for them to question candidates about their feelings regarding the autonomous, independent alternatives to which District 3 was committed. (See, for example, Board Minutes, 28 October 1992, 7 July 1994.) At the only interview session in which teachers were represented, the sole questions that could be posed to candidates – six in all – were formulated in advance and included no queries into how candidates felt about the non-traditional school structure called for by the design.

It proved difficult to find a principal with exactly the right credentials. The individual chosen was a former district director of special education. He had also served as a junior high school assistant principal. He is a tall, handsome, well-dressed African-American. Immediately before reporting to Wadleigh, he spent a week in the High School Division Office being instructed about his duties, but there does not seem to have been comparable advance time spent in the District 3 office.

The troubles began right away, when it became evident that the new principal would be claimimg the full prerogatives of the traditional principalship – a role not entirely compatible with those assigned school-within-a-school directors. He met regularly with the Superintendent and Deputy Superintendent of District 3, in accord with the matrix organization that has him reporting there as well as to the Manhattan High Schools office. But there was virtually no contact with the designer of the Wadleigh Complex, even though that individual was also by this time the titular head of alternative schools for District 3, and this principal presumably had responsibility for three such schools. Things got off to a bad start between the two when the new principal failed to keep an initial appointment with the alternative schools director, and each suggests that the other is the reason no subsequent meetings ever occurred. But difficulties between these two were not the only problem. And the new principal started off by rehiring a secretary who had been a key member of the office staff of the old Wadleigh – a staff of sufficient notoriety throughout District 3 as to have been carefully dispersed and relocated elsewhere.

The difficulties came fast. The principal immediately assumed control of all auxiliary service personnel and directed them to take instructions from his office and his alone. This meant that security guards, as well as other workers, would not respond to programme directors and their requests. The five or six uniformed guards rankled in particular. Upon occasion they challenged teachers' decisions and intervened in all incidents they deemed needful of their presence. Initially, they walked unbidden into classrooms, until the director of the school closest to their first floor station ordered them not to enter any of her classrooms again unless explicitly requested to do so. Not surprisingly, the guards talk and deal in a very different way with students than do the alternative school staff. And the adult–student relationships they generate are quite other than what the programme staff are striving to build. Furthermore, the guards are a constant source of irritation since their 'post' is situated only 50 feet down the hall from the Arts programme housed on the first floor; the result is often as many as four or five unoccupied people congregated there chatting.

The resulting morale level was not without irony. Here were three new teacher-designed programmes, ensconced in quarters that would turn most New York City teachers green with envy. Moreover, they had received just the facilities and equipment they asked for, probably with more resources potentially available. All they had lost, as they experienced it, was their freedom, dignity, and ability to operate their programme. They were forced constantly to deal with situations and events such as these:

- Although these were designed as small schools in part to permit personalization and reponsiveness to individual needs, the High School Division insisted on computer scheduling for all of their secondary students.
- During the first ten weeks in the new school, there were seven compulsory fire drills. Directors were told that 'Shelter Drills' would also begin shortly.
- For much of the first year in the New Wadleigh, the Library was unuseable since most of the books remained in the sealed cartons in which they had arrived. Since they have been shelved, the absence of a librarian has kept the Library locked for most of each school day.
- The assistant principal called late one afternoon to announce that the High School Division's regular report cards would have to be completed for all ninth and tenth graders – and by 9:00 the next morning.
- Teachers from all three schools are summoned over the PA system and must line up before the Payroll Clerk in the main office to obtain their pay cheques – despite their repeated requests that the cheques be entrusted to an emissary from each school.
- Locks for lockers failed to materialize, so until January or February youngsters were arriving in heavy coats and hats they had no place to store.
- The principal asked for curriculum outlines for all high school level courses taught.
- During the middle of a double emergency in the first November at the new Wadleigh – when ambulances for two students had been obtained and families contacted with dispatch – the principal told the middle school secretary who had done the calling that future emergencies must be reported only to his office, which would decide upon and take the action indicated.

As such reports imply, the principal was assuming standard detailed control of events and situations throughout the building. To the directors whose alternative school status had promised independence and autonomy, it meant betrayal. It also translated into the harrassment and assault combination described years earlier in the tragi-comic *Up to Down Staircase* (Kaufman 1965). Moreover, at least two of the directors were offended by the principal's demeanor and the way he treated them. He reportedly handled them with a combination of the courtliness that is his style, and the insistent assertion of the power of his office – prompting one director to comment disgustedly, 'He treats us like *wives*'.

From the principal's perspective, it was far from an easy situation. There were multiple start-up needs, decisions to be made, construction to be completed, auxiliary services and personnel to organize, new students and parents to initiate into the school, precedents to set, and conventions to be preserved while others were launched. And in the midst of all these urgencies, there was constant static from two of the programme directors who jealously guarded their separate terrains and stood alert to reject any intrusions. In his eyes, their resistance to whatever he proposed was 'total and abject'.

Even routine requests like submission of course outlines might be ignored or explicitly rejected. And there were objections to his attempts to execute policy set downtown, such as the scheduling of students or the holding of fire drills. He also experienced resistance to his efforts to fulfil his building responsibilities – e.g., seeing that people received their paycheques, and that calls, and cancellations of calls, for ambulances did not emanate from all over the school. The programme directors seemed to range from indifferent to hostile in their relationship to the rest of the school, and as the weeks went by their responses to situations and requests were increasingly negative. By Fall of the second year, the Cabinet Meetings involving the directors had become so contentious and unproductive that he stopped them altogether.

The principal is part wistful, part resentful about having come – and having stepped into a situation where he is held responsible for fulfilling promises made by others. He came because of an interest in innovation, although not necessarily in the particular innovations being foisted upon him. He has sometimes felt caught in a cross-fire with insufficient protection or support on either side.

Not surprisingly, then, the school has been the scene of growing irritation for all parties – teachers and directors, students, and administrators. It might have been resolved or allayed, some feel, by decisions from the District 3 central office that were not forthcoming. The superintendent who launched the Wadleigh Project had meanwhile retired. The former deputy superintendent became acting superintendent and a candidate for the permanent job. Although in his prior role he had been a strong and effective supporter – had, in fact, helped to create the new Wadleigh – in the seat of acting superintendent, he was evidently reluctant to continue in the same role. He saw his new role as maintaining harmonious relations, building collaboration, and helping the parties involved to arrive at arrangements they could find workable. Thus, his response to the directors who went to him with stories like those told above, pleading for his intervention, was that they would simply have to deal with and maintain peace with the principal, even if that meant re-negotiation of prior agreements.

His choice is understandable. Many high-level school administrators place the support of positive working relationships near the top of their agendas, giving this a priority superseding particular programmes. Moreover, in more personal terms, his own position brought considerable risk to tackling the Manhattan High Schools office (which enjoys more confidence among some local activists than does the District), or to opposing the unions supporting the principalship, or to becoming embroiled in the racial politics that challenging the African-American principal might invite. But this stance had a devastating effect on two of the three programmes. (By this time, a director of the Science and Technology program – its fourth – had been named: an African-American woman with whom the principal had worked previously and on whose support he could count. Since this individual has not moved towards developing an autonomous programme, there is less cause for tension between her and the principal. But neither has she moved toward the development of a substantive theme – a situation which continues to limit the distinctiveness and coherence, and hence the popularity, of the Science and Technology option.)

The directors completed their first year in the new building, reporting that there were good days with the kids as well as bad days with the administration. Meanwhile, the two distinctive schools-within-a-school were achieving external notice and various sorts of acclaim throughout the district, the city, and beyond. The director of the School for Writing and Publishing received two awards for innovation, from *Reader's Digest* and the Manhattan Institute for Policy Research. The Alternative Arts Middle School astounded the District with the quality of its first end-of-year performance, began receiving substantial grants from New York foundations, and struck alliances with Harvard's Project Zero, the Alvin Ailey Dance Group, and Warner Communications, as well as with its corporate sponsor Colgate-Palmolive. The advisory boards of both schools have functioned to buoy them up when morale sagged, and for the first year the two managed to maintain the demanded peace with the principal. As of this writing, however, an additional year has passed, and we are at the end of the new Wadleigh's second year.

The situation has deteriorated, and in reponse, key staff in both the successful schools-within-a-school have simply given up. The conclusive moment occurred at the end of last year, in June. At a meeting called by the middle school parent associations, there were criticisms of the two directors and their refusal to accede to the principal's direction. It was an occasion that might have been used to help the community understand the organizational structure of the new Wadleigh, supporting separate and autonomous programmes. Instead, however, the acting superintendent appeared to reinforce the notion that the directors were responsible to the principal as the building's top official. The two directors report that for them this marked the end. They heard it as official confirmation that the separate, autonomous status accorded other alternative schools in the district was not going to extend to Wadleigh. According to the acting superintendent, however (who is now the superintendent), the end had actually come earlier, when the two had made plain their intention to leave after another year. For him, then, the choice had lain between backing a duo who were leaving, or supporting the more permanent faction.

One gets conflicting reports about how good or bad things are at Wadleigh this year, and what would really be needed to resolve the difficulties. On the one hand, youngsters in the two popular school-within-a-school programmes continue to speak enthusiastically about their schools and one sees engagement in their classrooms. On the other hand, according to one staff member, the third school-within-a-school remains virtually themeless, and attendance is a problem. Middle school staff also report that high school students roam the halls unfettered and are intimidating them and their students. As one teacher put it, teen culture – which is street culture – has taken over the high school.

There has been recurring talk of District 3 assuming full control of Wadleigh, and the Division of High Schools withdrawing. Opinions are divided about how much that would solve. Staff of the two popular schools-within-a-school feel that such a solution is too little and too late, as well as quite uncertain. On the other hand, the Wadleigh parents who have remained closest to the matter tend to feel that such a solution would only prove tangential, since in their eyes the problems do not pertain primarily to external control but internal – largely, they feel, a matter of personality conflicts.

In early March, the forthcoming departure of the two directors was announced, their resignations to become effective at the end of the school year. The two directorships are now open and the selection process is under way. What is not yet clear is how many of the teachers from the two programmes will also be leaving Wadleigh. It appears that virtually all of the initiating staff in both programmes may go – one group opting for retirement or reassignment, and the other hoping to relocate their programme elsewhere in the city. In that event, Wadleigh's programmes will doubtless be extensively modified or replaced.

As several of these developments have suggested, vocal parents are figuring actively in the internal politics of Wadleigh. Middle school parent association officers have become a frequent presence in the school, and their understanding of the situation and the related programmes align them with a traditional organization position. They are upset by descriptive materials emanating from the programmes that fail to feature Wadleigh instead of a particular school within it. They want – and report that the community wants – a principal in charge of the whole school, an administrator who is involved in and has the final say on *all* decisions.

One of the root present difficulties, according to the middle school parents association president, is that the programme directors have too much power – gained in their temporary locations before the new building could open. They are uncooperative, insubordinate, and discourteous in their dealings with the principal and the High School Division, ignoring or blatantly refusing to comply with legitimate and reasonable requests, such as that they submit course outlines. Moreover, they lack the assistant principal certification necessary to evaluate their own teachers. The parents association officers interviewed align themselves with the principal and the High School Division and tend to find both the directors and the District 3 superintendent at fault. They feel that settling matters will require an outside mediator, and they report having attempted to function in that capacity. But both of the departing directors doubt that the situation can be resolved as long as the principal and his office staff remain. Thus, the two have resigned and the fate of the programmes is uncertain.

Understanding the trajectory

Locally, all sorts of explanations are being offered for these events. As might be expected, many are directed at individuals and identify a single villain or two. Some hold the downhill slide directly attributable to the principal's alleged incompetence – or to his determination to micro-manage each of the several schools-within-a-school. Some have claimed that the debacle was foretold when he brought back the old school secretary, who wields extraordinary power over all within the building. Others hold the superintendent responsible, claiming that in the course of his campaign to become superintendent, he abandoned the programmes and their directors. Still others look to the inexperience and political ineptitude of the directors, or to their intractable and insubordinate behaviour. And some lay the problems at the feet of the designer, for a scheme they believe that only he could have operated.

Broader explanations have also been proffered. One is that disaster was written into situating the school within two distinct jurisdictions, thus forcing it to report to and deal with two different bureaucracies with quite different, often incompatible, cultures and styles. Another is that the schools-within-a-school model is unworkable, at least short of relevantly well prepared and highly receptive administrators. And an all-embracing explanation nurtured by some is the indifference of the entire 'system', with its resulting willingness to simply stand by as spectator to the collapse.

A different order of context-centered explanation must also be considered: the particular environment and circumstances in which the events occurred. Harlem is a famous, and for many of its residents, a proud African-American community. It is divided among three school districts, two of which consist of fairly compact areas of extensive ethnic homogeneity, one almost exclusively Black and one approximately two-thirds Latino and one-third Black. The third school district represented in Harlem, however, is not confined there and extends South to include the upper West side of Manhattan. Within it (Community School District 3) housing patterns as well as the more formal geographical separation from Harlem divide the ethnic groups. Thus, within the District, mention of 'uptown' versus 'downtown' politics carries heavy racial overtones, and school board representation and discussion sometimes reflect these sectional and racial divisions. This context had at least three effects on the unfolding of the Wadleigh story.

First, although it cannot be said that the community was totally omitted from the planning process for the new Wadleigh, neither did it have a prominent role in developing – or in coming to understand – either the programme or the organizational structure of the new school. Community members had been the core of the task force which had saved Wadleigh from permanent closure and was thus responsible for the Wadleigh Project. But the design had been the work primarily of professionals and their business and civic collaborators. The plan that emerged was a collaborative product and far from the work of a single designer, which standard New York City schools procedure would have made it. But the process was patterned after District 4, where school design was in the province of a programme's prospective teachers – as augmented in this case by a cadre of experts and potential political supporters. There was no emphasis on local Harlem participation in composing the three advisory groups that produced the designs for the three programmes, and few locals were involved.

Whether by virtue of the resulting relative lack of input – or the failure subsequently to educate the community about the new programmes and structure – there are Harlem parents and others who feel they were left out of the planning process and who obviously have failed to understand the way the organization was designed to operate, or why.

The second important consequence of the ethnic division marking District 3 was the conviction that the new Harlem school must have an African-American principal. It had initially been thought by many within District 3 that the main designer of the new Wadleigh wanted to be, and was slated to become, its 'campus director', as the original proposal had it. But as time for selection neared, word was circulated that the individual named must be African-American. The designer did not even apply. And this certainly appeared reasonable: two of the first three programme directors were white, initially two women and one man (eventually, all three appointments were held by women). Thus, an African-American, and probably a male, seemed the appropriate choice.

Racial questions have continued to simmer, although largely unstated. One compelling question that has been raised is whether the same sort of demands for a traditional organizational format would have been advanced by community residents, had the roster been reversed racially: three African-American directors and a white principal. And one might also ask (though perhaps no one has) how a different gender line-up might have affected the situation. For instance, would a traditional organizational format have been championed if there had been a woman principal and three male programme directors?

Although we will never know, it does appear that racial and perhaps gender politics as well have played a part in Wadleigh events. Class politics may also have been involved. This has seemed particularly plausible in the case of one of the three schools-within-a-school – the one that is the least traditional in concept and operation. Its inspiration is the Progressive School/Open School tradition, and its intent is to make its students thoughtful, responsible makers of their own decisions. The relative lack of structure which results appears less compatible with the childrearing patterns and expectations of working class and poor families than with those of middle class families. However, it appears that parent support has been substantial in both of the innovative schools-within-schools, and that criticisms may have emanated more from other community residents than from parents.

Not all Harlemites had been ready to give up so completely on the old Wadleigh. Many remembered at least some of the proud years of the school's history – if not its initial years as the city's first high school for girls, then the middle school it became in 1957. As one alumnus fondly recalls, the Wadleigh of the 1960s was 'a family school' with lots of parent and community involvement. It was one which successfully taught its students to depend on themselves. Things reportedly began to fall apart in the 1970s, however, when warring camps erupted among the students, and there was daily fighting. There were also rapes and guns and, allegedly, alcoholic teachers who were drunk during the school day and who were 'busted for drugs'. And there were still other teachers who struck parents as simply incompetent. But it evidently remained debateable whether even such a state of affairs called for a new concept or simply renewed resolve to make the old one work – restructuring or reform. The Wadleigh principal is just one of a number who believe that the new leadership went too far in the direction of erasing the practices and traditions, and ignoring the rituals of the old Wadleigh.

Whatever may be the plausibility of these explanations for the story of Wadleigh, it is evident that its trajectory has taken it from a boldly innovative plan and beginning, back to what seems poised to become one more inner city middle school and high school. From the start, pressures in that direction have been strong. And 'the inexorable push toward homogenization' (Zucker 1987: 453) has come from multiple sources: the city bureaucracy, professional associations, and from parents as well.

Thus the brave new plan is giving way to the pressures exerted by the bureaucracy and the community. Community pressures toward a more orthodox structure and traditional trappings are particularly strong. As Meyer and Rowan pointed out, 'organizations which innovate in important structural ways bear considerable costs in legitimacy'. (1977: 353.) And this community is very much concerned with maximizing the legitimacy of Wadleigh. It may strike some observers as ironic that the small, teacher-designed, teacher-directed programmes that research recommends as offering maximal chances of success for these youngsters are being modified to conform in ways bound to compromise their effectiveness. As has been pointed out, however, organizations innovative enough to have to choose between traditional structures on the one hand, and mission success on the other, are frequently forced to select the former in the interests of enhancing their legitimacy (Meyer and Rowan 1977).

Legitimacy – acknowledged acceptability and status – is an attribute of particular value for institutions in the Harlem community. Minority status, poverty, and the history of many Harlem schools combine to place a premium on the importance of offering a fully 'legitimate' education in a school to be respected as identical on paper (e.g., as to table of organization and curriculum) to successful schools. The result is a strong press, as Mary Haywood Metz (1989) put it, for a school that is identifiable as a 'real' school. This means it must be organizationally structured in the manner of 'real' school, with the same officials (e.g., a principal) and departments (as contrasted with units that are themed schools-within-a-school). And it must offer a program – a *full* program – of the traditional disciplines. Despite evidence that this sort of school and program do not well serve disadvantaged students (Lee *et al.* 1993, Nafriello *et al.* 1990, Metz 1989), ironically the press for these arrangements may be strongest in a community where such youngsters predominate. That the school *look like*, and *follow the script of* schools that are successful provides important affirmation in the face of doubtful status (Metz 1989). In fact, the greater the possibility of school or personal failure, the stronger may be the push for 'real' school as a source of personal reassurance and affirmation. If it may not show in the results, it must be plain in other ways that this is 'real' school.

Further intensifying the desire for 'real' school, the adoption of traditional structure and program are seen as the 'guarantor of equity' (Metz 1989: 86) assuring equal opportunity to those enrolled. Thus, making the school as much like successful traditional schools as possible is of considerable symbolic value. Pressures motivated by such a concern are especially heightened in contexts such as that of District 3, where 'uptown' schools and their patrons have consistently felt they were not getting the concern and attention of 'downtown' schools. For these several reasons, a school that resembles the successful conventional model is a cultural value in and of itself, quite apart from how effective it proves in educating children. And it has certainly appeared to function this way with a part of the Wadleigh constituency. Thus, parents who might be expected to be among the most committed champions of new forms of education, and to new ways to organize schools in the interests of making them more successful, become instead the defenders of the very arrangements that need replacing.

Can it be otherwise? As David Tyack and William Tobin conclude from their comparison of enduring versus non-enduring institutional forms (1994), reforms that depart from a community's notion of 'real school' heighten the need for local support and input. Such a need poses considerable challenge for those who subscribe to the teacher-design model of creating new schools, in preference to the stakeholder-design approach. And a situation like Wadleigh's posed particular problems with the stakeholder model, for example the constitution of the Task Force, its need for handicapping compromises among members, and the necessity of accommodating union interests. But if the community is to support instead of remaining skeptical of the new arrangements, ways must be found to make it aware of the need for departures from 'real school'. Moreover, to complicate matters still further, ways must be found of doing so without offending sensibilities that can be roused by claims about how bad things are. But if community members are not to acquire such knowledge as participants in the design process, then other meaningful ways for providing it must be launched early on. Otherwise, when their conceptions of 'real school' are violated, they are likely to become champions of the *status quo* rather than defenders of significant reform. And we will over and over again simply reinforce Nona Prestine's conclusion that 'the traditional form of schooling... [possesses]... an awesome capacity to wait out and wear out reformers' (1994).

References

COMMUNITY SCHOOL BOARD 3 (1992) Minutes of Public Meeting, October 28.

COMMUNITY SCHOOL BOARD 3 (1994) Minutes of Public Meeting, July 7.

CONCEPT PAPER – The Wadleigh Educational Community. A Community District/High School Collaborative (1989).

DIMAGGIO, P. J. and POWELL, W. W. (1983) The iron cage revisited: institutional isomorphism and collective rationality in organizational fields, *American Sociological Review*, 48, 147–160.

ELWELL, J. W. Jr (1993) Planning as organizing: the planning process used in the startup of the Wadleigh Alternative Arts Middle School. Unpublished PhD dissertation, Teachers College, Columbia University.

ELWELL, J. W. Jr (1994) Dreaming and the rebirth of Wadleigh. Unpublished MS.

'Establishment of the Wadleigh Secondary School'. Resolution [n.d.].Unpublished MS.

KAUFMAN, B. (1965) *Up the Down Staircase* (Englewood Cliffs: Prentice-Hall).

LEE, V., BRYK, A. and SMITH, J. (1993) The organization of effective secondary schools, in Linda Darling-Hammond (ed.), *Review of Research in Education*, 19, 171–268.

Memorandum of understanding: Wadleigh Secondary School. A Community District 3/High School Collaborative. n.d. (Although this document bears no date, it reportedly represents the fifth and operative version, which was formally adopted on July 2, 1992.)

METZ, M. H. (1990) Real school: a universal drama amid disparate experience, in D. E. Mitchell and M. E. Goertz (eds), *Education Politics for the New Century*. Twentieth Anniversary Yearbook of the Politics of Education Association (Philadelphia: Falmer), pp. 75–91.

MEYER, J. W. and ROWAN, B. (1977) Institutionalized organizations: formal structure as myth and ceremony, *American Journal of Sociology*, 83(2), 340–363.

NATRIELLO, G., McDILL, E. L. and PALLAS, A. M. (1990) *Schooling Disadvantaged Children: Racing Against Catastrophe* (New York: Teachers College Press).

PRESTINE, N. (in press) Sorting it out: a tentative analysis of essential school change efforts in Illinois, in S. Stringfield (ed.), *Essential Schools, Essential Reform? Reports from the Field* (Buffalo: Suny Press).

SOSTRE, L. (1991) Variations on the implementation of an organizing model: the Wadleigh Schools. Unpublished MS, March.

SOSTRE, L. (1992) A second look at the implementation of an organizing model in the Science and Technology Middle School. Unpublished MS, December.

TYACK, D. and TOBIN, W. (1994) The 'grammar' of schooling: why has it been so hard to change? *American Educational Research Journal*, 31(3), 453–479.

TASK FORCE (1989) *Wadleigh... in the Year 2000: A Community and School Respond.*

ZUCKER, L. G. (1987) Institutional theories of organization, *Annual Review of Sociology*, 13, 443–464.

8.   *Intentional transformation in a small school district:*
the Turner School Initiative

William B. Thomas, Kevin J. Moran and Jeremy Resnick

Introduction

In states such as Colorado, Connecticut, Kentucky, Maryland, and Pennsylvania, some legislators, school boards, and advocacy groups are excited about prospects of charter schools, privatization, vouchers and home rule legislation. These kinds of reforms seek to reinvigorate public education by introducing a competitive dynamic that grants local communities educational options. Since these reforms will likely threaten longstanding monopolies and create rivalries for the delivery of instructional services, resistance to restructuring reforms is certain to follow.

This is a case study of how elected school directors in Wilkinsburg, Pennsylvania came to the decision to take draconian measures to restructure one of the borough's three public elementary schools. Their restructuring model was so unique that it catapulted the district into the national limelight. In its decision to select and pave the way for the best provider of education to operate Turner Elementary School, the board served furlough warning notices to 30 teachers and eventually dismissed 24 of them. Vigorous discussions that ensued demonstrate how threatening and political these kinds of reforms are to various stakeholders. In Wilkinsburg, concerns driving the discourse included dissatisfaction with schooling outcomes; rising taxes to help finance a school system in decline; rights of teachers to job security; and prerogatives of local officials to seek, and state authorities to enable, educational reforms.

Theoretical framework

The board's precedent-setting action illustrates that one way of initiating change in an institution might be to introduce the process of radical shock. Through the introduction of this revolutionary procedure, 'major structural changes in institutions', according to March and Olsen (1989: 64), 'are made in hopes that such changes will destabilize political arrangements and force a permanent realignment of the existing system'. In addition, there are impediments to institutional change through this type of intentional transformation. One barrier, they maintain, is the political institution's efficiency of history. March and Olsen characterize efficiency of history as an incremental process of adapting to environmental changes by employing practices that resolve problems which institutions encounter and eliminating those practices that do not contribute to institutional equilibrium. They further theorize that institutions with historical efficiency

0268–0939/95 $12 · 00 © 1995 Taylor & Francis Ltd

– in our case the schools – preserve themselves partly by being resistant to many forms of change, partly by developing their criteria of appropriateness and success, resource distribution, and constitutional rules. Routines are sustained by being embedded in a structure of routines, and by socialization.

Impediments of adaptation notwithstanding, radical shock applied to schools might be a viable process for provoking discourse on institutional change; for demonstrating the urgency of problems needing attention; for forcing people to examine critically existing structures and to consider alternatives; and for exposing group interests as yet another barrier to change. Typically, initiatives to correct educational problems originate with a renegade building administrator or a visionary superintendent. They seldom emanate from school boards, taxpayers or teacher unions. In our case study, we demonstrate what might occur when citizens experience a crisis of confidence in the power and ability of schools to restructure themselves. It highlights the activities of a grassroots, reform-minded core of citizens, who coalesced to become agents for institutional reform and revitalization of an inert community, previously complacent about local educational matters.

A community in transition

Changing demographics in Wilkinsburg over the last 20 years have transformed this suburban community. They have brought social and economic problems similar to those that impinge upon inner cities throughout the United States. Among these are white flight; spiraling welfare rolls; increases in the number of aging citizens and single-parent families; the exodus of manufacturing jobs; a regressive tax structure, with soaring expenses to pay for truncated public services; increases in the numbers of absentee landlords whose rental properties are falling into disrepair; deteriorating and abandoned family homes on delinquent tax rolls, which become havens for drug users; and rising juvenile crime, substance abuse, and random violence. Rival gang shootings and competition for drug trade have had chilling effects upon all segments of this community. Law enforcement officials describe the current situation in terms such as: 'This is a more violent generation'; 'Life is taken for granted'; and 'Kids do not believe that they will live beyond the ages of 23 or 24 years'.

In 1980, Willkinsburg was a community of 23,669 residents, 61% of whom were white and 37% were African-American. By 1990, there was an 11% decrease in its total population, with a 32% decrease in its white and a 27% increase in its African-American residents. The results of these demographic shifts over the decade were a population comprising 46% whites and 53% African-Americans. In addition, patterns of emigration contributed to a housing vacancy rate of 13%, with 56% of these residences having been built prior to 1939 (Health and Welfare Planning Association, 1983, University of Microfilms, 1993).

Contrasting statistics conceal the immediacy of a crisis in this community. On the one hand, the percentages of residents employed as professionals and managers increased between 1980 and 1990 from 27% to 32%, while those in skilled and semi-skilled positions decreased from 8% to 5% and 11% to 8%, respectively. As the region underwent shifts in its production, dramatic changes occurred in the percentages of residents employed in manufacturing industries, dropping from 19% to 9%. Levels of educational attainment rose concurrently. The percentage of residents 25 years and older with a high school education increased from 71% to 81%, as the percentage of college graduates increased from 19% to 23%.

On the other hand, the borough's level of poverty is at 65% above the average for Allegheny County, rising from 14% in 1980 to 17% in 1990. Police records show that juvenile crime increased by 22% from 1991 to 1993, averaging 22·7 offences monthly. In this community, recognized for having 'a church on every corner', offences ranged from homicide, rape, and assaults to burglary, arson, and auto theft. These statistics are indicative of a growing community-wide malaise rooted in urban abandonment, changes in social values, and withdrawal in social relations.

Pawn shops, second-hand clothing stores, and quick check-cashing establishments have replaced long-standing family businesses. Lower middle class white flight has left the school district with a 51% pupil population that receives Aid for Dependent Children, in contrast with an 8% state average. The cost per pupil in this district is $7,368, which places it in the highest 20% of the 501 districts in Pennsylvania. The local district bears responsibility for paying 55% of school costs, underwritten with property taxes. An eroding tax base, resulting from tax delinquency, deserted properties and state cut-backs on special education allotments, places an inordinate strain on limited resources. The 120·5 mills school tax, in a borough already in financial difficulties, is the highest rate in the county.

As members of the numerical racial majority in this community, African-American children comprise 96% of the public school population. The United States census shows that, in 1990, 19% of school-age children had opted out of the public schools to attend private institutions. By 1992, this number had risen to 23%. Less than 10% of the teaching corps reside in Wilkinsburg. All of these statistics give rise to citizens' crisis of confidence in institutions, such as politics, public services, the contemporary family structure, the police, and the public schools. When asked in a survey about reasons for residents not sending their children to the high school, one citizen sardonically responded: 'They want their children to read'.

A profile of school achievement at Turner Elementary School, targeted for restructuring, shows that 68·7%, 67·5%, and 72·1% in Grades 4, 5, and 6, respectively, scored in the lower-middle and bottom quartiles in reading on the Comprehensive Test of Basic Skills in 1993. In mathematics, 70·6%, 67·4%, and 67·5% scored in the lower-middle and bottom quartiles. These figures contrast with other Pennsylvanian schools, which show that only 32·5%, 33·1%, and 32·8% of the 4th, 5th, and 6th graders scored in the lower-middle and bottom quartiles in reading, and 33·8%, 33·7%, and 32·6%, respectively, in math. Low achievement in elementary schools has had a residual effect in high schools. Statistics demonstrate that as students proceed through the school system, their achievement levels remain below national norms. While an individual student or two may score 1000 on the Scholastic Aptitude Test, typically, the combined SAT average score for Wilkinsburg students is below 700, more than 250 points below the nation's average.

In response to these deteriorating conditions, local educational policy makers and analysts concur that systemic changes are imperative. One school board member commented: 'The bottom line is that things are terrible. You can't blame it on the teachers. There are a million different things that are responsible for the situation we're in. And if that's the case, we have to try a different approach' (Haynes 1995a). Recognizing that Wilkinsburg teachers have a difficult educational task, given the social conditions that impinge upon some pupils' lives, educational policy analyst William W. Cooley concluded: 'What *can* be said is that the educational program at Wilkinsburg is inadequate for the task it has. It is clearly possible for children from poverty homes to learn the basic skills, but it cannot be done by business as usual. It is going to require a greater effort, and different strategies than those currently in place' [emphasis in original] (Cooley 1994:5).

Citizens unite for action

In June 1992, a small contingent of citizens became outraged by prospects of a 28% property tax increase to finance a 21% teacher pay rise over a three-year period. They summoned homeowners to a school board meeting to protest the high cost of educational inadequacy in their schools. Their fliers, posted on telephone poles and distributed door-to-door, decried the shrinking numbers of high school graduates and the 2·7 grade point average (C +) for the graduating class valedictorian. Responding to a jeering overflow crowd in the high school auditorium, the board capitulated and lowered the proposed tax hike to 14%. Organizers then recruited homeowners to become more involved in the local politics of school reform. The Wilkinsburg Citizens for Action (WCA) became yet another of the 100 *ad hoc* citizen advocacy groups in Pennsylvania rising up to challenge the educational *status quo* (Temple 1993).

This grassroots organization drew largely from homeowners in Blackridge, Beacon Hill and Regent Square, enclaves of citizens from the professional and managerial classes. Shaken out of their past complacency, members of the new WCA met in July and formed three committees to investigate alternatives to the existing structure. The legal committee comprised lawyers residing in the borough. They explored the legal ramifications of secession from the borough, a tax revolt and mergers with contiguous school districts. Their investigations, however, uncovered state laws forbidding neighbourhoods' seceding from their community if abandonment created further financial hardship for the remaining community members. Other state codes frustrated merger attempts. For example, a majority of Wilkinsburg's and the receiving community's taxable inhabitants needed to sign a petition favouring such a transfer of territory (*PA School Code*, 24 P.S. Section 2–242). Given the borough's notoriety for gang activity and declining status, community members held little faith in their neighbouring districts' willingness to receive Wilkinsburg's youth. The legal committee, therefore, recommended working to change the schools within the existing educational structure. It then disbanded.

During this period Wilkinsburg had no newspaper, and the Pittsburgh newspapers were on strike. In response, WCA's second committee – communications – established a newsletter to articulate the mission of the organization and to keep citizens apprised of school and community developments.

Of the three committees, education had the greatest impact upon impending school reforms. A few of its members accepted an invitation from the superintendent to visit the schools. When they visited the high school, their observations verified suspicions about conditions in the district. They found classes with low teacher-student ratios and high absenteeism among students and teachers. Teachers relayed to the residents their concerns about the 'lack of consistent support structures to deal with the ongoing problems of discipline and truancy as well as the ever but equally important programmes dealing with motivation for learning and self esteem' (Tkacik 1992). In response to what they witnessed, the citizen group called for a major overhaul of educational programmes.

Twenty-one citizens, including businessmen and women, psychologists, artisans, public school teachers, homemakers, and professors of education convened as a working group to press for changes in the Wilkinsburg schools. Unlike many citizen advocacy groups that limit their energy to issues like smaller class size, teacher salaries and more field trips, the education committee pulled together parents and non-parents to build some community knowledge about education reform and restructuring initiatives. Representatives of very diverse neighbourhoods came together to find common ground on educational issues. They discussed fundamental changes during regular meetings, and read the national research on school restructuring, including Edward Fiske's *Smart Schools, Smart Kids* (1991), James Comer's *School Power* (1993), and Theodore Sizer's *Horace's School* (1992). Having studied reform possibilities, the group asked themselves, 'Why can't we have these good programs in Wilkinsburg?' They invited to their meetings the local state representative (who also chaired the state educational committee), the school superintendent and the coordinator of the state-mandated strategic planning committee. Several Wilkinsburg teachers, curious about the group's activities, attended a meeting.

Members of this committee were optimistic about the possibility that local school districts could make substantive changes, since Pennsylvania's Democratic Governor Robert Casey had relaxed some restrictive state education requirements. Opportunity for local school districts to redefine graduation requirements, to develop innovative assessment techniques and to involve the community energized the WCA. They jockeyed for membership on the district's strategic planning committee. To their dismay, they soon discovered, as one committee member commented, 'The mills of the gods of educational change grind slowly'. At times, planning seemed encumbered by various issues that arose: a breakdown in the level of community trust in teachers' willingness to explore reforms broadly and to meet during summer months; teacher requests for compensation to attend committee meetings; community complaints about a templated approach to restructuring; contention over committee membership criteria; and complaints that the WCA undermined the planning process by holding 'secret meetings' outside of scheduled regularly strategic planning sessions.

Meaningful strategic planning requires a school district to inform the planning committee about the state of its educational programme. This information includes budgetary, achievement, instructional, enrollment and demographic data. When shared with a vocal and impatient wing of the strartegic planning committee, these data validated their criticisms of the existing structure and a need for change. The dismal picture which the data painted spawned heated verbal confrontations. Teachers blamed uninvolved parents, unmotivated and transient pupils, and ineffective administrators for educational decline in the district. Citizens challenged school employees, asking how long they had been aware of student low achievement, and what innovations they had pursued to remedy it.

Occasionally, these community members demanded to be included on planning subcommittees, usually reserved for the professional staff. They hoped to oversee the planning and progress of these working groups. As one citizen advocate exclaimed at a meeting, 'Look, let's get it out on the table. We don't trust you and you don't trust us'. In the view of some WCA members, the most frustrating aspects of the planning process lay in their perceptions that some teachers resisted any educational innovation that was university-based, was rooted in educational literature, or was without a five-year track record. To WCA members, opposition to change signalled an institutional response toward maintaining the *status quo*. Sceptical at one point about educational planning, a teacher suggested, 'Let's continue to do what we are now doing, but call it something different'.

After one year, the WCA education committee became disillusioned with the pace of reform through strategic planning. They shifted their focus from a participatory role in strategic planning to one allowing members to gain a firmer grip on the change process and its outcomes. WCA sought control of the school board. To this end, they recruited from among their membership a slate of candidates to fill four seats on the board. In the 1993 primaries, their candidates ran unopposed. The 1,307 voters elected an accountant, a businessman, an engineer and a bank employee. A fifth candidate, a real estate developer who had lost in the election, was appointed to a vacated seat. The citizen group believed that with this victory, they now could hasten the tempo of educational change in Wilkinsburg.

The new board takes charge

By now, those who had participated in the early tax revolt and were still involved with the schools as either board members or strategic planners were no longer concerned about rising taxes. Nor were they philosophically wedded to the promises of school choice and competition as means to desired educational ends. Instead, the more expedient problem confronting the new board was obtaining quality education for the children of Wilkinsburg. According to the school board president, Ernest Neal Ramsey 'A stronger school system would augment efforts in Wilkinsburg to control its crime problems, revitalize its economic base, and shore up the housing market . . . if we don't improve the quality of the education we give our children, we have no future' (Frolik 1994).

Despite some citizen discontent with the process, long-range planning successfully brought consensus on a mission statement for the school district and several high priority goals. One of these priority goals was to 'restructure the entire educational program'. The pace at which this restructuring would move was frustrating to those who were initially optimistic about educational change in the district. Some new board members realized that traditional kinds of reforms by unions and school administrators in other districts were less likely to succeed in Wilkinsburg. At times, the bureaucratic infrastructure had undermined the reform initiatives. Nevertheless, the board forged ahead, advancing its agenda to restructure schools. In doing so, the board went beyond the boundaries of their prescribed role as educational policy-makers. They began to fill a void resulting from the Pennsylvania state legislature's failure to create alternative school regulations. Risking a protracted and costly court battle, the board sought a 'shock' that might force Wilkinsburg teachers and administrators to behave differently.

The new board's first major undertaking, therefore, was to apply what members had gleaned from their study group. They hired a consultant to devise a strategy that would institute a school of excellence in Wilkinsburg by 1995–96, with no increase in the annual per pupil allotment. Using a high risk-high gain strategy, the board issued a request for proposals (RFP) to any organization interested in school restructuring. In doing so, they hoped that their own teachers might accept this opportunity to revamp educational programmes. The RFP gave the successful respondents the option of either using the existing Wilkinsburg teacher corps, represented by their union, or hiring its own teachers at the prevailing union wage scale. Under the second option, the provider would give reasonable consideration to any current Wilkinsburg teacher interested in working with the provider without loss of pension or seniority.

The board selected Turner Elementary School, with a 99% African-American student population, as the initial target of reforms, since they felt that chances for success there were greatest. Turner was an ideal site when compared with the borough's two other elementary schools. According to the board's president, it employed fewer teachers. In the event that the provider used the second option, and the union sued, a successful lawsuit challenging teacher furloughs might be less costly to the district in back wages. Turner's relatively low enrollment of 375 students and location on an attractive landsite with a large playing field were also appealing features.

Sending out the RFP was a patent declaration that some board members believed the existing educational programme 'is not delivering the goods' (Haynes 1994). Brian Magan, Vice President of the school board commented: 'We have to do a better job of preparing these children for life after school' (Haynes 1995b). The newly hired consultant stated: 'Wilkinsburg is now saying, "We've got these kids and we just don't seem to be able to do what's needed, and we have to go out and find someone who can"' (Haynes 1994).

Reinventing school

On 23 April 1994, eleven potential contractors attended an informational meeting held at Turner Elementary. Five submitted proposals, which a consultant from Minnesota reviewed. This evaluator brought an extensive background in redesigning schools for improved educational outcomes and in the rating of educational proposals submitted to foundations for funding. By September, Alternative Public Schools (APS) was the top contender. APS, headed by two businessmen from Nashville, Tennessee, received very high marks for its accountability, parental involvement, innovation and assessment plans. The APS proposal called for an eleven-month, 212-day school calendar. Despite the school board's request that they operate the school with the existing workforce, APS insisted on recruiting and hiring its own teachers and principal. In addition, it promised to raise achievement test scores 5% after two years, 7·5% after three years, and 10% after four years. To accomplish these outcomes, APS proposed to the board a five year contract, unless terminated for non-performance. The student body would consist of the same students attending Turner on the date of the board's contracting with APS, including exceptional students. Student vacancies would be filled by lottery from those applying to attend. The cost per pupil in the first year would equal the $5,400 spent on those enrolled in the other two schools, and would increase by $100 annually over the five years of the contract. APS proposed also to meet all federal and state standards and to employ qualified professionals. An interesting accountability feature was a promise to escrow all money except out-of-pocket expenses and money for capital improvements until the specified academic and non-academic goals of the restructuring plan were achieved.

These contract managers seemed confident that they could meet the terms of the proposal. A spokesperson told the *New York Times* 'Our contention is not that a private business can always run schools better. All sorts of organizations could put together a separate legal entity to manage schools. What we do believe is that if you put together a team of people who share a common philosophy and are accountable for what they do, you can deliver a higher quality of education' (Applebome 1995).

On the surface, APS brought no experience in educational contract management. They had tried unsuccessfully to negotiate a similar concept with the Nashville Public Schools. For Wilkinsburg, they hired the services of an African-American principal, Elaine Mosley, of the Corporate Community School in inner-city Chicago to direct the tailor-made educational planning process. They created an instructional design team, including three principals from Pittsburgh elementary schools which had demonstrated success in educating urban African-American students.

Not surprisingly, there were flurries of rumours, accusations and concerns, including those that the board was going to bankrupt the community to underwrite the high costs of imminent lawsuits; that Turner would become a Catholic school; that the board only sought to repatriate the white professional class to the school district; that board members acted in the interest of financial gains through increased real estate value; that a high achieving elementary school would create an educational élite; that the company would abandon its commitment when profits declined, leaving the district in turmoil; that the move would destroy public schools; and that the board desired to break the teacher union.

To allay community suspicions of an outside agency operating a public school for profit, the communications committee of the WCA resurfaced. It distributed a newsletter contrasting the APS proposal with the current contractual arrangement with the local teacher union. It highlighted the lack of accountability in the union's contract. It reiterated the need for the community to focus on quality education for Wilkinsburg children and charged that 'the main concern of the WEA, PSEA, and NEA is their jobs – not our children'.

Interestingly, neither the board nor the teacher union seemed to have generated an outcry among parents of children enrolled at Turner Elementary. Parents have been conspicuously reserved in their support of or opposition to the initiative. One local resident and school district employee, however, observed:

> The bottom line is jobs. They want their paychecks raised, they want, they want, they want. I am a taxpayer and I'm an employee, so I am between the devil and the deep blue sea. But if I go to the store and want a loaf of bread, I can buy Italian bread or German bread or white bread, whatever kind of bread I want. Here . . . there's no selection. You've got what's here and most people don't think that's good enough. (Applebome, 1995:26)

Teacher union response to the Turner Initiative

News of the impending contract management of the Turner School aroused national attention. Understandably, the greatest opposition to the Turner Initiative came from the Wilkinsburg Educational Association (WEA), and its parent organizations, the Pennsylvania State Educational Association (PSEA) and the National Educational Association (NEA). When the board invited the WEA to participate in the competition for management of Turner, the association's leadership declined. The union's chief negotiator and a teacher at Turner, Barbara Bell, viewed the offer and the process as illegal. She asserted: 'This has nothing to do with education. It has to do with union busting, plain and simple' (Applebome 1995). In a news release to the press, PSEA protested vigorously that

> The Turner Initiative is in violation of existing laws, Department of Education regulations, and standards applicable in Pennsylvania. For the Wilkinsburg School Board to attempt implementation of this proposal may increase local tax levels, with outside private concerns taking the profits . . . [the union] will advocate strenuously to protect its collective bargaining contract, the rights of students, parents, and taxpayers. It is important for the WEA-PSEA-NEA, as well as support staff, parent organizations, and students, that control of our schools remain within the Wilkinsburg family. [WEA-PSEA-NEA] will oppose the Turner Initiative and consider alternate activities to meet the educational concerns and benefit all students. (PSEA 1994:1–2).

In this vein, WEA and the University of Pittsburgh's School of Education entered an agreement to submit an alternative to the competitive bidding for contract management of Turner School. A primary consideration was the accomplishment of the board's achievement goals using the existing teachers at Turner. WEA and the School of Education proposed to establish a professional development school in which student teachers and the existing faculty would share their expertise. The plan focused on intensive reading in primary grades, ongoing formative assessments and a curriculum to address the diverse needs of students in a multicultural society. It would draw upon community organizations with expertise in health and social work and would become an extension of a collaborative between the university and the Wilkinsburg School District, begun in 1992. A major feature of the restructuring would be the establishment of the Project Read/Inquiring School model, emphasizing high level thinking and problem-solving. The plan promised increased parental involvement and organizational change at the classroom level to facilitate a sense of belonging for at-risk students (Bean 1994).

The Associate Dean of the School of Education announced to the press

> The Pitt project is not a proposal . . . instead, the teachers and the university view it as a plan . . . the difference is, we are talking about the process where [Pitt] would be working with the teachers to collaborate and plan how they can change a school. We're not interested in taking over a school. We're not interested in running a school. We're intersted in working with the community to change the school.

The Dean projected that the collaboration would cost an additional $200,000 annually for the first five years. To quell community concerns about higher taxes, he reported that the university and the teachers' union would seek additional funding to underwrite the project.

When WEA and the University of Pittsburgh presented its proposal at a curriculum meeting of the board, some citizens expressed scepticism. One asserted, 'I have a difficult time with this, considering the history of the district. The teachers at Turner are all of a sudden interested in this. They could have done this earlier. What guarantee do we have from Pitt and the teachers to make it work?' (Houser 1994).

The board rejected the WEA–Pitt proposal, characterizing it as 'less than what we expected'. When the board requested further elaboration of the plan, they received no response from the union. In early March 1995, the school board offered to withdraw the RFP if the teachers' union agreed to match the APS proposal and to institute a merit pay system based on pupil achievement (Haynes 1995c). The board president asserted 'We are trying to bargain in good faith and we are trying to afford our teachers the opportunity to be involved in revitalizing the educational pursuits in Wilkinsburg'. The board's proposal also called for a 1994–95 school year wage freeze and a 4% retroactive raise for the next two years, but only if student achievement increased by 4% and 6% on standardized tests during those years.

The union rejected the board's offer and sought a temporary injunction to stop the board from contracting out instructional services and dismissing the teachers. Simultaneously, the board forged ahead, encouraged by activities at the state capitol.

State sanctioned reforms

The 1994 elections were a clarion call for reforms in the state and the nation. In his inaugural address, Pennsylvania Republican Governor Thomas Ridge pledged to remove existing barriers to quality education. He promised parents more control over where they sent their children to school and the type of education they would receive when they enrolled.

On 8 May 1995, Ridge visited Wilkinsburg and met with school board members, parents, students, and teachers. His conversation with a parent from Turner impressed upon him the need for educational reforms. He recounted her comments:

People talk about empowering me as a parent, and they say we need to work within the educational establishment to improve education. I think around here what they want me to do is to walk the halls as a monitor or hand out lunches. I want my child to have a better education than I did. They are not getting it here. I just want some options. (Pennsylvania Public Broadcast System 1995)

Following his visit, Ridge told an audience: 'It's time to change the existing structure, and people are resistant all over the place. I understand that. It's predictable human nature. All I'm saying is it's not about school boards, it's not about teachers' unions and it's not about budgets. It's not about anything other than children' (Liss 1995:5).

Within the first 100 days of his administration, he proposed to the legislature a plan for tuition vouchers, charter schools and a plan which would allow school boards to hire contract managers for public schools. State legislators, however, eliminated the contract management clause from the bill and voted against the remaining proposed legislation. They yielded to reform opponents who described the reforms as too costly and too detrimental to the well-being of public schools as they have been known. Legislative disapproval notwithstanding, the governor was resolute in his support of the Turner School Initiative.

Ridge permitted newly-appointed Secretary of Education Eugene Hickok to grant the Wilkinsburg school district's formal request to restructure its school. This endorsement seemed to remove any obstacle to the district's contracting with APS. Hickok wrote: 'This request is granted because I believe the change proposed by the Wilkinsburg School District will result in a more efficient and effective educational program for the children who attend the Turner Elementary School. The school district's statistics demonstrate that children are not receiving a quality education'. The secretary was particularly drawn to the opportunity for a longer school day and an expanded school year, the creation of programmes before and after school to help working families, and an increased focus on personalized instruction. As to the question of the legality of restructuring that would furlough teachers, the secretary of education cited the *Pennsylvania School Code* that grants school boards permission to 'suspend the necessary numbers of professional employees' in order to 'alter or curtail educational programs' should the secretary find that a school district's request is educationally sound and beneficial to students (Section 1124.2).

Commenting on this decision, the governor's press secretary asserted: 'Fundamental school reform has been a top priority for Governor Ridge [who] said that parents and their elected school leaders should have more options including privatization, as they try to improve their schools. Improving schools for children is far more important than protecting institutions and the *status quo*' (PR Newswire, 1995).

Outcomes of litigation

Between March and July of 1995, the board, the teacher union, and the State Department of Education were embroiled in court battles over the legality of teacher dismissals and the use of public funds to contract manage a school. On 17 July 1995, the Commonwealth Court of Pennsylvania voted 2–1 to uphold a lower court injunction against the operation of the new Turner School. Despite the ruling, Turner Elementary School opened on 5 September under the new management of APS, as the nation's first public, entrepreneurial contract-managed school that replaced existing teachers with its own teaching staff.

Discussion

This case study has shown how a citizens' group, dissatisfied with educational decline in their community, coalesced as advocates of institutional reform. Citizens had relied upon the traditional power and authority of schools to educate youth in this community, as schools had done under more stable conditions and times. Alarmed that children were not achieving under a *laissez-faire* educational management system and frustrated by the seemingly slow pace of change to remediate this, reformers sought and explored alternative paradigms. To effect the desired structural changes in their educational system, they first studied the problems confounding educational attainment in the district. When strategic planning negotiations became mired in suspicion and mistrust, this group gained control of the school board. Successful candidates, perceiving how children suffered in the system, pledged an end to their miseducation. They chided the administrative and teacher corps for seeing educational problems but doing nothing substantive about them as the system declined. To these citizens, the time seemed propitious for reforms that challenged existing institutional structures and laws that bolstered a failing school bureaucracy. Versed in educational reform literature and sustained by a belief that reforms are indeed possible and attainable, the board then tested the viability of alternatives which had not been used heretofore in Pennsylvania. Namely, they introduced reform by a process of radical shock. The board hoped to force a permanent realignment of a system which graduates, for a host of reasons, only about 25% of the number of pupils who enter the first grade. By hiring contract managers to operate a school with a new teaching staff, leading to the furlough of 24 elementary school teachers, the board destabilized a political arrangement between itself and the teachers' union.

These actions illustrate first that schools are political institutions with efficient histories. As such, the success or failure of intentional transformation initiatives within these institutions is inextricably tied to state and local politics. Second, these linkages, at times, frustrate reforms. Structural change, from the perspective of reformers, required something more than revitalizing the curriculum, adding new courses, infusing more technology, or 'doing the same thing but calling it something different'. It demanded the reshaping of structural boundaries and reinterpretation of rules by principal actors. However, without constituencies advocating change and armed with the necessary social capital, innovations tend to be implemented in ways which leave schools functioning as they always have. State laws may also frustrate reforms while protecting the interests of those who support the *status quo* and who have the most to lose under any major re-structuring.

Status quo proponents in larger cities can usually withstand, without feeling threatened, small numbers of actors who do not play by the rules. But what happens in smaller communities which seek major changes that challenge institutional arrangements and where there is less tolerance for citizen-generated reforms? In these communities, reform advocates may be dismissed as radicals, troublemakers, outsiders or interlopers. To the extent that school districts are inextricably tied to other entrenched bureaucracies with similar efficient histories, we can expect the effects of radical shock to be mitigated, thwarting institutional reforms to attenuate the plight of poor and working class African-American children. Perhaps at this historical juncture, the Turner story shows that this is the case even when an elected school board leads the effort at meaningful change.

References

APPLEBOME, P. (1995) Private company given power to pick teachers. *New York Times*, 9 April, p. 26.

BEAN, R. (1994) Conceptual plan for school restructuring in Wilkinsburg. Proposal submitted to the Wilkinsburg Board of Education, 29 August.

COMER, J. (1993) *School Power: Implications of an Intervention Project* (New York: Free).

COOLEY, W. W. (1994) The Regional Workforce: Asset or Liability? Position paper no. 19, Pennsylvania Educational Policy Studies.

FISKE, E. B. (1991) *Smart Schools, Smart Kids: Why Do Some Schools Work?* (New York: Simon & Schuster).

FROLIK, J. (1994) Pittsburgh area board would revitalize school. *Cleveland Plain Dealer*, 31 May, p. A1; 4.

HAYNES, M. L. (1994) Public School May Go Private. *Pittsburgh Post-Gazette*, 24 March, p. A1; 11.

HAYNES, M. L. (1995a) The revolution in education. *Pittsburgh Post-Gazette*, 19 March, p. A1; 14.

HAYNES, M. L. (1995b) Turner plan is termed righteous. *Pittsburgh Post-Gazette*, 16 February, p. A1; 14.

HAYNES, M. L. (1995c) Wilkinsburg school board offers to forgo private firm. *Pittsburgh Past-Gazette*, 3 March, p. B1; 6.

HEALTH AND WELFARE PLANNING ASSOCIATION (1983) *1984 Community Profile*, Pittsburgh: Health and Welfare Planning Association.

HOUSER, M. (1994) Pitt presents Wilkinsburg plan. *Tribune-Review*, 30 August, p. A9.

LISS, S. (1995) Ridge set to present educational reform plan. *Tribune-Review*, 9 May, p. A1; 5.

MARCH, J. E. and OLSEN, J. P. (1989) *Rediscovering Institutions: The Organizational Basis of Politics* (New York: Free).

PENNSYLVANIA PUBLIC BROADCAST SYSTEM (1995) Talk to the Governor. 15 June.

PENNSYLVANIA STATE EDUCATION ASSOCIATION (1994) Wilkinsburg Education Association: Turner Initiative response. News Release, 29 March.

PR NEWSWIRE (1995) Hickok clears way for Wilkinsburg privatization, 5 July.

SIZER, T. R. (1992) *Horace's School: Redesigning the American High School* (Boston: Houghton Mifflin).

TEMPLE, J. (1993) Taxpayers fighting mad over teacher salaries. *Tribune-Review*, 21 November, p. A1; 10.

TKACIK, D. (1992) Letter to superintendent and school board, 24 June.

UNIVERSITY MICROFILMS (1993) *1990 Census of Population and Housing*, Pennsylvania, Wilkinsburg Borough, Summary tape file 3A on CD-ROM.

9. *How the state should 'break up' the big-city district*

Ted Kolderie

The impulse to do something radical about the big urban school district is now visible in cities all across the country. Sometimes the impulse comes from within the board. More and more frequently, however, it is coming from the state. Witness these examples:

- In May 1995, the Illinois Legislature removed the Chicago board of education and its superintendent and gave the mayor sweeping powers to change and improve the schools, free of many of the usual constraints. The law also strengthened the local school councils. The legislature created the councils in 1988, at the urging of neighbourhood groups and business/civic organizations and over the objections of the board, superintendent and union.
- In New Jersey, the state has taken over school systems in Jersey City and Paterson and will now, it appears, take over Newark. Illinois has taken over East St Louis. In Ohio, the federal court has ordered the state to take over Cleveland.
- Baltimore hired a contract manager for a part of its system. Hartford has put its entire system out to private contract management. In Minneapolis, the board has gone to contract for 'district leadership services.'
- Bills to 'break up' Los Angeles Unified have so far been resisted successfully. Inside the district, the debate now is whether the district should continue to resist or should come forward with a plan of its own to pre-empt state action. In Milwaukee the resignation of Superintendent Howard Fuller revived the idea of a break up among some legislators. In Minnesota Representative John Sarna sponsored a bill to divide Minneapolis into wedges and to annex each wedge to an adjacent suburb. The Minneapolis district would dissolve.
- In Boston, the schools were moved back into the framework of general local government.
- The Pittsburgh area is debating a plan for a countywide board with oversight responsibility for autonomous schools.
- In New York City, the chancellor and local community districts are creating small, new high schools working without legislation and around the bureaucracy.

This activity is not the product of coincidence. There are strong and widespread feelings that the big-city district is too large and too bureaucratic, itself an obstacle to the improvement of learning. Too much has changed: the city; children and the youth culture, the economy, parents and technology. New models of organization are appearing in almost every other sector of society. People no longer believe that the corporate-public-utility model – a unitary organization that hires everyone and owns everything – is the best or the right way to organize public education in the city.

0268–0939/95 $12 · 00 © 1995 Taylor & Francis Ltd

Local elected officials increasingly call for change. Problems in the schools create problems for them. Mayors know that if costs drive the school tax rate higher and if families lose confidence in the public school system, their cities are in trouble. Under present arrangements most mayors cannot much affect the schools' costs or quality. They have found that a new board or superintendent makes little difference. Increasingly, they are looking for radical change. Their growing involvement increases pressure on the state to act.

The search for a new model

Initial efforts to restructure the big-city district were not radical. These efforts assumed the corporate model, but brought in someone new to run it, or tried to reduce its size, or change its organization. Not surprisingly, these efforts have not been particularly successful. Only recently has the discussion begun to challenge the traditional model itself.

'Reform' within the traditional model

The first reform impulse is often to change the people – to fire the superintendent or to elect a new 'reform' board. Legislative reforms alter school district representation from at-large to district elections (or vice versa) in the hope that this will produce 'better people.'

It looks radical when the state intervenes to turn over the district to the general city government or to take the district over itself. But this approach does not necessarily change the basic model either. Asked what it meant to take over Jersey City, a state official said, 'We sent in four people.'

The idea of breaking up the district geographically sounds radical. Again, however, the traditional model remains. The corporation becomes smaller, but smaller is not necessarily more responsive. There are also significant barriers to this approach. Cutting up a city into small pieces would create new fiscal, social and racial disparities. This approach would likely fail on equity grounds, either politically or in the courts.

The old appeal for fewer mandates ('give us the money and leave us alone') recently has become a cry for 'home rule.' Texas may try such an approach under pending legislation. It is not clear, however, that this approach will move districts out of the corporate model. It will simply allow those corporations to operate free of regulations. The model is essentially the same as an unregulated public utility. Whether it will work is not clear either.

An alternative: breaking up the old model non-geographically

The other idea is a non-geographic breakup of the school corporation. The board of education would lose the monopoly to own and run the learning-company. More than one organization could be operating public schools in the city.

Educators have been talking for some years now about the school becoming the unit of improvement, and the idea of autonomous schools is implicit in school-based management. There is broad agreement on this as a goal. 'A system of schools,' some are now saying, 'rather than a school system.' It is essentially a contract model.

Board, administration and union, however, are not always eager to make a real delegation of meaningful authority to the school. And schools do not always want the problems that come with making their own decisions. If the Legislature presses, the organizations in K–12 resist. 'Leave it an option. We're not ready yet. We need more time, more training,' they said in Minnesota this year.

When a board of education moves to become a buyer rather than a provider of educational services, the resistance can be fierce. In Wilkinsburg, Pennsylvania, the reform board elected in 1993 decided to bring in an outside firm to run Turner Elementary School. The board concluded that improvement required accountability and that accountability required the board to have some distance from the operation of the school. The President of the National Education Association went to Wilkinsburg (population 20,000) to try to back the board away from its decision. The board voted to proceed. The battle continues in the courts, in the legislature and in the campaign for board seats this fall. Similar battles occurred in Chelsea, Baltimore and Hartford.

For a district organized as a corporate public utility change is simply unnecessary. It is unrealistic and unproductive to exhort – or try to order – an organization to undertake difficult and stressful work that it does not want to do and that it knows it does not have to do. To achieve change and improvement, a different model is needed – one that makes performance necessary.

Talking about a different and better model is not enough. The critical discussion is not about what ought to be, but how to make change happen.

The 'challenge and response' strategy for change

One approach is for the state to act directly and simply put the new model into law. An alternative is for the state to act indirectly by making the new model available for the district and giving the district a reason to adopt the model in its own interest.

The first approach is easy to understand. The second requires some explanation. Dan Loritz, deputy chief of staff for Minnesota Governor Rudy Perpich from 1987 to 1991, put it this way:

> Over the years the state tried everything. We tried money. We tried mandates. We tried demonstrations in the hope good practice would spread. Nothing really worked. We concluded the state can't 'make em' improve. So we decided we'd try giving districts a reason. [Under the strategy evolving in Minnesota since 1985] nobody will have to do anything. The state will simply make it possible for people to offer new and different and hopefully better programs and the state will make it possible for students to go these programs if they wish. If you as a district want to add new and better programs, that's great: We hope you will. If you don't that's all right, too: Nobody has to do anything. But there will be consequences now, for what you do and don't do.

This is the first part of the indirect strategy: to give the district a reason to change. The second part is to design the new and different model the district can adopt when it decides to move.

The challenge: creating the pressure

The most effective way to create the pressure is to withdraw the district's exclusive franchise to offer public education in the city. The state does this by chartering other public bodies to run – or to sponsor teachers, parents or others to run – public schools that students can attend without charge.

The state can withdraw the exclusive franchise in several ways. Minnesota currently uses three. First, it makes the schools of other districts available to students through open enrollment. Second, it lets students in the 11th and 12th grades finish high school in a college or university. Third, it says a district, the state board of education (or, as of 1995, a public post secondary institution) may sponsor teachers to set up and run a public school of choice.

The major education organizations have resisted the charter laws, or at least strong versions that create real dynamics. In legislatures this year they supported the charter idea only if it occurs within the traditional model – with only the local board authorized to sponsor a school and with the schools remaining a part of, or the teachers remaining employees of, the local district. When a state does enact a charter law that contains real dynamics – providing for an alternate sponsor and for the school to be a discrete entity with its own teachers – the behavior of districts begins to change. It is easy to see why.

Before, if teachers or parents came in with a proposal and the district refused, that was the end of it. (The school district, as American Federation of Teachers President Albert Shanker said in Minnesota in 1988, has been 'an organization that can take its customers for granted.') With a strong charter law on the books, the district's rejection of a proposal will not be the end of it. The charter law provides a way for teachers, parents and students to get the programs they want within the framework of public education.

When this pressure exists, districts become noticeably responsive to proposals for change. In Minnesota and Colorado, local school boards that earlier had resisted proposals by teachers and parents suddenly were offering to work with these groups. Less than a year after Massachusetts enacted its charter law, the Boston schools came up with an in-district charter program of their own. High schools in Minnesota began offering more college-level programs once the state challenged the district's ability to take the students for granted.

Attitudes have changed as well. In 1993, the Colorado legislature passed a charter law over the opposition of the state association of school boards. This defeat caused the director of the association to reflect; a few months later, in his column in the association magazine, Randy Quinn suggested to members that the results might be a blessing in disguise. If the board were a purchaser rather than an owner/operator of schools, he argued, its ability to provide a quality program of education for the community would enlarge greatly. 'I began to see it during the legislative debate', he said.

A district that decides it wants to change finds itself restricted. Within the traditional model, it is hard to make the changes that improvement requires, and the district itself cannot change the model.

Cities have long had the freedom to choose the plan of organization they prefer for their municipal government or to write a 'home rule' plan of their own. This flexibility is not available to school districts. There are no optional forms and there is no concept of 'home rule.'

This is a serious policy omission. The state should make available an alternate form of organization that a district can adopt if it wishes.

The response: voluntary divestiture and unbundling

Under the strategy proposed by this paper, the key idea on the policy side is to get the board out of owning and running the learning-company. It is *divestiture.* The key on the operating side is to make available a variety of organizations – among which the board may choose – to run the schools. It is *unbundling.*

This is a radically different model. But the legislation to authorize its use can be simple. The legislation can create the essential dynamics of the model and leave the specifics to the board and to the new operating organizations.

The Board of Education will need to decide:

- *How many learning-organizations should the district have?* A board might have a single contract with its former school administration. At the other extreme it might want to have a contract with each of its schools. More likely, perhaps, it would decide to work with some number in between. For example, it might divide the old administration into three to five groups. Each group would become a discrete organization with its own teachers. Each would offer its program in every part of the district.
- *What method of accountability should apply to these learning organizations?* A district might use what the Carnegie Forum report in 1986 called 'administrative accountability.' Under this approach, the board would measure performance and enforce consequences itself. The board would assign students to schools. Over time the board would give more students to the groups it judged more successful, and reduce the number of students to groups it judged less successful.
- Alternatively, the board would decide to take the Carnegie Forum's other option and use parent choice as the mechanism for accountability. The size and distribution of the offerings then would vary with the pattern of student enrollment over time. While contract arrangements often involve choice, they do not have to involve choice. In Wilkinsburg, for example, the board of education proposes to contract out the operation of one school, but the district will continue to assign students to that school under an attendance-area concept.

The operating groups will need to decide:

- *Structure.* One group might set up on a traditional, centralized basis. Another group might decide to move decisions to its schools. Some might want to be membership organizations. One might choose to have its sites headed by a conventional principal. Another might want its sites to have, separately, an administrator and an instructional leader.
- *The learning program.* Some groups might emphasize basic approaches to learning. Other groups might move to student-centered methods or to the new digital-electronic technologies. Some groups might employ teachers. Others might allow teachers to form professional partnerships and then enter contracts to run the learning program.
- *Location.* Some groups might prefer to operate in buildings owned by the district. Others might want to operate smaller programs at a larger number of sites, leasing space from other owners in the community.
- *Support services.* Some organizations might buy accounting, purchasing, food service, insurance and other services entirely from the district office, to the

extent the district is able or willing to sell these services. Other groups might prefer to buy services elsewhere in the community or to provide them directly.

What if the district does not respond?

The strategy suggested here creates the incentive and the opportunity for the district to restructure. The district may respond and adopt the divestiture and unbundling plan. But it may not.

In the latter event the state has several choices. First, the state can increase the pressure. It can enlarge the number of schools the 'alternate sponsors' may create or charter more alternate sponsors. The state also may make it easier for teachers and others to get approval from these alternate sponsors, for example, by allowing teachers and others to apply to them directly.

If the district still does not respond, the state will have a further, more basic decision to make. The state could let the district live with the consequences of its decision not to unbundle. The state would then continue indefinitely to expand and diversify the range of other public organizations chartered to offer public education in the city.

Or the state could act directly to put the alternate arrangement into law: that is, *do* the divestiture and unbundling. The British make a good distinction between 'agreed' solutions, and 'imposed' solutions. Sometimes 'agreed' solutions are not possible. New York state acted directly for New York City in 1969. Illinois acted directly for Chicago in 1988 and again in 1995.

State-mandated divestiture and unbundling

Where a state already has taken over a district, as in Newark or Cleveland, it may be able to accomplish the divestiture and to carry out the unbundling without new legislation. As long as good state management is assumed to be the answer to bad local management, the implication is that the state will run the district indefinitely. By unbundling the district, however, the state can create a workable basis for returning the schools to local control.

When legislation is required, the key will be for the state to keep it simple: to set up just the framework and to leave it to the people involved to work out the specifics. The state needs to leave room to allow the dynamics to play out over time. This is what it means to be systemic.

In carrying out this strategy the hardest thing may be to get people to see that performance depends on system structure. Many people are impatient with talk about structure. They want to move directly to issues related to high standards, good teachers and better learning. They are critical of talk about structure as not dealing with what is really important.

The impatience is understandable. Of course it is the results that are important. But results are not obtained just by affirming their importance and by agreeing on their substance. There has to be a way to get there. So we have to talk about method. The real barrier to the changes everyone agrees need to occur in public schools is not people or lack of resources. It is the structure of the system itself.

The problem is in the basics of system-structure

Attendance in schools is mandatory. Geography divides the system into districts and students go to the school near where they live. Within each set of boundaries, there can be only one organization offering public education. The district does not have to earn its revenue. Its revenue is appropriated to it, usually on a per-pupil basis.

This structure assures the district of its success — its students, revenues, jobs, security, even existence. This guarantee by the state of the district's success in no significant way depends on whether students learn. This reward structure explains almost everything about the way the K–12 institutions behave: why change is resisted, why failure is tolerated, why standards and measurement are lacking, why adult interests are put first, why change is a risk, why the solutions offered are always 'fewer mandates' and 'more money.'

It is unrealistic to expect the districts and the people in them to do the hard things involved in change — in excellence — as long as they receive almost everything important to their material success whether they change or not. Public school districts are behaving as the state built them to behave. To change the behavior, the state must change the structure.

The heart of the problem is the conflict of roles in which state law presently traps the board of education. It requires board members to promise the best possible education. It denies them the ability to do any such thing. The board must put the children into the only learning-business in town, which the state requires it to own and run and in which its members serve as the officers and directors. It is a self-dealing arrangement, arguably corrupt.

Inevitably the board's 'producer' interests dominate. Realistically it must worry more about its employees (who can leave) than about its students (who cannot). The board sees the choice that parents so clearly want as competition for the schools owned by the board and so resists choice. When problems appear in the learning business, the board is drawn deeper into management. This creates conflict with the superintendent. As superintendents come and go more rapidly, the potential to make the changes that take a career to accomplish disappears.

The structural problem is a feature of state law. Changing state law can fix it. The state has to make the board's interest, like the public's interest, a consumer interest. It can accomplish this by making the board of education a buyer of educational services — by opening up choice for the board of education.

Until this structural problem is fixed, reform efforts will simply play at change. Public education could be lost in the process. It is wrong now not to be radical. The burden of proof is not on those who advocate the new model that the system needs but has not been tried. The burden of proof is on those who would stay with the old model that is failing.

Note

This piece first appeared in July, 1995, in a publication by the Education Commission of the States: *The New American Urban School District*. It is reprinted with permission from ECS.

10.   *This time it's serious: post-industrialism and the coming institutional change in education*

Joseph G. Weeres and Charles Taylor Kerchner

We have entered a long-wave cycle of revolutionary change in education. The conditions that existed at the end of the last century, when the structural and political basis of contemporary schools was founded, are reoccurring. Just as at the turn of the century, we are in the midst of reorganizing the economy. Then, it was industrialization; now it is the creation of the information society (Kerchner 1986, Reich 1991, Marshall and Tucker 1992, Drucker 1993). Now, as at the turn of the century, we witness large-scale migration and immigration that shapes both the sending and receiving communities and raises questions as to how we define our civil society and how people are socialized into it.

As a result, the capacity of exsiting institutions is being questioned (Block 1990, Chubb and Moe 1990). Both reforms on the political left and right originate from a critique which holds that existing institutions are *incapable* of performing as they should.

The long wave change in schools as institutions

The common criticism that nothing changes very much or very fast in education mis-states reality on two counts. The long-wave changes are extraordinary. When education takes on a different identity and purpose, as public schooling did in the first two decades in this century, things change rapidly around new structures and functions (Cremin 1962, Iannoccone and Lutz 1970). Also, the period *before* the shift to a new identity is one of great uncertainty, public debate and apparent confusion with competing proposals for reform and simultaneous consternation that not much is happening very fast (DiMaggio and Powell 1991). Rather than interpreting the school reforms of the last decade as a failed cycle of reform, it is possible to see the continuing debate as a search for answers that are not yet apparent. Within the current debate over reform, we find three historic elements that replicate those which were part of the last great wave of school reform in the first decades of this century.

First, there is a profound debate about learning. The conventional dimension of this debate is the schools' failure to perform on widely used tests (such as the SAT), in cross-national comparisons, and in casual observation on the streets and within work places (NCEE 1990). The conventional educational policy response has been to raise standards, and to try develop a national testing system to provide assurance that a high school graduate has mastered a particular body of knowledge and application.

This response misses the deeper dimension of the learning debate: what and how to learn. Post-industrial economies, and what may become our first genuinely pluralist democracy, require that analytic skills and a breadth of knowledge once reserved for the élite be more broadly distributed (Berryman and Bailey 1992). While high skills do not

0268–0939/95 $12 · 00 © 1995 Taylor & Francis Ltd

necessarily translate to high wages, skill becomes a necessary condition for grabbing the increasingly slippery ladder of the middle class (Ehrenreich 1990, NCEE 1990).

Second, there is a fundamental debate about public bureaucracy. Modern schools were founded on a belief that a scientific approach to management could increase quality and access while holding down costs. For much of the century it did exactly that, under a logic of economies of scale and industrial-style organization. The ability to standardize instruction across classrooms and across cities created an ability to increase quality and access simultaneously so long as students could be conveniently divided into classes or tracks and where the expectation of lower tracks was adjusted downward to meet some socially expected norm. Not every graduate was expected to perform to a high standard (Tyack 1974, Powell 1985, Tyack 1990, Toch 1991).

However, the logic of individual differences defeats the ability of bureaucracies to perform. In situations such as those driven by modern pedagogies (where learning is to begin with an individual and his or her social context), the level of flexibility required of teachers and schools is far greater than conventional bureaucracies can provide. Authority over rather fundamental decisions needs to be devolved from central authorities to schools and classrooms. Students need to become managers of their own instruction in ways that are foreign and hostile to existing organizations. Once the logic of instruction takes hold, it challenges the logic of organization. Everyone's role is rethought, and as one principal put it, 'This is no business for those who are hung up about power and authority.'

Third, changing organizations challenges our ideas of governance. The schools we know were founded on the basis of an élite divorced from day-to-day machine politics but representing the culture and ethos of the community leadership. Democracy in this context meant the application of a dominant culture to the schools. Schools were to be above politics; but the politics of equity powerfully changed school governance and, within the last two decades, the attack on public bureaucracy as both inequitable and inflexible has created a dysfunctional cycle of external change and bureaucratic response (Chubb and Moe 1990). Interest group politics replaced the politics of community élites. The three largest public policy interventions in the last 50 years were of this type: school desegregation, teacher unionism and categorical programmes. When interest groups organize, schools and governments respond. They create a bureaucratic mechanism to monitor compliance, to deliver programmes, and to handle disputes. The result is a vast increase in the size and apparent inflexibility of school bureaucracies and the beginning of the assertion that fundamental changes in the operation and control of schools are needed.

A century ago, school reformers succeeded in devising an institutional system for public education that married developmental and redistributive purposes. By coupling education to the newly emerging industrial economy, progressives not only markedly improved quality but also substantially broadened access. The result arguably was the best mass education system in the world. Now, however, the transition from an industrial to a knowledge society has called into question the capacity of existing institutions to provide both excellence and equity. Embedded in the current debates about markets and politics, efficiency and fairness, individual choice and collective decisions, resides a deeper struggle to define the relationship of education to democracy. Addressing this relationship requires placing the current debate about school reform within an institutional perspective.

Parallels with the progressive era

We live in what has been called the age of parenthesis, something between an industrial society and what has been described as the coming knowledge society, a society influenced by globalism, computerization and flexible manufacturing (Block 1990). To understand why existing modes of schooling are being challenged necessitates retracing our steps to the beginning of this century.

A new economy

Schumpeter (1942) described capitalism as a process of creative destruction. Destruction is an apt term for what took place in America's rural communities during the latter half of the nineteenth century. As the application of machines to farming vastly increased the economic efficiency of agriculture, millions of small subsistence farmers were pushed into debt and eventual bankruptcy. In 1880 it took more than 20 man-hours to harvest an acre of wheatland. By 1936 only 6.1 hours were required. One leading agriculturist of the day noted, 'We no longer raise wheat here, we manufacture it . . . We are not husbandrymen, we are not farmers. We are producing a product to sell' (Rifking 1995: 109).

Today, new information-based technologies are imposing similar destructive efficiencies on the industrial sector of our economy. Millions of workers already are, and have been, losing jobs due to corporate downsizing, outsource contracting of personnel and offshore manufacturing. Figure 1 shows these parallel patterns in employment. Between 1870 and 1910, the percentage of the labour force employed in farming declined from 53 to 35%, and from 1950 to 1990 employment in the goods-producing sector fell

Figure 1.   Percentage of workers employed in sector: 1870–1910 and 1950–1990.   ■ , Percentage of workers employed in agriculture: 1870–1910; O, percentage of workers employed in goods-producing: 1950–1990.

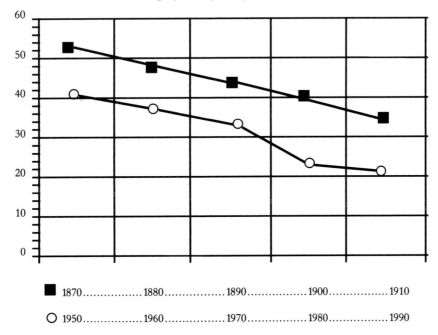

Sources: US Bureau of the Census, *Historical Statistics of the United States: Colonial Times to 1970* and *Statistical Abstracts of the United States: 1992*, 112th edn.

Figure 2.   Economic sector's percentage of GNP: 1870–1910 and 1950–1990. ■ , Agriculture as percentage of GNP: 1870–1910; ○, goods-producing as percentage of GNP: 1950–1990.

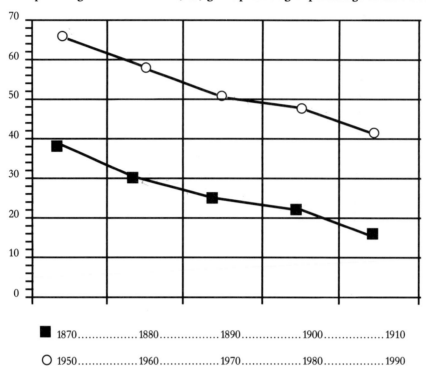

■ 1870................1880.................1890.................1900.................1910

○ 1950................1960.................1970.................1980.................1990

Sources: US Bureau of the Census, *Historical Statistics of the United States: Colonial Times to 1970* and *Statistical Abstracts of the United States: 1992*, 112th edn.

from 40 to 20% of nonagricultural payrolls. Similar patterns present themselves when one compares the sector's relative contribution to GNP during these time periods (figure 2). The industrial sector will experience even greater declines if future trends parallel what happened in agriculture. In less than a century, the percentage of the labour force working on farms declined from approximately 65% in 1850 to less than 5% today.

There is, however, as Schumpeter noted, a creative force in capitalism. The gains in economic efficiency which destroy the existing economy produce a new one. While millions of farmers were losing work in agriculture, whole new industries were arising which eventually provided employment and higher standards of living. Likewise, new information-based technologies are producing new wealth, though the future distribution of that wealth remains a matter of uncertainty and debate (Reich 1991, Berryman and Bailey 1992).

A wave of migration

These economic shifts created social dislocations. Large segments of the population moved to the geographical areas being occupied by the emerging growth sectors. For example, from 1870 to 1910 the percentage of the population living in urban areas increased from 25 to 47%. By the 1940s, nearly 70% of the manufacturing jobs in the country were located

Figure 3.   Distribution of population: 1870–1910 and 1950–1990.   ■ , Percentage of population living in urban areas: 1870–1910; and O, percentage of metropolitan population living outside central cities: 1950–1990.

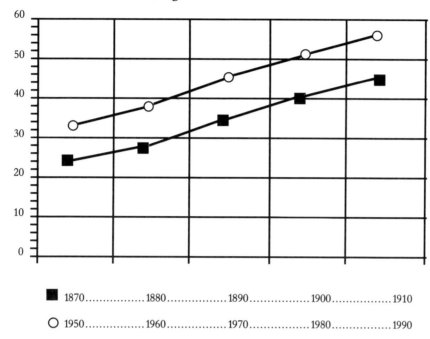

■ 1870.................1880.................1890.................1900.................1910

O 1950.................1960.................1970.................1980.................1990

Sources: US Bureau of the Census, *Historical Statistics of the United States: Colonial Times to 1970* and *Statistical Abstracts of the United States: 1992*, 112th edn.

in cities with populations greater than one million people. Now we see a parallel trend accompanying the shift from the industrial to the knowledge society (figure 3). The flight from central cities to the suburbs was the beginning of this process. But as availability of telecommunications increases and costs of usage diminish we may see population declines even in suburban communities as people follow jobs to exurban locations.

Immigration has also contributed to the migration wave (figure 4). Approximately 23 million new immigrants were admitted during the period 1870–1910, and 18 million (*not* counting those who arrived illegally) between 1950 and 1990. Controversy surrounded each of these periods of immigration as public education sought to define its nation-building function.

Learning and the institutional crisis

The fundamental change in educational purpose and direction that will be called for by the coming knowledge society will require the kind of sweeping institutional transformation that occurred in public education a century ago with the transition from an agrarian to an industrial society. Then, as now, the central task is to redesign the instructional core of public education to meet the human and social capital needs of the new society, and then to construct governance, funding and organizational systems to support this core.

Figure 4.   New immigrants: 1870–1910 and 1950–1990. ■ **, Immigrants: 1870–1910;** ○**,**
immigrants: 1950–1990. Chart calibrated in millions.

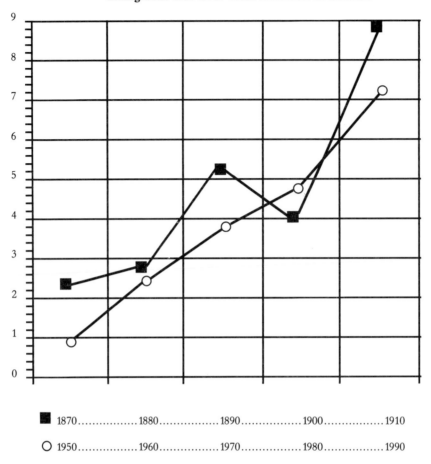

■ 1870................1880................1890................1900................1910

○ 1950................1960................1970................1980................1990

Sources: US Bureau of the Census, *Historical Statistics of the United States: Colonial Times to 1970* and
Statistical Abstracts of the United States: 1992, 112th edn.

Redesigning the instructional core: circa 1910

Attention to the instructional core preceded the changes in governance and organization
that were to mark the modern school system. By the 1890s the curriculum began to
resemble an 'academic jungle creeper, spreading thickly and quickly in many directions at
once' (Powell 1985: 240). Industrialization demanded essential changes in the purposes of
schools, the pedagogy and the organization of teaching. The revolution in technology, the
rise of urbanization and the emergence of the large scale, bureaucratic corporation required
that public education serve functions not envisioned when the common school was
created. The separation of work from family life, the intensification of labor specialization,
the shift in the locus of work from natural groups to formal organizations and the rise of a
nation state interconnected by rail, roads, and waterways necessitated a fundamental
change in what children learned in school. And this change was associated with
urbanization. As Cubberly (1916: 61) noted then, 'It is not too much to say that the great

educational advance which we, as a nation, have made during the past half-century has been, to a very large degree, the advance which our cities have made in the organization, administration, equipment, instruction, and the extension of educational advantages'.

Whereas rural schools had sought to impart basic literacy skills, industrialization called for a much broader and more specialized range of curricular content.

> The grading of schools, the development of high schools, the introduction of instruction in special subjects, night and continuation schools, vacation schools, playgrounds, evening lectures, schools for adults, the kindergarten, schools for dependents and delinquents, compulsory education, health supervision, vocational guidance and vocational instruction, free textbooks and supplies, the establishment of the value of good supervision and business organization, and the working-out and establishment of sound principles in educational organization and administration – these have been distinctive contributions which the city school district has made to our educational theory and practice. (61)

In addition to reading, writing and arithmetic, urban reformers expanded the curriculum to include formal training in such subjects as spelling, geography, literature, history, physiology, natural science and mathematics. They also called upon schools to prepare students for an occupation, something that was not necessary in agrarian society when virtually all jobs involved simple manual labor. Given the occupational differentiation accompanying industrialization, this prescription invariably meant some form of curricular tracking, i.e., vocational education for those who would be going into the trades and more advanced training in the academic disciplines for those moving into the professions and management. Schools also needed to socialize students for entry into the workplace, so they placed great emphasis upon inculcating habits of punctuality, discipline, obedience, regularity, attention and silence. This new socialization function set aside the kind of voluntary school attendance that had been associated with rural education and resulted in the establishment and enforcement of strict compulsory attendance laws. Schools also sought to transcend the allegiances of particular groups and communities and to instill in students common national values of citizenship, loyalty and submission to the rule of law. Liberal immigration policies and the mass migration from the farm to the city made nation-building an essential purpose of schools in an industrialized society.

The imposition of this agenda on public education necessitated profound changes in pedagogy and the organization of teaching. The ungraded classroom of the one-room schoolhouse and the jack-of-all-trades teacher were no longer appropriate for a curriculum with the scope and specialization associated with industrialization. The effectiveness of the transmittal of each curriculum subject required specialized pedagogical approaches and the knowledge base teachers needed to master demanded a much greater degree of formal, specialized education.

To say that nineteenth century Americans were unschooled was not to say that they were uneducated. Even in colonial Massachusetts, about 80% of the adult males were literate, about twice the level in England at the time (Bellah et al. 1991: 146). But until late in the nineteenth century, formal education beyond basic literacy was not necessary to prepare for an occupation. Even the professions relied on apprenticeships and learning on the job. This was easily accomplished because most families were economic units, either farmers (50% of families in 1900), merchants or manufacturers.

By 1910 however, education was rapidly becoming institutionalized. The earliest education still took place at the hearth, but the child was becoming rapidly a creature of the state rather than of the household as families relied on or were coerced into sending their children to school for extended periods (Tyack and Hansot 1982, Bellah et al. 1991). Dewey saw the need to change because children were no longer exposed to processes such as getting illumination by first killing an animal, rendering the fat, making the wicks and dipping candles. It was not the escape from hardship that alarmed Dewey but the loss of training in ingenuity, imagination, logical thought and a sense of reality through experience (Bellah *et al.* 1991: 151). Schools, he thought, would have to take up the slack. Others thought so too. During the last three decades of the nineteenth century, almost all the northern states passed compulsory attendance laws, largely under the leadership of Republican governors who took the lead in extending the powers of government (Tyack and Hansot 1982: 102).

To meet the needs of rapidly growing cities, urban reformers sought to institute (and only achieved moderate success until the late 1930s) an extensive state certified credentialing process, established normal school to prepare prospective teachers for the pedagogical challenges they would face, and developed elaborate curricular guides to control the sequencing and presentation of lessons within the classroom. Knowledgeable teachers were recruited into special curriculum committees to help develop these curricular materials, and while this could be interpreted as a process of deskilling (Braverman 1974), it almost certainly was necessary given the comparatively low level of education and training most teachers brought to the classroom at the turn of the century.

The structure and formality of the school day also needed to be made much more intensive to meet both curricular and socialization purposes. The ungraded classroom worked reasonably well for a rural student clientele that moved in and out of school depending on the weather, season and personal whim. Age-graded classrooms provided the possibility of breaking the academic disciplines down into digestible, sequentially appropriate bits. It reduced the range of material a given teacher needed to master and allowed for far greater specialization within the teaching force. Graded and specialized classrooms also facilitated occupational placement. By making knowledge a scarce commodity and requiring a bell-shaped distribution of academic grades, schools greatly facilitated the process of sorting students into occupational tracks.

The precise scheduling of time, classroom assignments and seating patterns gave schools formal organizational mechanisms for socializing students and controlling their behaviour (Waller 1961). The expansion of extracurricular activities induced students to stay in school and to learn the lessons of this hidden curriculum. The daily pledge of allegiance to the flag, the memorization of selected passages from the Constitution and the storybook approach to history helped impart a sense of national identity and pride. Eventually, most states required prospective teachers to complete courses in USA and state history as part of their formal credentialing process.

Industrialism and behaviourism

The rise of industry and the decline of agrarianism in the United States coincided with a change in the psychology that underlay both schooling and industrial management. Both teaching and management as we know them reflect the triumph of behaviourism over what in the nineteenth century was called introspection. At the turn of the century, just as psychology and the other human sciences were being recognized, a group of aggressive young, mostly American scientists staked out the territory that was to shape society during this century.

Behaviourists established two propositions. First, science ought to be public and observable. 'No subjective ruminations or private introspection: if a discipline were to be a science, its elements should be as observable as a physicist's cloud chamber or a chemist's flask' (Gardner 1985: 11). Second, science ought to focus on behaviour. The mind became a black box. Rather than individuals acting because of their ideas or mental constructions, they reacted to external stimuli. The tradition of Pavlov, Skinner, and Thorndike held that behavioural models could explain not only what people did but also how they learned.

Behaviourist learning theory emphasized arranging and manipulating a student's world so that teachers would create the desired stimulus-response chains.

> Teachers would present lessons in small, manageable pieces (stimuli), ask students to give answers (responses), and then dispense reinforcement (preferably positive rather than negative) until their students become conditioned to give the right responses. (Bruer 1993: 8)

This view of the world is perhaps best captured by the homemade sign we encountered on a classroom door: 'Knowledge dispensed; bring your own container'. It is a view that emphasizes coverage and prescribed curriculum, practice and repetition.

Since World War II, what became known as the process-product view of teaching transferred behaviourism into a template for teaching. The logic was that all teachers could become effective if they would just do what teachers who were found to be effective did. The voluminous research on teaching has come close to codifying good teaching (Brophy and Good 1986). Good teachers frequently present information through lecture and demonstration. They get feedback and they supervise student work. Consultants and staff development experts, such as Madeline Hunter, have turned these practices into keys that schools have turned into evaluation schemes for teachers.

Management had a parallel application. Copying the behaviours of successful managers would transfer success to one's own organization. From the 1920s principles-of-management movement to the current search for excellence, the assumption has been that following the same behavioural steps will recreate good organizations (Peters and Waterman 1982). In schooling this practice reduced research about the differential effects of inner-city London schools to the effective schools mantra for American schools (Rutter 1983). It is this world view that cognitive science has come to challenge, both in schools and in organizations.

The history of the effective schools movement presents a good example of the differences between the ways cognitive construction and behaviouristic approaches are applied. Resting on the work of Rutter, Brookover, Edmonds and others, the effective schools message was widely welcomed following the school-doesn't-matter conclusions of the Coleman Report and Jenck's *Inequality* in the 1970s. Effective schools researchers found that the patterns of use of school resources mattered a great deal, and they revived hope that schools could be useful bodies for social intervention in the lives of inner-city children.

Edmonds (1982) reduced the research to five principles; these took on a shorthand character of their own as they were incorporated into school reform programmes:

- instructional leadership: principals pay attention to the quality of instruction.
- academic press: schools have a broadly understood instructional focus.
- order: a safe and orderly environment.
- high expectations: teachers convey the expectation that all students are to obtain at least a minimum level of mastery.
- accountability: pupil achievement is the basis for programme evaluation.

Within months the elements of a description of schools found to be effective were translated into programmes for rescuing failing schools. Programmes were created to increase time-on-task, raise teacher expectations, and institute discipline programmes for students. While some of the programmes built on effective schools principles attended to the creation of strong organizational cultures or common beliefs, most did not.

Brookover's admonition that an effective school learning climate is the 'collective norms, organization and practice' often went unheeded (Brookover 1982: 8). Most continued to treat schools and teachers as mindless black boxes.

The challenge of cognitivism

Cognitive science challenges the black box view of learning. Rather than storing facts, the mind creates representations of reality. It stores and uses these mental representations, which we recognize as a system of symbols, to solve problems. Since the Second World War cognitive science has developed an increasingly complex representation of the mind's operations. Studies of experts and novices as they solve problems reveal the complex schemas or associative structures that link knowledge and data together into networks of related information. Chess experts, for example, see their opponents' pieces in groups; novices see them one at a time. These networks are extraordinarily powerful and important to learning because of the severe limitations on short-term memory, as George Miller suggested in the title of his 1956 essay, 'The Magical Number Seven, Plus or Minus Two'.

Because our capacity for processing information is limited, our ability to solve problems rests largely on the mental representations or schemas we have developed. A glance at an animal rustling in the bush evokes a classification system that distinguishes robin from canary while ruling out bears and snakes. The relationship between working memory and long-term memory makes it possible to integrate bits of current data with long-term sense-making schemes, using not simply facts but facts integrated into patterns (figure 5). Our senses present us with problems for active consideration by our working memory.

Figure 5.   Standard picture of the human cognitive architecture.

Problem	→	Working Memory	←	Long Term Memory
Task		Meta-Level Processes		Metacognitive Knowledge & Skills
Environment		planning		
		monitoring		Procedural
		evaluation		Knowledge
				(production rules)
		Active Representations	→	
		from environment		Schema
		from long term memory		Knowledge
		new symbol		world knowledge
		structures created		factual knowledge
		in working memory		

Source: Bruer (1993: 24).

Our ability to solve problems, however, rests largely on the ability to call schemas or patterns of information from long-term memory. It is there that associated chunks of information are stored – knowledge of problem solving procedures, as well as associated facts. Yes, facts matter. Cultural literacy, or literacy in any other domain, is impossible without them, but what matters most to the solution of higher order problems is the capacity to associate patterns of facts with one another.

Although short-term memory is highly limited in the number of representations of reality it can hold, long-term memory is thought to be virtually unlimited. But unlike a computer, which has a digital address for each chunk of information, our memories function through an associative structure that links bits of information together in stuctures. Cognitive science validated what William James (1918) knew: 'When we wish to fix a new thing in either our own mind or a pupil's, our conscious effort should not be so much to impress and retain it as to connect it with something else already there'.

Cognitive approaches to education become relevant when one moves from simple to complex tasks, exactly the point where the American education experiences break down. Using the National Assessment of Educational Progress as a reference, we see high levels of competence in basic numeracy and literacy. Increases in basic skill levels correspond to the political and organizational attention given to basic skills over the last 20 years and suggest that long term gains can result from focused educational policy. But many fewer examinees can solve high-level, complex problems. Only 7.5% of high school students could draw correct conclusions using detailed scientific data. Fewer than 5% of 17-year-olds could integrate specialized information and state their own views about what they had read (Bruer 1993: 5). When behavioural training is capable of producing additions to human memory that can be reproduced on tests of basic skills, they help little with *ill-defined problems* characteristic of higher order cognitive tasks and real-world applications.

With ill-defined problems, such as writing an essay, we begin to have an idea of the solution only after we start solving the problem. Most every-day problems and virtually all creative tasks in work, higher education and civic life are ill-defined. Teaching is one of these ambiguous problems. 'Teaching a classroom lesson presents an ill-defined problem that the teacher has to solve on the spot, where every student-teacher interaction can change the teacher's goals and choice of operators' (Bruer 1993: 32). Good teachers have a quality of 'doublemindedness', the ability to carry out a task while trying to define it at the same time, a dynamic of putting things together that goes beyond the structure of the lesson and makes a mockery of the plan filed in the principal's office (Mitchell *et al.* 1987).

Cognitive learning and the new economy

Just as behaviourism was perfectly linked to the requirements of mass manufacturing, cognitive approaches to learning coincide with the requirements of working in a post-industrial world (figure 6).

The cognitive problem of creating knowledge essentially returns the focus of education to the classroom, to the activities of learners rather than legislatures. It raises anew the learning problems addressed by Dewey as the country moved from an agrarian society to an industrial one, namely how to create a context in which children could learn naturally. The principles of Dewey's school frame the problem that has to be solved anew today:

- Instruction focused on development of a student's mind, not on coverage of subject matter. The emphasis was on learning how to learn rather than on recitation.
- Instruction had a context, started with active projects, was integrated and resulted in a substantial project.

Figure 6.   The contrast between the nature of work in industrial and post-industrial society.

Ideal-Type Characteristics of Industrial Roles	Ideal-Type Characteristics of Post-Industrial Roles
1. physical activity	1. mental activity
2. transformation of material objects (e.g., picking fruit, smelting iron, assembling toasters, ironing clothes, transporting plywood, selling shoes)	2. information gathering and problem solving
3. roles defined in terms of a narrow range of prescribed tasks and routine activities for which goals and procedures are clearly specified	3. roles defined by goals for which no certain procedure can be specified, consequently involving a relatively wide range of nonroutine tasks
4. time and place for role performance are tightly constrained and there is freedom from role-related concerns when outside that place in time and space	4. the time and place for role activity are not tightly constrained, and people have difficulty insulating one social domain (e.g., family or work) from worries or demands emanating from other domains
5. humans as appendages of machines: machines determine how the work is to be done, how long it will take, and what the finished product will look like	5. people determine how work will be done, how much time will be spent, and what the finished product will look like; machines are tools
6. satisfactory job performance produces a sense of completion	6. satisfactory job performance produces a sense of mastery
7. non-ephemeral aspects of roles resist change	7. roles are frequently and substantially redefined via negotiation and even conflict
8. low interaction rates, even for managers; that is, the role-set is small and contained	8. high interaction rates; that is, the role set is large and demanding
9. service is a small component of most jobs	9. service is a significant component of many roles

Source: Hage and Powers (1992: 13).

- Instruction began in the learner's world, and the teacher made connections between the student's background and experience and the more abstract and disciplinary knowledge (Farham-Diggory 1990).

Almost all the contemporary urban success stories have returned to these principles: Theodore Sizer's Essential Schools, Henry Levin's Accelerated Schools, the Central Park East Academy in New York. 'Practicing any art or any science means circling around a subject, trying this and trying that, asking questions that simply cannot be answered in a trivial way', says Sizer (quoted in Cushman 1992: 1). Each of these schools works on the basis of creating strong internal values, connecting the school to the surrounding environment and having a clear organizational identity. What is significant in this context is that leading examples of successful learning have largely been originated by teachers, either acting alone or cooperating with university-based scholars. Although they may have made use of computer technologies, the successful examples were not packaged by computer software manufacturers, or textbook publishers or state departments of education.

One need look no further than the examples of labour-management invention over the last decade (Shedd and Bacharach 1991, Kerchner and Koppich 1993, Bascia 1994). Those settings that intensified bureaucratic routines made only shallow reforms. Those that invoked command-and-control changes were resisted (Fowler 1988, McNeil 1988).

Those that involved teachers and first-line administrators actively in reworking their schools, and provided the institutional stability to protect them, made decent progress.

Industrial work was built around creating integrated sequences of largely physical work. What we call 'scientific management' was the technology that took complex processes, reduced them to relatively simple steps, and thus allowed them to be transferred from person to person. Simplification and specialization became the backbone of pedagogy in schools and workplace skill in industry. Compartmentalization of knowledge created expertise. Both work and knowledge became more specialized as expressed in the subject-oriented high school curriculum.

In the knowledge society, abstractions and representations of reality become important. Just as cognitive psychologists create symbolic representations that mirror the brain, every day occupations increasingly use and manipulate symbols. Reich (1991) coined the phrase 'symbolic analysts' to describe the people who control and analyze distant situations based on their understanding of abstract symbol systems. Those persons hold a range of occupational titles from research scientist to lawyers, consultants, film editors, journalists, marketing strategists and even university professors. 'They simplify reality into abstract images that can be rearranged, juggled, experimented with, communicated to other specialists, and then, eventually, transformed back into reality' (Reich 1991: 178). While they may sit in front of computer screens, their tools are the building blocks of cognitive construction: mathematical algorithms, psychological theories, legal principles. From spreadsheets to video images, these workers have the capacity to create and manipulate virtual realities. They intertwine invention and calculation. And they account for the most affluent 20% of the work force.

The cognitive revolution has enormous implications for the definition of quality and the organization of teaching. In behaviouristic teaching, the learner can be passive; school is even arranged to encourage passivity. Cognitive approaches to learning require experimentation and engagement. Teaching settings – classrooms, laboratories, playgrounds, communities – become more situationally responsive, the curriculum and the teaching process more fluid. These schools have to devolve more authority and responsibility to individuals and teams of teachers, and teachers need to be more knowledgeable and better educated.

The structure of behaviouristic learning is hierarchical. Learners follow a teacher's script through a set of lessons that places the teacher in control; the lessons themselves assume that one set of facts in a body of knowledge needs to come before another. Cognitive approaches to learning allow branching and networking. They begin with a student connecting what he or she already knows to that which is being studied. This type of learning is possible only through enquiry and suggests that passive learning is no learning at all.

A confluence of distributive and developmental

The age we are entering opens a new possibility of marrying the redistributive and developmental purposes, which was the largely achieved promise of the current institution of public education. The progressives brought with them a belief that things could simultaneously get better and fairer, a virtual joining of what political scientists were later to call developmental and redistributive politics. In the sweep of history, the promise was largely kept. Between 1870 and 1947 living standards *doubled* every 36 years, and during the post-war boom they doubled in 27 years (Peterson 1994). The society also became fairer. In the years after the 1930s New Deal labor legislation and activist government and the rise of industrial unions, income gains accrued more rapidly to the lower half of the economy. But as we know, the escalator of industrial process came to a dead stop in the 1970s.

From the beginning, the relation of education to national progress has been a driving theme in the establishment and maintenance of public support for public education. The common school was not to be a school for the common people, but a school common to all the people. It was to embrace both rich and poor and to provide an educational experience as good as, and perhaps even better than, that provided by private education. It expressed the Jeffersonian belief that democratic institutions depend upon a knowledgeable citizenry making intelligent decisions in their personal lives, in their civic engagement, and in their economic choices. It also was to be an engine for social mobility, enabling persons from every social strata and background to realize their own potential, and thereby contribute to national economic prosperity.

The public educational system that evolved reflected these redistributive and developmental aspirations. Constructed as a pyramid, the system presupposed that an expanding base of primary and secondary education would produce the human capital, and thereby the growth in economic resources, to allow for the extension of the pyramid upward (Figure 7). Universal primary education, for example, would make possible the provision of high quality secondary education to students who desired and qualified for it. The extension of compulsory education through the middle grades would strengthen further the quality of high schools and make possible an expansion of post-secondary education. Expanding the base of students entering college, in turn, would improve the quality of graduate education.

Figure 7. The pyramid of education: circa 1987.

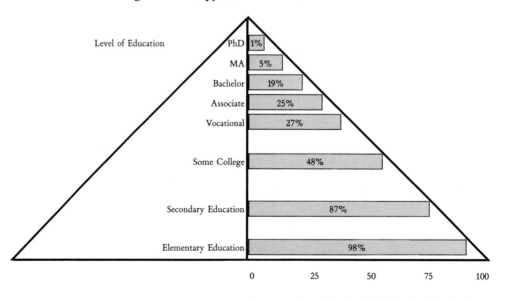

Percentage of Population Ages 18–88 Who Have Completed
Designated Level

Sources: US Bureau of the Census, *Historical Statistics of the United States: Colonial Times to 1970* and *Statistical Abstracts of the United States: 1992*, 112th edn.

The entire system was to be designed so that, in principle, opportunities for individual advancement up the pyramid would be driven by individual performance, discipline and commitment. It aspired to be a system that tightly coupled democratic values (through expansion of the base), individual freedom (through mobility within the pyramid) and educational quality (through extension of the top of the pyramid). It was to be at once a sorting machine, an expression of egalitarian values and an institution for national economic progress.

This institutional design departed rapidly from the idea of uniform standards for all. In 1893, the so-called Committee of Ten [experts] commissioned by the National Education Association and chaired by Harvard president Charles W. Eliot advocated a modernized curriculum, including choices, but 'every subject which is taught at all in a secondary school should be taught in the same way and to the same extent to every pupil so long as he pursues it, no matter what the probable destination of the pupil may be or at what point his education is to cease' (quoted in Toch 191: 42).

Within a decade, however, uniform standards gave way to what we now recognize as tracking. Expanding access to school, it was thought, required tailoring school to what were termed the endowments and the social condition of children. In a phrase made famous by psychologist Stanley Hall, the school should be fitted to the child and not the other way around. Schools became fitted to the child through the development of alternative pathways.

This institutional design was not without its critics. At each juncture in the expansion of the base of the pyramid some argued that universality would dilute educational quality. These arguments were heard when universal primary education was introduced over a century and a half ago, and they have been replayed in more recent years when the country committed itself to providing every youngster with a complete high school education.

The argument that élitism is necessary for quality applies, however, only to a given level within the pyramid, not the system as a whole. The quality of secondary education would be improved, as Singal (1991) has argued, if public high schools cast aside 50% of their students, as they once did, and retained only the most academically proficient. But this improvement does not necessarily hold when education is viewed in its entirety. The skills those previously cast-off students acquire in high school can make them more economically productive, and the wealth created by their productivity can be used to pay for an increase in the numbers allowed to matriculate into higher education. The structure and logic of the system, in other words, is predicated on the most fundamental of democratic beliefs: that a society that expands the scope of opportunity accorded to ordinary men and women will be more prosperous than one that restricts choice to an élite. This supplementary wealth pushes up the top of the pyramid, conferring on the system as a whole higher educational quality than it would otherwise have if opportunities for primary and secondary education were more constricted by exclusionary values. Achieving these developmental and redistributive purposes in the knowledge society will require reconstructing the instructional core of education – what is taught, how it is taught, to whom it is taught and how teaching is organized.

Education as a basic industry

In the industrial age, wealth was created through integrating capital and labour in the manufacture of products. Schools served as prime socializing agents. By the late 1920s

Robert and Helen Lynd were able to remark that while children continued to live at home, and while religious training took a limited part in their lives, starting at age six 'for four to six hours a day, five days a week, nine months of the year, his life becomes almost as definitely routinized as his father's in the machine shop, and even more so than his mother's at home; he "goes to school" ' (Lynd and Lynd 1929: 181).

We, of course, take this behaviour, along with high school graduation and entrance into college as being unremarkable, but the mass socialization of the young, and the attachment of educational credentials, particularly high school graduation, to employment, firmly locked the schools into the orb of industry. But the schools also became something more. The Lynds found schools were the social hub of the community for young people, and while education was taken for granted by children from the business class, 'it is no exaggeration to say that it evokes the fervor of a religion, a means of salvation, among a large section of the working class' (187).

Of course, schools still play a socializing role, and they are brokers to employment and further education. However, in a post-industrial setting, schools and colleges – the institution of education – serve a more central role. In a society where knowledge is rapidly the key ingredient in creating goods and services, education becomes a basic industry rather than a service to other industries.

Early in this century schools were important to cities because they socialized workers into the routines of an industrial economy. Now schools are important because they generate both economies and civil societies. Basic industries, steel and auto-making in industrial societies, occupy central positions in the economy and ripple wealth through the society. Knowledge-generating institutions fill this role in post-industrial cities and the role of universities is well recognized. Stanford University and the University of California at Berkeley were the handmaidens of the Silicon Valley microelectronics revolution, and the proximity of Harvard and MIT are frequently associated with the recent prosperity of the Boston region (Castells and Hall 1994). Colleges and schools frequently serve as the largest employers. The Unified School District is the second largest employer in Los Angeles, after the city itself. The University of Southern California is Los Angeles' largest private employer.

However, despite the fact that the real estate market values schools highly, the instrumental value of elementary and secondary schools in building economies and cities is seldom mentioned, except in the negative. Yet, the effects of relatively small changes in schooling outcomes can be substantial. For example, a recent economic simulation in Pennsylvania suggests substantial effects on population and regional economics from just a one per cent increase in worker productivity, a decline in births to teenage mothers or an increase in the quality-of-life index (Passmore 1994).

Schools obviously work in synergistic ways with economies: Good schools attract talented people and give communities the 'quality-of-life' label treasured by the mobile and critical professional middle class. Good schools create stability in working class and poor neighbourhoods that allows community organization. Schools contribute to the general production of human capital; a generation of economists has documented the positive rates of return from schooling that accrue both to individuals and society. However, by positing schools as basic industries we wish to explore more instrumental and purposive connections between schools and communities, connections that should be developed and reflected in educational policy.

References

BASCIA, N. (1994) *Unions in Teachers' Professional Lives: Social, Intellectual, and Practical Concerns* (New York: Teachers College Press).

BELLAH, R. N., MADSEN, R., SULLIVAN, W. M., SWIDLER, A., and TIPTON, S. M. (1991) *The Good Society* (New York: Knopf).

BERRYMAN, S. E. and BAILEY, T. R. (1992) *The Double Helix of Education and the Economy* (New York: Institute on Education and the Economy, Teachers College, Columbia University).

BLOCK, F. (1990) *Postindustrial Possibilities: A Critique of Economic Discourse* (Berkeley: University of California Press).

BRAVERMAN, H. (1974) *Labor and Monopoly Capital* (New York: Monthly Review Press).

BROOKOVER, W. B. (1982) *Creating Effective Schools: An In-Service Program for Enhancing School Learning Climate and Achievement* (Holmes Beach: Learning Publ.).

BROPHY, J. E. and GOOD, T. L. (1986) Teacher behavior and student achievement, in M. C. Wittrock (ed.), *Handbook of Research on Teaching* (New York: Macmillan), 328–76.

BRUER, J. T. (1993) *Schools for Thought: A Science of Learning in the Classroom* (Cambridge, MA: MIT Press).

CASTELLS, M. and HALL, P. (1994) *Technopoles of the World: The Making of Twenty-first Century Industrial Complexes* (London: Routledge).

CHUBB, J. E and MOE, T. M. (1990) *Politics, Markets and America's Schools* (Washington: Brookings Institution).

CREMIN, L. A. (1962) *The Transformation of the School: Progressivism in American Education, 1876–1957* (New York: Knopf).

CUBBERLY, E. P. (1916) *Public School Administration: A Statement of the Fundamental Principles Underlying the Organization and Administration of Public Education* (Boston: Houghton Mifflin).

CUSHMAN, K. (1992) What works, what doesn't: Lessons from essential school reform. *Horace*, 9(2), 1–8.

DIMAGGIO, P. J. and POWELL, W. W. (1991) Introduction, in W. W. Powell and P. J. DiMaggio (eds), *The New Institutionalism in Organizational Analysis* (Chicago: University of Chicago Press), 1–38.

DRUCKER, P. F. (1993) *Post-Capitalist Society* (New York: Harper Collins).

EHRENREICH, B. (1990) *Fear of Falling: The Inner Life of the Middle Class* (New York: Harper).

FARHAM-DIGGORY, S. (1990) *Schooling* (Cambridge, MA: Harvard University Press).

FOWLER, F. C. (1988) The politics of school reform in Tennessee:Aa view from the classroom, in W Q. L. Boyd and C. T. Kerchner (eds), *The Politics of Excellence and Choice in Education* (Philadelphia: Falmer), 183–99.

GARDNER, H. (1985) *The Mind's New Science: A History of the Cognitive Revolution* (New York: Basic).

HAGE, J., POWERS, C. H. and HENRY, J. (1992) *Post-Industrial Lives: Roles and Relationships in the 21st Century* (Newbury Park: Sage).

IANNOCCONE, L. and LUTZ, F. W. (1970) *Politics, Power and Policy: The Governing of Local School Districts* (Columbus: Merrill).

JAMES, W. (1918) *The Principles of Psychology* (New York: Dover).

KERCHNER, C. T. (1986) Union made teaching: The effects of labor relations on teaching work, in E. Rothkopf (ed.), *Review of Research in Education* (Washington: American Educational Research Association), 317–52.

KERCHNER, C. T. and KOPPICH, J. E. (1993) *A Union of Professionals: Unions and Management in Turbulent Times* (New York: Teachers College Press).

LYND, R. S. and LYND, H. M. (1929) *Middletown: A Study in Contemporary American Culture* (New York: Harcourt, Brace).

MARSHALL, R. and TUCKER, M. (1992) *Thinking For A Living: Education and the Wealth of Nations* (New York: Basic).

MCNEIL, L. M. (1988) The politics of Texas school reform, in W. L. Boyd and C. T. Kerchner (eds), *The Politics of Excellence and Choice in Education* (Philadelphia: Falmer), 199–216.

MILLER, G. A. (1956) Human memory and the storage of information. *IRE Transactions of Information Theory*, 2–3, 129–37.

MITCHELL, D., ORTIZ, F. and MITCHELL, T. (1987) *Work Orientation and Job Performance: The Cultural Basis of Teaching Rewards and Incentives* (Albany: State University of New York).

NATIONAL COMMISSION ON EDUCATION AND THE ECONOMY (1990) *America's Choice: High Skills or Low Wages* (Rochester: Author).

PASSMORE, D. and WILLIAM, A. (1994) Linking school reform and the economy in Pennsylvania, in *Pennsylvania Educational Research Association* (University Park: Penn State), 10.

PETERS, T. J. and WATERMAN, R. H., Jr. (1982) *In Search of Excellence: Lessons from America's Best-Run Companies* (New York: Harper & Row).

PETERSON, P. G. (1994) *Facing Up: Paying Our Nation's Debt and Saving Our Children's Future* (New York: Simon & Schuster).

POWELL, A. F., FARRAR, E. and COHEN, D. (1985) *The Shopping Mall High School: Winners and Losers in the Educational Marketplace* (Boston: Houghton Mifflin).

REICH, R. B. (1991) *The Work of Nations: Preparing Ourselves for 21st Century Capitalism* (New York: Knopf).

RUTTER, M. (1983) School effects on pupil progress: research findings and policy impressions, in L. Schulman and G. Sykes (eds), *Handbook of Teaching and Policy* (New York: Longman), pp. 3–42.

SCHUMPETER, J. (1942) *Capitalism, Socialism and Democracy* (New York: Harper).

SHEDD, J. B. and BACHARACH, S. B. (1991) *Tangled Hierarchies: Teachers as Professionals and the Management of Schools* (San Francisco: Jossey-Bass).

SINGAL, D. J. (1991) The other education. *Atlantic* 268(November), 59–76.

TOCH, T. (1991) *In the Name of Excellence* (New York: Oxford University Press).

TYACK, D. (1990) 'Restructuring' in historical perspective: Tinkering toward Utopia. *Teachers College Record*, 92(2), 170–91.

TYACK, D. (1974) *The One Best System: A History of American Urban Education* (Cambridge, MA: Harvard University Press).

TYACK, D. and HANSOT, E. (1982) *Managers of Virtue: Public School Leadership in America, 1820–1980* (New York: Basic).

WALLER, W. (1961) *Sociology of Teaching* (New York: Russell & Russell).

11.   *The new institutionalism, the new science,*
        persistence and change: the power of faith in schools

Rick Ginsberg

No it isn't strange
After changes upon change
We are more or less the same
After changes we are more or less the same
        'The Boxer,' by Paul Simon

Introduction

Americans in the 1990s are obsessed with the idea of change, both for individuals and organizations. Popular books implore us to reframe organizations (Bolman and Deal 1991), reinvent government (Osborne and Gaebler 1993), reinvent our lives (Young and Klesko 1994), restructure business (Barker 1992), reconceptualize our ideas about leadership (Wheatley 1992), even to reconsider our understanding of faith and religion as espoused in the New Testament (Frank and Hoover 1994). Perhaps the most significant changes that have occurred in modern thinking come in mathematics and the sciences, fields which Thomas Kuhn (1971) referred to as mature paradigm disciplines, where scholars apply ideas on chaos theory (Gleick 1987, Kellert 1993), quantum physics (Capra 1976, Wolf 1989) and complex adaptive systems (Lewin 1992, Waldorp 1992), in ways that alter our understanding of how the world operates. Even in the social sciences, in what Kuhn referred to as the pre-paradigm disciplines, various and often unrelated work in what is commonly referred to as the 'new institutionalism' (Zucker 1977, March and Olson 1989, Powell and Dimaggio 1991) is reshaping the analysis of organizational behavior.

In education, a field which derives its theoretical base from integrating aspects of the work in both the mature paradigm and pre-paradigm discipline, an exhaustive literature on change has emerged. From critics who decry the current system (e.g., Chubb and Moe 1990, Kozol 1991, Perelson 1992), to supporters who find models for others to emulate (Fiske 1991, Martz 1991), the need for reform of education is widely accepted. In fact, an entire literature on the restructuring of schools appeared in the 1990s (e.g., Elmore *et al.* 1990, Murphy 1990, Schlecty 1990).

A good deal of research in education has scrutinized the problems with implementing and understanding change in schools. Change is depicted as a difficult and often futile process. We learn, for example, of the great resistance to change in educational organizations at all phases in the cycle of innovation—e.g. adoption, implementation, institutionalization (Fullan 1991); of the need for understanding and impacting on the culture of those who work in schools (Sarason 1990, Cuban 1992); of the importance of 'mutual adaptation' of any reform and those whom the reform affects

0268–0939/95 $12 · 00 © 1995 Taylor & Francis Ltd

(Berman and McLaughlin 1986), partially because of the power of the 'street level bureaucrats' at the point of implementation (Weatherley and Lipsky 1977); and of the need for relevance, clarity, will and skill to successfully implement change (Miles and Louis 1990).

Change in schools is further complicated by the impact of state regulations and constraints related to the professions of teaching and administration. Certainly, schools and their employees are governed by state regulations. Much insight on how this affects schools is derived from the emerging work on the 'new institutionalism', which shows how the regularities of institutional and bureaucratic life imposed by the state, along with the restrictions derived from professional norms, leads to much similarity across organizations (Dimaggio and Powell 1983). Thus, any understanding of change must account for both the natural individual resistance and organizational constraints related to the change process.

On of the more enlightening treatments of the whole change process comes from work outside of education by Peter Marris (1974). His studies of bereaved widows in London and slum clearance in Nigeria and America, resulted in startling similarities, that the response to change in each instance was ambivalence, because the will to change must overcome the natural impulse to restore the past. Human beings have a need for continuity, thus part of the ability to survive is derived from a normal tendency towards conservatism, to defend the predictability of life. Marris argues, 'We assimilate new experiences by placing them in the context of a familiar, reliable construction of reality. This structure in turn rests not only the regularity of events themselves, but on the continuity of their meaning' (6). Thus, whenever change is disruptive to our accepted ways of thinking, we face the predicament of having our understanding of the world challenged. For the context of schools, this implies that changing cherished ways of teaching or thinking or organizing will naturally be difficult.

Developing an understanding of change involves recognition that varying levels of change do occur. Watzlawick *et al.* (1974) distinguished between what they refer to as first- and second-order change. First-order change occurs within a system which itself remains unchanged, while second-order change changes the system itself. For example, a person having a nightmare can scream or hide or jump in the dream, but they remain in the dream. Only by termininating the dream does one make a substantive change from dreaming to waking. Thus, the things one does in a dream are first-order changes, but only by waking does one experience the more extensive second-order change. Hammer and Champy (1993:31), in their influential book on reengineering corporations, described a phenomenon similar to second-order change. Reengineering, they argue,

> doesn't mean tinkering with what already exists or making incremental changes that leave basic structures intact. It isn't about making patchwork fixes—jury rigging existing systems so they work better. It does mean abandoning long-established procedures and looking afresh at the work required.

Given all the recent efforts to reform schools, such a description of change implies that we in education, using the dream metaphor, haven't yet awakened from our nightmare. That is, while some changes have been made to the prevalent state of schools, the system itself persists largely intact.

Interestingly, the distinction between first- and second-order changes has been widely adopted by scholars in education as a means of describing change in schools. Cuban (1988, 1992), for example, describes changes in education as either first-order (what he also calls incremental) or second-order (what he also refers to as fundamental). In his historical analysis of schooling, incremental changes are most likely in the core of schooling aimed at the average student, while more fundamental changes are most likely in peripheral settings, those programmes at the margins for students outside of the mainstream.

Categorizing change into only two classifications probably oversimplifies the degrees of change that schools regularly experience. Others, therefore, have adopted variations of this classification to describe diferent kinds of change efforts. Rosenholtz (1989) described schools in the process of improvement as being in one of three stages—stuck, between, or moving. Moving schools don't necessarily encompass a systemic change, but rather have a learning-enriched environment for staff and students, with a higher sense of shared purpose, commitment to teacher collaboration and continuous improvement. Both Cory (1991) and Bork (1993) described several stages of technology utilization in schools, with few, if any, reaching the final stage they depict (ostensibly, second-order). Ginsberg (1995) identified five degrees of change characteristic of school reform efforts, with only the last analalgous to Watzlawick et al.'s (1974) notion of second-order change. Describing the degrees of change as non-linear, he characterized the five degrees in terms of varying levels of four factors: inputs into the system; alteration of processes or products used; reconceptualization of processes or practices; dramatic improvements in outputs. Most change efforts were described as falling into the second or third category of change, with few if any reaching the most dramatic fifth level, called transformation.

Scholarship in a variety of other fields also classifies change into different categories or stages, especially studies of significant cultural, societal and scientific innovations. Marxist-Leninist analyses of the development of societies, for example, depict an evolution from the slave and feudal modes of production to capitalism, characterized by several stages (simple capitalist cooperation, large-scale manufacture, capitalist machine inductry, monopoly capitalism), resulting in the inevitable collapse of capitalism and the emergence of socialism (Kozlov 1977). Hernes (1976) discussion of structural   models of social change posited four change processes (simple reproduction, extended reproduction, transition and transformation) characterized by differing changes in output structure, parameter values and the process structure. Anthropologist Anthony F.C. Wallace (1972) suggested five components of change in which a paradigmatic core development process occurs—innovation, paradigmatic core development, exploitation, functional consequences, and rationalization.

Many scholars do underscore the inevitability of change in organizations. March (1981), for example, in an analysis of organizational change and adaption, pointed out that organizations change routinely and easily, though change cannot be easily controlled or the results of undramatic organizational life predicted. Thus, the paradox that the pessimistic verses of Paul Simon's 'The Boxer' highlight, the tendency for individuals to change but largely remain the same, appears true of organizations as well. Schools in particular regularly attempt change, but apparently remain 'more or less the same'. Indeed, Lortie (1975), in his landmark analysis of the teaching profession, emphasized this consistent result in his descripton of the conservative inclination and pattern of continuity in teaching. Thus, the question raised by Dimaggio and Powell (1983:148) over ten years ago remains relevant for understanding the issue of change in schools, namely, why is there 'such startling homogeneity of organizational forms and practices?'

This chapter seeks to broaden our understanding of both persistence and change in schools by drawing from very diverse and seemingly unrelated strands of literature from the social and hard sciences. Specifically, the implications of viewing schools from an institutional perspective derived from literature loosely described as the 'new institutionalism,' as well as the implications of understanding schools as complex adaptive systems in an emerging literature on what is referred to as the 'science of complexity,' suggest constraints that underscore key systemic characteristics of schools as organizations and institutions that limit their ability to change in significant ways. Though the accounts drawn from both strands of research overly simplify very complex areas of inquiry, interesting areas of intersection are highlighted. Specifically, the concept of faith as an underlying characteristic constraining school change efforts is developed. The implications of this synthesis for potentially changing schools are derived.

The new institutionalism

Over the past decades, an emerging line of inquiry which can be broadly labeled as institutional research has emerged in sociology, political science, economics, and other fields (Dimaggio and Powell 1983, Moe 1984, 1990, Zucker 1987, March and Olson 1989, 1984, Powell and Dimaggio 1991). Though research on institutions is not new, this recent scholarship has placed renewed emphasis on examining institutional characteristics in order to understand both organizational and individual behaviour. Simply put, the collective body of research emphasizing institutions argues that institutions matter, as March and Olsen (1989) clearly implied when they titled their book *Rediscovering Institutions*. Given the variety of fields in which institutional theory is utilized, along with the diversity of focus and interpretation of institutionalism both within and between fields, setting out a simple description of the 'new institutionalism' is difficult (Zucker 1987, Jepperson 1991). Other chapters in this volume offer a discussion and synthesis of these writings. However, since this chapter relates to change, several general characteristics can be set forth.

First, the research of the new institutionalism comes in reaction to the limitations of prior studies relying on individual rationality, behaviourism, functionalism and similarly oriented theories which posit rational individual decision-making based on knowledge of choices available. As Dimaggio and Powell (1991:5) explain,

> a new institutionalism has emerged in the field of politics in reaction to earlier conceptions of political behavior that were atomistic not only in their view of action as the product of goal-oriented, rational individuals . . . but in an abstract, social conception of the contexts in which these goals are pursued.

In some quarters, they suggest, the development of new institutionalism is a direct response to the advance of behaviorism in the social sciences, 'which interpreted collective political and economic behavior as the aggregate consequence of individual choice' (2). Similarly, Zucker (1987:459) explained, 'until recently, most work in economics and political science has treated organizations as black boxes that simply reflect aggregate interlocking individual choices'. March and Olsen's (1989) discussion of the new institutionalism in political science summarized the point as follows: 'Without denying the importance of both the social context of politics and the motives of individual actors—institutional analysis posits a more independent role for political institutions' (17).

Implied in this critique of other approaches for examining organizational, political, and economic behavior is a concern with the lack of practical applicability of the prior studies and the concomitant acceptance of institutions as the appropriate unit of analysis to remedy this problem. March and Olsen (1984:747) tell us that the new institutionalism is 'an assertion that what we observe in the world is inconsistent with the way in which contemporary theories ask us to talk'. Dimaggio and Powell (1991) agree, explaining that case-based research describing organizational reality does not always jibe with the prior models and theories. For example, programmes are established but not implemented; information may be gathered by administrators but not analyzed; experts are hired, commissions appointed, but recommendations may be ignored. Such events do not match the rationality inherent in other theories.

With institutions as the focus of analysis, according to supporters of the new institutionalism, such incongruities can be more clearly explained. Though the concept of institution is differentially defined within the broad 'new institutionalism' umbrella (Zucker 1987, Dimaggio and Powell 1991, Jepperson 1991), institutional theorists agree that focusing on institutions helps explain what previously was theoretically inconsistent behavior. As March and Olsen (1991, 1984) suggest in discussing political institutions, such institutions set a framework within which politics takes place, where the state not only is affected by society, but affects society itself. They call for treating institutions as political actors. In other words, institutional arrangements and structures can affect organizations in ways that help explain various behaviors, long-term stability and attempts at change.

Perhaps the most significant commonality among the institutional theorists is the recognition that institutions play a significant role in shaping individual and collective behaviour. Dimaggio and Powell (1991:3) go so far as to suggest that 'individual preferences and such basic categories of thought as the self, social action, the state, and citizenship are shaped by institutional forces'. Scott (1991) explains that institutionalization of cognitive systems defines social reality and consciousness, building on Meyer and Rowan's (1977) recognition that facets of environments—institutionalized beliefs—can affect organizations in dramatic ways. Similarly, Powell (1991) argues that institutional patterns limit future options, both for social structures and individuals. As March and Olsen (1984:743) conclude, 'institutional thinking emphasizes the part played by institutional structures in imposing elements of order on a potentially inchoate world'.

These three characteristics of the new institutionalism—a critique of prior approaches to analyzing behaviour, a means for explaining heretofore ignored behavior, and an appreciation of the ways that institutions can shape behavior—all converge to underscore the importance of recognizing how institutions constrain the behaviour of organizations and individuals. Prior approaches ignored the powerful ways that individual and collective behaviour are limited at the institutional level and how these institutional limits help explain less than optimal behavior by individuals. That is not to suggest that individuals, organizations, or institutions do not change. Both Fligstein's (1991) analysis of the structural transformation and the diversification of American industry, and Brint and Karabel's (1991) study on the transformation of the American community college from being predominantly liberal arts to being predominantly vocationally-oriented, underscore the fact that significant change does occur. But the nature of that change is severely constrained by institutional limitations. As Peterson's (1976) analysis of school politics in Chicago revealed, powerful constraints imposed on school districts by the cities and states restricted the options available to school policy makers.

How do institutions change? Jepperson (1991) offers four processes of institutional change: institutional formation, institutional development, reinstitutionalization, and deinstitutionalization. Simply, these are the processes of forming institutions, continuing or developing present institutions, moving from one institutional form to another, or ceasing to exist as an institution. According to Jepperson institutions change because of contradictions (e.g. with the environment, other institutions, or with social behavior). Such 'exogenous shocks', explains Jepperon, 'can force institutional change' (p. 153). Similarly, Powell (1991), Stinchcombe (1965), and Polsby (1984), all argue that political upheavals or crises can be the catalyst for significant reform.

But despite the realization that change does occur even at the institutional level, the constraining powers of institutional arrangements are more significant for understanding degrees of persistence and change in organizations. Dimaggio and Powell (1983) provided important insights about the constraints institutions pose by elaborating the concepts of institutional isomorphism and organizational fields. Organizational fields, according to Dimaggio and Powell, are those organizations that 'in the aggregate, constitute a recognized area of institutional life: key suppliers, resource and product consumers, regulatory agencies, and other organizations that produce similar services or products' (148). Disparate organizations are structured into an organizational field, then become homogenized in terms of organizational forms and practices. Once organized, organizations in these fields tend to resemble one another and do not change much. As Dimaggio and Powell (1983:148) explain, 'powerful forces emerge that lead them to become more similar to one another . . . in the long run, organizational actors making rational decisions construct around themselves an environment that constrains their ability to change further in later years'.

This process of homogenization is labeled by Dimaggio and Powell as isomorphism. Institutional isomorphism occurs through three mechanisms. First, coercive isomorphism is the result of formal and informal pressures foisted on organizations by other organizations, such as government mandates or needs related to increasing respect from others. Second, mimetic processes emerge in situations characterized by uncertainty. For example, when technologies are weak or goals ambiguous, modeling of other organizations is the appropriate response to uncertainty. Third, normative pressures, especially in areas with a high degree of professionalization, are powerful as a mean of making individuals behave in similar ways. Together, the three processes work to limit individual and collective behaviour, even though such behaviour may have no bearing on organizational effectiveness.

We consistently see examples of this institutional isomorphism in education. Whether it be the legal mandates of the states or federal government (e.g. U.S. Public Law 94–142 – "The education for all handicapped persons act" PL94-142), the mimetic behavior so common across schools districts (e.g. the development of present US administrative structures [Tyack 1976] or the spread of reforms like school effectiveness or site-based management) of the development of present U.S. administrative structures [Tyack, 1976] or the spread of reforms like school effectiveness or site-based management), or the licensure and certification rituals perpetuated collectively by state mandates and professional norms, institutional isomorphism is obvious in the organizational field of public education.

Powell (1991) further developed these concepts by suggesting four patterns of institutional reproduction. First is the exercise of power. That is, élites who benefit from present arrangements, professional organizations that impact on practices related to recruitment and socialization of members, and other forms of control, generally support prevailing conventions.

Second, due to the complex interdependencies that certain practices or structures entail, change is nearly impossible without reinventing the entire organization or field. Such interdependence, sometimes resulting in inertia, implies high switching costs. Powell (1991:192) contends 'a host of political, financial, and cognitive considerations mitigate against making such changes'.

Third, a good number of taken-for-granted assumptions permeate organizational behavior. Once practices and structures are taken for granted, once they are considered natural and legitimate, a search for alternative approaches is uncommon. This reasoning is similar to March and Olsen's (1989:22) discussion of routines and rules in organizations. They explain:

> By 'rules' we mean the routines, procedures, conventions, roles, strategies, organizational forms, and technologies around which political activity is constructed. We also mean the beliefs, paradigms, codes, cultures and knowledge that surround, support, elaborate, and contradict those roles and routines. It is a commonplace observation in empirical social science that behavior is constrained or dictated by such cultural dicta and social norms. Action is often based more on identifying the normatively appropriate behavior than on calculating the return expected from alternative choices. Routines are independent of the individual actors who execute them and are capable of surviving considerable turnover in individuals.

To March and Olsen, a criterion of appropriateness guides behavior.

The final avenue Powell (1991) derives for institutional reproduction is what he calls path-dependent development processes. This refers to how initial choices, either individual or collective, often constrain later options. In Powell's words 'organizational memory and learning processes not only record history, they shape its future path' (192). Economists have extended this idea of path-dependent processes by focusing on how economic history can engage a form of lock-in whereby future choices are governed by past decisions. Thus, work by Arthur (1990), interestingly a former fellow at the Santa Fe Institute for the Study of Complexity, emphasizes what he refers to as 'increasing returns', a concept which encompasses the idea that once a technology is adopted, it can capture a market as adoption accumulates, whereby the technology becomes rigid and locked-in, at times closing out other, more efficient technologies. Institutional arrangements, then, often result in a lack of any flexibility. Similarly, March and Olsen (1989) discuss how understanding of events in political systems are intimately connected to previous understandings.

These characteristics of institutional reproduction, then, show how institutions and their forms may persist despite being less than optimal. And the arrangements may entail what Dimagio and Powell (1991) refer to as 'cognitive sunk costs', which, in Powell's (1991:194) terms, impede change efforts 'because they threaten individuals' sense of security, increase the cost of information processing, and disrupt routines'.

This discussion exemplifies how an institutional approach implies a constraint theory about change in organizations. The 'new institutionalism', with its emphasis on organizational fields, rules and routines, institutional homogenity and isomorphism, and factors asociated with institutional reproduction, fosters serious constraints on change for organizations and the individuals who inhabit them. The 'new institutionalism' suggests that institutions create constraints analagous to the instinctual behaviour of animals in the wild, whose entire frame of reference is governed by past behaviour and practices comfortable for their environment. In human terms, institutional approaches foster a faith about ways to behave. The next section turns to research on complex adaptive systems which converges with the 'new institutionalism' in substantiating a kind of faith as a constraining feature of organizational life.

Complex adaptive systems: the science of complexity

The most significant new insights related to the functioning of human systems comes from research in the physical and other hard sciences. The revolution that has changed physics, chemistry, mathematics, biology and other fields is only slowly impacting on the social sciences. Simply put, Newtonian and Cartesian notions of predictability and reductionism have given way to a world of complexity, characterized by disorder, instability, diversity, disequilibrium, nonlinear relationships and temporality (Capra 1982, Prigogine and Stengers 1984, Nicolis and Prigogine 1989, Waldrop 1993). Using Karl Popper's (1965) metaphor of clouds and clocks, three hundred years of Newtonian thinking resulted in systems built on predictability, operating on the assumption that organizations and mankind could reduce any operation to that of a precision machine, a clock. But what quantum and atomic physics have revealed is the cloud–like nature of reality. Capra (1982:47) explains:

> Like human-made machines, the cosmic machine was thought to consist of elementary parts. Consequently, it was believed that complex phenomena could always be understood by reducing them to their basic building blocks and by looking for mechanisms through which these interacted. This attitude, known as reductionism, has become so deeply ingrained in our culture that it has often been identified with the scientific method. The other sciences accepted the mechanistic and reductionistic views of the classical physics as the correct description of reality and modeled their own theories accordingly. Whenever psychologists, sociologists, or economists wanted to be scientific, they naturally turned toward the basic concepts of Newtonian physics.

Specifically, complexity teaches us that the old universal laws, the ideas of physical determinism, are not universal at all. Instead, they apply only to closed systems. But human organizations are open systems, which exchange materials, energy and information with the environment. For such systems, a new understanding is in order. Complex systems are complex in the sense that large numbers of agents (individual) interact with one another in a great many ways. This happens in cells, in organs, even in organizations. Such systems, though in a state of disequilibrium, find order through their interactions as a result of spontaneous self-organization, known as emergence, a process of unconsciously organizing themselves. As Waldorp (1993:11) explains, 'groups of agents seeking mutual accomodation and self-consistency somehow manage to transcend themselves, acquiring collective properties such as life, thought, and purpose that they might never have possessed individually'.

Some complex systems are also adaptive, in the sense of actively organizing and reorganizing to enhance survival. Thus the human brain constantly reorganizes its neural connections, just as corporations respond to market influences. Finally, complex systems are dynamic, disorderly, irreversible and spontaneous. Unlike the limitations of ideas from chaos or dynamical systems theory, with its keen sensitivity to initial conditions leading to highly unpredictable behaviour (Gleick 1987, Hall 1991), complex systems somehow bring order and chaos together. At some points in time, these dynamic complex systems grow, overthrow the *status quo* and move in new directions. Prigogine's Nobel winning work in chemistry (Prigogine and Sellers 1984) referred to these as dissapative systems, because the loss of energy in a system (entropy) doesn't necessarily lead to its demise, but instead can foster the release of present forms so a new structure can emerge, one better suited to the environment. Thus, the universe was formed, apartheid was dismantled, the Berlin wall came down, animal species transform and the Soviet Union split apart. Such happenings are never completely predictable, and turbulence gives way to new systems.

Research in a variety of social scientific fields is beginning to apply ideas related to complexity. Thus, Senge's (1990) work on learning organizations and systems thinking, Fullan's (1994) adaptation of Senge's work to schools, Wheatley's (1992) application of the research in physics, chemistry, mathematics and biology to ideas on leadership, Arthur's (1990) economic theories on positive feedbacks, and work in economics by the Sante Fe Institute on Studies in the Sciences of Complexity (Anderson *et al.* 1988) are examples of this emerging tradition of challenging long held views.

What are the implications for understanding organizations? Wheatley (1992:7), in her treatment of the new sciences, argues that the ramifications are enormous:

> I no longer believe that organizations can be changed by imposing a model developed elsewhere. So little transfers to, or even inspires, those trying to work at change in their own organization . . . and much more important, the new physics cogently explains that there is no objective reality out there waiting to reveal its secrets. There are no recipes or formulae, no checklists or advice that describe 'reality'. There is only what we create through our engagement with others and with events. Nothing really transfers; everything is always new and different and unique to each of us.

This new science, the new vision of reality, has dramatic implications for our understanding of the workings of organizations like schools. Indeed, scientists working through the Sante Fe Institute for Studies in the Sciences of Complexity have offered a set of characteristics for complex adaptive systems, including human organizatons, which reconceptualize ideas about such systems (Arthur 1988, Holland 1988, Kaufman 1991, Waldrop 1992). Several properties are posed for these systems, what Holland (1988) calls adaptive nonlinear networks (ANN).

First, such systems have many agents or units acting in parallel, whose interactions shape the direction of the system. Actions of any unit are always dependent on the state and action of some other agents or units. These agents may be cells in an embryo or individuals in a firm.

Second, usually, there are very few controls on the interactions among the units. Control emerges from coordination, stated procedures, roles and the like. It is highly dispersed. But the difficulty of controlling an economic recession, or even the behaviour of children in a classroom setting, illustrates the importance of cooperation and coordination among the agents in the system. The individuals or agents act with and react to one another, implying that nothing is fixed. Obviously, at the macro level of human interaction, powerful norms must be created to control anarchy and chaos.

Third, complex adaptive systems have many levels of organization and interaction. Units at any one level serve as building blocks for units at higher levels. As Waldrop (1992:145) explains, 'a group of proteins, lipids, and nucleic acids will form a cell, a group of cells will form a tissue, a collection of tissues will form an organ, an association of organs will form a whole organism, and a group of organisms will form an ecosystem'. In a school, students form a class, classes form a department, departments form a school, schools form a district and so on.

Fourth, these building blocks are constantly revised as a system gains experience. This adaptation may involve promoting good workers or rearranging departments. But systems learn and adapt.

Fifth, all ANNs operate by anticipating the future. They are not like a behaviourist experiment involving stimulus and response. In fact, systems anticipate and predict the future based upon implicit or explicit internal models of how the work will operate. As Holland (1988:119) explains, 'Participants in the economy build up models of the rest of the economy and use them to make predictions. These models, sometimes called internal models, are rarely explicit. They are usually more prescriptive (prescribing what should be done in a given situation) than descriptive (describing the options in a given situation)'.

Finally, complex adaptive systems have many niches. An agent adapted to that niche can fill it, but no agent/unit can fill all niches. In fact, niches are constantly being created by new technologies and once a niche is filled it opens up new niches for new predators or partnerships. The result is perpetual novelty in these systems, implying that equilibrium can never be attained. Because systems are always creating new niches, they always operate far from an optimum. In other words, improvements are always possible.

Schools are complex adaptive systems. These properties—multiple agents which require control, building blocks, internal models and perpetual novelty—are clearly characteristic of schools. And the notion of never reaching equilibrium, with its implications about the potential for continual improvements, is significant for those interested in school reform. Why, then, is change so difficult for schools? Three implications of this understanding of complex adaptive systems related to schools are raised: how we lead and control, structural constraints and the concept of faith.

Together, the properties of complex adaptive systems imply a very different kind of leadership than is traditional in schools. Wheatley (1992), in reaction to ideas about complex adaptive systems, called for leaders to use a participatory approach to assist in creating reality, to focus on relationships, to freely generate and freely exchange information, to promote autonomy at all levels, and most important, to foster self-reference by accepting that order will evolve from continuous dialogue about core values and vision. In education today aspects of this kind of leadership are promoted. But greater sharing of information, more development of relationships, more autonomy for teachers, and greater attention to self-reference are still in order. Leaders who pursue such ends will lead schools in ways better fitted to the properties of complex adaptive systems.

Second, related to leadership, the constraints imposed by state and local policies unnaturally limit the cooperation and coordination among agents in schools, and worse, constrain the needed adaptabilty between the agents and building blocks of the system. Some leaders, as pointed out by Morris et al. (1984), do ignore many restraints by being 'creatively insubordinate' in dealing with mandates in order to free their teachers to perform as they think best. But state regulations regarding curriculum, textbooks, testing, evaluation, certification of personnel and the like impose controls and are obvious limitations on an individual's ability to adapt to other agents and the environment.

Most significant, however, is the problem related to the concept of internal models. Usually individuals who become teachers have been in school all their lives—as K–12 pupils, as college students training for their career and as professionals on the job. Administrators have been associated with schools in similar ways. In fact, board members, even members of the community (as students themselves and parents) have all had considerable personal experiences with schools. Most have a very strong sense, developed over a long period of time, of what schools should look like, of how teachers should teach, of how administrators should administrate. These internal models that individuals who work in schools bring to their jobs are very potent. For many, they operate with a power equivalent to spiritual faith. And faith is hard to change. This notion of faith, inculcating implications of both the literature on complex adaptive systems and the 'new institutionalism', is developed next as a means of understanding the constraints on organizational change.

The power of faith

What is faith? We read in Hebrews 11:1 that 'Faith is the substance of things hoped for, the evidence of things not seen'. In a spiritual sense it is a powerful force, the 'leap of faith' in Kierkegaard's terms, that allows men to become true Christians (Jolivet 1946). Faith, according to Smith (1979:160), is a quality of the whole person. 'One's conceptualization of faith,' he asserts, 'and of the universe perceived from faith, if it is itself to be faithful, must be the closest approximation to the truth to which one is capable of rising'. Historians and sociologists examining religion have refered to sacred and profane norms, those sacred being essentially immutable, those profane being temporary adjustments made to everyday living (Eliade, 1959, Berger 1967). When applied to schools, sacred and profane norms represent the accepted patterns of thinking and practicing in schools (Sarason 1971, Rossman *et al.* 1988).

The argument here is that the internal models driving teachers' and administrators' behaviour must be thought of as the equivalent of faith. For many, these are as powerful as sacred norms. No wonder change in schools is so difficult! It follows, then, that contemplating change in schools must be considered as the equivalent of undertaking a religious conversion. William James (1902:157) defined conversion as 'the process, gradual or sudden by which a self hitherto divided, consciously wrong, inferior and unhappy, becomes unified and consciously right, superior and happy in consequence of its firmer hold upon religious realities'. Conversions involve discernible changes in beliefs and attitudes. The changes include degree of commitment as well as the content of the new beliefs. The experience usually results in alterations of obvious behavioural manifestations (Ullman 1989). Converting to a new religion is a highly emotional and difficult experience. It stems from dissatisfaction and aims to find comfort. If there is any basis to the analogy between religious conversion and undertaking fundamental changes in school practices, then the immense difficulty of the process is clear.

Developing the concept of faith as a constraining force on organizational change can certainly draw from literature beyond that from the 'new institutionalism' and science of complexity areas. Toffler, for example, in *Future Shock* (1970), talked of durational expectancies or assumptions, culturally bred ideas about how long certain processes should take. Similarly, Marris' (1974) work on loss and change highlighted the difficulty of accepting reform in the face of one's expected notions of continuity. But the research on the 'new institutionalism' emphasized the effects that institutions can have on individual and collective behaviour. Organizational fields characterized by homogeneity (isomorphism) result in powerful norms for maintaining the *status quo*. The patterns of institutional reproduction, especially the idea of routines and path-dependent processes, work to create a powerful faith, what was referred to as sunk costs. As Dimaggio and Powell (1991:10–11) explained,

> Institutionalized arrangements are reproduced because individuals often cannot even conceive of appropriate alternatives (or because they regard as unrealistic the alternatives they can imagine). Institutions do not just constrain options: they establish the very criteria by which people discover their preferences. In other words, some of the most important sunk costs are cognitive.

The work on complex adaptive systems also promotes the sense of a power like faith operating as an internal model within the agents (individuals) in schools. And feedback, it appears, is a key for altering an internal model (Waldrop 1992). In a field like teaching, characterized by a weak technology, where cause and effect relationships are loose, feedback is an inefficient mechanism for forging new paths in individuals' internal models. Indeed, given the long years of being a student, being trained and inducted, then being reinforced on the job, a property as powerful as spiritual faith characterizes the internal models of school people.

Final word

The thinking about analyzing organizational behaviour as well as more fundamental ideas about how our world operates are undergoing dramatic revisions. Scholars taking an institutional approach offer fresh ideas about why organizations and the individuals in them behave as they do. In science (drawing from discoveries in physics, chemistry, biology and mathematics) a new world order characterizes open systems as complex and adaptive, leaving behind the reductionist and deterministic leanings of the past. Yet schools and other organizations have been built on the ideas and assumptions of the Newtonian age, while more traditional scholars continue to focus exclusively on rationality and social-choice in examining organizational behavior. The analysis offered in this chapter implies that dramatic change in schools—transformation—is very unlikely. Constraints on both the system and on the individuals in the system have acted to deter any reengineering of schools. Utilizing an institutional spy glass and conceptualizing schools as complex adaptive systems offers insight into the kinds of new ideas and methods which must be employed to offer hope for dramatic school reform. Leadership must change to meet the demands of the characteristics of complex adaptive systems. Schools must be freed up to adapt to changing needs. Finally, the depth of the sacred norms which guide individual behaviour must be recognized and treated with the core sensitivity they deserve. Nothing short of a religious conversion of the faith guiding behaviour in schools will result in a transformation of practice. Without understanding the power of faith in schools, and treating the task of change as the equivalent of religious conversion, it will not be surprising if our schools, as Paul Simon wrote, remain more or less the same.

References

ANDERSON, P. W., ARROW, K. J. and PINES, D. (1988) *The economy as an Evolving Complex System* (Redwood City: Addison-Wesley).

ARTHUR, B. (1990) Positive feedbacks in the economy. *Scientific American*, 262, 92–99.

ARTHUR, B. (1988) Self-reinforcing mechanisms in economics, in P. W. Anderson, K. J. Arrow and D. Pines, *The Economy as an Evolving Complex System* (Redwood City: Addison-Wesley).

BARKER, J. A. (1992) *Paradigms* (New York: Harper Business).

BERGER, P. L. (1967) *The Sacred Canopy* (Garden City: Doubleday).

BERMAN, P. and McLAUGHLIN, M. (1976) Implementation of educational innovation. *Educational Forum*, 40, 345–370.

BOLMAN, L. G. and DEAL, T. E. (1991) *Reframing Organizations: Artistic Choice and Leadership* (San Francisco: Jossey-Bass).

BORK, A. (1993) Technology in education: an historical perspective, in R. Muffoletto and N. N. Knupher, *Computers in Education* (Cresskill: Hampton).

BRINT, S. and KARABEL, J. (1991) Institutional origins and transformations: the case of American community colleges, in W. W. Powell and P. J. Dimaggio, *The New Institutionalism in Organizatonal Analysis* (Chicago: University of Chicago Press).

CAPRA, F. (1976) *The Tao of Physics* (Berkeley: Shambhala).

CAPRA, F. (1982) *The Turning Point* (New York: Bantam Books).

CHUBB, J. E. and MOE, T. M. (1990) *Politics, Markets and American Schools* (Washington: Brookings Institution).

CORY, S. (1991) Technology in schools: Who'll provide the leadership? *Computers in School*, 8, 27–43.

CUBAN, L. (1988) Constancy and change in schools, in P. W. Jackson, *Contributing to Educational Change* (Berkeley: McCutchan).

CUBAN, L. (1992) What happens to reforms that last? The case of the junior high school. *American Educational Research Journal*, 29, 227–251.

DIMAGGIO, P. J. and POWELL, W. W. (1983) The iron cage revisited: institutional isomorphism and collective rationality in organizational fields. *American Sociological Review*, 48, 147–160.

DIMAGGIO, P. J. and POWELL, W. W. (1991) Introduction, in W. W. Powell and P. J. Dimaggio, *The New Institutionalism in Organizational Analysis* (Chicago: University of Chicago Press).

ELIADE, M. (1959) *The Sacred and the Profane* (New York: Harcourt Brace Jovanovich).

ELMORE, R. and associates (1990) *Restructuring Schools: The Next Generation of Reform* (San Francisco: Jossey-Bass).

FISKE, E. B. (1991) *Smart Schools, Smart Kids* (New York: Touchstone/Simon & Schuster).

FLIGSTEIN, N. (1991) The structural transformation of American industry: an institutional analysis of the causes of diversification in the largest firms, 1919–1970, in W. W. Powell and P. J. Dimaggio, *The New Institutionalism in Organizational Analysis* (Chicago: University of Chicago Press).

FUNK, R. W. and HOOVER, R. W. (1994) *The Five Gospels: The Search for the Authentic Works of Jesus* (New York: Macmillan).

FULLAN, M. (1991) *The New Meaning of Educational Change* (New York: Teachers College, Columbia University Press).

FULLAN, M. (1994) *Change Forces: Probing the Depths of Educational Reform* (London: Falmer).

GINSBERG, R. (1995) Understanding degrees of persistence and change in schools. Presentation at the Annual Meeting of the American Educational research Association, San Francisco, April.

GLEICK, J. (1987) *Chaos: Making a New Science* (New York: Penguin).

HALL, N. (1991) *Exploring Chaos* (New York: W. W. Norton).

HAMMER, M. and CHAMPY, J. (1993) *Reengineering the Corporation* (New York: Harper Businesss).

HERNES, G. (1976) Structural changes in social process. *American Journal of Sociology*, 82, 513–547.

HOLLAND, J. H. (1988) The global economy as an adaptive system, in P.W. Anderson, K. J. Arrow and D. Pines, *The Economy as an Evolving Complex System* (Redwood City: Addison-Wesley).

JAMES, W. (1902) *The Varieties of Religious Experience: A Study in Human Nature* (New York: Longmans, Green).

JEPPERSON, R. L. (1991) Institutions, institutional effects and institutionalism, in W. W. Powell and P. J. Dimaggio, *The New Institutionalism in Organizational Analysis* (Chicago: University of Chicago Press).

JOLIVET, R. (1946) *Introduction to Kierkegaard* (New York: E. P. Dutton).

KAUFMAN, S. A. (1991) Antichaos and adaption. *Scientific American*, 265, 78–84.

KELLERT, S. H. (1993) *In the Wake of Chaos: Unpredictable Order in Dynamical Systems* (Chicago: University of Chicago Press).

KOZLOV, G. A. (1977) *Political Economy: Capitalism* (Moscow: Progress).

KOZOL, J. (1991) *Savage Inequalities* (New York: Crown).

KUHN, T. S. (1970) *The Structure of Scientific Revolutions* (Chicago: University of Chicago Press).

LEWIN, R. (1992) *Complexity: Life at the Edge of Chaos* (New York: Macmillan).

LORTIE, D. (1975) *Schoolteacher: A Sociological Study* (Chicago: University of Chicago Press).

MARCH, J. G. (1981) Footnotes to organizational change. *Administrative Science Quarterly*, 26, 563–577.

MARCH, J. G. and OLSON, D. (1989) The new institutionalism: organizational factors in political life. *American Political Science Review*, 78, 734–749.

MARCH, J. G. and OLSON, D. (1989) *Rediscovering Institutions* (New York: Free Press).

MARRIS, P. (1974) *Loss and Change* (New York: Anchor).

MARTZ, L. (1991) *Making Schools Better* (New York: Times Books).

MEYER, J. and ROWAN, B. (1977) Institutionalized organizations: formal structure as myth and ceremony. *American Journal of Sociology*, 83, 340–363.

MILES, M.R. and LOUIS, K. S. (1990) Mustering the will and skill for change. *Educational Leadership*, 47, 57–61.

MOE, T. M. (1984) The new economics of organizations. *American Journal of Political Science*, 28, 739–777.

MOE, T. M. (1990) Political institutions: the neglected side of the story. *Journal of Law, Economics and Organizations*, 6, 213–253.

MORRIS, V. C., CROWSON, R. L., PORTER-GEHRIE, C. and HURWITZ, E. (1984) *Principals in Action* (Columbus: Charles Merrill).

MURPHY, J. (1990) *The Educational Reform Movement of the 1980s* (Berkeley: McCutchan).

NICHOLIS, G. and PRIGOGINE, I. (1989) *Exploring Complexity: An Introduction* (New York: W. H. Freeman).

OSBORNE, D. and GAEBLER, T. (1993) *Reinventing Government* (New York: Plume/Penguin).

PERELMAN, L. J. (1992) *School's Out* (New York: William Morrow).

PETERSON, P. E. (1976) *School Politics Chicago Style* (Chicago: University of Chicago Press).

POLSBY, N.W. (1984) *Political Innovation in America: The Politics of Political Innovation* (New Haven: Yale University Press).

POPPER, SIR K. R. (1965) *Of Clouds and Clocks*, Arthur Holly Compton Memorial Lecture (St Louis: Washington University).

POWELL, W. W. (1991) Expanding the scope of institutional analysis, in. W. W. Powell and P. J. Dimaggio, *The New Institutionalism in Organizational Analysis* (Chicago: University of Chicago Press).

POWELL, W. W. and DIMAGGIO, P. J. (1991) *The New Institutionalism in Organizational Analysis* (Chicago: University of Chicago Press).

PRIGOGINE, I. and STENGERS, I. (1985) *Order out of Chaos: Man's New Dialogue with Nature* (New York: Bantam).

ROSENHOLTZ, S. (1989) *Teachers' Workplace: The Social Organization of Schools* (New York: Longman).

ROSSMAN, G. B., CORBETT, H. D. and FIRESTONE, W. A. (1988) *Change and Effectiveness in Schools: A Cultural Perspective* (Albany: State University of New York Press).

SARASON, S. (1971) *The Culture of the School and the Problem of Change* (Boston: Allyn & Bacon).

SARASON, S. (1990) *The Predictable Failure of School Reform* (San Francisco: Jossey-Bass).

SCHLECTY, P. (1990) *Schools for the 21st Century* (San Francisco: Jossey-Bass).

SCOTT, W. R. (1991) Unpacking institutional arrangements, in W. W. Powell and P. J. Dimaggio, *The New Institutionalism in Organizational Analysis* (Chicago: University of Chicago Press).

SENGE, P. (1990) *The Fifth Discipline: The Art and Practice of the Learning Organization* (New York: Doubleday).

SMITH, W. C. (1979) *Faith and Belief* (Princeton: Princeton University Press).

STINCHCOMBE, A.L. (1965) Social structure and organizations, in J.G. March, *Handbook of Organizations* (Chicago: Rand McNally).

TOFFLER, A. (1970) *Future Shock* (New York: Bantam).

TYACK, D. (1974) *The One Best System* (Cambridge: Harvard University Press).

ULLMAN, C. (1989) *The Transformed Self: The Psychology of Religious Conversion* (New York: Plenum).

WALDROP, M. (1992) *Complexity: The Emerging Science at the Edge of Order and Chaos* (New York: Simon & Schuster).

WALLACE, A. F. C. (1972) Paradigmatic processes in cultural change. *American Anthropologist*, 74, 467–478.

WATZLAWICK, P., WEAKLNAD, J. and FISCH, R. (1974) *Change: Principles of Problem Formulation and Problem Resolution* (New York: Horton).

WEATHERLEY, R. and LIPSKY, M. (1977) Street level bureaucrats and institutional innovation: implementing special education reform. *Harvard Educational Review*, 47, 171–197.

WHEATLEY, M. J. (1992) *Leadership and the New Science* (San Francisco: Berrett-Koehler Publishers).

WOLF, F. A. (1989) *Taking the Quantum Leap* (New York: Harper & Row).

YOUNG, J. E. and KLESKO, J. S. (1994) *Reinventing your Life* (New York: Dutton).

ZUCKER, L. G. (1987) Institutional theories of organization. *American Review of Sociology*, 13, 443–464.

Part 3

12. *Institutional theory and the social structure of education*

Douglas E. Mitchell

Introduction

The rise of institutional theory and the fall of organization analysis

Institutional theory is one of the hottest topics in contemporary sociology and political science. Dozens of articles and several important book length treatments of the elements and aims of this theoretical perspective have been published in the last several years. In sociology, the seminal work by Powell and Dimaggio (1991) has brought the major elements of this work together in a single volume that is receiving widespread, and well deserved, attention. Institutional theory is also appearing in graduate programmes – new courses covering its theoretical and empirical foundations are being designed in sociology, education and other fields emphasizing the study of complex social organizations.

Before jumping on this bandwagon, however, it might be well to step back for a moment and put all this excitement into perspective: to contemplate the possibility that major insights developed using earlier theoretical frameworks might be lost and to examine whether competing theoretical concepts might be as well (or possibly even better) suited to grappling with issues lying at the heart of the new institutionalism. This chapter offers a preliminary effort at this kind of stock taking. It begins by identifying seven milestone scholarly works that mark out the trail of organization theory development in the last half century. These works undercut confidence in the functionalist theories of social organization that guided research and policy development during most of the twentieth century. They gradually unraveled the central proposition of functionalist theory – a proposition articulated explicitly by Max Weber (1947) and implicitly endorsed by 'scientific management' theorists beginning with Frederick Taylor (1911) – that *centrally controlled, hierarchically structured and rationally managed bureaucracies are the archetypical modern organizations*.

Disenchantment with classical bureaucratic theory began with the discovery that work-related human relations processes, largely ignored by Weber and the scientific management theorists, substantially influence worker productivity. Subsequent steps in the dismantling of classical theory are traced through works describing how: worker professionalization reshapes the division of labour; standardization of processes and routines inhibits optimal task performance; marginal adjustment can lead to better decisions than comprehensive rational planning; hierarchical organization structures may not be tightly linked or behave as cohesive systems; decision-making involves political and social processes unconnected to rational pursuit of goals; and ultimately, organizations can be legitimated in the eyes of their clients and the larger political community on the basis of confidence rather than productivity.

0268–0939/95 $12 · 00 © 1995 Taylor & Francis Ltd

Following the listing of key milestones in the collapse of classical theory, the central problems addressed by institutional theory are summarized. Resolving these theoretically nettlesome and intellectually challenging problems requires a whole new perspective on how complex organizations are structured and how they influence social behaviour. Developing this new perspective helps institutional theorists account for the reasons why the sweeping programme and policy changes such as those made in public education over the last few decades are having only modest impact on the overall learning and socialization of school-aged children. The review of institutional theory ends with a short discussion of what losses in understanding might result if the new institutionalism is allowed to completely override or replace interpretations of organizational behaviour developed within the classical tradition. Institutional theory, for all its potency in explaining the contextual and non-rational aspects of social behaviour that confound more rationalist and bureaucratic interpretations of complex organizations, tends to deflect attention away from structural and technical dimensions of action, obscuring rather than illuminating issues of effective and efficient action.

With this concern in mind, a major section in this chapter is devoted to inquiring into whether recent theory development in the physical sciences might not provide a useful and more balanced treatment of the relationship between the social, political and cultural dimensions highlighted by institution theory and the technical, structural and rational elements emphasized in older theoretical traditions. The natural science theory elements that are the focus of this inquiry are extensions of a theoretical structuralism which identifies fundamental elements and studies how they are linked together through the operation of equally elemental forces that follow relatively simple rules of interaction and combination to produce the enormous complexity of experienced reality.

The breakdown of classical bureaucratic theory

Classical organization theory is synonymous with the concept of bureacracy. Kelly (1974: 59) offers a typical summary of the origins of classical theory,

> The classical theory as we know it today had its origins in the political changes introduced in France after the Revolution of 1789, which were seized upon by the Prussians as a means of unifying their nation into an efficient instrument of military and industrial power. Max Weber . . . made the most significant contribution to the development of classical theory by setting out his ideas on the 'ideal organization', which he called bureaucracy.

Weber, himself, traces the origins of bureaucracy to the preservation of Roman legalism and formal social organization by the Roman Catholic Church, the only important social institution to survive the Dark Ages (Weber 1947). Talcott Parsons (1971) confirms Weber's analysis in his discussion of the emergence of modern societies.

During the first few decades of the twentieth century, however, bureaucracy lost its lustre as a conception of the ideal social organization. Just as the term bureaucracy was working its way into the common vernacular for describing organizations in all social sectors and for explaining how modern economies and political states could function to deliver social and economic goods to citizens and workers, classical bureaucratic theory began to encounter serious problems in accounting for actual behaviour. At first, it was thought that documented failures of bureaucratic theory could be overcome with relatively modest amendments – amendments that left intact the central bureaucratic concepts: rational decision-making, fixed jurisdictional domains, official offices and duties, meritocratic promotion to status and centralized authoritative control. As time went on, however, the amendments out-weighed the original concepts and the whole idea of bureaucratic control in modern social organizations came to be equated with social systems that were ineffective, inefficient and abusive to both their workers and their clients. Seven scholarly milestones (perhaps they could be called tombstones) mark the development of modern organizational theory and show why classical organization theory ultimately collapsed. They are:

1. Mayo's 'Hawthorne Effect' and the emergence of human relations theory
When Elton Mayo and his colleagues published their seminal study of the bank wiring room of the Hawthorne electric plant, few recognized it as the beginning of the end for classical organization theory (Mayo 1933, Roethlisberger 1943). Indeed, for nearly half a century, their demonstration that worker behaviour requires psychological as well as technical explanation produced a 'human relations' approach to organization and management that was seen as only an amendment to classical theory rather than a fundamental challenge to its basic tenets.

2. Herbert Simon's concept of 'satisficing'
Herbert Simon (1945) established his place in organizational theory development by demonstrating that organizations and their leaders compromise the bureaucratic ideal of rationality by 'satisficing' rather than 'optimizing' decisions. The 'satisficing' behaviour which he described does not represent a moral failure of individual decision makers, however, but it is a feature endemic to large scale bureaucratic social organization.

3. Talcott Parsons' recognition of the dilemma of professionalism
In introducing his English translation of Weber's classic works, Talcott Parsons (1947) was the first to recognize that Weber's ideal-type bureaucracies had no place for a professionalized work force. In Weber's conception, merit based promotion requires that management jobs go to those who master the technological knowledge and operational requirements for organizational productivity – the idea of a separation between production skill and management skill was not recognized.

4. Charles Lindblom's 'Science of muddling through'
In his classic essay, Charles Lindblom (1959) announced that managers can and frequently do make better decisions if they eschew the rationalist perspective implicit in classical theory and rely on 'muddling through' – making marginal adjustments at the margins of ongoing organizational practice rather than lifting decisions out of context and considering them in an abstractly rational way.

5. Cohen, March and Olsen's 'garbage can' decision making
Cohen et al. (1972) contributed to this thread in organizational re-analysis by pointing out that important interests in organizational decisions and actions are not limited to those who are in leadership positions.[1] Indeed, participants at all levels approach organizational interaction as an array of constraints on, or opportunities to pursue, their own fundamental interests. Decisions, rather than being made once at the centre or top of the organizational hierarchy, are constantly being made and remade as problems are moved to the places where they are expected to get the most favourable hearing, and decisions made in one arena are easily deflected or overruled by those made in another.

6. Karl Weick's 'loosely coupled systems'
Karl Weick (1976) carried the issue beyond the limits of individual decision makers and

specific decision making processes to observe that the Weberian ideal of centralized control over hierarchically linked action systems tying all parts of an organization into a cohesive unified whole simply does not apply to most complex organizations. Actions taken at one place in an organization often do not actually affect the perceptions or actions of members in other parts of the same organization.

7. Meyer and Rowan's 'logic of confidence'
Once it became evident that rationality in complex bureaucratic organizations is tenuous and compromised, attention was fruitfully shifted to the question of how dependability and orderliness can be maintained. Meyer and Rowan (1977) bring us nearly full circle in the analysis by highlighting the reemergence and importance of informal, taken-for-granted traditional *gemeinschaftlich* values and social characteristics. They argue that social order is preserved less by rationality and formal systems of social control than by the creation of an *élan*, a 'logic of confidence', that keeps organizational members loyal to their images of organizational action and maintains organizational legitimacy in the eyes of various stakeholders in the environment – even when the organizations do not actually follow the logic of action which they formally espouse.

With this *coup de grace* the Weberian ideal has all but disappeared. Organizations are no longer defined by their rationality but by non-rational and cultural properties. Interest expression and interest conflict are seen as commonplace, leadership and decision making are as much concerned with the preservation of organizational form and the maintenance of power by those who are now in leadership positions as by the rational pursuit of goals or the moral representation of member interests. Institutional theory grapples with this issue by distinguishing the ethos of social systems from their organizational structures and asserts that social form is secured and maintained on the basis of the ethos produced by institutional histories and value systems rather than by control over roles and organizational resources.[2]

Putting culture, regime and profession at the centre

Declining support for hierarchical structures of authority and the Weberian bureaucratic model of organization has moved the concepts of civic culture, political regime and occupational professionalism to the centre of attention in efforts to analyze how organizations establish order and produce results. By emphasizing environmental impacts on institutional identity formation and the symbolic incorporation of individual identities and meaning systems into an overall system of coherent and cooperative action, new theories of social organization account for organizational behaviour that is inconsistent with rationalist frameworks. Pursuit of the classical image of rational management and leadership is not only unrealistic, it tends to promote a demeaning conception of both the members and the clients of formal organizations. The image of all participants accepting the rationalist ideals of a Weberian bureaucracy has given way to the realization that actual behaviour is less coherent, more ritualized and more socially idiosyncratic than classical theory predicts.

The shift to a focus on the cultural foundations of organizational and leadership effectiveness has been broadly supported by political leadership scholars. Since World War II political theory has given much attention to the moral and ethical dimensions of leadership. Illustrated by Hannah Arendt's (1968) attempt to account for the totalitarianism of Nazi Germany and James McGregor Burns's (1978) effort to focus attention on the transformational potential of moral leadership, political theorists have been trying to bring some type of cultural norms and belief structures into the leadership equation. A few political scholars, notably the late Aaron Wildavsky (1993), have brought the term culture directly into the discussion of leadership theory. As this work unfolds, it becomes increasingly evident that it represents a broad-based reconsideration of the power equalization theories of democracy that characterized French, British and American liberalism in the seventeenth and eighteenth centuries. With the introduction of morality and culture into the leadership equation comes a reconsideration of the relationship-based authority systems rejected by Renaissance democrats.

The new institutionalism

As classical theory failed to account for central features of modern complex organizations, the initial reaction was to adjust the theory to account for unexpected behaviours. These modifications gradually produced a theory so cumbersome it lost its ability to generate intellectual understanding or lay the foundations for sound management and policy. Theoretical and empirical work by the new institutionalists has addressed five of the most troublesome shortcomings of classical theory. The responses to these problems are, of course, interconnected, but a brief review of the significance of each helps to reveal what institutional theory is seeking to accomplish.

1. Persistent non-rational and sub-optimal behaviours

Classical bureaucratic theory hypothesized that organizations would develop structures and productive technologies optimizing 'means-ends' rationality. That is, management was expected to consider various alternative mechanisms and procedures for reaching organizational goals, and then choose those that were most efficient and effective. This type of means-ends rationality was expected to emerge for two reasons. First, the principle of meritocratic appointment and promotion – a bedrock of the classical definition of bureaucracy – was expected to put organizational control in the hands of those executives who best understand the processes and techniques needed to optimize organizational effectiveness. Second, the development of competitive markets was expected to eliminate from the field any organizations that failed to rely on technically competent managers to control their operations. In combination, these two factors were expected to support norms of continuous innovation and improvement in organizational structures and productive processes.

As the twentieth century unfolded, however, it became increasingly obvious that this ideal of optimal pursuit of organizational goals was not being achieved. Initially it was thought that organizations were being tainted by the self-interest of irresponsible managers, subjected to undue political influence, or possibly protected by a failure of competition in the marketplace. By mid-century it had become obvious that these excuses were insufficient to account for the nearly universal failure of ideal-type bureaucracies to optimize means-ends rationality in decision-making and production processes. Indeed, the term bureaucracy itself came to be virtually synonymous with inefficient and ineffective social organizations, consumed with serving the interests of workers or overpowered by political pressure groups, rather than pursuing their intended goals. Within the space of half a century, bureaucracies moved from being heralded as the archetypal modern organization to being seen as a primary impediment to economic and social development.

Rather than seeking explanations in the failure of managers or of the social environment, institutional theory offers to explain the development of non-rational and sub-optimal behaviour in modern organizations by revising basic assumptions about human behaviour in complex organizational settings. As social and technical systems become more complex, the institutionalists note, the very possibility of cooperation among members of an organization comes to depend more and more upon the establishment of simplifying social norms and standardized routines and practices. On both the social and the technical levels, organizations operate by making large capital investments. Just as changing machinery requires new capital investment in plant and equipment, changing workers' understanding of their tasks and responsibilities requires large investments in training and socialization. Managers are, therefore, motivated to 'satisfice' rather than 'optimize'. That is, they are motivated to preserve existing practices and technologies so long as there is a positive margin between cost and benefits, even when they know that there are superior productive techniques that could increase overall organizational efficiency. Moreover, increasing complexity makes it less and less certain what changes in structure or technology would be most efficient. And the risks associated with making the wrong capital investments are far from trivial.

2. Organizational history as a determinant of social meaning and practice

A second problem with classical theory is its failure to recognize the importance of specific historical factors controlling organizational structures and operations. Classical bureaucracies evolved, of course, changing much more rapidly and dramatically than the patrimonial and sacradotal systems which they replaced. But classical theory attributed to these changes to the functional means-ends rationalism identified as the essence of modern organization. Organizational growth and decline, and the location and timing of changes in form or function were all presumed to depend on the logic of tightly linked technical and organizational processes – attributing logical necessity to processes now recognized as the products of historical accidents rather than rational decisions.

Institutional theorists, by attributing social regularity to processes of collective sense-making and identity formation among organization members, were able to give organizational history its proper weight as a factor responsible for creating and sustaining social order. Institutionalists recognized that many members of the most complex organizations do not have any personal knowledge of the immediate purposes or overall technical rationality of the organizations to which they give their work efforts and loyalties. These individuals learn to accept the purposes and routines of the organization by accepting its historical significance rather than by identifying with, or perhaps even understanding, its technical processes and rational goals.

3. Ordering social behaviour through myth, ritual, ethical and moral rules

The third problem addressed by institutional theory is often seen as its most important contribution to rethinking organizational behaviour. Although Weber had recognized the importance of religious beliefs in creating a spiritual foundation for modern organizations, the scientific management theorists who took over the development of classical theory largely ignored this aspect of his work. As a result, the importance of social belief systems embodied in myths and rituals and in moral and ethical norms, were seen as epiphenomena – sources of inefficiency and control problems – rather than forces responsible for defining and stabilizing effective organizational action.

Tonnies (1957) classical formulation of the mixture of *gemeinschaft* and *gesellschaft* elements in all social and political organizations preserved a place in general theory for the more affective components of any stable social system. Durkheim's (1933) formulation of the place of religion in society was also influential in keeping the concepts of myth and morality at the centre of general social theory. But these theorists had much less influence on the development of organization and management theories than did the scientific managers. Political scientists, despite the neglect of affective solidarity in Machiavelli's classic work and an overt hostility toward mythic social order in Marx's analysis, continued to credit the importance of affective belief systems. Indeed, political theorists not only recognized the value of symbolic and mythic communication, they debated the adequacy of specific belief systems for the creation of just political regimes. In organization analysis, positive perspectives on myth and symbol were marginalized by a dedication to the idea that *gesellschaftlich* formal organizations were the essence of Renaissance economic and political reforms.

Early institutional theorists (e.g., Selznick 1949) raised ritualization to the status of core concept, but continued to see affectively potent ideas as impediments to organizational efficiency. More recent institutional theories – what Powell and Dimaggio call the 'new institutionalism' – adopt a much more positive view of the place of the symbol systems embodied in myth and ritual. These theorists see powerful symbol systems as essential for engendering loyalty among workers and garnering public legitimacy for organizations. In this sense, the new institutionalists are recapturing Tonnies's sense of the *gemeinschaftlich* or communitarian side of complex organizations – a perspective fully compatible with their focus on non-rational action and the crucial role of organizational histories. The symbol systems that give a *gemeinschaftlich* foundation to organizational life are only effective if their affective components are stronger than their rational ones. They have to be created within specific organizations through the development of interpretive stories that provide a moral basis for organization goals and the operational norms that give members a sense of identity and participation. The interpretive stories are created by abstracting them from specific historical events and then highlighting and reinforcing the corporate significance of these events.

4. A tendency toward isomorphic rather than divergent organizational forms

One of the more paradoxical features of modern organizational development is that direct competition for market share and public support within a given sector tends to encourage organizations to converge on common organizational forms and to adopt similar technical and social operations. According to classical theory, such competition should generate differentiation, not isomorphic convergence, as organizations concentrate on developing competitive advantage rather than reproducing the operational characteristics of their competitors. But isomorphic convergence appears to be the rule – network television offerings converge in form and substance as do automobile designs and supermarket operations. Classical theory would predict, for example, that automobile dealers would seek to reduce immediate competition by distributing themselves sparsely across population centres, but their tendency has been to congregate in the giant 'auto rows' that dot the landscapes of urban America.

Institutional theory accounts for this convergence by pointing out that institutional legitimacy is every bit as important as technical adequacy in this kind of competition. Whenever innovation becomes sufficiently novel or radical to call into question continuity with other organizations in the same sector, organization members, clients or the legitimating public may lose confidence in the legitimacy or efficacy of the organization. Additionally, clients or customers who accept services from a totally unique organization lose their competitive position in the marketplace because they cannot easily move or threaten to move to a competitor. Thus, both producers and customers have an interest in 'institutionalizing' productivity by creating several sources for functionally equivalent goods and services and then limiting innovation to a relatively narrow range of marginal improvements on a common base product or service. This institutionalization proceeds by setting norms and value parameters that constrain organizational practices – norms that encourage all organizations to move at about the same pace and in roughly the same direction in the development of improved services. The process of institutionalization involves creating a broad cultural or social symbol system for defining legitimate organizational forms and product or service parameters. Thus, for example, the oil embargo of the 1970s created a society-wide interest in automobile fuel efficiency and home insulation. This broad social interest was converted into pressure on buyers and sellers alike to give symbolic attention to energy conservation and stimulated a large number of marginal innovations, but left the basic structure of private automobile commuting and single family suburban housing developments largely in tact.

5. Responsiveness to professional norms, political regimes and socio-cultural contexts
Perhaps the most profound contribution of institutional theory is its accounting for the role of environmental forces in shaping organizational behaviour. For several decades it has been clear that organizations respond to their environments in substantial ways. In its original form, classical bureaucratic theory concentrated almost entirely on the internal logic of organizational life – productive processes, organizational structure development, managerial planning and decision-making – and largely ignored environmental influences. This over-concentration on internal processes was modified substantially by the development of 'open systems' conceptions of organization–environment transactions. While correcting the neglect of environmental influence, open systems theory did not go far enough in developing a robust account of the symbiotic relationships between organizations and their environments. Open systems analysis concentrates on analyzing boundary *transactions* rather than recognizing the convergence of organizational and environmental structures. Thus, open systems theory identifies *processes* of environmental influence, but leaves organizational transformation to be explained as a consequence of particular environmental transactions. As a result, while open systems theory explains how organizations are tied to their environments, it gives insufficient weight to the fact that basic organizational forms reflect environmental contexts.

Institutional theories are more direct in their assertions about environmental influence. As institutions, complex organizations are the creatures of the professional regimes and cultural patterns that surround them. Organizational managers are unable to move their professional workers very far from the environmental norms of their profession. All organizations operating within a common political regime are drawn toward standard practices that correspond to the political pressures and formal regulations produced by the regime. And all participants within an organization, together with their clients and attentive publics, hold expectations about the roles of individuals as well as the social roles of the organizational units that highlight and sanction deviant actions.

Implications for further problems that could be addressed

Public schools display all of the features addressed by institutional theory:

- responsiveness to context rather than productivity in the development of new programs

- a tendency toward isomorphic adjustment of organizational design and practices
- infused with the myth and ritual of 'secular religion' (Iannaccone 1967)
- constrained in responding to change initiatives by unique organizational histories
- persistence of sub-optimal educational practices and routines

Despite the fact that these are common features of institutions throughout the advanced modern world, they have been repeatedly cited as the reasons why schools have become the focus of the harshest, most sweeping, sustained and expensive organizational reform effort in history.

In addition to offering substantial insight into why schools display these institutional properties, institutional theory addresses three additional features of organizational life that are of particular importance to analyzing public school policies and operations. These three features are: the failure of successful educational programmes and practices to produce predictable results when adopted by other school organizations; the prominent role of constitutional law litigation in shaping the delivery of educational services; and the use of conventional and arbitrary practices and socially legitimated organizational routines to control the high costs of responding to individual preferences regarding the form or content of children's education. By applying the concepts of institutional theory to analyze and interpret these three persistent problems, we can recognize ways in which they become meaningful features of institutional life, and also extend and clarify some basic features of the institutional paradigm itself. While each of the three issues deserves fuller treatment that can be provided here, the following brief comments indicate where the fuller analysis would lead.

1. The failure of control systems to give predictable results

Failure in the dissemination and replication of successful educational programmes and techniques is universally recognized, but its explanation is far from obvious. Individual schools and school systems appear to pursue innovation at a great rate – so much so, in fact, that educators are frequently charged with taking up every fad or fancy that comes along. Successful practices developed in one location, however, typically fail to produce similar effects at other sites. Even when innovative practices are well supported by funding incentives and legal mandates, schools are characterized by *pro forma* compliance rather than substantive implementation. As a result, schools are seen as simultaneously wasting resources on an enormous number of untested and unsuccessful practices and remaining impervious to substantive change.

This curious situation of altering everything while changing nothing becomes easier to explain if we adopt the institutional perspective. For public schools, the three environmental contexts identified by institutional theorists are diverse and often in tension with one another. The political regime environment has been purposefully fragmented through constitutional and statutory decentralization of authority. Local school districts, the traditional loci of political authority, have been substantially overrun by state and federal policy makers' attempts to impose narrowly focused but extremely potent constraints on local practice. The federal government has explicitly eschewed responsibility for the creation and maintenance of a viable system of local schools, concentrating instead on imposing innovation and equity constraints on a system which is presumed to have already attained local viability. That is, federal policy is characterized by the use of mandates and funding incentives to *redirect* local school systems which are presumed to be relatively strong but highly resistant to the values and priorities of federal policy makers. State policy systems, by contrast, have substantial constitutional authority and responsibility for the public schools. State authority is an overlay, however, on an older tradition of local initiative and responsibility. Typically, local school districts are constitutionally immunized against direct state-level management of their affairs and are expected to respond to the political values and interests of local constituencies. This preference for political localism is severely compromised, however, by the fact that local school districts lack critical features of regime-based political control. Progressive and urban reform activists in the first part of the twentieth century succeeded in separating most schools from political party structures, issue-oriented elections and ward-based representation systems – the basic machinery of local regime politics.

The professional norm environment for public education has always been weak. Partly this is the result of the political vulnerability created by extreme localism in the political regime, but it is more directly the result of the fact that educators have always been deeply divided over basic questions about the professional goals and processes of education. Indeed, many of the most widely read textbooks on the history of American public education present their stories largely in terms of basic tensions in the professional culture (Cremin 1961, Tyack 1974, Tyack and Hansot 1982). Professional educators have continued to debate whether American education should be for the masses or for an intellectual élite, whether it should be grounded in classical literature or vocational skill development, whether it should be organized by academic discipline or practical art, whether it should be grounded in behavioural or cognitive psychology, whether it should be socially activist or protected from social controversy, and, above all, whether it should be grounded in professional wisdom or in the cultural and social interests of local communities.

When it comes to the third institutional context factor – socio-cultural norms and beliefs – public schools face the exquisite agony of being the organization toward which cultural conflict is most often directed. Schools have been asked to bear the brunt of a national movement to create a more open and integrated culture. Schools are expected to both honour the principle of equal opportunity that is regularly violated in such areas as property ownership and economic access, and be the agency that provides children with understanding and tolerance for competing sub-cultures – often against the wishes of families and community groups. Moreover, the geographic boundaries of local schools and school districts often include multiple sub-cultures and cut across neighbourhood and community sub-cultural boundaries. As a result, the socio-cultural environment for American education is more a source of tension and stress than of positive guidance regarding appropriate educational purposes and practices.

Given their fragmentary political, professional and cultural environments, it is not surprising that schools are unable to move effective programmes and practices from one setting to another.

2. Constitutional law and organizational control

Throughout the twentieth century adjudicating competing demands on educational institutions has been a mainstay of state and federal litigation. To a remarkable extent, court decisions constraining school policy formation over a broad range of liberty and equity issues have been made on the basis of constitutional, rather than statutory, law. From the perspective of classical theory, this predilection for constitutional litigation is quite baffling. Neither the arguments offered nor the remedies adopted by the courts emphasize the principles of efficient pursuit of agreed upon goals – a central ingredient in the classical model. Nor do judicial actions give uniform support to the principles of hierarchical control and meritocratic status assignments classically presumed to be the very essence of sound organizational actions.

What, then, are we to conclude? That the courts are the enemies of effective schooling? Or that constitutional principle is at odds with social efficiency? While many observers have objected to judicial interference with public education on the grounds that some such conclusion is appropriate, institutional theory offers another possibility. If constitutional law is seen as an environmental force comparable in character with the political regimes, professional norms and socio-cultural value systems already being explored by institutional theorists, it can be seen that this environmental factor is also working to develop operational standards and encourage isomorphic organizational development. Constitutionalism is a deep structure in the institutional environment. Constitutions serve as the 'fly wheels' of political regimes, encouraging continuity and stability while resisting episodic change in regime values and aims.

Constitutionalism is an important point of contact between political regime and socio-cultural environments. Fundamental societal values are expressly articulated in the constitutional text, but, like other cultural forces, these values are most powerful when they are unconsciously applied to guide individual and organizational actions. To the extent that the courts are called upon to consciously elaborate and tightly rationalize constitutional principles in order to resolve social conflicts, their decisions become vulnerable to covert cynicism and overt resistance. From an institutional perspective, it is reasonable to suggest that schools have had to rely too much on constitutional litigation to force attention to the underlying principles of liberty and equity. The result is a reduced confidence in the government as a civic institution as well as an increased attention to basic social values.

3. Capitalized investment in conventional rationality

Schools are widely recognized for their tendency toward ritualized and routinized activity structures. Non-substantive ritual responses to desegregation pressures were early recognized by Crain and his colleagues (1968). The importance of rituals as a source of public confidence was highlighted by Meyer and Rowan (1977). Their importance in the micro-politics of relations among teachers, administrators and families are described in the various chapters of Blase's edited volume (1991). At the classroom level, this tendency was highlighted in Willard Waller's (1932) early sociology of school life. More recently the importance of ritual structures in the formation of lessons has been highlighted by Mehan (1979) and elaborated by Mitchell *et al.* (1987). The deflecting and trivializing impact of these ritual forms of instruction have been documented in Sedlak *et al.* (1986) and Page (1991).

Since they often involve sub-optimal or even technically unproductive activity structures, it is often assumed that these ritualized forms of action are caused by incompetence and insensitivity on the part of educators, or undue influence over education by special interests outside the schools. Institutional theory offers another possible line of interpretation, however. From an institutional perspective, the establishment and maintenance of an orderly social system that efficiently distributes status and assigns role responsibilities is a major accomplishment. Life in an institution is made possible by the social legitimacy of its structures rather than by its technical productivity. Institutional order relies on *conventional* rather than *technical* rationality. That is, institutions arise by *imposing* rational form on actions that could easily be seen as arbitrary. Where technical rationality is a matter of *discovering* effective means-ends links that make organized actions productive, conventional rationality involves providing reasonable order in situations that require cooperation to be successful, but do not make one form of cooperation more effective than another. Classical theory emphasized the stabilization of organizational structures and production systems through capitalization of technical rationality; institutional theory recognizes the importance of legitimating and stabilizing conventional rationality.

Neo-structuralist solutions to institutionalist problems

While institutionalism addresses the most glaring weaknesses in classical organization theory, it has yet to integrate these insights into a balanced account of social behaviour in complex organizations. In its present form, institutional theory is facing limitations on two related fronts. First, by displacing rationality away from organizations – locating it in the cultural, regime and professional environments surrounding organizations (Meyer and Scott 1992) – and by stressing the symbolic meaning of these environmental contexts for organizational action systems, institutional theory pushes technical means-ends rationality into the background and gives an ultimately unsatisfactory account of when and how technical realism will emerge to dominate organizational decision-making and action (see Scott 1992 for a discussion of how organizations become less rational as their environments become more so). To give a proper account of technical realism we need to synthesize institutional insights with the rationalism of classical theory in order to specify how symbolism and realism are integrated into an overall control system. While classical theory gave too much emphasis to organization-level rationalism, institutional theories give too little.

The second weakness in institutional theory involves its failure to develop a satisfactory account of how symbolic thought is effectively grounded in an underlying reality structure within the natural or social world. Typically, institutional analysts examine the values and symbol systems that guide social relationships and actions (i.e., myths, rituals, social norms and institutional legitimacy) from a *functional* rather than a *phenomenological* perspective. They inquire into how various symbol systems influence the timing, form or character of organized social activity, but generally ignore the knotty problem of how particular symbol systems acquire the personal or social significance needed to generate the influence patterns under study. Where theologians and political theorists devote substantial energy to interpeting how specific elements in the underlying logic of various mythic idea systems make them ontologically and epistemologically correct or socially compelling, institutionalists tend to treat competing systems of thought and belief as functionally inter-changeable and do not often inquire into which systems possess the characteristics needed to strengthen or weaken organizational cohesion and direction. To overcome this limitation, institutional theory needs to be integrated into a social analysis framework capable of describing how both symbolic and rational elements are grounded in the concrete realities of complex human action systems – capable of evaluating symbolic idea systems on the basis of their essential character rather than confining attention to their functional contributions to organizational operations and outcomes.

The tasks of integrating symbolic and rationalist control schema and of grounding symbolic reality in underlying social system characteristics may not be as difficult as it at first appears. Recent developments in the natural sciences have given rise to a new form of structuralist theory that promises to overcome these challenges to institutional theory, while retaining its important advances over classical organization analysis. This new approach in the physical sciences is appropriately described as 'structural' in the sense that 'explanation' is equated with the identification of a relatively small number of basic elements and forces that, in combination, are responsible for the enormous complexity and variety encountered in both laboratories and everyday experience (Levine and Bernstein 1987). Nobel laureate Richard Feynman (1995: 23) describes this structural perspective as follows,

> Curiosity demands that we ask questions, that we try to put things together and try to understand this multitude of aspects as perhaps resulting from the action of a relatively small number of elemental things and forces acting in an infinite variety of combinations.

The basic building blocks of the structuralist sciences are conceptualized in a variety of ways (e.g., energy waves, fundamental particles or basic elements). These building blocks are linked together through the operation of an even smaller number of basic forces of cohesion and repulsion (e.g., electromagnetism or gravity). All large scale physical entities are hypothesized to be composed entirely of these basic elements. As the basic building block elements are aggregated into larger and more complex entities, however, they begin to display new characteristics. These emergent properties, while related to the characteristics of the component elements, are fundamentally new and can only be studied by examining the behaviours of the aggregated wholes. For example, while molecular biology accounts for all of the *content* of living organisms, the biological *cell* is the smallest unit of *living* tissue – an emergent and highly complex phenomenon that results from, but radically transcends, its molecular foundations. Or, to take another example, studying the chemistry of an unstable metal, sodium, and a poisonous gas, chlorine, reveals how these elements can unite to form common table salt, but it is impossible to guess the character and behaviour of table salt without examining the compound itself. Feynman (1995: 56) makes the point in this way,

> One of the great triumphs in recent times (since 1960) was at last to discover the exact spatial atomic arrangement of certain proteins . . . . The first was hemoglobin. *One of the sad aspects of this discovery is that we cannot see anything from the pattern; we do not understand why it works the way it does.* [emphasis added]

Uniting bonding theory with the study of mechanics

For many purposes physical scientists find it both appropriate and necessary to separate the study of micro-structural elements and elementary forces from the study of emergent macro-structures into which they are incorporated. The concepts and techniques used to identify basic elements and explain how they interact to form larger aggregated entities are often not helpful in trying to study the properties and actions of the resulting macro-structures. The study of micro-structural elements might be called, using the language of chemistry, 'bonding' theory. At this level, the micro-structures are examined for their essential properties, and the processes governing their interaction and combination are documented. The basic elements are defined on the basis of how they interact and join to form aggregated structures.

Analysis of large scale, macro-structures is generally called the study of 'mechanics' – the name used in introductory physics courses devoted to the dynamics of interaction among ordinary physical objects (sometimes the term 'classical' or 'Newtonian' is used to avoid confusion with the quantum mechanics of micro-structures). At this level, the emergent characteristics of the organized aggregates are studied to determine how they will interact with each other and how they transcend or transform the properties of their component basic elements. Thus, while *bonding theory* describes how aggregate entities are produced from the basic building blocks of nature, *mechanics* describes how the resulting macro-entities interact to produce the complex universe of forms and experiences we encounter in the natural world.

In recent years, it has become clear that separating the study of elemental bonding processes from the study of macro-structure mechanics masks some of nature's most important features. At the boundaries, where collections of basic elements begin to combine into identifiable organized structures lie complex, non-linear processes of great importance. Complex systems become self organizing and develop localized equilibria which can remain stable through a broad range of conditions and over extended periods of time. These non-linear processes can be recognized on both sides of the boundary separating micro and macro structural processes.

Micro-structural bonding processes not only create the complex aggregates that become the focus of study in mechanics, they establish boundary conditions limiting the applicability of all mechanical principles. The mechanics of aggregated macro-structures are transformed fundamentally and unpredictably whenever conditions are such that bonding processes breakdown or become transformed. When, for example, paper reaches a temperature of 451 degrees Fahrenheit, it suddenly burns and can no longer be used as a communications or record keeping medium. Similarly, pressure from an ice-skater's blades, overcomes the ordinarily crystalline structure of ice and turns it into a self-lubricating slippery surface. These phenomena are direct outgrowths of the micro-structural atomic bonding processes found in water and paper, but they are only understood as these micro-level processes are examined in conjunction with the macro-level phenomena of ambient temperature and pressure.

As a result of the recent emphasis on the study of non-linear and complex processes, a new structuralism has emerged in many branches of the physical sciences. These neo-structural theories emphasize the importance of modeling the unpredictable chaotic behaviour of aggregated systems. Two important ideas are at the centre of the neo-structuralist theories: (a) micro-structural elements are linked together in simple (but often non-linear) ways to form large-scale complex phenomena, and (b) the behaviour of the large-scale aggregates follows a logic that, while grounded on the behaviour of the micro-structures, cannot be directly predicted from them. The chaotic complexity linking the micro- and macro-structural levels is captured in the infinite variety of 'fractal' geometric patterns and in the 'strange attractors' that constitute the mathematical solutions to autocatalytic and other non-linear processes. Where understanding global systems is important, advances in knowledge depend on finding analytic methods that bridge between the micro- and macro-structural levels and illuminate the transitional points where aggregated micro-structures give rise to macro-patterns of action. That is, the bonding theories developed for micro-structures become meaningfully linked to the mechanics of macro-structures only when we understand the phase transition points where one form of analysis reaches its limits and the other form cannot fully account for the phenomena being investigated.

Adapting neo-structuralist theories to social phenomena

Figure 1 outlines a neo-structuralist framework for the analysis of social action systems drawing upon the concepts developed within the new structuralism of the natural sciences. The three columns in the figure describe, respectively: (a) theories of social

Figure 1.   A Framework for Neo-Structural Theory Development

	The **Bonding** of Micro-Structures Parameterized Mathematical *Functions*	Phase Transitions ⟶ ⟶ ⟶ ⟶ Emergent Non-linear Complexities	The **Mechanics** of Macro-Structures Pattern Stabilizing *Strange Attractors*
Affectivity Morals Ethics Emotions Feelings Experienced as Legitimacy	**Symbolic Interaction** Purposes Identities Cognitivism Personal Meanings	From personal meanings to assumptive worlds of action *Fractal Complexity* ⟶ ⟶ ⟶ ⟶ Truth is compelling goodness or beauty	**Functional Authority Structures** Norms Myths Culture Regime Profession Institutions *Gemeinschaft* Community
Rationality Means-Ends Reasoning Experienced as Potency	**Exchange Theory** Contracts Expectancy Theory Behaviorism Reinforcement Individual Incentives Utilitarianism	From individual rationality to coordinated inter-dependent actions *Autocatalytic Dynamics* ⟶ ⟶ ⟶ ⟶ Truth is reliable predictability	**Power Structures** Resource & Technical controls Economics Group Incentives Class Conflicts Organizations *Gesellschaft* Society

bonding that account for the linking of individuals and small groups into complex social structures, (b) phase transition theories describing the dynamic shifts that occur as the logic of individual and small group action gives way to the logic of social aggregate behaviours, and (c) theories of social mechanics which examine social dynamics that emerge when aggregate units interact.

Social bonding – linking individuals into social groups to create a web of relationships and establish a social fabric of mutual interdependence and stabilize regular patterns of social action – is rooted in the social psychology of everyday life. Individual needs, interests, desires and capacities create predilections toward specific actions. These predilections create forces of both cohesion and differentiation. Since psychic as well as physical security, interpersonal intimacy, feelings of self-worth and a sense of competence are all dependent upon the creation of interpersonal relationships, individuals come into the world with a certain amount of 'bonding energy' and a positive valence toward others. At the same time, the classical problems of scarcity in material goods and social prestige combine with clashes of values and desires to create interpersonal competition and the centrifugal forces that tear apart social groups. Like molecular bonds in chemistry, human social bonds are created when the attractive forces of mutual interdependence are stronger than the repelling forces of self-interest. There is nothing novel or profound about this insight. The point to be remembered, however, is that individuals become vested in these bonding relationships, moving from nominal independence into relationships rich with capitalized energy investments that lead individuals to presume, and rely upon, the stability of the social configuration. They cease to act as independent social actors and, instead, become component parts of the social molecule into which they have become bonded. The social unit, like a chemical molecule, displays emergent characteristics that depend upon, but cannot be directly predicted from, the characteristics of the participating individuals. Moreover, the social structures thus created display an array of social mechanics that have a logic and a predictability that are analytically distinct from the component individuals and social sub-groups. At the level of social bonding, the relevant questions concern how self-interests, personal meanings and individual identities among diverse individuals can be linked into chains of shared meaning, mutual interest and collective identity. But it is important to recognize that these bonding processes do not fully explain the emergent social structures. Once individuals have entered into a web of shared meanings, the logic of control shifts away from the bonding process itself and becomes focused on the logic of the social system. Thus, for example, shared religious beliefs create communities of faith, but contrasting theologies lay the foundations for sectarian conflict and schism even as they are linking followers into church organizations.

Phase transitions – the movement of social systems between an emphasis on bonding individuals and sub-groups into larger social aggregates and engagement in the mechanics of macro-structural interaction – are non-linear and complex. During phase transitions, attention can be focused on either the mechanics of the social aggregates or on the processing of generating individual engagement in them. Bonding processes become rich textured and auto-catalytic as social aggregates emerge. Once the aggregate structures become fully developed and become the taken-for-granted structures of social life for their members, they serve as the 'strange attractors' for social action – envelopes of limited variability which encompass but do not fully specify the actions of individual members.

The two horizontal rows shown in Figure 1 distinguish two basic forces at work in all social relationships – affection and rationality. These forces play vital but distinctive roles in the dynamics of both bonding and social mechanics. Affectivity – expressed in the form of moral commitments, social and ethical norms, motivating emotions, and feelings of desire or repulsion – creates the bonding energy that is the focus of symbolic interaction theories of social organization and action. Symbolic interaction theories account for the development of shared meanings, purposes, identities and the establishment of collective consciousness within social groups. As social aggregates emerge, affectivity becomes capitalized in myth and ritual forms – beliefs about the transcendental meaning and ultimate Truth expressed in the social aggregates. Because these affections are stabilized by raising them to transcendental significance, the resulting symbol systems move to the level of civic culture, political regime and professionalized occupational norms. The embraced macro-structures are infused with the sense of shared meanings that Tonnies (1957) called *gemeinschaftlich* or communal.

The rational energy found in both bonding and social mechanics is linked to the human capacities for accepting conventional rationalization of action and generating technical means-ends reasoning. Rational bonding processes are generally the focus of analysis in public choice and exchange theories. These theories identify the inherent capacity of human beings to calculate the consequences of their actions and to moderate activity based on expected outcomes. Social contract theories beginning with Rousseau's (1987) classic formulation have accounted for the creation of cohesive social structures in terms of the capacity of coordinated activity to produce more wealth, more security and more opportunity than individual actions. Typically, these bonding conceptions presuppose a behaviourist psychology in which utilitarian reward structures are linked to fundamental pleasure and pain processes. Incentives are, therefore, conceptualized in universalistic categories, shaping individual action through calculated optimization (or at least satisficing) of means-ends relationships.

Once individuals have been brought together in mutually reinforcing aggregate social structures, rationality takes on a new role in the social mechanics of interaction among these emergent structures. Power structures are created and sustained by the ability of rationally aggregated social groups to use their collective control over technical and economic resources to influence aggregated reward and punishment systems. Group incentive structures create class and caste social aggregates, and influence the stability and maintenance of formal organizations. The resulting social systems are characterized by what Tonnies (1957) describes as *gesellschaftlich* social relationships – relationships in which coalition building, formal contracts and abiding systems of exchange or domination determine how rewards and benefits will be distributed.

The non-linear phase transition between rational bonding and rational social system dynamics is characterized by the emergence of 'autocatalytic' organizational structures and interaction patterns. They are autocatalytic in the sense that the distribution of rewards and incentives become self-reinforcing and self-sustaining. The social mechanics of aggregated rationality include systems of private and corporate property systems, political entities, formal and informal organizations and marketplace contractual relationships. The common underlying principle is best captured in the economic conceptualization of capital formation. By controlling the formation and utilization of economic and social capital, these aggregated structures acquire the capacity to coordinate the active participation of individuals and to pyramid individual resources to form powerful centres of social stability.

The foregoing discussion has been too brief and cryptic to present a full blown model of how the neo-structuralist concepts of the new physical sciences can be appropriated by contemporary sociological and political theories. The central point is that affection and rationality are equally important in both bonding and social mechanisms. Classical theory put too much emphasis on the bonding aspects of affection and on the mechanical aspects of rationality, but this imbalance is not corrected by merely shifting the emphasis, it requires reconceptualizing the relationship between micro and macro level action systems. That is, rather than emphasizing the role of symbolic thought and human affectivity in creating and sustaining institutional norms, this approach emphasizes the importance of distinguishing the micro-structural study of social bonding from the macro-structural analysis of social mechanics. By conceptualizing social systems as involving distinctive systems of social bonding and structural mechanics, separated by phase transaction dynamics that involve non-linear and emergent social processes, the neo-structural paradigm is able to provide a more balanced treatment of both affectivity and rationalism.

The fundamental elements in both symbolic and rational processes can now be examined for their ability to contribute to individual bonding into social aggregates and their ability to provide social aggregates with just, reliable and orderly systems of social interaction. From this perspective, legitimacy is not just a matter of social approval for established systems of control. Legitimacy can be critically appraised on the basis of whether the aggregated systems are able to create and sustain bonding patterns among the individuals who participate in them.

Conclusion: future directions for neo-structural analysis

Before the neo-structuralist perspective sketched out in the preceding section can become a powerful tool for research design, professional practice improvement and educational policy development it will need to be elaborated and clarified. This concluding section is aimed at suggesting how future developments might give neo-structuralist theory the power needed to place it alongside classical bureaucratic theory and the insights generated by the new institutionalism as a basic framework for interpreting the behaviour of complex social organizations. To illustrate the kind of theoretical work that remains to be done, three areas of development – methodology for non-linear function analysis, conceptualization of 'fractal' textures and order producing 'strange attractors' in social action systems, and development of professional practices that might constrain social complexity – are briefly reviewed.

Methodological development of non-linear function analysis

At the methodological level, neo-structural theory challenges both interpretivist and linear modeling research strategies to become much more explicit about the theoretical bases for data collection and analysis. The need for more explicit theory is driven by the fact that the distinction between bonding and mechanics is more conceptual than empirical. Bonding is a problem that exists at many different levels – personality elements need to be bonded together to create a personal identity, individuals bonded to create groups, and groups to create organizational units which are, in turn, bonded into larger organizational and societal macro-structures. Thus, any given structural element can be studied from the perspective of either its bonding dynamics or its emergent structural mechanics. The two levels are thoroughly linked, but are joined by complex, non-linear processes rather than by predictable and conventionally studied linearities. We presently lack needed methodological tools for effective inquiry. Non-linear research in the physical sciences is clarifying at least a few aspects of the methods of inquiry that might be useful. It is clear, for example, that data collected to study non-linear phenomena can only be used to fit parameters that are *already* apprehended theoretically. Non-linear data is indistinguishable from random noise data without an hypothesized causal model to organize it for analysis. Thus, the factor and multiple regression techniques so often used to search for meaningful patterns and eliminate untenable causal propositions in contemporary social science research cannot be used to study truly non-linear problems. Interpretivist and ethnographic research strategies often advanced as tools for developing 'grounded theories' requiring no theoretical presuppositions are equally untenable for the study of phase transition problems. Without an intelligent hypothesis to fit, the complexities of phase transition data remain impenetrable.

Conceptual development of fractal textures and strange attractor controls

Two dimensions of the neo-structuralism guiding complexity and non-linear systems analysis in the physical sciences are particularly suggestive of new directions in social science research. The first is the recognition of infinitely varied textures and patterns within fractal geometric designs. Fractal geometries rely on simple underlying mathematical functions to produce richly textured patterns with surprising macro-structural regularities. To the extent that social action systems are fractal in structure, it is reasonable to assume that relatively simple micro-structure dynamics are responsible for highly complex aggregate system properties. Student and family cultures, for example, might well be fractal dimensions of school and classroom cultures. If so, the complex patterns of classroom life are to be explained by non-linear interactions among the cultures, rather than the linear impact of either cultural system on the other. While fractal interaction is a good metaphor for the relationship among classroom and school sub-cultures, it remains to be seen, however, whether new research methods can be found to delineate the fractal texture and demonstrate that this is more than simply a metaphor for aspects of schooling that are currently confusing.

The concept of a 'strange attractor' in non-linear mathematics is another provocative idea that may prove especially powerful in interpreting macro-structural behaviour in schools and other social institutions. Strange attractors are identified in non-linear systems to describe the ways in which some variables enable us to predict the general domain within which other variables will be found, but without actually producing specific point predictions of the values to be assumed by the dependent variables. This is not, as Weick (1976) might be interpreted as suggesting, that the causal and consequential variables are only 'loosely coupled', but rather because non-linear relationships are so dependent on the precise values taken on by the causal variables that no measurement system can be precise enough to give more than a broad envelope of predictability.

Professional practice development

Neo-structuralist theory has the potential of redirecting inquiry into professional practice. To the extent that educators need to be concerned with the phase transitions between the bonding of individual students and families into the social organization of the school and the mechanics through which pedagogy, curriculum and student assessment govern aggregate teaching and learning action systems, educators can expect to encounter important non-linear relationships between professional practice and student attainment. It may be helpful to point out that there are a number of mechanisms available for establishing professional control over non-linear processes. Three possibilities of great interest to teachers and school administrators might be called: (a) the pacing strategy, (b) the umbrella strategy and (c) the picket fence strategy.

Pacing for control over the timing of expected events
A particularly intriguing discovery in recent non-linear dynamics research was clarification of the role of the pacing signal in establishing complex regularity in the human heart beat. Heart beat regularity is far from perfect. Indeed, fibrillation – the development of a perfectly regular fluttering of the heart muscles – is potentially deadly because it fails to circulate the blood properly. Moving large quantities of blood requires a sequence of relaxation and contraction movement timed to allow blood to accumulate in specific heart

chambers and then be forced into the rest of the circulatory system. To accomplish blood circulation, the heart muscles must undergo non-linear contraction and relaxation cycles of a sort that only succeeds if a specific, appropriately timed pacing signal is generated to assure the proper sequence of muscle contractions. The result is a truly complex process in which a chaotic stream of muscle actions is made productive through the action of a very low energy timing signal. The overall system is not at all regular in its basic high energy muscle actions, but is made to function with a complex regularity through external control. The control mechanism is so completely external to the basic operation that battery operated pacemakers can be rather easily substituted for the original nerve system controls.

Application of this model of controlling chaotic processes through pacing signal timing offers some intriguing new lines of research for complex systems. Whether we are looking at student learning in classrooms or lawmaking by legislative bodies, it is now quite reasonable to think of the process as heavily influenced by relatively low energy pacing signals generated by key actors – signals which turn otherwise unproductive convulsions in the complex systems into orderly sequences of meaningful action. The resulting orderliness would never arise without the pacing signal overlay, and it can be as easily disrupted and made unproductive by pacing signals that are ill-timed or inappropriately applied. To the extent that this model accurately depicts control in social as well as biological systems, professional expertise would consist of knowing how to generate appropriate pacing signals and how to time their release to influence the performance of the underlying system. Both the exact nature of pacing signals and the time and place linkages between their release and the responses of the otherwise chaotic behaviour in the larger system could well become the focus of future research on professional service delivery. Educators and politicians may come to recognize what comedians have always known – the difference between success and failure is more in the timing than in the substance of the materials used.

Umbrella strategies to cope with unpredictable certainty

A second area for extending the insights generated by the neo-structuralist paradigm into professional practice involves accommodating rather than controlling non-linear processes. Since Edward Lorenz's (1963) work on weather forecasting models made a major contribution to the analysis of non-linear phenomena, we might call these accommodations of chaos 'umbrella' strategies. We purchase and carry umbrellas for the simple reason that non-linearities in the system make it impossible to accurately predict the time and amount of rainfall that will be encountered, even when we can predict with virtual certainty that rain is headed our way. Thus, rather than alter our work and travel schedules, we develop umbrellas that can be folded away until the moment when they are needed and then pop up to protect us against rainstorms that are certain to arrive but uncertain as to time, place and duration.

In elementary school classrooms, teachers need to have their umbrella strategies for coping with conflict and disruption. Every teacher knows that some children can create disturbances at any time (the disruptions may be responses to jealousy, boredom, health or family stress or an almost limitless variety of other causal forces). Like the rain, it is impossible to prevent the disruptions, or to predict exactly who will be involved, or when they will occur. Instead of prevention or control, teachers need response strategies that protect the integrity of the classroom and keep the disruptions from splashing over to uninvolved students. These strategies, identified as 'desist' strategies by Kounin (1970), are effective because they can be instantly generated whenever disruption is immanent or has begun.

Picket fence strategies to contain unpredictability

A third form of professional expertise implicit in the neo-structural paradigm might be called the 'picket fence' strategy for control of complex systems. Picket fences serve to set boundaries within which complex behaviour remains uncontrolled. Small children confront the fences surrounding family swimming pools as devices intersecting the 'strange attractors' for their behaviour. That is, the fences create explicit boundaries for complex behaviour that would otherwise include random visits to the pool area. The fences are needed because the naturally complex behaviour of children includes at least this one area which is too dangerous to permit them to follow their natural course of action. Complexity theories, by defining the strange attractor envelopes within which unconstrained behaviour can be expected to range, alert us to the fact that responsible parenting, like responsible professionalism in work environments, includes behaviour management at the points where intervention may be necessary to cut off some part of the behavioural domain that would otherwise be included in normal range of complex activity. Thus, for example, excited students can be expected to make noise and act energetically within the normal processes of learning. If the excitement leads to behaviours too far from the established social pattern of the classroom, however, the result can be a transformation of the classroom from a well-paced learning environment into a high noise, chaotic environment. Teachers have to intercept behaviours that would alter the classroom operating environment, while allowing spontaneous and energetic involvement in the learning process.

In very brief summary, this chapter has chronicled the breakdown of classic organization theory and explored ways in which the new institutionalists have grappled with the problems responsible for its demise. Despite the substantial advances of institutional theory, the neo-structuralism of the contemporary physical sciences have been presented as a potent alternative perspective on the study of how individuals become integrated into social systems and how the resulting systems establish regularity and stability in their operations.

Notes

1. I am indebted to Rodney Ogawa who pointed out that the Cohen, March and Olsen's conceptualization of organized anarchies and garbage can decision making has its roots in Herbert Simon's notion of constrained or 'bounded' rationality.

2. Public choice theorists are also carrying a torch for the more qualitative character of organizational decision and action systems by moving the centre of rationality away from the organization itself and onto the actions of individual members. Unfortunately, discussion of how choice theories could be used to resolve the issues raised by the work challenging classical theory must be left for another paper.

References

ARENDT, H. (1968) *Between Past and Future* (New York: Viking).

BLASE, J. (ed.) (1991) *The Politics of Life in Schools: Power, Conflict, and Cooperation* (Newbury Park: Sage).

BURNS, J. M. (1978) *Leadership* (New York: Harper & Row).

COHEN, M. D., MARCH, J. C. and OLSEN, J. P. (1972) A garbage can model of organizational choice. *Administrative Science Quarterly*, 17 (1), 1–25.

CRAIN, R. L. with assistance from INGER, M., MCWORTER, G. A. and VANECKO, J. J. (1968) *The Politics of School Desegregation: Comparative Case Studies of Community Structure and Policy-making* (Chicago: Aldine).

CREMIN, L. (1961) *The Transformation of the School: Progressivism in American Education, 1876–1957* (New York: Knopf).

DURKHEIM, E. (1933) *The Division of Labor in Society* (New York: Free).

FEYNMAN, R. P. (1995) *Six Easy Pieces: Essentials of Physics Explained by Its Most Briliant Teacher*, originally prepared for publication by R. B. Leighton and M. Sands (Reading, MA: Addison-Wesley).

IANNACCONE, L. (1967) *Politics in Education* (New York: Center for Applied Research in Education).

KELLY, J. (1974) *Organizational Behavior: An Existential-Systems Approach* (Homewood: Irwin).

KOUNIN, J. (1970) *Discipline and Group Management in Classrooms* (New York: Holt, Rinehart and Winston).

LEVINE, R. D. and BERNSTEIN, R. B. (1987) *Molecular Reaction: Dynamics and Chemical Reactivity* (New York: Oxford University Press).

LINDBLOM, C. E. (1959) The science of muddling through. *Public Administration Review,* 19, 79–88.

LORENZ, E. (1963) Deterministic nonperiodic flow. *Journal of Atmospheric Sciences*, 20, 130–41.

MAYO, E. (1933) *The Human Problems of an Industrial Civilization* (New York: Macmillan).

MEHAN, H. (1979) *Learning Lessons: Social Organization in the Classroom* (Cambridge, MA: Harvard University Press).

MEYER, J. and ROWAN, B. (1977) Institutionalized organizations: formal structure as myth and ceremony. *American Journal of Sociology*, 83, 340–63.

MEYER, J. W. and SCOTT, W. R. (1992) *Organizational Environments: Ritual and Rationality* (Newbury Park: Sage).

MITCHELL, D. E., ORTIZ, F. I. and MITCHELL, T. K. (1987) *Work Orientation and Job Performance: The Cultural Basis of Teaching Rewards and Incentives* (Albany: State University of New York Press).

PAGE, R. N. (1991) *Lower-track Classrooms: A Curricular and Cultural Perspective* (New York: Teachers College Press).

PARSONS, T. (ed.) (1947) Introduction, in M. Weber (ed.) *The Theory of Social and Economic Organization*, trans. A. M. Henderson and T. Parsons (New York: Free).

PARSONS, T. (1971) *The System of Modern Societies* (Englewood Cliffs: Prentice Hall).

POWELL, W. W. and DIMAGGIO, P. J. (eds) (1991) *The New Institutionalism in Organizational Analysis* (Chicago: University of Chicago Press).

ROETHLISBERGER, F. J. (1943) *Management and Morale* (Cambridge, MA: Harvard University Press).

ROUSSEAU, J.-J. (1987) *On The Social Contract*. Trans. and ed. Donald A. Cress, introduced by Peter Gay (Indianapolis: Hackett).

SCOTT, W. R. (1992) 'The organization of environments: network, culture, and historic elements', in J. W. Meyer and W. R. Scott (eds) *Organizational Environments Ritual and Rationality* (Newbury Park: Sage).

SEDLAK, M. W. *et al.* (1986) *Selling Students Short: Classroom Bargains and Academiuc Reform in the American High School* (New York: Teachers College Press).

SELZNICK, P. (1949) *TVA and the Grass Roots* (Berkeley: University of California Press).

SIMON, H. (1945) *Administrative Behavior* (New York: Free).

TAYLOR, F. (1911) *The Principles of Scientific Management* (New York: Harper).

TONNIES, F. (1957) *Community and Society*, trans. C. P. Loomis (East Lansing: Michigan State University Press). (Originally *Gemeinschaft und Gesellschaft*, 1912).

TRUHLAR, D. G. (ed.) (1981) *Potential Energy Surfaces and Dynamics: Calculations for Chemical Reactions and Molecular Energy Transfer* (New York: Plenum).

TYACK, D. B. (1974) *The One Best System: a History of American Urban Education* (Cambridge, MA: Harvard University Press).

TYACK, D. and HANSOT, E. (1982) *Managers of Virtue: Public School Leadership in America* (New York: Basic).

WALLER, W. (1932) *The Sociology of Teaching* (New York: Wiley).

WEBER, M. (1947) *The Theory of Social and Economic Organization*, trans. A. M. Henderson and T. Parsons (eds) (New York: Free).

WEICK, K. (1976) Educational organizations as loosely coupled systems. *Administrative Science Quarterly*, 21, 1–19.

WILDAVSKY, A. (1993) Democracy as a coalition of cultures, *Society,* 31 (1), 80–83.

13. The new institutionalism in postmodern times: de-differentiation and the study of institutions

James Ryan

For many of us in the Western world, the 1960s were a time of questioning. During this decade many young men and women took a hard look at the world about them, and they did not like all that they saw. Among many other things, they looked with disfavour on what they believed to be impersonal, oppressive and omnipotent institutions. Educational institutions did not escape this scrutiny. Students targeted many university campuses across the USA and Canada, staging protests and in some cases occupying administrative offices. But the assaults on educational institutions at this time cannot all be traced to unruly students. In fact considerable damage to the image of schools was produced, ironically enough, within the institution itself, in the form of a court-commissioned empirical study. Subsequently known as the Coleman Report (Coleman *et al.* 1966), its findings surprised many. What the researchers concluded from this wide-ranging survey was that the school itself had only a minimal impact on student achievement. The data told them that schools seemed relatively powerless to counteract the powerful social conditioning that young men and women were subject to 'outside of' educational institutions. Among other things, Coleman *et al.* (1966) contended that the socio-economic situation of students proved to be a better predictor of educational achievement than any in-school 'variables'. The assaults on our educational institutions did not stop here, however. In the next decade, Bowles and Gintis (1976) assembled an impressive array of empirical studies that more-or-less supported the Coleman findings. They concluded that instead of providing equal opportunities for all students, regardless of background, schools merely reproduced the unequal relations that already existed in the wider society.

Needless to say not all supporters of our educational institutions accepted these findings. Some proponents simply could not embrace the fact that schools did not matter. Many of these people could not bring themselves to believe that schools were incapable of acting apart from the social conditions that surrounded them. Still others were determined to hold onto the myth that our educational institutions were in fact the beacons of hope and opportunity that our dominant liberal ideology had led many of us to believe. Not surprisingly, groups of academics set about to prove detractors wrong by illustrating once and for all that schools do make a difference. Researchers in what subsequently came to be known as the effective schools movement, for example, went about this task by identifying the common characteristics of (academically) successful schools (Brookover *et al.* 1979, Rutter *et al.* 1979) and districts (Coleman and LaRoque 1989). The hope was that once these characteristics were identified then all that not-so-successful schools had to do was to adopt these practices. Unfortunately, advocates of the movement under-estimated the complexity of the social phenomena which they were exploring, including for example the often unique cultural contexts within which these school practices

0268–0939/95 $12 · 00 © 1995 Taylor & Francis Ltd

occurred. Subsequent efforts to parachute in so-called successful practices to these institutions met with minimal success (Holmes 1989, Ryan 1993).

But even as the influence of the effective schools movement wains and our institutions continue to come under attack in the media and from the public, efforts to bolster our apparently flagging educational institutions persist. The most recent efforts have emerged under the label 'The New Institutionalism'. Already taking root in such diverse fields as economics, political science, organization theory and sociology, they employ a wide and disparate range of concepts and assumptions. Despite this diversity most advocates of the new institutionalism would probably agree that institutions do play a substantial role in shaping life, and as a consequence they see value in directing much of their analytic efforts at institutions, sometimes at the expense of other social phenomena, including for example, the wider social context (March and Olsen 1984). The hope for those importing this concept into education would seem to be that a focus on institutions thus conceived will help us get a better read on just how schools work so that reformers will eventually get their efforts at restructuring right. An approach of this nature, it is hoped, will provide an appropriate framework for scholars to explore schooling so that they will eventually be able to supply practitioners and politicians with the information that will help them in their efforts to provide meaningful education for all.

While it is difficult to assess the potential of this approach at this time, particularly given the wide range of perspectives, there are nevertheless dangers in conceptualizing institutions too narrowly, de-emphasizing, for example, the importance of social context, as some – but not all – branches of the new institutionalism are apt to do (March and Olsen 1984). Such a practice runs the risk of overlooking the sweeping changes that are occurring in our social and cultural fabric and that are part of what some refer to as postmodernity. In particular, efforts to separate out elements of this fabric, be they institutions or elements of institutions, will be difficult, if not impossible, in a world that is becoming increasingly 'de-differentiated' (Lash 1990), a progressively shrinking or 'imploding' world (McLuhan 1973) where what were once thought to be unique realms of experience continue to collapse into one another. Institutions are as much a part of this changing landscape as other realms of existence, and efforts to ignore or de-emphasize the social and cultural contexts of contemporary institutions will only leave us with a limited and inadequate understanding of how schools work. In what follows I describe these aspects of our postmodern world, illustrate how institutional life is changing, and comment on how we can best go about analyzing these changes. First, however, I briefly describe selected aspects of the modern era and compare them with the new institutional analyses.

Modernity and differentiation

Lash (1990) believes that our postmodern world can best be characterized by its *de-differentiating* tendencies. He contrasts this phenomenon with the *differentiation* common to the modern age. But this differentiation of life was not always the prevailing norm in human affairs. Indeed, before the onset of mass industrialization, the invention of the printing press and the technology that made these and other phenomena possible, men, women and children lived their lives free from what eventually were to become boundaries (Lash 1990, Bauman 1992). All aspects of their lives were inseparably intertwined. Separating out or identifying single elements or aspects of existence would have been difficult, since everything they did melded into a holistic life experience. What we would now think of as an economic sphere was also in many respects part of the familial, educational and religious or spiritual spheres. Hunting, for example, which today would probably be considered part of an economic institution, was inevitably a family enterprise. It would also have involved the education of younger members and most often had profound religious or spiritual significance. Life would also have been conducted primarily within an oral as opposed to a literate tradition which would have made it difficult to separate out elements of experience. The spoken word was inextricably fused with all other aspects of existence (Goody and Watt 1968, Ryan 1994).

Life began to change dramatically as humanity learned to fashion tools and employ them effectively. Europeans were the first to take advantage of technology on a large scale. In doing so they ushered in an era that subsequent generations have referred to as modernity. Mass production of goods, the invention of the rifle and the printing press, the rise of the nation state, the emergence of science, the rapid increase in populations (among many other phenomena) all characterized this modern era. Also symptomatic of the age was something that Durkheim (1964) and others who followed his lead, including Lash (1990) and other commentators on the postmodern age, would refer to as differentiation. By this they meant that modern society displayed a tendency to compartmentalize itself. Increasingly different aspects of life were seen as distinct from others. Unlike premodern times the economy, education, religion and the family all took on lives of their own as institutions in their own right. Men, women (and sometimes children) now travelled to places of work that had little to do with their family lives. Education was something that took place in a building, and spiritual fulfilment occurred as an organized activity on a specified day. People now *went to* work, school and church. But these divisions did not end here. Social phenomena, from these overarching institutions to the most insignificant personal acts, continued to be broken down into finer and finer categories. Nash (1993: 19), for example, maintains that

> As society modernizes there is a tendency for activities to become broken into smaller and more specialized parts. Each part is given a special task (specialization) and each part is supposed to shape its energy and organization to fit the work it does (differentiation). Indeed most of our daily lives are specialized and differentiated. Our jobs require that we know more and more about less. When we want something fixed we seek out a person who specializes in the kind of repair we need and whose knowledge and skills are differentiated to the solution of our problem.

Lash (1990) looks at this differentiation from another perspective. He contends that modernization brought on divisions that had a profound effect on things cultural. As the world began to modernize, men and women started to see distinctions between types of cultural objects, the social and cultural, the conditions of production and consumption, and between symbols, signs and objects. According to Lash, humanity now drew distinctions between aesthetic, theoretical and ethical realms, believed that culture was contained in activities or objects quite removed from everyday practices, could no longer see connections between production of cultural objects and their consumption, and increasingly relied on the separation of signs from the objects to which they supposedly referred. The rise of literacy in fact facilitated this latter division. Words could now be separated out from the flux of time and made to stand for unique objects and events. As a consequence literacy accelerated the compartmentalization of life and went hand in hand with the drive for control that was behind this process.

A preoccupation with controlling human activity was also closely associated with this differentiation. This relationship is perhaps best captured by Weber (1968) and Foucault (1979, 1980). For Weber rational bureaucratic structures with their divisions of labour, specialization and hierarchy provided the most efficient means for successful operation. Foucault, on the other hand, noted that captains of industry, administrators and politicians increasingly employed disciplinary measures that included perpetual surveillance and exhaustive divisions of space and time, to achieve optimal levels of production. For both Weber and Foucault this segmentation or division of life, from society's major institutions to the most trivial activity, played a pivotal role in controlling the actions and lives of men and women.

Foucault (1979, 1980) also recognized that knowledge played an important part in this control. The separation of 'words and things' played a key role. A theoretical discourse made possible in part by a literate society that took for granted the ability of signs to stand apart from an object world, and in turn account for it, enabled scholars to construct a picture of institutions which they believed would help them collect information that would eventually facilitate this control. Many scholars found that a machine metaphor was particularly useful in this endeavour. Some believed that its interlocking and distinct parts provided an ideal model for analyzing institutions and their constituent organizations, and for eventually supplying managers with the information necessary to get workers, students, or public servants to produce efficiently and at optimal levels (Ryan 1988). Assumed in such a model was a bounded organization or institution, a tendency for the institution to gravitate toward consistency and uniformity, and the possibility of a uniform interpretation of organizational phenomena. Clegg (1990: 19), for example, contends that organizational analysis has traditionally centred

> on the systematically bounded world of organizations. Organization, conceived in terms of its modernist antecedents implies a degree of legal and more normative unity, a single center of calculation and classification, a relatively unambiguous distribution of power and influence, and a setting for action sufficiently uniform for *similar actions* to be expected to bring *similar consequences* for the whole and thus to be interpreted in a similar way. Moreover, the modernist anchorage of the concept of organization allowed it to be situated in an endless play of determinations, between inherent developmental tendencies, self-sustained and self-propelled, inexorably naturalized as being *inside* organization, such as 'size' and 'technology' and those factors *outside* such as the 'environment', which have a precarious, contingent relation to these interior forces.

Modern analysis and the new institutionalism

How does new institutional analysis conform, if at all, to the traditional modernist organizational approach? And if it does, what are the implications? First of all, it is difficult to say whether or not the new institutionalism as a whole reflects these aspects of modernist differentiation simply because of the diversity in the approaches generally grouped under this rubric. Even so, there is a tendency in many branches of the new institutionalism to display, if not explicitly then implicitly, traditional modernist analytic assumptions and techniques. Indeed, selected theorists of this persuasion subscribe to ideas that revolve around the assumptions outlined above by Clegg – a world view that separates, compartmentalizes and breaks down social phenomena into unique categories. A number of these individuals want to advertise a concept of institution that is bounded, set apart in good measure from, while at the same time maintaining a precarious relation to, the social context within which it exists. Other proponents see value in emphasizing distinct, common and enduring patterns which they believe are endemic to institutions. Finally most approaches foresee few difficulties in the interpretation of organizational phenomena. Many who adopt this approach continue to believe in the ability of scientific discourse to capture or mirror the objective world of organizations and institutions.

Some branches of the new institutionalism seek to feature a bounded institution. Not all proponents subscribe to this view, however. Indeed, the degree to which a particular strand adheres to this view depends on how its advocates conceptualize institutions. And as Dimaggio and Powell (1991) point out, there are a wide range of such definitions. On the one hand, 'sociological' approaches tend to see institutions in all sorts of phenomena. The organization theory branch, on the other hand, holds a more restrictive view of institutions. It focuses on organizational structures and processes that are industry-wide, national or international in scope, and takes as its starting point arrangements in the labour market, schools, states and corporations. March and Olsen (1984, 1989) perhaps typify efforts to re-focus organizational analysis on institutions from an organization theory perspective. They maintain that explorations of the polity, for example, have for some time now paid too little attention to institutions. Their contention is that those who explore political activity attribute too much importance to the effect of 'society' and to the social context of politics. March and Olsen (1984: 735) state that political scientists are 'inclined to see politics as an integral part of society, less inclined to differentiate the polity from the rest of society'. This view reflects an 'inclination to see causal links between society and polity as running from the former to the latter, rather than the other way around'. March and Olsen feel that this is a mistake, and seek to reestablish a more autonomous role for institutions and to de-emphasize the social context. Indeed they go so far as to say that institutions

> are political actors in their own right. The argument that institutions can be treated as political actors is a claim of institutional coherence and autonomy. The claim of coherence is necessary in order to treat institutions as decision makers. (March and Olsen 1984: 738)

Not all branches of the new institutionalism would support, without question, a view that boldly reifies institutions in this manner. Even so, most proponents would probably endorse a more autonomous role for institutions, while at the same time making room for at least some 'societal' influence. Mawhinney (1994: 7), for example, claims that 'although not rejecting the importance of the social context of politics and the motives of individual actors, the new institutionalism insists on a more autonomous role for institutions'. The nature of this context, however, may know considerably more limits than the one acknowledged by the political scientists whom March and Olsen criticize. Dimaggio and Powell (1991: 13), for example, recognize that the new institutionalism admits 'environments' into their analyses, but these 'non-local environments' are strictly bounded entities.

> The new institutionalism focuses instead on non local environments, either organization sectors or fields roughly coterminous with the *boundaries* of industries, professions, or national societies. Environments, in this view, are more subtle in their influence; rather than being co-opted by organizations, they penetrate the organization, creating lenses through which actors view the world and the very categories of structure, action, and thought. [My emphasis]

The new institutionalism displays a second tendency towards differentiation. In the modernist tradition, and in addition to the distinctions it establishes between institutions and their social context, it is preoccupied with distinctions *within* institutions. In particular, those who employ this perspective commonly draw distinctions between and among different types of institutional components (or practices). They routinely separate out those practices which repeat themselves in a variety of contexts from other apparently random practices, and from each other. In other words, they work at identifying and extracting patterns and regularities in institutional performance and practice. In doing so, they routinely direct their efforts toward the uniform and coherent, while de-emphasizing or overlooking the diverse and chaotic. The emphasis here is on the persistence of these phenomena rather than on their transformation, on stability as opposed to change. Dimaggio and Powell (1991: 14), for example, summarize these tendencies in a helpful way.

> In the new view, institutionalization tends to reduce variety, operating across organizations to override diversity in
> local environments . . . . The organization's *standardized components*, however, are loosely coupled, often displaying
> minimal functional integration. . . . Not only does neoinstitutionalism emphasize the homogeneity of
> organizations; it also tends to stress the stability of institutional components. By contrast, for the old
> Institutionalism, change was an endemic part of the organizations evolving adaptive relationship to its local
> environment. [My emphasis]

The emphasis on uniformity finds expression in both March and Olsen (1984) and in Dimaggio and Powell (1983). March and Olsen (1984: 743) explore the 'part played by institutional structures in imposing elements of order on a potentially inchoate order'. In doing so they identify six conceptions of order; historical, temporal, endogenous, normative, demographic and symbolic. Dimaggio and Powell (1983), on the other hand, are interested in the concept of 'homogenization'. As a consequence, they seek to identify the means through which organizations tend to display similar characteristics. For example, they note that the greater participation of professional managers in professional associations and the increasing reliance on academic credentials can lead to greater uniformity of practice across organizations and within institutions.

The new institutionalism reflects modern differentiation in one final way. Unlike the other two aspects, it is not addressed directly by its proponents. Instead, they endorse this aspect of differentiation more by what they fail to say. They do this by taking for granted the utility of empirical research. Virtually all of the supporters of this perspective employ unproblematically the results of empirical research to support what they claim. They also call for more empirical research into the areas they deem to be appropriate. Nowhere in these papers do we find a critical discussion of the research or analytic process. This is largely because these theorists, like many others in the 'realist' tradition, take for granted the separation of analyst and researcher from that which is being explored. They assume, in other words, that there is an object world of institutions 'out there' that can be captured in a straightforward way by astute investigators, provided of course that they employ the correct methodology. Also taken for granted here is the capability of scientific discourse to map out a one-to-one correspondence between its signs or elements and the components of the object world under investigation.

Unfortunately those branches of the new institutionalism that reflect these aspects of differentiation fail to acknowledge key aspects of our contemporary world. In particular they do not take into account that life is becoming increasingly de-differentiated. Proponents of the new institutionalism who subscribe to this view of institutions overlook the fact that institutional life is becoming increasingly dependent on other (global) forms of life; organizational life is becoming more spontaneous and organic in nature and is susceptible to sometimes fast and dramatic change; and the relationship between the researcher/analyst, scientific discourse and the phenomenon under scrutiny is more complex than most realist social scientists have assumed.

De-differentiation

Any analysis of contemporary institutional forms, or for that matter any social analysis, must take into consideration our rapidly changing world. Prominent among these changes is a shift from differentiation to de-differentiation. Among the first to recognize this transformation was Marshall McLuhan (1973). His notion of a global village provides a useful metaphor for understanding this shift. McLuhan acknowledged that our world was getting smaller. He did not mean that the world was physically shrinking, of course. Instead he pointed out that technology, and in particular the electronic media, was bringing humanity closer together. The following citation employed by many observers of the postmodern condition including Harvey (1989), Smart (1992) and Hargreaves (in press) illustrates the phenomenon associated with McLuhan's global village.

> After three thousand years of explosion, by means of fragmentation and mechanical technologies, the Western World is imploding. During the mechanical ages we had extended our bodies in space. Today, after more than a century of electronic technology, we have extended our central nervous system itself in a global embrace, abolishing both space and time as far as our planet is concerned.

Here McLuhan (1973: 11) contrasts the social forms associated with mechanical technologies with those that are now accompanying electronic technologies. Specifically, he notes that the former is synonymous with differentiation and separation, while the latter is connected with de-differentiation and inter-dependence. Smart (1992: 118), borrowing from McLuhan, makes this same observation.

> Where mechanization is synonymous with differentiation, fragmentation and specialization, electrification is precipitating de-differentiation, creating if not requiring a high degree of inter-dependence. Where 'the typographic extension of man brought in rationalism, industrialism, mass markets and universal literacy and education', the implosion of the electronic age is eroding national boundaries and precipitating an 'organic structuring of the global economy' and in turn is rendering the 'uniformily trained and homogenized citizenry . . . a burden to an automated society'.

This process of globalization, and its associated compression of space and time (Harvey 1989), renders compartmentalization and separation difficult, if not impossible. Institutions, organizations and divisions of all sorts will find it increasingly difficult to escape the influence of this implosion. Under these postmodern conditions of 'extreme inter-dependence' (Smart 1992), elements of this global culture will continue to find their way into even the most isolated pockets of existence, contaminating those characteristics which at one time set them apart from other facets of life. Technological advances are responsible, at least in part, for this condition. They have made it possible for us to experience how others around the world live, not only by facilitating transportation to these places, but also by bringing these places to us. Changes in the economy have rendered national borders meaningless (Reich 1991). Multinational corporations circulate goods, services, capital and labour among their subsidiaries around the globe with little if any regard for national boundaries. Improved and cheaper transportation capabilities further enhance the permeability of these borders as natural disasters, civil strife and changing immigration policies prompt men and women to pick up and move to distant lands. The electronic media also have a powerful role to play in bringing us all closer together. Harvey (1989: 293) maintains, for example, that

> Mass television ownership coupled with satellite communication makes it possible to experience a rush of images from different spaces almost simultaneously, collapsing the world's spaces into a series of images on a television set. The whole world can watch the Olympic Games, the World Cup, the fall of a dictator, a political summit, deadly tragedy . . . while mass tourism, films made in spectacular locations, make a wide range of simulated or vicarious experiences of what the world contains available to many people.

The bringing together of different worlds in the same space and time, whether it be in the form of simulated images, auditory transmissions, sets of electronic figures, goods and services, or people themselves, will have a considerable impact on the shape that our institutions will take. Most importantly, for future analyses of institutions, it will be difficult to carve out bounded institutional forms from an increasingly inter-dependent world, single out distinct and enduring patterns of interaction, and separate scholarly and scientific discourse from the social phenomenon under scrutiny.

Unbounded institutions

Theoretical efforts to construct a bounded – albeit permeable – entity for the purposes of analysis or empirical study, ignore the ways in which our experiences of work, leisure and life have changed over the past two decades. Among other things, these enterprises overlook the way in which 'culture' constitutes an important part of institutions and organizations. While organization theorists and gurus have brought a notion of culture into their analyses over the last decade (for example, Peters and Waterman 1982, Deal and Kennedy 1983), it has not always been one that captures the complexities of organization life in a helpful way. Instead these scholars perceive culture as something endemic to the organization, a phenomenon that can be created and shaped by managers to control the actions of those who work in these institutions (Bates 1987). Clegg (1990) provides us with a more useful perspective on the role of culture. In his analysis of postmodern economic institutions in Asia, he illustrates how local and national cultures become *part of* what happens in institutions. Drawing on Granovetter (1985), he employs the concept of 'economic embeddedness' to show hwo a more broadly conceived notion of culture 'fuses' with institutional practices. Clegg demonstrates how the family, the state and pre-war networks influence profoundly the character of organization life in economic institutions in Taiwan, Korea and Japan, arguing that 'organizational sovereignty' loses credibility and conviction as a privileged space for economic activity. Clegg (1990: 150), maintains that

> In organizational terms culture works through framing the assumptions that agencies are able to operate with. It frames and enables; it enables and it constrains. The crucial factor is not that a manager or an organization is Japanese rather than American or Australian. It is what being Japanese makes available in terms of normal ways of accounting for action, of calculating strategy, of constituting rationalities, of mapping cognitively, which is important. These matters are not just cultural: they depend upon distinct and nationally variable institutional frameworks. By such frameworks one is referring to nationally specific, hence variable, conditions within which managerial and organizational action is constituted.

But Clegg (1990) perhaps understates the impact of the electronic media in this regard. It is not just local and national culture and institutions that influence action in these settings. We now know that thanks to this technology men and women have a much wider repertoire of potential practices and discourses from which to draw than they once had. They are perpetually bombarded with ideas, norms, values and practices from a multitude of sources and lands, and are more than occasionally influenced by them. The importation of quality circles into American companies illustrates the ease with which these practices circulate globally.

Another way of illustrating the interdependence of contemporary social practices is to highlight the increasingly overlapping spheres of production and consumption, not only of goods, but of services, information and knowledge. Sociologists such as Bauman (1992), Smart (1992) and Baudrillard (1983) suggest that perhaps social analysts should direct their energies toward consumption rather than production, the traditional object of scrutiny. They make these suggestions because they believe that the processes associated with consumption are more important in shaping, and in turn understanding, what men and women do than those institutions responsible for producing material goods or services. Others want to include both production and consumption within a single framework in a way that captures the interdependence of both spheres. Knights and Morgan (1993) for example, want to acknowledge the 'interdependence and social constitution of the market, the consumer and the organization'. They consider the powerful influence of cultural consumption values over organizations and in turn institutional attempts to shape these same values. Knights and Morgan (1993: 217) maintain that 'connections between the organization of production and the organization of consumption either privately or within households through kinship, power, ethnic and gender relationships cannot be ignored'. One of their linking concepts is identity. They contend that institutions actively attempt to create market niches by shaping consumer identities in, for example, the area of youth culture. This is not a one-way process, however, as Knight and Morgan (1993: 223–4) note.

> Organizations participate in the construction of needs or use-values through the way in which they advertise and market products but they are by no means omnipotent in this regard, nor are consumers passive recipients of their propaganda. On the contrary as suggested earlier, organizational failure is frequent as consumers resist particular products and services. In seeking to overcome such resistance to consumption, organizations continually appeal to or seek to create specific identities.

Educational institutions are as much a part of this de-differentiating world as economic institutions. We can expect local and global cultures to become fused with educational practice and the lines between the 'production' of knowledge and skills and their 'consumption' to become increasingly blurred. In grappling with these issues, however, we must acknowledge that the latter boundaries have always been more complex in the area of education because of the nature of the clientele and the so-called product. Are students the clients or beneficiaries of educational activities? Parents? The immediate community? The larger society? The economy? Teachers? Recent efforts to involve the community in more fundamental ways in the process of formal education (Crowson 1992, Government of Ontario 1995), a focus on teacher learning and development (Government of Ontario 1995, Hargreaves 1994), initiatives to 'de-institutionalize' teacher training institutions (Hargreaves, in press), calls to move toward education as a 'life-long experience' or to move out of a formal setting, increasing associations with businesses and other institutions (Alladini 1995), the increase in numbers involved in home schooling, among many other practices, will no doubt continue to frustrate those who want to draw a line around educational institutions.

The nature of educational 'products' also demands that analyses not be too narrowly defined. Since knowledge is something that is constructed and not discovered, the experiences that students bring to school will play an important role in the kinds of things they learn or fail to learn. Indeed a good teacher is often one that will find ways to tap into student experience and build on it (Ryan *et al.* 1995). These experiences, however, are becoming increasingly varied, due in part to exposure to the electronic media and, at least in Canada and the United States, increasing migration of men, women and children from all parts of the world. As a consequence, young men and women used to perpetual visual stimulation may find standard lessons less than stimulating (Hargreaves 1994), while those newly arrived from distant shores may have trouble adjusting to authority conventions (Ryan *et al.* 1995). Rapidly changing knowledge bases may also have an impact on what happens in educational institutions. In order to prepare their students to keep up with the recent explosion in knowledge, some medical schools, for example, have moved away from teaching their students 'facts' to helping them learn how to go about searching for knowledge that changes on a daily basis. Schools are also sites where identities are built, demolished and fought over. Indeed this process of identity formation can have a considerable impact on the ways in which students respond to formal schooling (Ryan 1989, Solomon 1992).

Cooper and Burrell (1988) provide an alternate conception of organization that attempts to acknowledge some of these changes. They believe that analyses of organizations and institutions should not be directed at an ontological entity, an envelope as it were, in which one enters and leaves (Clegg 1990). Instead, as characterized by Parker

(1993), analysts should look at organization as a *verb* rather than a noun. In doing so they would direct their efforts at the social production of organization, rather than the organization of production. They will necessarily have to include networks of social relations of considerably wider scope than those suggested as appropriate by March and Olsen (1984), for example. Cooper and Burrell (1988: 106) maintain that

> We need to see organization as a *process* that occurs within the wider 'body' of society and which is concerned with the construction of objects of theoretical knowledge centered on the 'social body': health, disease, emotion, alienation, labor, etc. In other words, to understand organizations it is necessary to analyze them from the outside, as it were, and not from what is already organized. It becomes a question of analyzing, let us say, the production of organization rather than the organization of production.

Unstable and organic institutions

The de-differentiating tendencies of contemporary social life will likely continue to frustrate the efforts of social scientists to identify enduring and endemic patterns of institutional practice. Indeed the accelerating rate of change and moves towards organic rather than fragmented approaches to solving problems bring to the surface the contingent rather than stable aspects of institutional life. Analysts have invariably characterized contemporary organizational practice as 'disorganized, untidy, and fragile' (Hassard 1993: 18); 'ambiguous, heterogeneous, and discordant' (Jeffcut 1993: 38); 'fluid and under-patterned' (Clegg 1990: 22); 'contingent and arbitrary' (Reed 1993: 164); and made reference to its 'innate capriciousness and uncertainty in all its multifarious forms' (Reed 1993: 164). This instability is due, in part, to the accelerated pace of life. Things appear to happen so much faster today than they once did. This speed-up is perhaps best reflected in changes in the production of goods and services. Over the past two decades the turnover rate of production and consumption has dramatically increased. Economic institutions and organizations race to cultivate, target and exploit market niches. Technological advances in transportation and electronic communication now make it possible for producers to appraise volatile markets, make adjustments in their productive apparatus, and move goods and services to consumers in a matter of weeks and sometimes days (Harvey, 1989, Toffler 1990). Timing in these cases is not just a matter of convenience. The very survival of companies may depend on the speed with which they can adjust to quickly changing market preferences. Many of those organizations that survive employ flexible manufacturing practices which may include such things as extensive sub-contracting, adjustable productive apparatus, and decentralized decision-making. This flexibility in turn enhances unpredictability. Product lines may change dramatically from week to week, employees may come and go on a moment's notice, and entire operations may move to other more distant locations overnight (Ryan 1995). Indeed it would seem that a focus on transformation or 'deinstitutionalization' rather than 'institutionalization' would perhaps be more appropriate here (Oliver 1992).

The changes in the speed with which things occur are often accompanied by more organic work arrangements. The traditional modern emphasis on job specialization, stable roles and functional divisions are now being replaced by moves toward more fluid divisions. Hargreaves (1994: 164), for example, contends that 'the postmodern organization is characterized by networks, alliances, tasks and projects, rather than by relatively stable roles and responsibilities which are assigned by function and department, and regulated through hierarchical supervision'. Clegg (1990: 187) notes that Japanese economic institutions display overlapping work roles, extensive job rotation, team-based and relatively flexible production lines. Generalists now are the order of the day. Clegg (1990: 193) maintains that the move toward generalists may even blur distinctions between managers and line personnel.

> Managers will not usually be specialists in accounting or finance, for instance, but will more likely be generalists who can rotate between positions. Management rotation results in flexibility and learning by doing similar to that experienced on the shopfloor. This blurs the distinction between line and staff managers, and between management and workers.

The fast pace of life in institutions and the move away from rigidly prescribed roles engenders conditions that prompt men and women to act in ways that are often unpredictable and that resist conformity to patterns. Clegg (1990) for example sees those who work in institutions as 'practical experimentalists' forced to solve problems in a world that is more uncertain, ambivalent, contradictory and ambiguous that any natural scientist would anticipate finding in the lab. Cooper and Burrell (1988: 91), on the other hand, see organization as 'less the expression of planned thought and calculative action and more of a defensive reaction to forces intrinsic to the social body which constantly threaten the stability of organized life'. They see the process of organization as 'self-originating and automatic', and consider that organized rationality, 'far from originating in *beau-ideals* and consummate logics of efficiency is founded on sleight-of-hand, vicious agonisms and *pudenda origo* (shameful origins)' (Cooper and Burrell 1988: 108). Marquard (1991: 5–6) undermines further the prospect of establishing underlying regularities in institutions, suggesting in fact that life is more a product of our accidents than our plans.

> We are not only our accomplishments, but also our accidents – our fateful accidents. To which I make only one additional qualification: we are always more our accidents than our accomplishments. So we have to be able to bear what is accidental, because living with what is accidental is not a result of failing to reach the absolute, but is our historically normal condition.

What then are the chances of identifying stable patterns of interaction in educational institutions? Have the frantic pace of change and holistic organization patterns found their way into education? On the one hand, educators have for some time now been subject to waves of reform (Cuban 1990). Legislatures and school districts have mandated changes of various sorts, and teachers and administrators have been forced to adopt many of them. Some (Sarason 1990, Tye 1992, Lewington and Orpwood 1993) argue, however, that reforms have in fact done little to change the actual structure of education. They say, for example, that little has changed in the classroom itself. Some teachers, however, would maintain that much has changed in the classroom over the last ten, and even five years (Ryan *et al.* 1995), even though such changes would probably have little to do with reform efforts. Teaching has changed because students and teachers have changed. Students bring with them to the classroom ideas and values, some of which they have acquired through the electronic media, among a host of other sources. As these images and influences change so do students, along with classroom practices, at a rate much faster than ten years ago. Also changing is the ethnic composition of many classrooms. The current wave of immigration, particularly in the larger cities in North America, has changed dramatically the nature of the student body. Five to ten years ago teachers were instructing students of primarily Anglo-European background; now they can encounter up to sixty different ethnic groups in one day (Ryan *et al.* 1995).

Job and subject specialization, however, vary depending upon the level of education. Elementary teachers often tend to treat subject matter in a holistic manner, even though they would commonly direct their efforts to one particular and often similar group of children. Many secondary schools, on the other hand, display balkanized organization

(Hargreaves 1994). Teachers tend to instruct students in their speciality, rarely straying far from their area of specialization. Nevertheless there have recently been moves toward more holistic approaches to education at this level (Miller 1994), and towards more cooperative ventures between teachers (Hargreaves 1994). Furthermore, Hargreaves (1994) maintains that schools will eventually have to adopt more flexible practices – like other institutions – if they are to keep up with the world around them. These realities, coupled with the failure to identify underlying regularities in schools (Ryan 1988), would seem to signal difficulties for those interested in identifying underlying institutional patterns. Fraatz (1989: 4) for example maintains that schools are in fact places where individual action is just as unpredictable as in other institutions.

> People in schools spend their days carrying out difficult tasks with uncertain consequences; they pursue vague and often conflicting objectives with highly variable and conflicting resources; they rely on poorly specified 'technology' to identify problems and to discriminate among solutions; and they are connected with one another in ways which appear structured and predictable, but which are in fact tenuous and circumstantial.

Emphases on uniformity or efforts to identify common traits or regularities within and across institutions cannot always capture the tenuous and circumstantial, the messy and multifarious nature of contemporary educational institutions. In fact many social scientists acknowledge problems in the analytic or research process.

Conclusion

There is little doubt that institutions are *the* dominant contemporary social form. In one way or another they influence virtually everything we do and say. But the institutions of today are not the institutions that we knew twenty or even ten years ago. In the space of two decades many of these organizations and institutions have undergone considerable change. Among other things, contemporary de-differentiation tendencies have engendered a high degree of inter-dependence between and among organizations, institutions and aspects of them, and other forms of life. Institutional practice no longer confines itself to clearly identifiable boundaries, as scholars once assumed. Moreover, institutions are becoming more organic, flexible and subject to more rapid changes than ever before. Educational institutions have also changed over the last two decades, although many of these changes have not necessarily resulted from planned reform efforts. Unfortunately, the conceptual entities constructed by organization theorists and others a quarter of a century ago are often less than helpful in providing us with insight in postmodern institutional and school practice. Further to this, contemporary social scientists now question traditional approaches to the study of organizations that strive for factual accuracy. This is not to say that we should not seek to understand education by directing our efforts to institutional aspects of education. We should, and I believe that the new institutionalists are right in calling for greater attention to institutions. But if we are to move ahead with this programme then we must do so in ways that allow us to tap into the changes that they are undergoing. In particular, those who direct their efforts to exploring institutions must employ a sufficiently broad conception of organizations and institutions and methods to allow for credible inquiry into these new forms.

Ethnography is one approach that fulfils some of these conditions. It enables scholars to capture unbounded social phenomena, and bring to the surface the disorderly aspects of organizations not normally highlighted. One way ethnography is able to do this is by allowing those under scrutiny, particularly traditionally marginal groups, to speak their minds. Ethnographic approaches also provide a useful alternative to approaches that mistakenly seek to provide accurate descriptions of institutions by assuming that social scientists can separate themselves from the phenomena which they explore. Rejecting notions of objectivity and accuracy, ethnographers construct texts in ways that permit readers to judge for themselves the sensibility of the contained descriptions. Here the authority of any claim rests not with the text, the research design or the researcher, but with the reader (Erickson 1992). Linstead (1993) sees the function of texts of this nature as being one of *evocation* rather than reference. In the tradition of poetic discourse, he looks to these texts for their ability to evoke that which escapes reference. While such an approach to the study of education is not a panacea, it does represent a credible option to more restrictive and dated perspectives that fail to acknowledge our rapidly changing social and cultural landscape. It offers all those interested in the education of young and old alike a chance to gain insight into the process of education and to eventually make changes to improve it.

References

ALLADINI, Nourandini (1995) Private resources for public education. Unpublished doctoral thesis, University of Toronto.

BATES, R. (1987) Corporate culture, schooling and educational administration. *Educational Administration Quarterly*, 23 (4), 79–115.

BAUDRILLARD, J. (1983) *Simulations* (New York: Semiotext).

BAUMAN, Z. (1992) *Intimations of Postmodernity* (New York: Routledge).

BOWLES, S. and GINTIS, H. (1976) *Schooling in Capitalist America: Educational Reform and the Contradictions of Economic Life* (New York: Basic).

BROOKOVER, W., BEADY, C., FLOOD, P., SCHWEITZER, Z. and WISENBAKER, J. (1979) *School Social Systems and Student Achievement* (New York: Begin).

CLEGG, S. (1990) *Modern Organizations: Organizations Studies in the Postmodern World* (London: Sage).

COLEMAN, J.S., CAMPBELL, E.Q., HOBSON, C.J., McPARTLAND, J., MOOD, A.M., WEITFIELD, F.D., and YORK, R.L. (1966) *Equality of Educational Opportunity* (Washington: US Department of Health, Education and Welfare).

COLEMAN, P. and LEROQUE, L. (1989) *Struggling to be Good Enough: Administrative Practices and School District Ethos* (New York: Falmer).

COOPER, P. and BURRELL, G. (1988) Modernism, postmodernism and organizational analysis: an introduction. *Organization Studies*, 9 (1), 91–112.

CROWSON, R. (1992) *School-Community Relations Under Reform* (Berkeley: McCutchan).

CUBAN, L. (1990) Reforming again, again, and again. *Educational Researcher*, 19 (1), 3–13.

DiMAGGIO, P.J. and POWELL, W.W. (1983) The iron cage revisited: institutional isomorphism and collective rationality in organizational fields. *American Sociological Review*, 35, 147–160.

DiMAGGIO, P.J. and POWELL, W.W. (1991) Introduction, in W.W. Powell and P.J. DiMaggio (eds), *The New Institutionalism in Organizational Analysis* (Chicago: University of Chicago Press), 1–38.

DURKHEIM, E. (1964) *The Division of Labour in Society* (New York: Free Press).

ERICKSON, F. (1992) Why the clinical trial doesn't work as a metaphor for educational research: a response to Schrag. *Educational Researchers*, 21 (5), 9–10.

FOUCAULT, M. (1979) *Discipline and Punish: The Birth of the Prison* (New York: Pantheon).

FOUCAULT, M. (1980) *Power/Knowledge: Selected Interviews and Other Writings* (New York: Pantheon).

FRAATZ, J.M.B. (1989) Political principals: efficiency, effectiveness, and the political dynamics of school administration. *Qualitative Studies in Education*, 2 (1), 3–25.

GOODY, J. and WATT, I. (1968) The consequences of literacy, in J. Goody (ed.), *Literacy in Traditional Societies* (Cambridge: Cambridge University Press).

GOVERNMENT OF ONTARIO (1995) *For the Love of Learning: Report of the Royal Commission on Learning* (Toronto: Queen's Printer).

GRANOVETTER, M. (1985) Economic action and social structure: the problem of embeddedness. *American Journal of Sociology*, 91, 481–510.

HARGREAVES, A. (1994) *Changing Teachers, Changing Times* (Toronto: OISE Press).

HARGREAVES, A. (in press) Towards a social geography of teacher education, in N. K. Shimahara and I. Z. Holowins (eds), *Teacher Education in Industrialized Nations* (New York: Garland).

HARVEY, D. (1989) *The Condition of Postmodernity* (Oxford: Blackwell).

HASSARD, J. (1993) Postmodernism and organizational analysis: an overview, in J. Hassard and M. Parker (eds), *Postmodernism and Organizations* (London: Sage).

HOLMES, M. (1989) School effectiveness: from research to implementation to improvement, in M. Holmes, K. Leithwood and D. Musella (eds) *Educational Policy for Effective Schools* (Toronto: OISE Press).

JEFFCUT, P. (1993) Towards postmodernism: from interpretation to representations, in J. Hassard and M. Parker (eds), *Postmodernism and Organizations* (London: Sage).

KNIGHTS, D. and MORGAN, G. (1993) Organization theory and consumption in a post-modern era. *Organization Studies*, 14 (2), 211–234.

LASH, S. (1990) *Sociology of Postmodernism* (New York: Routledge).

LEWINGTON, J. and ORPWOOD, G. (1993) *Overdue Assignment: Taking Responsibility for Canada's Schools* (Rexdale: Wiley).

LINSTEAD, S. (1993) Deconstruction in the study of organizations, in J. Hassard and M. Parker (eds) *Postmodernism and Organizations* (London: Sage).

MCLUHAN, M. (1973) *Understanding Media* (London: Abacus).

MARCH, J. G. and OLSEN, J. P. (1984) The new institutionalism: organizational factors in political life. *American Political Science Review*, 78 (3), 734–749.

MARCH, J. G. and OLSEN, J. P. (1989) *Rediscovering Institutions: The Organizational Basis of Politics* (New York: Free Press).

MARQUARD, O. (1991) *In Defense of the Accidental* (New York: Oxford University Press).

MAWHINNEY, H. (1994) Bringing the state back into theorizing on educational policy making: a neo-institutional perspective. *Organization Theory Dialogue*, 1, 6–13.

MILLER, J. (1994) *The Holistic Teacher* (Toronto: OISE Press).

NASH, J. E. and CALONICO, J. M. (1993) *Institutions in Modern Society: Meanings, Forms and Character* (New York: General Hall).

OLIVER, C. (1992) The antecedents of deinstitutionalism. *Organization Studies*, 13 (4), 563–588.

PARKER, M. (1992) Post-modern organizations or Postmodern organization theory? *Organization Studies*, 13 (1), 1–17.

PETERS, T. J. and WATERMAN, R. H. (1982) *In Search of Excellence* (New York: Harper & Row).

REED, M. I. (1993) Organizations and modernity: continuity and discontinuity in organization theory, in J. Hassard and M. Parker (eds), *Postmodernism and Organizations* (London: Sage).

REICH, R. (1991) *The Work of Nations* (New York: Random House).

RUTTER, M., MAUGHAN, B., MORTIMORE, P. and OUSTON, J. (1979) *Fifteen Thousand Hours* (London: Open Books).

RYAN, J. (1988) Conservative science in educational administration: knowledge, power and truth. *Journal of Educational Administration and Foundations*, 3 (2), 5–22.

RYAN, J. (1989) Disciplining the Innut: normalization, characterization and schooling. *Curriculum Inquiry*, 19 (4), 397–403.

RYAN, J. (1993) Studying effective schools and districts. *Canadian Journal of Education*, 18 (1), 79–85.

RYAN, J. (1994) Organizing the facts: aboriginal education and cultural differences in school discourse and knowledge. *Language and Education*, 8 (4), 251–271.

RYAN, J. (1995) Order, anarchy and inquiry in educational administration. *McGill Journal of Education*, 30 (1), 37–59.

RYAN, J., WIGNALL, R. and MOORE, S. (1995) *Teaching and Learning in a Multi-ethnic School* (Toronto: Ontario Ministry of Education and Training).

SARASON, S. (1990) *The Predictable Failure of Educational Reform* (San Francisco: Jossey Bass).

SMART, B. (1992) *Modern Conditions, Postmodern Controversies* (New York: Routledge).

SOLOMON, P. (1992) *Black Resistance in High School: Forging a Separatist Culture* (New York: SUNY Press).

TOFFLER, A. (1990) *Power Shift* (Toronto: Bantam).

TYE, K. E. (1992) Restructuring our schools: beyond the rhetoric. *Phi Delta Kappan*, September, 8–14.

WEBER, M. (1968) *Economy and Society: An Outline of Interpretive Sociology* (New York: Bedminster).

14.   *The politics of education, the new institutionalism, and reinvented schooling: some concluding observations*

Robert L. Crowson and William Lowe Boyd

Introduction

As Chicago began its summer of 1995, yet another chapter unfolded in the eventful history of 'Windy City' school reform. With legislative approval, Mayor Richard M. Daley took over direct control of that city's public schools. The old Board of Education was abolished, to be replaced by a mayor's-office, 'handpicked' five-member panel. The Superintendent of Schools quickly resigned, and 'potential leaders of the new system were being discussed behind the scenes' (Kass 1995: 1).

Broad powers for the new governing panel were established in the enabling state legislation, accompanied by a tough-minded curtailment of union preogatives and a clear message of 'war' against the city's recalitrant educational 'interests' and 'petty bureaucrats'. As of mid-summer 1995 the Mayor had already appointed his 'A-team' to manage the schools – a recognized group of some of the 'best people' in Chicago government and business leadership, sending the city a clear message of seriousness of purpose (Bradley 1995a: 3).

By all accounts, Mayor Daley's takeover of the Chicago schools should represent a move toward the reinvention of schooling that this yearbook addresses. Curiously, however, the Chicago schools had already been dramatically 'reinvented' just seven years earlier. Widely recognized as an extremely radical change, the reform of the Chicago schools in 1988 decentralized significant decision-making power throughout the city to the individual school-sites, by creating a parent-and-community dominated council for every city school, and by marshalling major resources (political, intellectual, financial) around the concept of a bottom-up, community-controlled strategy of school-improvement.

Why has it seemed necessary to Chicagoans to reinvent their school system twice in less than ten years? Has the first decentralizing reform so thoroughly failed to meet school-improvement expectations that a mayoral takeover, while radical, seemed to be the only solution left? Had the first reform been effectively slowed and even sabotaged (as many critics have claimed) by an entrenched bureaucracy and powerful, unyielding unions? Or, had the first reform begun to succeed a bit too well by starting to rearrange the community-based politics of the city away from institutionalized political norms? Or, is it possible that because the first, decentralizing reform had begun to succeed by mid-1995, the Mayor's initiative provided a complementary effort to help cement the gains made?

0268–0939/95 $12 · 00 © 1995 Taylor & Francis Ltd

These are the kinds of events, questions, and issues that this yearbook has examined. Growing interest in new institutional theorizing in education comes at a time of demands for the 'reinvention' of American public education. Indeed, educational 'reform' in its numerous waves is too mild a term to describe the mid-1990s agenda calling for fundamental structural changes: in schools and in school district governance and finance; in who (using what measures) is to assess the schools; in how and by whom the schools are to be managed; in how professionalism in education is to be taught and rewarded; and in how schools are to connect with other institutions and particularly with their clientele. The central significance of new institutional theorizing amidst all of this lies in its instructive focus upon persistence amidst change, in its broader view of schooling beyond the organizational, and in its insights into what it might possibly take to 'reinvent' anything in the human-services arena.

What the Chicago story reminds us, though, is that the politics of education continues to exist at the very foundation of reinvention, renewal, or restructuring of institutions and organizations. Mayor Daley is quintessentially a political actor, indeed a member of a legendary dynasty of Chicago politicians. In Chicago, school reform, the educational system and city politics all come together inseparably in the city's struggle to improve its schools. It is no accident that mayors (and Daley is far from alone), state governors, and other elected officials are newly and directly entering the fray of school reform (Mazzoni 1995). Public education is now clearly recognized by politicians for its vital society- and community-building functions.

With its combined emphasis upon environmental and organizational forces, the study of educational politics provides an appropriate vehicle for an institutions-minded approach to inquiry. The open-systems frame of reference of this field has long challenged a strong tendency towards closed-system thinking in much of the literature on school administration (Boyd and Immegart 1979, Peterson 1995).

Nevertheless, the study of educational politics also finds itself engaged in transition and redefinition (Scribner and Layton 1995). Many of the key issues in Chicago's struggle are at the head of current reassessments of the politics of education. These issues touch the intersection of policy/politics and school-improvement, the multi-layered and 'systemic' influences upon schooling, the politics of cross-organizational 'networks' in education, and of course questions of democratic participation and change in large-urban districts (Cibulka 1995, Iannaccone and Lutz 1995, Mazzoni 1995, Wong 1995).

In an effort to bring new institutional theorizing into somewhat sharper focus in a framework of educational politics, this volume has also had to confront the nation's continuing struggles, as in Chicago, over school-improvement. The attempt to consider simultaneously the politics-of-education lessons of new institutional thinking *and* some insights into school reform has been a very ambitious and thoroughly daunting exercise. Still, the assembled contributions in this yearbook do offer, we believe, some important ideas to those now trying to rethink the field and to those attempting to consider what it might indeed mean to 'reinvent' American schooling.

Institutions and the politics of education

Students of political science have long been aware of some of the major ideas which new institutional theorizing reinforces. The recognition that the 'state' (i.e. legislative and executive government) is not just another actor in the environments of organizations is paramount. As W. Richard Scott (1995: 93) observes, 'the state is set apart'. It has the capacity to use legitimate coercion; it has the power to shape other institutional features; it can define and enforce conditions of ownership and control; it fuses, often powerfully, the collective will (93–95). Thus, not by accident has governmental policy-making (from local to national) formed a foundation for much of the study of educational politics, and not by accident do many reformers in education continue to seek 'state' remedies for education's many deficiencies (Mazzoni 1995). Indeed, there is discussion of a new 'intrusion' of politics into education, much of it now centered upon deep ideological cleavages at the state level (Lindsay 1995).

Paradoxically, students of educational politics are also fully aware of a present-day 'flight' from the state in school governance. Marshall and Anderson (1995: 177) write of a 'privatization of the public sphere' (e.g., school-business partnerships, contracting-out, market and 'choice' options), wherein the logics of economic and market principles are substituted for 'public discussion of profound normative issues'.

Similarly, Plank and Boyd (1994: 264) note the growth of an 'antipolitics' of education internationally, as well as in America – a retreat from the rigours and uncertainties of traditional democratic governance toward arenas 'that are less "political" and more authoritative, such as courts and markets'. Among the currently attractive alternatives to traditional democratic governance, interestingly, are a renewed fascination with the development of professional expertise and a renewed faith in the power of competition to change and improve education, as well as the phenomenon of de-centralizing schools to grassroots 'communities' that 'will prove to be homogeneous in culture and values' (273).

One might argue, paradoxically, on both sides of the question as to whether the Mayor's takeover in Chicago represents 'antipolitics' or a return-to-politics. While Mayor Daley is quintessentially a political actor, by no means is the takeover necessarily a thrust toward democratic governance. Is the push and pull of interest-mobilization and coalition-building around public education about to increase or decrease in Chicago? Is a singular mayoral ideology (e.g., increase the city's attractiveness to middle-class families) about to replace a more pluralist (albeit divisive) set of negotiations around 'what's-to-be-done' with the schools? Is the city- and economic-development value of urban public education now too important to be left to 'chance'?

Whatever its direction (towards more or less democracy), the Chicago case and the nation's current ambivalence about the role of 'the state' in education suggest two key politics-of-education observations from the new-institutional thinking in this volume. The state is more than just another actor, yet there is a 'flight' from 'state'-oriented traditions. A flight from tradition finds new, 'reinvented' approaches aplenty under experimentation in American education, yet the 'hold' of traditional legitimizing structures and values may be only minimally challenged. What are the implications, in these trade-offs, *vis-à-vis* renewed inquiry into the politics of legitimacy in American education, and the politics of institutional and organizational 'structures' in public schooling?

A new politics of institutional legitimacy

Why have many of the 'structures and rules that organize the work of instruction' in our public schools remained so stable over time, ask David Tyack and William Tobin (1994: 454), despite repeated efforts to 'reform' them? One answer, they suggest, is to be found in an enduring tie between many organizational forms of schooling and cultural beliefs held by the general public, a match that Metz (1990) has termed 'real school' and that Tyack and Tobin (1994: 456) claim 'provides legitimacy and public support'.

A return to community-level legitimacy (even if it means changing simulta-neously from a boldly innovative to just another inner-city school) is the message delivered in Mary Anne Raywid's chapter. An old Wadleigh, orthodox and traditional, represented a proud past to the school's Harlem community. A new Wadleigh, even renovated, failed to meet the community's definition of 'real school'. Reforms that stray rather far from community notions of 'real', warns Raywid, are advised to attend carefully to 'stakeholder' politics, even when the stakeholder model represents by far the most troublesome of routes toward change.

Interestingly, relatively few students of failed reform have discovered roots in inadequate community-level legitimizing. More commonly, failure has been found in 'insider' intransigence, weak leadership, or resistant organization structures. Nevertheless, those who tend to think broadly have long warned (as do Grant and Murray in this volume) that widespread public support (typically around very basic historical values) is at the heart of both non-productive educational change and the likelihood of successful reform. From this perspective, Tyack and Tobin (1994: 478) urge the current need for a new round of 'intense and continual public dialogue about the ends and means of schooling', reaching far 'beyond a cadre of committed reformers to involve the public in a broad commitment to change'.

However, 'widespread public support' can easily lead to state standardization, warns Mary Driscoll in a chapter comparing institutionalism and communitarianism. Indeed, it would certainly not be compatible with Etzioni's call for a new nationwide commitment to democratic education, she argues, to employ coercive mechanisms to achieve such an ideal. On the other hand, from a reform-mindedness 'upward' to society, Driscoll observes that individual schools and systems have been 'extraordinarily myopic' in failing to turn institutional forces to their own advantage and in failing to understand the impact of societal context upon such efforts as a community reshaping of teacher professionalism.

It is on the same note of a 'strategic' consideration of 'what-it-takes' for reform that Grant and Murray find a likelihood of 'widespread institutional change' in the current technological revolution of our society and perhaps in the 'rise of competing systems' in American education. One of the most critical of the competing interpretations, argues James Ryan, must be a philosophic recognition that today's institutions are increasingly interdependent. They are not as differentiated as a language of 'educational' institutions, 'health-care' institutions, 'banking' institutions, 'public-safety' institutions would have us believe. Thus, to talk of a politics of institutional legitimacy in that separate arena we call 'education' narrows the scope of attention dangerously.

While recognizing Ryan's important point, Rodney Ogawa (1992) and W. Richard Scott (1995) both note, however, that some commonalities as well as differ-ences in organizational structure (e.g., organizations lacking specific goals and clear technologies) can be analyzed effectively across institutional domains.

From this perspective, Ellen Goldring's chapter on environmental adaptation employs Scott's (1995) three 'pillars' of institutions informatively, in an analysis that examines schools, parents and the public. Goldring observes, for example, that a 'regulatory pillar' of institutional environments can press toward an evolution of orga-nizational structures *vis-à-vis* state rules-and-regulations conformity, without much affecting 'what actually takes place inside the organization'. A 'cognitive pillar', however, does represent an inside-the-organization internalization of the symbols/meanings of the environment, but this 'construction of social reality' may or may not fit well with the regulatory frame. Most disturbing of all, concludes Goldring, is the sense that this framework for legitimation in education seems generally to operate as if parents and the public are not 'fundamental parts' of the institutional environment of schools. Paradoxically, while reform can fail under the scrutiny of a community's sense of 'real school', those who press toward reform often proceed as if parents and the public are not essential in a change-the-schools equation.

What does all of this mean toward inquiry into a new politics of institutional legitimacy in education? Especially, what does all of this mean for a new politics that is fully appreciative of the current context of wide-ranging reinvention,from Mayoral takeovers, to privatization, to an 'antipolitics' of education, to a new drive toward professionalism?

To be sure, the politics of education as a field of study has long recognized the importance of legitimacy. From the pathbreaking work of McCarty and Ramsey (1971) to the 'dissatisfaction' theorizing of Lutz and Iannaccone (1978) and the governing-élites work of Harmon Zeigler and his colleagues (1974, 1985), a legitimizing function has been at the heart of political inquiry in education.

Nevertheless, the papers in this volume, and some of the additional literature rapidly developing around the new institutionalism, suggest to us three concluding observations. *First*, as Meyer and Rowan (1977) pointed out years ago, the politics of reform/reinvention at the site level is far from just a local politics of education. There *is* a systemic character to schooling – albeit a strange and confusing character, wherein the logic of formal policymaking may show few marks of the reality of organizational life but where the reality of organizational life nevertheless displays a breadth far beyond any of its immediate environments.

This is not to say that an understanding of the neighborhood politics of education is unimportant, for Raywid's work clearly demonstrates the site-level impact of institutionalized forces. But, it is to say (with Mary Driscoll) that 'a sophisticated rendering of the institutional environments of school communities must be developed if we are to comprehend fully their consequences or explore their potential'.

Second, the politics of legitimation is far more than a politics (or even an antipolitics) of power, conflict, negotiation, and the various 'games' (Scribner *et al.* 1995) of educational reform. To be sure, questions of influence and activism, of differences in values, of strategies and stakes, of purposive behavior and the like are still vitally important. But, a deeper politics of institutionalized rules, 'things-taken-for-granted', and long-established myths form much of this added perspective (Cibulka 1995). It is a perspective that requires a full sense of historical processes, for myth-building is a key element in the politics of legitimation, an element that Ritti and Silver (1986) suggest arises in a 'dramaturgy of exchange' between major organizational participants.

We find an example of this in the Wilkinsburg case. Wilkinsburg's attempt to privatize the Turner School may or may not succeed, as we learn from William Thomas, Kevin Moran and Jeremy Resnick. The traditional political forces of state and national professional opposition, charges of union-busting and a general skepticism *vis-à-vis* business motives could prove to be far too formidable for the potential of this experiment to receive a test.

Aware of important institutional values, the private management firm has offered to hire only qualified professionals, to escrow the payments, to be highly accountable and to be guided by well-regarded experts in urban schooling. But, a true test for the Wilkinsburg case is far more likely to be found in the salability of its delightful insight into the politics of institutionalism, wherein the suggestion was that perhaps a bit of radical shock, under apparently no-hope conditions, might indeed stir a new mythology and even a new 'contagion' of institutional legitimacy (Zucker 1987). Such a 'what-else-is-left-to-be-tried' mood is very much to be found elsewhere in the spate of mayor's-office and state-level takeovers of urban districts.

Third, there should be renewed consideration (for public education) of a key point made by Yeheskel Hasenfeld (1992). Hasenfeld noted that institutional theory includes an important, and very different perspective on the question of organizational 'effectiveness'. From an institutional point-of-view, the long-honored criterion of goal-attainment may not be the most salient of effectiveness measures. Indeed, particularly for most human-service organizations, goal-attainment is difficult to evaluate, and it furthermore does not tend to be the focus of attention of external groups. Rather, the practices and symbols that communicate organizational *legitimacy* are key effectiveness measures for the public. Thus, it is not at all hard to understand why savvy school districts superintendents have long valued the newly-built school, the award-winning marching band, and the top-ranked basketball team.

If political legitimacy is a measure of effectiveness, one understands more clearly the dilemmas in this volume posed by Goldring, by Kerchner and Weeres, and by Ginsberg. How much public (especially parental) support, asks Ellen Goldring, is to be found for many of the reforms that the professional community holds most dear, e.g. site-based management, national curricular standards, portfolio assessment? The public is probably much more 'concerned with safe and orderly schools and a return to basics', she notes. Thus, Goldring concludes that, curiously, the legitimating thrust in much of the reform movement thus far has been toward enlisting public support for professions-based changes, and not toward adapting the schools 'more effectively to parents' expectations'.

An even deeper dimension of a very serious legitimation issue in school reform, Kerchner and Weeres observe, derives from the radically changing nature of education's post-industrial playing-field wherein both parental expectations and organizational adaptations are forged. Somehow, a new learning debate around public education must take place, they contend, a debate that may help to rebuild the institution of education around knowledge, as newly 'basic industry'. It is not just a matter of reform or of adaptation that is before us, but a legitimation imperative connected to the very core of a much-changed economy. What we are talking about here, adds Rick Ginsberg's chapter, is a legitimating effort that could reach 'the equivalent   of undertaking a religious conversion'. A 'powerful faith' may prove to be far more reconstructive than the numerous mechanisms and technologies now under experimentation around school-to-school 'reform'.

A new politics of institutional structures

Thus, politics-of-legimation dilemmas persist in school reform, and nothing short of a renewed faith in public education may be necessary for its very survival. A paradox is that amidst warnings regarding legitimacy, new institutional theorizing at the same time refocuses our attention upon the many structural aspects of schooling that do indeed tie educational organizations to their environments. Time-honoured, much-valued structures in education (e.g., a marks-oriented reward system, a school day and a school year, a "graded" curriculum) have long been at the foundation of our nation's sense of 'real school'.

A key insight in new institutional thinking is that much of the structural order of educational and other public-service institutions is far less directed toward means-ends rationality and goal-attainment than toward a politics of organization in relation to environment (March and Olsen 1984). James Cibulka's chapter demonstrates the special power and the special politics of an institutional interpretation, in our efforts to understand the incapacity of public schooling to reform. Thus, new institutional theorizing brings neatly together the deep structures of educational organizations with the legitimation foci of the politics-of-education. The stable 'structures and rules' noted by Tyack and Tobin (1994) are now highly important politically. And we already know how very difficult they are to change (Sarason 1990).

Douglas Mitchell's chapter captures both of these key points with creative and informative insights. Mitchell suggests that central structural features of educational organizations can include: a responsiveness to context rather than productivity in the development of new programs; an isomorphic 'sameness', lest innovation become 'sufficiently novel or radical to call into question continuity with other organizations in the same sector', a 'garnering' of public legitimacy through powerful symbol systems embodied in myth and ritual; the importance of 'historical significance' as a 'determinant of social meaning and practice', and a 'sub-optimization' of practice in the face of constraining interests both in the organization and its environment.

At a deeper level of analysis, Mitchell identifies three key 'features of organizational life' for schools that tie directly into this vital, but hard to change, quality of an institutional/political context. The features include: the difficult to replicate impact of overlapping and often-in-tension environments (a political regime, a professional norm, cultural norms-and-beliefs; an over-reliance upon the courts to resolve social conflicts, thus bringing constitutionalism 'down' to the level of just another political actor in education; and the impact of 'social legitimacy' far more than technical productivity upon day-by-day lifeways and conventions in schooling.

Beyond such insights as these, the papers in this volume suggest to us two central conclusions. *First*, it would not be at all difficult to conclude from neo-institutional theorizing that 'change the structure' is indeed the central message for school renewal. This conclusion converges with Allan Odden's (1994) observation that advocates of educational reform have failed to adequately address the management and organization structures that successful reform requires.

Indeed, even in the new institutional literature, studies of 'macrostructures' (or structures of environments) have proceeded further to date than have studies of micro-level structural effects (Lant and Baum, 1995). Nevertheless, a developing literature is now beginning to improve our understanding about how deep-structures do operate under reform, and how they might be altered. Some good examples are: Barker's (1993) discovery of self-managing workgroups drawing themselves back into their own 'iron cages' of highly rationalized rules; Pentland and Rueter's (1994) observation that organizational routines are not as fixed or habitual as is often believed; and Ritti and Silver's (1986) finding that the myth-building stage of institutional change can be a confused, complicated, even dramatic process of environmental exchange.

As this literature continues to develop, understandings about how to change the structure of schools could well take off in newly creative and insightful directions. Indeed, Douglas Mitchell's suggestions in this volume about theorizing from the physical sciences go far beyond traditional structuralism to introduce social-bonding theory and structural mechanics' reasoning to our analysis. He shows how a new respect for non-linear and complex systems might better instruct our understanding of such phenomena as the pacing of events and the use of 'umbrella' and/or 'picket fence' strategies to cope with unpredictability or disruption. Similarly, Mary Driscoll reasons that there is something vital in the 'soft-structures' concept of community that, in its complexity, goes well beyond our current understanding of institutional forces, an observation supported empirically by Stone and Wehlage (1995), who found an important symbiosis of professional community with structural change.

A *second*, central conclusion, however, is that looking first to structure may *not* be the key message of new institutional theorizing. An insight has been supplied by Christensen and Molin (1995), in their history-of-the-institution approach to a study of the Danish Red Cross. They found that in the one hundred and twenty-five year resiliency of this organization, the essential structure and governance of the Red Cross had changed remarkably little. What *has* provided the key to that organization's survival is its capacity to infuse into its own core values (its very identity) the changing societal demands of Danish society. Thomas Payzant (1994) has made much the same point with forceful clarity, observing that educators tend to assume, in restructuring reform, that structural change will result in cultural change. It usually fails to do so, he notes (194), leading 'to the interesting hypothesis that reculturing leads to restructuring more effectively than the reverse'.

From Payzant's (1994) insight and from the Danish Red Cross example, we can see how to resolve the paradox of our competing conclusions: rather than being contradictory, they are actually interrelated; the politics of changing structures may parallel and, indeed, may flow out of a politics of legitimation and reculturing. It is no accident that increased attention in many quarters is now being paid to new-style polling in education, eliciting the 'public's voice' and 'rebuilding public relationships' as an essential first step in school reform (Bradley 1995b, Harwood 1995). Institutions need 'to listen to the public differently', observes Harwood (59), through listening carefully to the cultural messages flowing out of the *patterns* of what people say and the *meanings* in their voices, in order 'to *understand* both the particular points that they make and how those points fit together'.

A special structural interconnectedness with the public has also been a conclusion reached by Terry Moe (1990) about the essence of politics and its link with legitimacy. Moe (215) observes that most political institutions arise from a politics of structural choice. More specifically, 'institutions arise out of the struggle to control and exercise public authority' (214). He (221) explains that

> voting is not what is fundamental or distinctive about politics. People vote on all sorts of things in the private sector, just as they do in the public sector. Politics is distinguished by what people in the public sector are voting *about*: they are voting to determine how public authority will be exercised.

Furthermore, observes Moe (1990), the key class of political institutions, for our understanding of public authority, may be less importantly the legislative arena than the group of political institutions we classify as public bureaucracy. Public agencies are created through the exercise of public authority and are loaded with structures that reflect some political interests above others; that reflect the public's efforts to control the exercise of bureaucratic authority; and that simultaneously reflect each agency's own efforts to insulate itself from this control, seeking protection through structure from their political enemies (Moe, 1990). Seymour Sarason (1995: 84) puts it even more clearly and distinctly when he writes that

> an alteration of power relationships – in the classroom, school, or system – is a necessary but not sufficient condition for change. This assertion is justified by theory, research, and (most important) the history of institutional and social change.

Emerging from this backdrop of structural choice and the control of public authority, Moe and other authors in this volume now advocate not reform, but a radical reinvention of schooling. Thus, in their critique of Charles Manski's (1992) computer simulation of the impact of a voucher system, Moe and Shotts argue that public schools are heavily bureaucratic, wasteful and unresponsive, especially in urban areas. They note that we are now 'struck with educational arrangements that are highly stable and yet wholly unsatisfactory'. Little short of something radical (e.g., vouchers), they believe, is likely to alter a structure of control in education whose effects are now at their worst for low-income communities.

In his chapter, Ted Kolderie makes a similar argument, calling bluntly for the breakup of large urban school systems. He contends that a new model of 'divestiture and unbundling' must now guide the design of state legislation for the public schools. A potentially radical structural choice is also represented in the chapter on the privatization of the management of Turner Elementary School in Wilkinsburg, Pennsylvania (Thomas, Moran and Resnick). Amidst on-and off-again court decisions, Alternative Public Schools, Inc. did manage to open the 1995–96 school year at Turner Elementary, with a completely new *teaching* staff as well as *administrative* staff. The challenge to the property rights of tenured, unionized teachers is paramount in this case which represents a threat to union power and to restrictions upon the entry of "outsiders" into the professional domain. The very 'constitution' of the unionized organization may be at stake here (Knudsen, 1995).

The new institutionalism and reinventing American schools

In sum, one can see direct linkages between new institutional theorizing and issues central to the reinvention of American schooling. A concern with legitimacy is one focus here, with a reminder that the reform movement in America may not have paid enough attention to community-legitimation imperatives, or to the connections between change-targeted structures and their institutionalized roots. A 'structures' emphasis in the new institutionalism is a second focus. One key message is the notion that a politics of 'structural choice' (Moe, 1990) may well require far deeper forays into the exercise of public authority than has been heretofore understood. Kenneth Wilson and Bennett Daviss have worded it forcefully in *Redesigning Education* (1994: 4), observing that

> America's national inadequacies, which we sense and which we attribute to our failing schools, have arisen not because our schools have changed, but precisely because *they continue to do what they always have, in the same ways they always have*. The authors of *A Nation at Risk*, like most of the reformers that their report has inspired, have failed to understand that genuine reform is not about repairing the dilapidated structure of traditional schooling. Instead, it is about discerning a new vision of what it means to educate and be educated in a world that is fundamentally different from the one our schools still believe themselves to inhabit.

New visions are beginning to gain momentum, while on a parallel course there appears to be a developing consensus that old-vision educational reform has languished. Mayor Daley's takeover of the Chicago schools and Wilkinsburg,

Pennsylvania's privatization of professional property rights are just two examples of a new radicalization that appears to be gaining a foothold in the nation.

As Ted Kolderie puts it, it is time to 'withdraw the exclusive franchise' over public schooling held by public school districts within their boundaries and to move towards an opening up of opportunities for organizations other than school districts to operate public schools, and for school attendance decisions to be transferred to students, i.e., school choice. Additional phraseology now in evidence speaks of 'organizational trans-formation' (Tewel 1995); of reinvention, redesign and renewal; of a re-drafting of state school codes; and of state takeovers of school districts guilty of sustained academic fail-ure. This phraseology (now alongside serious experimentation with charters, vouchers and privatization) appears to be rapidly replacing calls for 'school restructuring', 'site-based management', or even 'systemic' reform.

However, there is a decided danger, as Hanne Mawhinney warns in this volume, if we fail to apply the same scepticism to the new institutional paradigm that we would apply to any other theorizing. While much of the current analysis of educational change has begun to move deeply into problems of altering institutional structures and processes – and could probably benefit much from more explicit linkages with new institutional theorizing – Mawhinney notes that there are key 'challenges on the frontiers of institutional theorizing': in defining the relationship between institutions and organizations, in defining the specific role of the state in an institutionalized society, and in deciding how contested values and ideologies fit into institutional change in schooling. In a more pointed restatement of much the same message, William Boyd (1995: 18) writes that:

> Calls are mounting in the United State to 'breakup', 'privatize', or otherwise radically reform troubled urban school districts. Increasingly, it appears that major surgery is required. But *what surgery* and *with what consequences* for the patient?

It is not at all clear, for example, just what surgery is yet to come with what conse-quences in the newest takeover phase of Chicago school reform. There were some indi-cations, by as early as September of 1995, that sharpened scalpels had already been at work on many of the district's programmes, employee rolls and spending plans. The city's newspapers began carrying reports of a successful 'battle against waste' by a man-agement team which discovered, for instance, such matters as millions of dollars of spoiled food and unused equipment in the district's warehouses (Schmidt 1995). A legitimation imperative in this battle against waste was clearly on the agenda, fueled by the hope enunciated by Mayor Daley's press secretary that these management efforts would 'send a message to state lawmakers', in recognition of 'a new day at the board of education' (11).

However, it remains to be seen whether Chicago-styled reinvention, or any of today's more radical proposals for educational reform, can go very far beyond a mes-sage here and there. Does a Daley's Office politicization of Chicago reform offer a chance to step forward into important new citywide linkages for the industry of public education (as Kerchner and Weeres argue)? Is there a powerful new value of quality and accountability in Chicago's efforts, as well as others, to 'reinvent', that (as Mawhinney suggests) is at long last beginning to drive legitimation imperatives? Or, does the takeover suggest a political step backward in Chicago into a schooling recaptured by special interests (perhaps business élites in place of the political machine)?

Can reinvention, however radical, succeed in breaking the hold of such institu-tionalized structures and 'property rights' as Chicago's central-office bureaucracy or

Wilkinsburg's organized teachers? And, of course, amidst such a politics-of-reinvention, it also remains to be seen whether new institutional theorizing around questions of legitimation and structures can help us to understand better than before either the new surgery now underway in American education or the patient's likelihood of survival.

References

BARKER, J. R. (1993) Tightening the iron cage: coercive control in self-managing teams. *Administrative Science Quarterly*, 38, 408–37.

BOYD, W. L. (1995) Productive schools from a policy perspective: desiderata, designs, and dilemmas. Keynote address presented at the annual conference of the International Congress for School Effectiveness and Improvement (Leeuwarden, The Netherlands, January 3–6).

BOYD, W. L. and IMMEGART, G. L. (1979) Education's turbulent environment and problem-finding: lines of convergence, in G. L. Immegart and W. L. Boyd (eds), *Problem-finding in Educational Administration* (Lexington: Lexington Books), pp. 275–289.

BRADLEY, A. (1995a) Daley names team in takeover of Chicago schools. *Education Week*, 12 July, 3.

BRADLEY, A. (1995b) Public agenda captures voice of the people. *Education Week*, 11 October, 1, 12–13.

CHRISTENSEN, S. and MOLIN, J. (1995) Origin and transformation of organizations: institutional analysis of the Danish Red Cross, in W. R. Scott and S. Christensen (eds), *The Institutional Construction of Organizations* (Thousand Oaks: Sage), 67–90.

CIBULKA, J. G. (1995) Policy analysis and the study of the politics of education, in J. D. Scribner and D. H. Layton (eds), *The Study of Educational Politics* (Washington: Falmer), 105–25.

HARWOOD, R. C. (1995) Rebuilding public relationships. *Kettering Review*, Spring, 51–62.

HASENFELD, Y. (1992), *Human Services as Complex Organizations* (Newbury Park: Sage).

IANNACCONE, L. and LUTZ, F. W. (1995) The Crucible of democracy: the Local arena, in J. D. Scribner and D. H. Layton (eds), *The Study of Educational Politics* (Washington: Falmer), 39–52.

KASS, J. (1995) Bell's about to ring on Daley-run schools. *Chicago Tribune*, 24 May, 1, 20.

KNUDSEN, C. (1995) The competence view of the firm, in W. R. Scott and S. Christensen (eds), *The Institutional Construction of Organizations* (Thousand Oaks: Sage), 135–63.

LANT, T. K. and BAUM, J. A. C. (1995) Cognitive sources of socially constructed competitive groups: examples from the Manhattan hotel industry, in W. R. Scott and S. Christensen (eds), *The Institutional Construction of Organizations* (Thousand Oaks: Sage), 15–38.

LINDSAY, D. (1995) "Citing Politics, 2 States Pull Out of Chiefs' Group," *Education Week*, 13 September, 1, 17.

LUTZ, F. W. and IANNACCONE, L. (1978) *Public Participation in Local Schools: The Dissatisfaction Theory of American Democracy* (Lexington: Lexington Books).

MCCARTY, D. and RAMSEY, C. (1971) *The School Managers: Power and Conflict in American Public Education* (Westport: Greenwood Publishing).

MANSKI, C. F. (1992) Educational choice (vouchers) and social mobility. *Economics of Education Review*, 11, 351–369.

MARCH, J. G. and OLSEN, J. P. (1984) The new institutionalism: organizational factors in political life. *American Political Science Review*, 78, 734–49.

MARSHALL, C. and ANDERSON, G. L. (1995) Rethinking the public and private spheres: feminist and cultural studies perspectives on the politics of education, in J. D. Scribner and D. H. Layton (eds), *The Study of Educational Politics* (Washington: Falmer), 169–82.

MAZZONI, T. L. (1995) State policy-making and school reform: influences and influentials, in J. D. Scribner and D. H. Layton (eds), *The Study of Educational Politics* (Washington: Falmer), 53–73.

METZ, M. H. (1990) Real school: a universal drama and disparate experience, in D.E. Mitchell and M.E. Goertz (eds), *Education Politics for the New Century* (New York: Falmer), 75–91.

MEYER, J. W. and ROWAN, B. (1977) Institutionalized organizations: formal structure as myth and ceremony. *American Journal of Sociology*, 83, 340–63.

MOE, T. M. (1990) Political institutions: the neglected side of the story. *Journal of Law, Economics, and Organization*, 6, 213–53.

ODDEN, A. (1994) Decentralized management and school finance. *Theory Into Practice*, 32, 104–11.

OGAWA, R. T. (1992) Institutional theory and examining leadership in schools. *International Journal of Educational Management*, 6, 14–21.

PAYZANT, T. W. (1994) Commentary on the district and school roles in curriculum reform: a superintendent's perspective, in R. F. Elmore and S. H. Fuhrman (eds), *The Governance of Curriculum: 1994 Yearbook of the Association for Supervision and Curriculum Development* (Alexandria: ASCD), pp. 203–209.

PENTLAND, B. T. and RUETER, H. H. (1994) Organizational routines as grammars of action. *Administrative Science Quarterly*, 39, 484–510.

PETERSON, P. E. (1995) Foreword, in J. D. Scribner and D. H. Layton (eds), *The Study of Educational Politics* (Washington: Falmer), xiii–xiv.

PIPHO, C. (1995) The changing governance scene. *Phi Delta Kappan*, 77, 6–7.

PLANK, D. N. and BOYD, W. L. (1994) Anti-politics, education, and institutional choice: the flight from democracy. *American Educational Research Journal*, 31, 263–81.

RITTI, R. R. and SILVER, J. H. (1986) Early processes of institutionalization: the dramaturgy of exchange in inter-organizational relations. *Administrative Science Quarterly*, 31, 25–42.

SARASON, S. B. (1990) *The Predictable Failure of Educational Reform* (San Francisco: Jossey-Bass).

SARASON, S. B. (1995) Some reactions to what we have learned. *Phi Delta Kappan*, 77, 84–85.

SCOTT, W. R. (1995) *Institutions and Organizations* (Thousand Oaks, CA: Sage).

SCRIBNER, J. D., REYES, P. and FUSARELLI, L. D. (1995) Educational politics and policy: and the game goes on, in J. D. Scribner and D. H. Layton (eds), *The Study of Educational Politics* (Washington: Falmer), 201–12.

SCRIBNER, J. D. and LAYTON, D. J. (1995) (eds) *The Study of Educational Politics* (Washington: Falmer).

SCHMIDT, P. (1995) Chicago 'superboard' negotiates teacher pact, pares budget. *Education Week*, 15, 6 September, 10–11.

STONE, C. R. and WEHLAGE, G. G. (1995) Restructuring and school-based student support services. Paper presented at the Center on Organization and Restructuring of Schools, University of Wisconsin, Madison.

TEWEL, K. J. (1995) The new American school district: we can have it now with the knowledge we already have. In *The New Urban School District* (Denver: Education Commission of the States), pp. 1–5.

TYACK, D. and TOBIN, W. (1994) The 'grammar' of schooling: why has it been so hard to change? *American Educational Research Journal*, 31, 453–79.

WILSON, K. G. and DAVISS, B. (1994) *Redesigning Education* (New York: Holt).

WONG, K. K. (1995) The politics of education: from political science to multi-disciplinary inquiry, in J. D. Scribner and D. H. Layton (eds), *The Study of Educational Politics* (Washington: Falmer), 21–35.

ZEIGLER, L. H., JENNINGS, M. K. and PEAK, G. W. (1974) *Governing American Schools: Political Interaction in Local School Districts* (North Scituate, MA: Duxbury Press).

ZEIGLER, H., KEHOE, E. and REISMAN, J. (1985) *City Managers and School Superintendents: Responses to Community Conflict* (New York: Praeger).

ZUCKER, L. G. (1987) Institutional Theories of Organization. *American Review of Sociology*, 13, 443–64.

Index